Oracle Essbase 9 Implementation Guide

Develop high-performance multidimensional analytic OLAP solutions with Oracle Essbase

Sarma Anantapantula

Joseph Sydney Gomez

[PACKT] PUBLISHING

BIRMINGHAM - MUMBAI

Oracle Essbase 9 Implementation Guide

First published: June 2009

Production Reference: 1190609

Published by Packt Publishing Ltd.
32 Lincoln Road
Olton
Birmingham, B27 6PA, UK.

ISBN 978-1-847196-86-6

www.packtpub.com

Cover Image by Faiz Fattohi (faizfattohi@gmail.com)

Credits

About the Authors

Sarma Anantapantula currently works as an Essbase Consultant in the OLAP Center of Excellence at the Ford Motor Company. He has over 11 years of experience in the Software industry as a developer, designer, and administrator and has worked in various technologies involving client-server architecture, and Data Warehousing projects (tools like HOLOS and Essbase). Sarma also has expertise in web interface development (with both Microsoft and J2EE).

Sarma is a board member of the Hyperion User Group (`http://www.hug-mi.org`), and has presented on how Essbase is implemented at the Ford Motor Company. He has also published an article on "Executing DTS Packages from ASP" in ASP Today.

Sarma is well known for his magic fixes. He has a fix for any kind of issue in any technology. In his free time, Sarma likes to spend time answering new technology questions in user forums. If he is not in front of computer, he will be playing ping pong or chess with family and friends. He also likes listening to The Beatles, and reading English novels. Sarma is known for being ever smiling and friendly, and can be reached at `sarmaa@gmail.com`.

Joseph Sydney Gomez has been an Essbase developer, designer, and administrator for almost 10 years. Originally educated as a Graphic Designer in the field of Computer Graphics Technology, Joe took a job as a mainframe Y2K bug fixer and the rest is history.

Joe currently works as an Essbase technical specialist and is his company's OLAP Center of Excellence lead. Not a complete computer geek, Joe also enjoys basketball, fishing, bicycle riding, and photography. To fill out the picture, Joe does volunteer work at a senior citizen apartment and occasionally takes free-lance design jobs. Oh yes, Joe has a special interest in collecting antique glass telegraph insulators. Joe can be reached at `jgomez16@gmail.com`.

About the Reviewer

Shekar Kadur has over 23 years experience in Information Systems specifically managing complete system development life cycle of projects involving Databases, Data warehousing, Business Intelligence, OLAP, SAP, and Enterprise Management Reporting applications in the automotive, finance, utility, retail, and health care industries.

He is a certified PMP (Project Management Professional), a certified Hyperion instructor and a consultant proficient with all Oracle and Hyperion toolsets (Essbase, Planning). He is extremely proficient in project/program management of applications using Oracle, Hyperion, SAP, SAPBW, Business Objects, and Web-based technologies. He has consulted, deployed, and managed IT projects in Ford Motor Company, Ford Motor Credit Corporation (Ford Credit), General Motors, Daimler Chrysler Financial Corporation, Daimler Chrysler, Consumers Energy, Guardian Industries, Oakwood Health Systems, General Dynamics, Management Technologies Inc, TRW, Constellation Brands Inc, Johnson Controls Inc, Deloitte Consulting, and Capgemini Inc.

He has delivered lectures on Data Warehousing, Datamarts, Oracle, and Hyperion toolset in Michigan, USA, and London, UK.

Venkatakrishnan J is a well-known Oracle Business Intelligence expert who has diverse customer implementation experience. He has contributed over 350 technical articles through his blog `http://oraclebizint.wordpress.com`. He is well known for his custom integration techniques across different toolsets. He has over 7 years of Oracle Business Intelligence experience.

Acknowledgements

We met as co-workers working together to build Essbase systems for the company we are employed by. Along the way we became more than co-workers, we became friends. Here we are today, co-workers, friends, and now co-authors.

Hi all, this is Sarma here, first I would like to thank my beloved Lord Sri Sathya Sai Baba for giving me an opportunity to write this book. Huge thanks to my wonderful wife Kalyani for being so patient with my late nights, and for her faithful support in writing this book, without her tremendous support this book would not be possible. Special thanks to my sweet kids Sai (8 years old) and Saranya (3 years old) for sacrificing their fun and playtime with me. Many thanks to my father and mother for giving me sincere encouragement while writing this book. Thanks to all my special friends who supported me while writing this book. Lastly my utmost thanks to my dearest friend Joe Gomez for his help and cooperation during this challenging period.

Hi everyone, Joe here. Boy, that's a tough act to follow but I'll try. First and foremost, I would like to thank my lovely wife Rita, my beautiful daughter Ashley and my son Joey for putting up with me (or avoiding me), encouraging me, and supporting me during my distracted state while I was involved in writing this book. I especially want to thank my true friend Sarma Anantapantula for asking me if I would like to join him on this venture because I certainly wouldn't have thought of it on my own!

Collectively, we would like to thank James Lumsden, Acquisition Editor, without whom we would have never written this book or very likely, any other book! Our special thanks go to Bhupali Khule, Technical Editor, for seamlessly working with us to complete this book and Pallavi Kachare, Technical Editor, for performing the code reviews. Our special thanks also go to Ved Prakash Jha, Development Editor, and Rajashree Hamine, Project Coordinator, for making sure we are on target for the launch. We would also like to thank the entire Packt staff for all of their help and guidance throughout the completion of this book. We would also like to thank the reviewers for their reviews and suggestions.

Finally we really want to thank all of you who purchased this book. We have put every bit of our Essbase knowledge and experience into this book so you can avoid some of the inevitable pitfalls of learning a new piece of technology. We hope you feel that you made a worthwhile purchase. We certainly feel you did!

Table of Contents

Preface

Thank you for selecting this book. We assure you we will do our very best to make it entirely worth your while. The goal is to demystify the multidimensional database world and have you comfortable with designing, building, and coding Essbase systems.

Always remember, Essbase is an art not a science!

A brief history on Essbase

Essbase is a multidimensional database management system. The name Essbase stands for Extended Spread Sheet dataBASE. Using the custom add-in provides the end-user with near seamless compatibility in the Microsoft Excel spreadsheet program.

Essbase as we know it today evolved from software components developed by Arbor Software Corporation and through the acquisition of additional components or tools from other OLAP and Business Intelligence product development companies. In some cases Arbor Software Corporation purchased the entire company to acquire the needed components as was the case with App Source in late 1997. It is generally agreed that the release of Essbase version 3.2 in 1995 set Essbase as the standard for OLAP and Business Intelligence and Analytics enterprise software.

Rapid growth and popularity of the Essbase product led to the merger of Arbor Software Corporation and Hyperion Software becoming Hyperion Solutions Corporation in 1998. This new company achieved near global leadership in the OLAP and Business Intelligence (BI) software arena and ultimately attracted the attention of Oracle Corporation. Oracle completed the purchase of Hyperion Solutions in 2007 for $3.3 Billion. Hyperion Solutions is now a subsidiary of Oracle Corporation and offers a complete line of integrated Business Intelligence and Business Performance Management products.

Why Essbase

In addition to being the leading global provider of OLAP and Business Intelligence software, Essbase also offers incomparable value as a **RAD (Rapid Application Development)** tool. As will be demonstrated in the following pages the complete cycle from concept to design to build to implement can be only a fraction of what a traditional system may require. Further, enhancements to reporting or other functionality are fast, accurate and easy to code.

What this book covers

Chapter 1 guides you through a typical Essbase installation which includes the Essbase Agent on an analytic server, the Essbase API on the server, the Essbase Administration Services, and the Essbase Add-in for Microsoft Excel.

Chapter 2 covers Essbase database design considerations and how to apply them to a multidimensional database as opposed to the traditional row and column relational database.

Chapter 3 we begin to build in Essbase (hooray!). Using the information learned in the previous chapter we build the Essbase outline which is the foundation of the Essbase database. Instead of rows and columns an Essbase database contains dimensions and members in a hierarchical parent-child structure.

Chapter 4 dives right into loading data into your Essbase database. From user inputted data to flat file data manipulation and loading to direct database access all forms of data loading are explained and demonstrated.

Chapter 5 explains the varied and simple ways to calculate your data. Once data is loaded it is time to demonstrate one of the largest benefits of Essbase. Unlike relational databases, Essbase data can be calculated in many different ways. Instead of writing complex programs to calculate and derive data elements from existing elements or loading excessive amounts of data to derive the needed elements Essbase can calculate and derive data from a minimal amount of loaded data. Essbase has powerful yet simple to use tools that calculate the data

Chapter 6 goes over the use of the data for reporting, presentation, or data extracts to feed other systems. Simple steps explain how to create dynamic reporting abilities or user interfaces with a minimum of effort.

Chapter 7 jumps feet first into the Essbase Add-in for Microsoft Excel. As Microsoft Excel seems to have become the dominant spreadsheet program used by business today the Essbase Add-in for Microsoft Excel has evolved into a very powerful tool indeed. This is one of the main reasons Essbase is so popular today. Even the most novice end user can quickly create professional and dynamic reports with relative ease. We explain these features as well as how the addition of very little code can make the spreadsheet very powerful.

Chapter 8 we cover automating your Essbase cube. Depending on the requirements of your user community it is possible to design, build, and automate an Essbase application to where there is virtually no need for IT intervention.

Chapter 9 explains advanced techniques that can be used to keep your Essbase application running at peak performance. You know, those little things not usually covered in the user guide but learned with experience. Cache settings, server configuration, memory management are just a few topics covered.

Chapter 10 explains the **Block Storage Option (BSO)** and the **Aggregate Storage Option (ASO)** for storing data in its database cubes. For the most part this book deals with the BSO. Since the release of version 7.x Essbase has also offered the ASO. As this method of storing the data has substantial differences we felt it needed its own chapter to explain it.

Chapter 11 gives a high level view of the optional Essbase System 9 components that are available in the System 9 Suite with the Essbase database the common foundation for all the other components to launch from. With components like Essbase Planning or Hyperion Smart Office there's enough to make even the stodgiest accountant's head spin.

Appendix explains the significance of Oracle's new product Smart View.

Who this book is for

This book is aimed at the IT professional who has an understanding of typical client-server applications but is new to Essbase and the concept of multidimensional database management systems.

Occasionally explaining the concept of a multidimensional database to someone who only has experience with traditional row/column relational databases can make their head explode! This book will show you the common sense approach to designing, building, and most importantly understanding Essbase and the cube concept.

Versions covered in this book

As of this writing, Essbase System 9.x is the latest offering from Oracle Corporation. Essbase System 9.x itself is an integrated suite of Business Intelligence software. The Essbase module in System 9.x is substantially similar to Hyperion Essbase 7.x. Hyperion Essbase 7.x is still widely used and supported.

Since this book primarily covers the Essbase component where screen captures are used, they will be version 9.x however most all examples in this book will work in versions 7.x and 9.x unless otherwise noted.

Before we drill down into Essbase let us quickly take a minute to refresh some accepted data warehousing concepts.

Data warehousing concepts

Data warehousing is not a new concept. In fact, it has been around for many years now. Traditionally a data warehouse has been constructed with some sort of relational database structure. What is relatively new is the addition of the multidimensional database architecture to data warehousing family.

The following information is designed to give you a high level understanding of data warehousing and how it can be used in your business. Once you understand the basic principles and concepts of data warehousing it will be easier to understand where Essbase fits into the picture.

The fathers of the data warehouse

We guess we shouldn't tell you about the data warehousing concept without first telling you who is widely recognized as the creator or father of the modern data warehouse.

Bill Inmon is a world-renowned expert on data warehousing and is also widely recognized as the Father of Data Warehousing. With 35+ years of experience in the Information Technology field and more specifically database technology management and data warehouse design, Bill has been a highly sought after speaker for many major computing associations and industry conferences, seminars, and tradeshows.

Another widely recognized name in the data warehousing arena is Ralph Kimball. Ralph Kimball is an author on the subject of data warehousing and business intelligence and received a Ph.D. in 1972 from Stanford University in Electrical Engineering specializing in man-machine systems. He is widely regarded as the Guru of Data Warehousing and is known for long-term convictions that data warehouses must be designed to be understandable and fast. Ralph's methodology is also known as dimensional modeling or the Kimball methodology.

The similarities between Mr. Inmon and Mr. Kimball are many and so are the differences. The following paradigm statements illustrate just how Mr. Inmon and Mr. Kimball are perceived in the world of Data Warehousing.

Bill Inmon's paradigm: The enterprise data warehouse is one part of the overall business intelligence system. An enterprise should have just one data warehouse and one to many data marts. The data marts then source their information from the data warehouse. In the data warehouse, information is stored in third normal form.

Ralph Kimball's paradigm: The enterprise data warehouse is the conglomerate of all data marts within the enterprise. Information is always stored in the dimensional model.

There is no right way or wrong way between either of these two ideas. They each represent different data warehousing philosophies. In reality, the data warehouse philosophy used in most enterprises is closer to Ralph Kimball's idea. This is because most data warehouses started out as department level efforts, and as such they originated as an activity specific data mart. Only when more data marts are built later do they evolve into a data warehouse.

What is a data warehouse

Just what is a data warehouse really? According to Bill Inmon, you know, the famous author of several data warehouse books, "A data warehouse is a subject oriented, integrated, time variant, non volatile collection of data in support of management's decision making process."

A data warehouse is typically a relational database that is designed using dimensional modeling and is used for querying and data analysis rather than business transaction processing. It usually contains relevant historical data that is derived from transactional data. The data warehouse separates data analysis overhead from transactional overhead and enables an enterprise to consolidate its data from several sources or activities.

In simpler terms an enterprise-wide data warehouse is a centralized data store where integral and mission critical data that is relevant and necessary to the decision making processes of the different business units can be stored and accessed real-time by the various business activities.

One of the primary benefits of the enterprise data warehouse is the use of — One Number — across the enterprise. This means that what is called a part in one activity is the same part in another activity. Everyone is speaking the same language and is on the same page.

Different types of data warehouses

In addition to the relational database, an enterprise data warehouse environment often consists of an Extract Transform and Load (ETL) solution, an OLAP engine (hooray Essbase), client analysis tools, and other web or desktop applications that manage the gathering of data and delivering it to business users.

There are three types of data warehouses:

1. **Enterprise Data Warehouse:** An enterprise data warehouse provides a central database for decision support throughout the enterprise. It is recommended that there is only one data warehouse across the enterprise.

2. **Operational Data Store:** This has a broad enterprise wide scope, but unlike the real enterprise data warehouse, data is refreshed in near real time and used for routine business activity. One of the typical applications of the Operational Data Store (ODS) is to hold the recent data before migration to the data warehouse. Typically, the ODS are not conceptually equivalent to the data warehouse albeit do store the data that have a deeper level of the history than that of the OLTP data.

3. **Data Mart:** The data mart is a subset of the data warehouse and it supports a particular region, business unit, or business function. The data mart receives its source data from the data warehouse. There can be many data marts sourcing data from the one data warehouse.

In case you're wondering, here are a few words about an OLAP solution and an OLTP solution. An OLAP solution stands for On-Line Analytical Processing, which in a nutshell means that the data you are using for your analysis is mainly considered reporting or presentation data and any updates or write-backs are solely for analytical purposes. The source data is rarely updated in this method.

The OLTP solution stands for On-Line Transactional Processing which means that the base or source data is directly updated with factual and historical data as an output of the analysis or data entry processes. Conventional straight line reporting can be performed and there is very little, if any, slice-and-dice analysis or what-if scenarios.

Data warehouses and data marts are usually built on dimensional data modeling where fact tables are connected with dimension tables. This is most useful for users to access data since a database can be visualized as a cube containing many dimensions. A data warehouse and its smaller, more specific data mart provide an opportunity for slicing and dicing that visualize cube along any one of its dimensions.

Data warehouse data modeling

As mentioned above, even the so-called masters of the data warehouse have differing ideas as to the data modeling methodology that should be used in a data warehouse. There is general agreement that seem to have the choices narrowed down to just two popular architectures. There is the Third Normal Form and the Dimensional Data Model.

Of the two main types of data modeling most popularly used in data warehousing the more common of the two is the Dimensional Data Model. Read on as we briefly explain the differences between the two.

The Third Normal Form (3NF)

The Third Normal Form or 3NF method of database modeling in a nutshell is all about the primary key. What this means is there is no data element in the database that cannot be referenced by the primary key. To achieve 3NF a database must also pass the first levels on normalization.

In the First Normal Form or 1NF the theory is that all of the data in all of the columns must be atomic. This means there can be no sets of data in one column. For instance, a name column that contains both first and last names has sets of data. It is better to have one column for the first name and a separate column for the last name.

To pass the Second Normal Form or 2NF the data must be 1NF compliant and now must also be more key dependent. Where the 1NF model focuses on the atomic nature of the data the 2NF model is more key dependent. What this means is that data in non-key columns cannot depend on the composite or primary key.

Finally there is the Third Normal Form or 3NF which now, on top of organizing the data at the atomic level as well as identifying the data in conjunction with other supporting data, must now be completely primary key dependent. To be 3NF all data in non-key columns must be dependent on the primary key. No more can the data in one column or table be dependent on data in another column or table that is dependent on the primary key.

As we said earlier, there is no right or wrong reason to use either data modeling methodology. Both have their merits and their demerits.

Being the least popular of the data warehousing data models, the 3NF model is actually the most popular data modeling methodology used in active online transactional processing systems.

Ironically, when data is exported from an Essbase cube to a flat file for load to a relational database, it more closely resembles a 3NF data model than a Dimensional Data Model.

The Dimensional Data Model

The Dimensional Data Model is the data modeling methodology most commonly used in data warehousing systems. The Dimensional Data Model differs substantially from the Third Normal Form, more commonly used for transactional systems. As you can imagine, the same data would then be stored much differently in a dimensional model than in a 3NF model.

The Dimensional Data Model consists of Fact and Dimension tables. The Fact tables store the numerical values of the business unit and contain numerical or additive measures of the business like Gross Sales, Gross Units. The Fact table also contains columns which link to the Dimension table. The Dimension table stores the descriptive information about the dimension and some times these are joined to other dimension tables to define the hierarchy of a dimension like Market (Geographical information) or Time information.

To understand Dimensional Data Modeling, we'll define some of the terms commonly used. Pay attention here as you may notice a definite similarity here with the terms used to describe data in an Essbase database

- **Dimension:** A category of information, for example, the Time dimension. The Time dimension would contain data relative to time periods such as days or months or years.
- **Attribute:** A distinct level within a dimension. For example, Year is an attribute in the Time dimension.

- **Hierarchy:** The specification of levels that represents relationship between different attributes within a dimension. For example, one possible hierarchy in the `Time` dimension is Year | Quarter | Month | Day.

When the data in the data warehouse is modelled using the Dimension Data Model method instead of being organized like the 3NF method, which is in neat rows and columns with primary keys to identify everything, it usually follows the line of the dimensions that are included as necessary components of your data. The resultant structure of the dimensional data method resembles more of a multidimensional cube than two dimensional rows and columns.

Where does Essbase fit in this

Okay, now for the big question. Where does Essbase fit in with all this data warehouse mumbo jumbo?

Well if you were paying attention a few paragraphs back you would notice that we mentioned that a necessary tool in your enterprise data warehouse toolbox included an OLAP solution. Well, Essbase is it!

Essbase is the perfect multidimensional OLAP database tool to use as your function specific reporting and analysis data mart tool. Consider this, if your data is stored in your relational database data warehouse under the Dimensional Data Model methodology what better tool is there that has the power and capability to perform in the multidimensional arena. Essbase is a natural.

Consider this, with the proper hardware, Essbase is designed to support even the largest cubes with vast numbers of users so scalability is not an issue. Essbase is also the superior real time analysis and reporting tool that performs complex calculations. It can also be updated from the source database, in this case the data warehouse, quickly and effortlessly and depending on the technology you use for your data warehouse, Essbase can also connect directly to the data warehouse database to draw its data.

Knowing all this what other choice is there besides Essbase?

Conventions

In this book, you will find a number of styles of text that distinguish between different kinds of information. Here are some examples of these styles, and an explanation of their meaning.

Code words in text are shown as follows: "Note that the Time dimension contains the calendar periods used in the EssCar system"

A block of code will be set as follows:

```
[default]
IF (@ISMBR ("PRICE"))
    "TOTAL NET REVENUE" ="TOTAL REVENUE" - "TOTAL DISCOUNTS";
ELSEIF (@ISMBR ("UNIT"))
    "TOTAL NET REVENUE" = 0;
ENDIF
```

When we wish to draw your attention to a particular part of a code block, the relevant lines or items will be shown in bold:

```
[default]
[Thu Sep 11 00:40:45 2008]Local/ESSBASE0///Info(1051061)
Application Demo loaded - connection established
[Thu Sep 11 00:40:45 2008]Local/ESSBASE0///Info(1054027)
Application [Demo] started with process id [4744]
[Thu Sep 11 00:40:45 2008]Local/ESSBASE0///Info(1056090)
```

Any command-line input or output is written as follows:

```
ESSCMD C:\Batch.SCR
```

New terms and **important words** are shown in bold. Words that you see on the screen, in menus or dialog boxes for example, appear in our text like this: "clicking the **Next** button moves you to the next screen".

[Warnings or important notes appear in a box like this.]

[Tips and tricks appear like this.]

Let's get started

If you're still holding onto this book then you are ready to embark on your journey towards Essbase Nirvana.

We begin by covering the installation of Essbase on both the client and the server and end with you having created a fully functional Essbase cube. This is where you usually read some form of good luck statement. With this book you don't need it! Let's GO!

Reader feedback

Feedback from our readers is always welcome. Let us know what you think about this book — what you liked or may have disliked. Reader feedback is important for us to develop titles that you really get the most out of.

To send us general feedback, simply drop an email to feedback@packtpub.com, and mention the book title in the subject of your message.

If there is a book that you need and would like to see us publish, please send us a note in the **SUGGEST A TITLE** form on www.packtpub.com or email suggest@packtpub.com.

If there is a topic that you have expertise in and you are interested in either writing or contributing to a book, see our author guide on www.packtpub.com/authors.

Customer support

Now that you are the proud owner of a Packt book, we have a number of things to help you to get the most from your purchase.

Errata

Although we have taken every care to ensure the accuracy of our contents, mistakes do happen. If you find a mistake in one of our books — maybe a mistake in text or code — we would be grateful if you would report this to us. By doing so, you can save other readers from frustration, and help us to improve subsequent versions of this book. If you find any errata, please report them by visiting http://www.packtpub.com/support, selecting your book, clicking on the **let us know** link, and entering the details of your errata. Once your errata are verified, your submission will be accepted and the errata added to any list of existing errata. Any existing errata can be viewed by selecting your title from http://www.packtpub.com/support.

Piracy

Piracy of copyright material on the Internet is an ongoing problem across all media. At Packt, we take the protection of our copyright and licenses very seriously. If you come across any illegal copies of our works in any form on the Internet, please provide us with the location address or website name immediately so that we can pursue a remedy.

Please contact us at copyright@packtpub.com with a link to the suspected pirated material.

We appreciate your help in protecting our authors, and our ability to bring you valuable content.

Questions

You can contact us at questions@packtpub.com if you are having a problem with any aspect of the book, and we will do our best to address it.

1
Installing Oracle Essbase

Welcome to the exciting world of Oracle Essbase! You have bought this book so you must be anxious to get started, and you can hardly wait. Well, not until you install the software. Yes, this is where we actually get going. This chapter will assist you in installing Oracle Essbase server (aka the Essbase agent), **Essbase Administration Services** (**EAS**), and the Essbase Add-in for Microsoft Excel.

Oracle Essbase server can be installed on several platforms like Unix, Windows, and Linux. For the most part, this book discusses a typical Windows installation.

Installing the Essbase analytic server

In this book, we will be focusing on version 9.x of Oracle Essbase. For your Windows installation, the minimum recommended system requirements are shown.

Operating system and processor requirements:

Operating system	Platform	Processor
Windows 2003 SP1		
Windows 2000 SP4	32-bit	x86
Windows 2003 SP1	64-bit	Itanium 2
Server Enterprise Edition		x64

Disk space and RAM requirements:

Component	Disk Space	RAM
Essbase Server	1GB	1GB
API	20MB	256MB (minimum)

You now know the recommended system requirements to install Essbase and we assume you have the software in hand, therefore, let's install Essbase.

1. Double-click the **setup** file for Oracle Essbase. After installing the Java Runtime Environment and initializing the install wizard, you will be presented with a screen asking you to select a language to be used by the installation wizard. This is the language that the rest of the installation screens will display. We recommend English as it is the only choice available in the list box.

2. The next is the Oracle Essbase welcome screen. As welcome screens go it's fairly tale and contains the standard blah blah blah, read it and then click **Next** whenever you are ready.

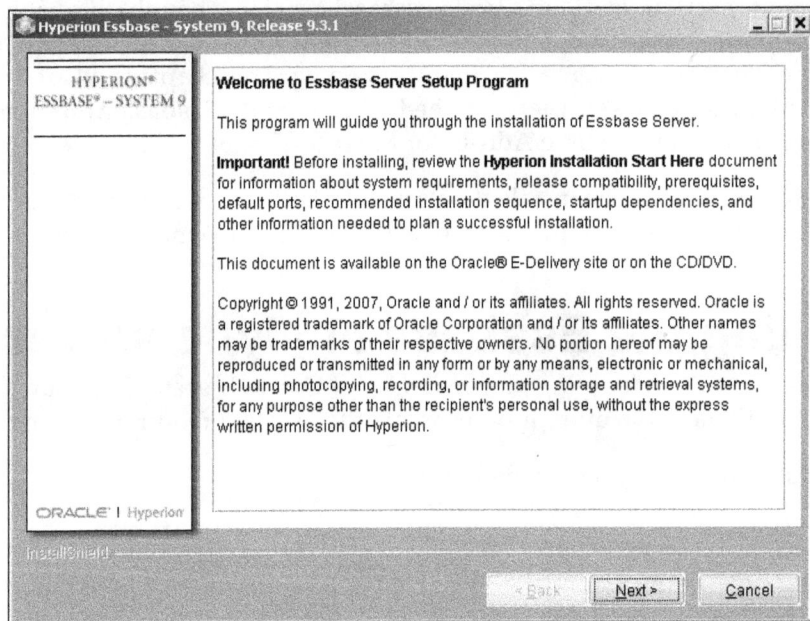

3. On the next screen, you are asked to select a country. Please select the appropriate country for your application, as this selection sets the country variable in the system. This country variable is used for currency calculations.

4. The next step is the license agreement screen, which you should read very carefully. When you have finished, select **I AGREE,** then click **Next** to proceed.

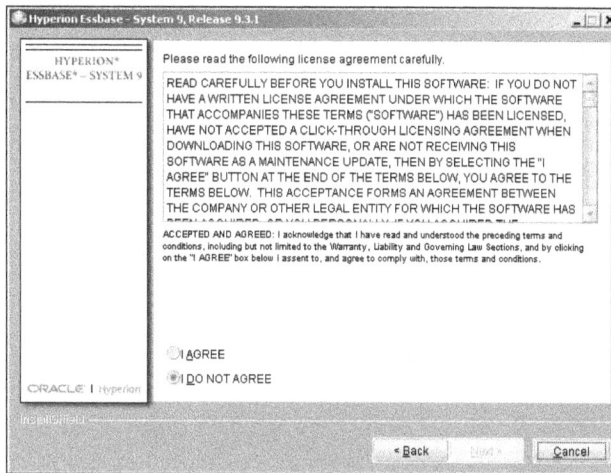

5. In this step, you need to specify the Hyperion home directory which defaults to `c:\Hyperion`. It is in this folder that all of the required and optional Essbase System 9 common components will be installed. If you choose to select a different path, please do so here.

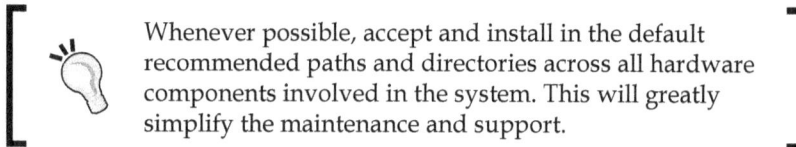

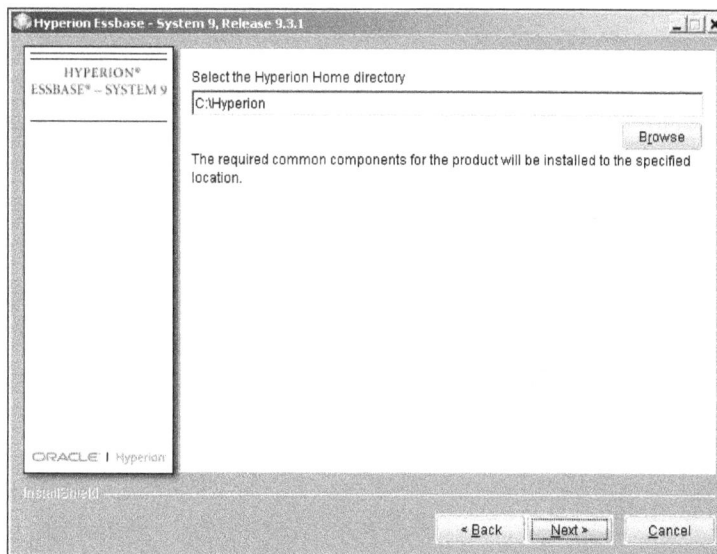

> Whenever possible, accept and install in the default recommended paths and directories across all hardware components involved in the system. This will greatly simplify the maintenance and support.

6. In this step, you need to specify the Essbase server directory. If you do nothing, it will default to the home directory you selected in the previous step.

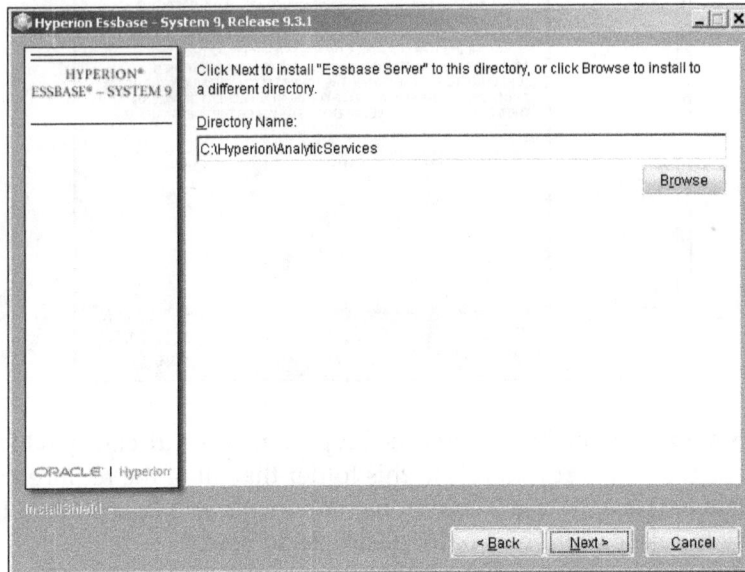

7. In this step, you are asked to select either the **Typical** or **Custom** installation. The **Custom** installation includes all of the components and allows you to pick which ones are required for your installation. We suggest you select the **Typical** installation for now as you can add other components at anytime in the future.

8. In this step, you are asking the wizard to update your system environment variables with the new Essbase system variables you have chosen in the previous two steps. The new environment variables, PATH and ARBORPATH, will be set in the system and the Essbase server configuration file. We will discuss this file and the settings later in the book. By default, the installer wizard is set to update the environment variables. Please leave it as is and click **Next**.

9. In this step, you are required to select the ESSLANG. The ESSLANG language variable defines the locale of the computer. For example, for US English, it is **ENGLISH (LATIN1)**. This is to ensure proper communication with other applications and is the Unicode setting.

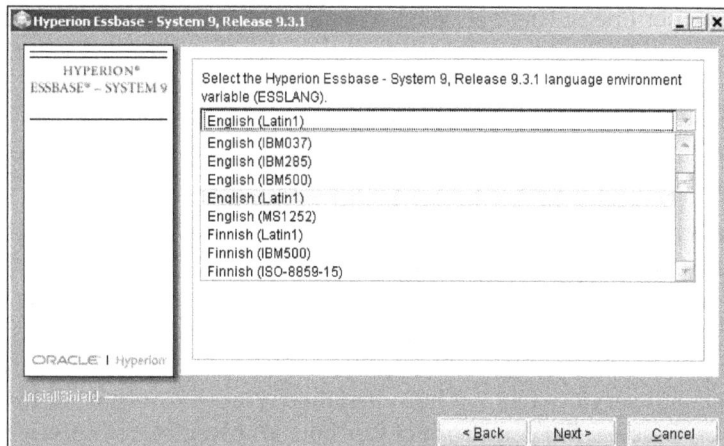

10. This step summarizes all of the components that are to be installed during this present installation. Check the information carefully to confirm you have the locations correct, as well as the selected Oracle Essbase components. If there are any corrections that need to be made, use the **Back** button to go back and fix what is needed. This is your last chance before the wizard begins the actual installation.

11. This step basically tells you that the Essbase installation is in progress. Take a break, read the install notes as they flash on the screen. Of course, you could click **Cancel** to halt the process, but why would you ever do that?

12. Upon successful installation (you'll know it's successful because you will see the following screen), you are now asked if you want to launch the system configuration tool. The default is selected and it is recommended you use it now to confirm your configuration one more time (it doesn't hurt to be careful here). This tool can also be used to configure any optional System 9 components you may have elected to install now or at anytime in the future.

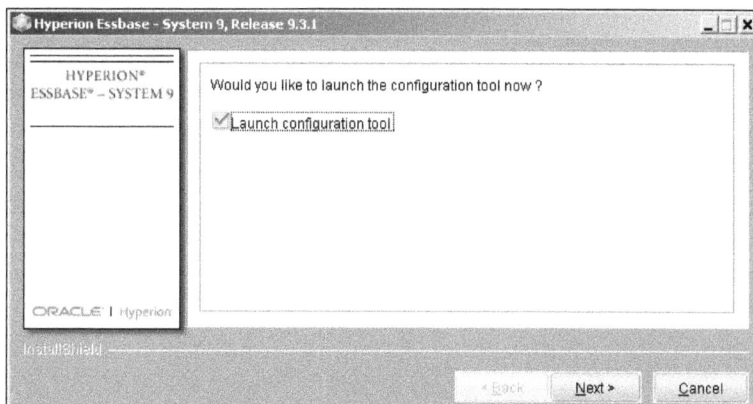

13. Yes, another one of these screens. This is now the configuration tool wizard. You are again asked to select the language for the wizard. Even though it is part of the Essbase analytics server software, what the heck, you may want to use a different language. Select **English** or the system will select **English** for you. Once again, this will determine what language the installation screens are presented in.

14. On the screen below, you are presented with the Essbase System 9 components you have installed on your server and their configuration status. Place a check mark next to all of the components that are flagged as pending, as now is the best time to set up your components and verify their proper configuration. Looking at the following screenshot, you can see that all choices are pending. Since shared services has not been installed, you will only want to place a check on **Essbase Server, Product Options** and **Register Analytic Services Server as Windows Service** at this time.

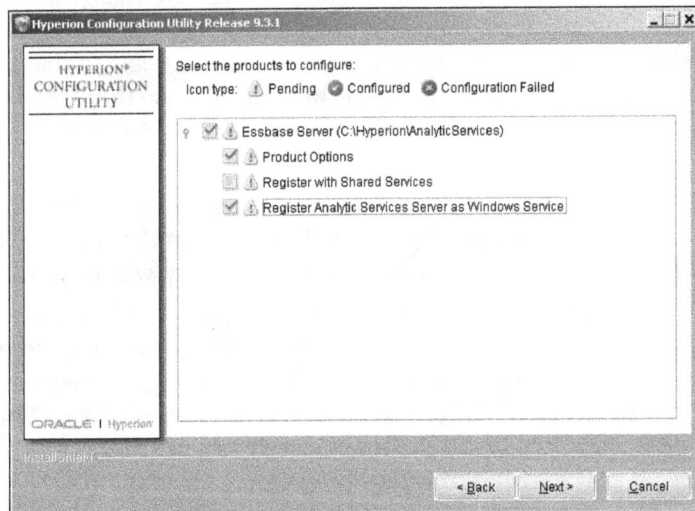

Clicking **Next** will open screens to you which will walk you through the configuration steps for the components you've selected. This is also where you will enter your initial supervisor account ID and password, so make sure you do not forget it.

15. After successful installation and configuration, you will see the following screen. Congratulations! You now have a fully functioning Essbase service installed on your server, complete with full Essbase API functionality. See the next step for what to do at the initial start up.

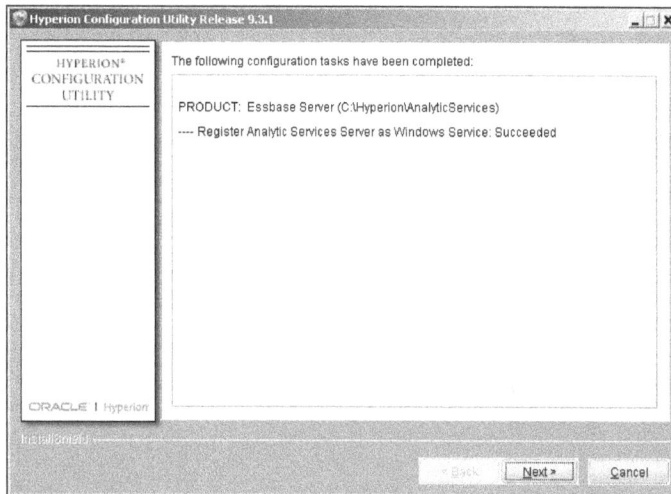

16. After the successful installation of Essbase server, please click on the **START | Programs | Hyperion | Essbase | Essbase** to start the service for the very first time. You will be asked for the ID and password you supplied in the configuration tool for Essbase installation. When the service starts, you want to see the line on the following screen—**Waiting for Client Requests....**

This is the *money* line. Your Essbase analytic server is installed correctly and ready to go to work.

That was not bad. The software practically installed itself. We will now install the EAS.

Installing Essbase Administration Services

Now that you have installed the Essbase analytic server, you need a tool which will enable you to play with your Essbase databases (commonly referred to as cubes) as you create, configure, and maintain them. The tool used for this purpose is called Essbase Administration Services. In earlier versions of Essbase, this tool is known as the Application manager or just App manager.

> Essbase databases are commonly called cubes after the Rubik's Cube style structure of how the data is conceptually stored.

The EAS user interface runs on any client and that is where you will install the software. The EAS talks to the Essbase service using TCP/IP and a web-based server. The servers recommended by Oracle are Tomcat, WebLogic, WebSphere, and Oracle Application Server. To simplify matters, Oracle includes a small Tomcat server with the installation package of the EAS service. In our example, we will be installing Tomcat as our administration server on the client with the EAS installation:

1. To get started, double-click the EAS executable file **setup** which is supplied by Oracle. Wouldn't you know that the very first screen to pleasure your eyes is the familiar old language selection screen. As always, this is where you select the language to be used with the installation wizard. Again, as always, select **English** as it is the only language option available. Click **OK** when you are ready.

2. As in the server software installation, you are now treated to the setup program welcome screen. Read this as you usually would and then click **Next**.

3. You may be noticing several similarities by now. This screen prompts you to select a country where, ideally, the software will be used.

> It is extremely important that the installation of all components of a system be installed using the same country selection. The primary benefits being the assurance of accuracy of the calculations and the ease of possible future root cause analysis.

For our example, we are using the United States. Select the country of your choice and click **Next**.

4. This step asks you to read and agree to the **End User License Agreement** (**EULA**). Read it carefully, and if you agree and wish to continue, click **Next**.

5. This step will ask you to accept or select the location for the Hyperion home directory (folder). Even though this software is being installed on a different physical machine than the Essbase analytics, ideally, it is a good idea to always install to consistent locations across the individual machines involved in the construction of the system.

> Whenever possible, accept and install in the default recommended paths and directories across all hardware components involved in the system. This will greatly simplify maintenance and support.

Make your selection and click **Next**.

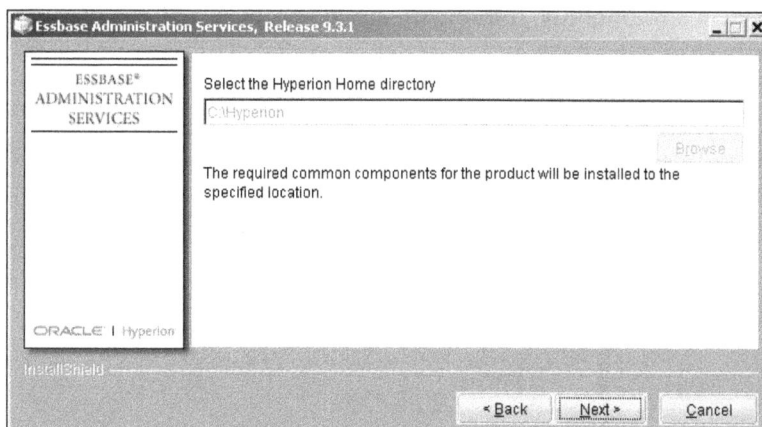

6. Here, you are asked to select your path for EAS. As suggested in previous steps, make your selection and then click **Next**.

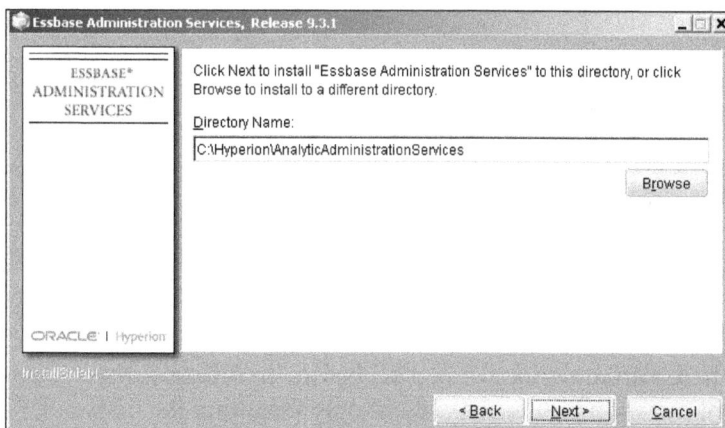

7. Here again, it will be best to accept the **Typical** installation to get you started. If you realize there is some feature missing that you must have, you can always reinstall the software at a later date and select the **Custom** option.

    For the most part, the difference between the **Typical** and the **Custom** installation is the ability to select sample scripts. The actual Essbase administrative functionality is the same.

8. Just like Step 9 of the Essbase analytics installation, this requires you to select ESSLANG. The ESSLANG variable defines the locale of the computer. For example, for US English it is **ENGLISH (LATIN1)**. This is to ensure proper communication with other applications and is the Unicode setting.

9. This step summarizes the current installation. Check the information carefully to confirm you have the locations correct as well as the selected Hyperion components. If there are any corrections to be made, use the **Back** button to go back and fix what is needed. This is your last chance before the wizard begins the actual installation.

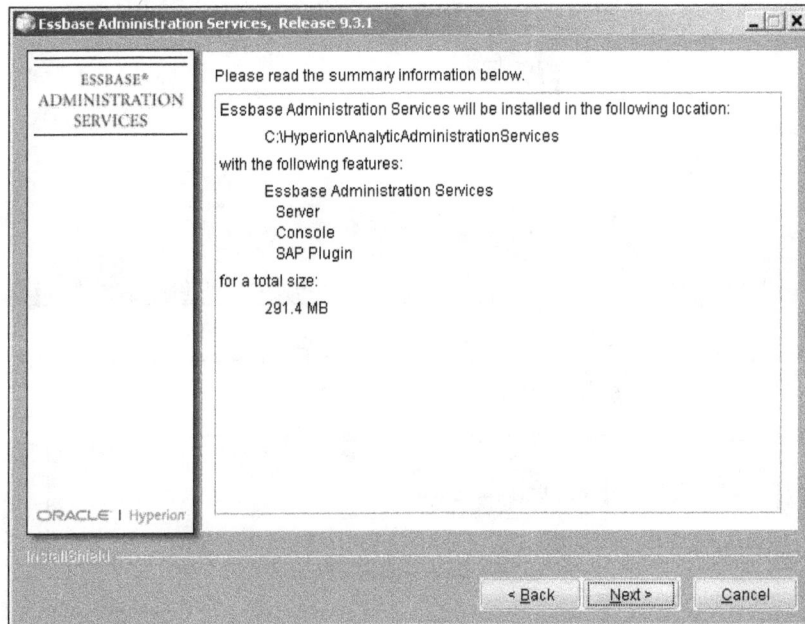

10. This step basically tells you that the EAS installation is in progress. Take a break, read the installations notes as they flash on the screen. Seems like Déjà vu.

11. Now, here's another one we've seen before. In this case, there is no need for the configuration tool, since you are only installing the EAS tool. *Do not* check the box on the screen labeled **Launch Configuration Tool**. Simply click **Finish**.

Your EAS is now installed and ready for use. The next few steps briefly describe how to start the EAS and login for the first time.

Starting the EAS

Your EAS tool requires the use of a web server to communicate with the Essbase agent on the analytic server. You can install EAS on a bona fide web server, but in this example, we will use the small web admin server included with the Essbase set up package. This small web server allows you to install the EAS directly on your client.

The starting of the Tomcat administration server and the EAS tool is a two step process:

1. Locate the admin server start executable (the location is dependent on system paths chosen by you during installation). The server executable is located in the `Hyperion\EAS\Server\Bin` path. Start the server by double-clicking the executable (it's handy to create a shortcut to this file on your desktop).

2. Locate the EAS console executable (again, the location is dependent on the installation paths you have chosen). This path is usually located in the `Hyperion\EAS\Console\Bin` path. Start the console by double-clicking on it (it's also handy to create a shortcut to this file on your desktop).

    When the EAS console opens, you will see the following screen. Initially you will need to supply the server name (network name of client), the default ID of **admin,** and the default password of **password**. It is highly recommended you immediately use the User Setup Wizard to create a supervisor account for yourself.

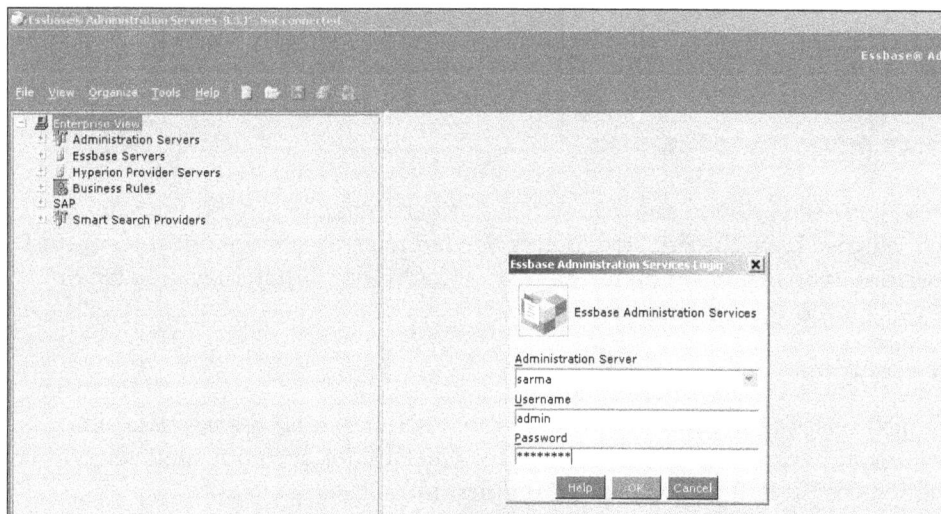

Following the documentation, connect to the Essbase server to test the installation. Using your mouse, right-click on **Add Essbase Server**. In the text boxes of the login screen, enter the Essbase server name as it is known on the network, the initial user ID (in our case **Hypuser**) and the initial password (ours is **password**, all lower case).

> This is the password that you have provided to the Essbase server upon the completion of the installation (Please refer to Step 14 of the Essbase Installation steps).

If your connection is successful, you will see the Essbase server listed in the left pane. You should be able to expand the server to see many options that are available.

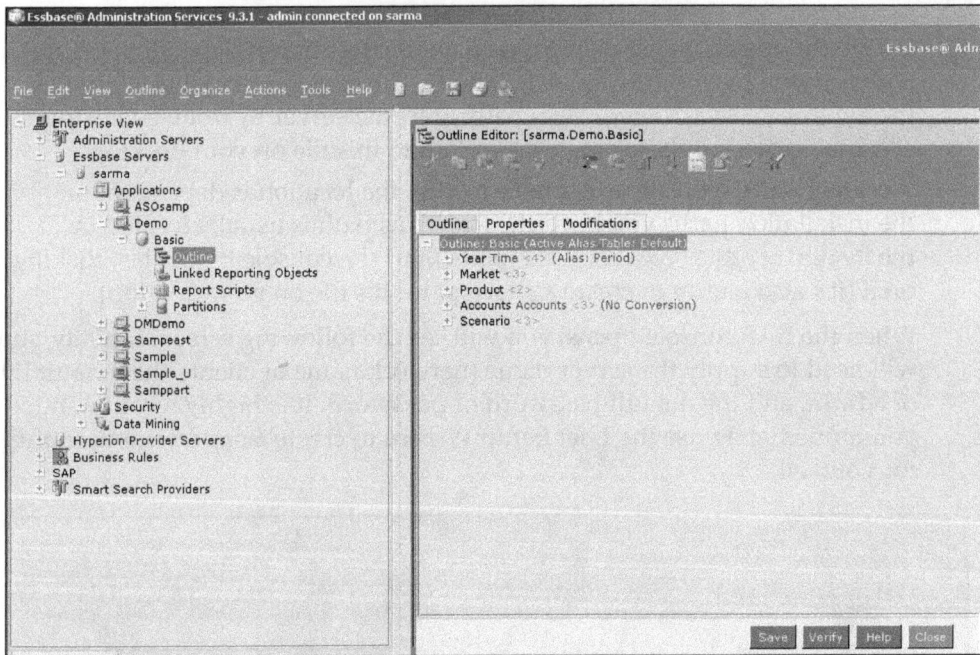

We now have the Essbase analytic server software installed on the analytic server. We also have the EAS tool that is needed to create, maintain, and support Essbase databases installed on the desktop PC. On top of that, they are able to talk to each other.

There is only one tool left to install!

In the next series of steps, we will install the much heralded Essbase Add-in for Microsoft Excel to complete the toolbox. Once that is accomplished, we will be ready to begin building and programming in Essbase.

Installing the Essbase Add-in for Microsoft Excel

We have installed Essbase analytic server and EAS and we are left only with the reporting tool. It's well known that most financial analysts are also Microsoft Excel experts (or believe they are). When you tell them the reporting tool they will be using is Microsoft Excel-based, you are almost certain to get your budget approved.

1. To get started, double-click on the Essbase client executable file supplied by Oracle. Huh? This screen looks familiar from the previous component installations. You know which language to select. Click **OK** when you are ready.

2. This step welcomes you to the installation of the Essbase client software, also known as the Essbase add-in. As usual, there are some recommendations and warnings, please click **Next** after you finish reading it.

3. In this step, as we have suggested before, please select the same country that you have chosen in the Essbase analytics server and EAS installations. In case you have forgotten, keeping the country variable consistent across all installed components will make your life easier. Once done, please click **Next**.

4. This step asks to read and agree to the EULA. Read it carefully, and if you agree and wish to continue, click **Next**.

5. This step has already detected the Hyperion home directory from a previous installation. If your home directory is different, select your home directory and then click **Next**.

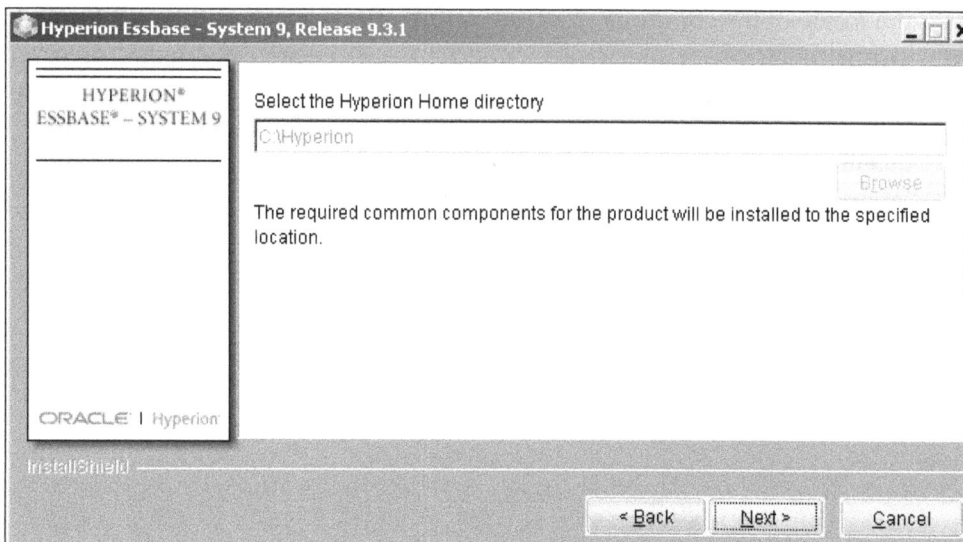

6. In this step, you are creating a directory for the Essbase client installation. Please choose `c:\Hyperion` and click **Next** when you are done.

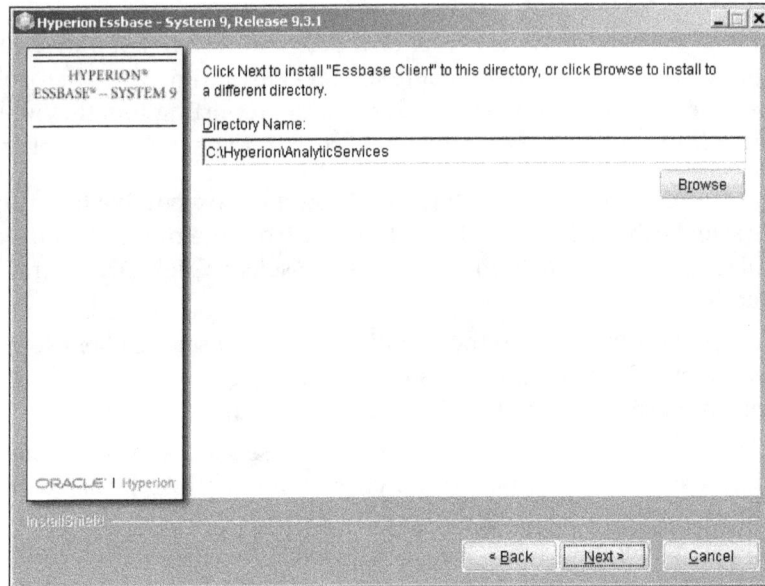

7. We recommend that you select **Typical** and click **Next**. As stated earlier, the **Typical** installation gives you all of the tools included with the software. Choosing **Custom** will really only provide more choices for samples.

8. This step requires you to select ESSLANG. The ESSLANG variable defines the locale of the computer. Just like before, please feel free to select **English**.

9. This step summarizes all of the components required for the client installation as well as the path. Please look them over carefully. Most importantly, verify the path and that it is correct with consideration to the other components installed on this machine. Click **Next** when you are satisfied that everything is correct.

10. This steps shows that the Essbase client installation is in progress and we recommend you not to take any more coffee breaks since you have already taken a lot of breaks in the previous installations.

[💡 **STATUTORY WARNING:**
Too much coffee drinking is injurious to health!]

When the installation wizard finishes installing the software, the **Next** button will be enabled. Please click **Next** to continue.

11. This step tells you that the Essbase client installation is completed. Click **Next** when you are ready.

12. Now, open Microsoft Excel. As it loads you should briefly see a **HYPERION ESSBASE SPREADSHEET ADD-IN** splash screen (shown below). Once Microsoft Excel has finished loading, you should see a brand new menu pick named **Essbase** that is usually located between the **Window** pick and the **Help** pick. This tells you that the Essbase client is successfully installed.

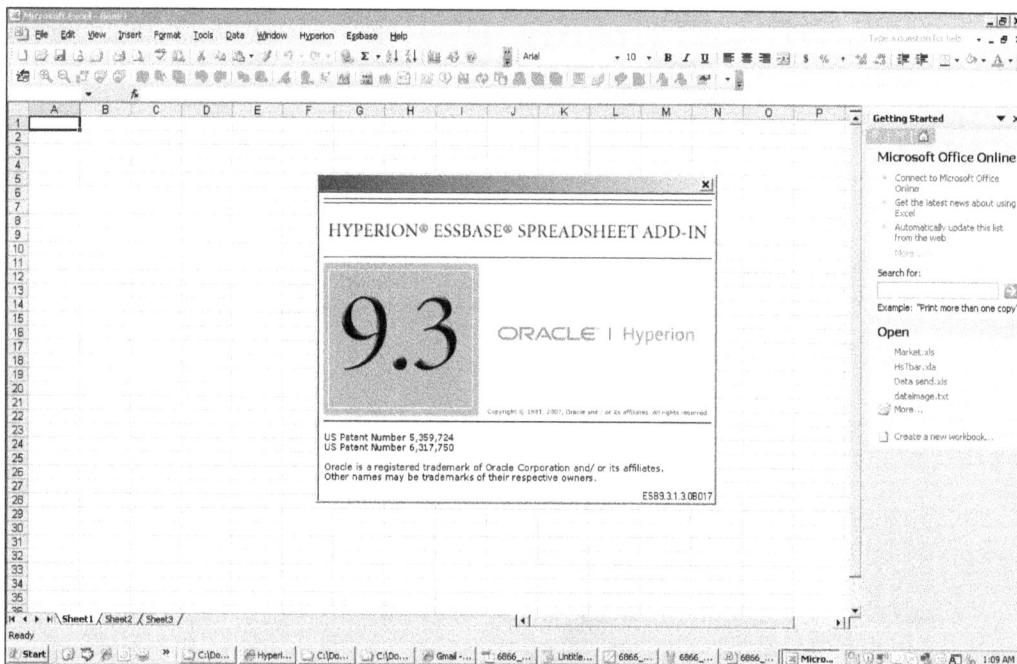

A typical network setup

In the following diagram, we show you a high-level image of the Essbase installation you have just completed. This is a very typical set up for most operations.

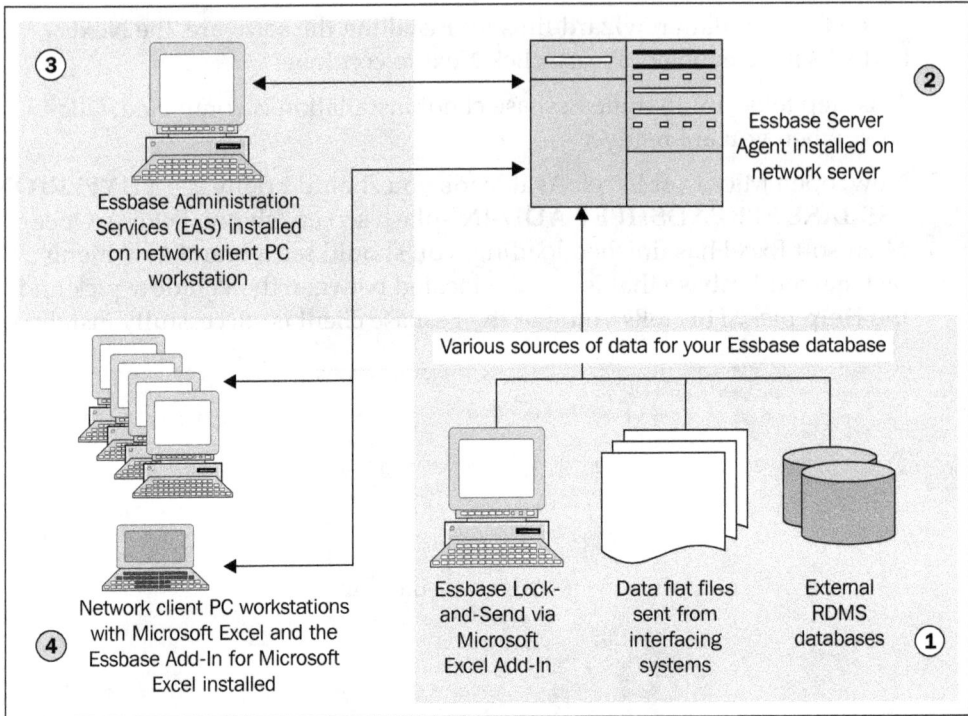

(3) Essbase Administration Services (EAS) installed on network client PC workstation

(2) Essbase Server Agent installed on network server

Various sources of data for your Essbase database

(4) Network client PC workstations with Microsoft Excel and the Essbase Add-In for Microsoft Excel installed

Essbase Lock-and-Send via Microsoft Excel Add-In

Data flat files sent from interfacing systems

(1) External RDMS databases

To help you understand and recognize your creation, the network diagram is divided into four sections which are explained below:

1. **Raw data**: Loading data from a little to a lot is easy in Essbase. Data can be sent directly to the database using the "Lock and Send" feature of the Oracle Essbase Add-in for Microsoft Excel. Flat files received from other systems can be easily rendered Essbase-friendly, using convenient and easy to use data load rules. Finally, vast amounts of data can be loaded using SQL data load rules that interface directly with relational databases.

2. **The Essbase server**: Running on the Essbase server is also something known as the Essbase agent. Depending on your needs, it is always best to try and use a dedicated server for your Essbase service. But don't worry, if that's not possible, we've found that Essbase does integrate nicely with other applications that have been installed.

3. **The developer client**: This is on the desktop workstation that EAS is installed on. You will also want to have Microsoft Excel and the Oracle Essbase Add-in for Microsoft Excel installed on this machine as well. A setup like this allows the developer to quickly create and test many pieces of an Essbase application, such as calculation results, data load validations, and so on.

4. **End-user PC**: This is your typical networked workstation that has decent computing power and storage. Having Microsoft Excel and the Oracle Essbase Add-in for Microsoft Excel installed are all that is necessary to provide the end-user with an extremely capable analysis and reporting tool.

Summary

You did it! You've made it this far and haven't run away. While the individual installations have probably seemed routine or even mundane at times, we wanted to give you the benefit of our experience. This should have helped you avoid small mistakes now that can cause big problems later.

What we have created is a very capable basic Essbase installation. Very basic in Oracle Essbase terms means a very powerful set up. Of course, there are many optional configuration settings and tweaks that can make your Essbase system virtually limitless. All this and more, will be discussed in future chapters.

Now that we have successfully installed Essbase, it is time for us to dive deeply into the world of Essbase. In our next chapter, we will talk more about Essbase cube design consideration, Essbase application and database types, data storage options. By the end of the next chapter, you will be able to create your first Essbase application and database.

2
Essbase Data and Design Considerations

We have successfully performed the installation of Oracle's Essbase software and it is functioning correctly. Let's cross-check for a minute, we have the server agent installed and running, the EAS installed on our client and operating correctly, and the Oracle Essbase Add-in for Microsoft Excel is also installed on our client in Microsoft Excel. We are now ready to begin learning and exploring Oracle Essbase!

In this chapter, we will discuss how to use the data elements required by the customer and transform them from the usual row and column relational schema into Essbase-friendly meta-data dimensions and data members.

Moving ahead, we will use the Esscar Motor Company as the fictitious business customer for all of our examples throughout this book. The Esscar Motor Company is a traditional multinational automobile manufacturing enterprise.

Introduction to OLAP

OLAP is the common term for Online Analytical Processing and is generally known to be a multidimensional, client-server computing environment.

The differences between OLAP analytical solutions and traditional data analysis applications containing backend relational databases are stark. The most obvious being an OLAP analytical application's ability to provide speedy analysis of broad slices of data. Programs which are complex and expensive to write would be required to perform even a fraction of the functionality provided by a simple Oracle Essbase OLAP application.

Another notable difference is OLAP's ability to drill-down to the lowest level of granularity with ease. You will even hear phrases like, **slice and dice**, and **multidimensionality**, which means having the ability to view the data from virtually any perspective. Finally, the ability to calculate large amounts of data on the fly gives users a superior advantage over traditional applications with relational databases when it comes to "what if" and "cause-and-effect" data analysis and reporting.

> Oracle Essbase is widely known as a financial analytical tool. We want to change the mindset just a bit, right here and now. Oracle Essbase absolutely is a superior financial OLAP tool, but it is an equally superior OLAP tool for just about *any* type of data analysis.

Determining the data requirements

One of the most important factors for any successful Essbase database design is to determine up-front what data elements and attributes are required.

Our business customer is the director of sales forecasting and production planning for the Esscar Motor Company. What if our customer would like to have the ability to create a monthly sales forecast for the vehicles manufactured by Esscar Motor Company and then sold in the various markets they compete in? The customer also needs to see the effects of the sales forecast on the planned production volumes and the required stock of vehicles. In addition, with regard to future monthly planning, the data needs to be robust enough to provide historical looks at the data and year over year comparisons. As you can see in the following screenshot, you can use Oracle Essbase for predictive analysis for future or forecast periods:

	Four Door Sedan								
	<-- Historical Periods			Future Periods -->					
	Jan 2009	Feb 2009	Mar 2009	Apr 2009	May 2009	Jun 2009	Jul 2009	Aug 2009	Sep 2009
Units Built	21335	15998	14789	21573	22864	19002	10123	22541	25148
Units Built Year Ago	*18898*	*16916*	*15992*	*20184*	*21143*	*19580*	*9649*	*20446*	*22152*
Variance to Year Ago +(-)	2437	(918)	(1203)	1389	1721	(578)	474	2095	2996
Total Sales	7771	17332	20887	24158	33672	19554	16879	16544	13152
Total Sales Year Ago	*8751*	*16304*	*21312*	*24000*	*32757*	*18118*	*15332*	*16521*	*10468*
Variance to Year Ago +(-)	(980)	1028	(425)	158	915	1436	1547	23	2684
Total Vehicle Stock Units	55490	49254	46383	41028	40594	37141	31974	35238	36494
Total Vehicle Stock Units Year Ago	*47445*	*48009*	*43414*	*39147*	*28760*	*28859*	*21862*	*28036*	*38791*
Variance to Year Ago +(-)	8045	1245	2969	1881	11834	8282	10112	7202	(2297)

Let us see what we have learned about data requirements from our customer. What data elements are important and must be included in the database? Our customer has indicated that they need to track vehicle sales, vehicle production, gross stocks, and profits. Chances are that there will be more data elements, but because we are working with Essbase, they can be added quickly and easily at anytime in the future.

The elements listed in the previous paragraph will become members under a dimension, which we will call Measures. These elements are what the customer is using to measure his business. It is the attributes of these data elements which will help us determine the rest of the necessary dimensions in the Essbase outline.

> The dimensions described in an Essbase outline can best be described as a category of information used to organize your data. For example, Calendar Periods can be a dimension in an Oracle Essbase database and can also be used to describe the frequency of your data. Dimensions will be discussed in depth in the next chapter.
>
> The Measures dimension is included in most databases as it contains the customer-required measurables. The other dimensions can be thought of as the necessary descriptors of the measurable data, such as Calendar Periods, product lines, markets.

When we talk about the data elements and their categories, we ask many questions. Typically, each critical data descriptor or data member category, needs to be created as a dimension in the Essbase database outline. Keep reading to see how this plays out.

Although we go into great detail on exactly what a database outline is and the purpose it serves, for the time being, consider the Essbase database outline to be similar to a logical data model you create for a standard relational database.

One use of your new system is to track the company's performance based on sales and profits. What is the frequency of the data? Is it safe to figure that we need a Calendar Periods dimension in the database outline? Depending on how we build the Calendar Periods dimension, we will be able to work with the data on a monthly, quarterly, or yearly basis.

What is it that our customer produces? Why, it's automobiles of course! Wouldn't our customer want to track the company's performance in many ways? We are probably safe in assuming that we need to create a Total Vehicle dimension that allows us to look at the data by an individual vehicle line or by the total of all vehicles.

One feature or characteristic of our customer's product that may not be applicable to all types of manufacturing companies is the model year. Typically, automobile manufacturers produce the same vehicle line year after year, but introduce a new model year for every calendar year. It's a pretty safe bet that our customer would like a `Total Model Year` dimension in the database.

Another consideration with our customer's data is the type of customers. You will find this to be true in many situations when dealing with an enterprise that manufactures and sells a product. In the case of the Esscar Motor Company, vehicles are marketed to retail customers and fleet customers. Retail customers are the typical private consumers who buy one car at a time and the fleet customer is usually another company or entity, that purchases many vehicles at once. The customer agrees he needs a `Total Customer` dimension.

The Esscar Motor Company produces and markets vehicles in several countries. Would it be safe to say we need a `Total Market` dimension? If we structure the `Total Market` dimension properly, we can look at company performance by individual country (`Market`) or by total country (`Total Market`).

Now that we have gathered the data attributes necessary for reporting, we have one last requirement to fulfill. Our customer has asked if there is a way he can have his data "as is", and prepare different versions of the data to help with analyzing and strategizing. In other words, our customer needs to have the ability to create full looks at the data with many different versions or *scenarios*. Thus, we provide a `Scenario` dimension. The customer can now create a forecast that has several looks at the same data with only "what if" changes made and see the effects side-by-side with the other scenarios. It's a beautiful thing!

The following is a quick visual that, we hope, gives you an idea of how the Essbase outline will look. Please study it carefully. Understanding the hierarchical or parent-child relationship between the members of the outline is critical with respect to successful programming with Oracle Essbase.

Notice that the high level names are the data members or categories or as you will soon come to know them, the dimensions, in the database outline that we have discussed previously. Observe how the children members of the `Total Market` dimension will be added to summarize the value in the `Total Market` database outline member.

```
Outline    Properties    Modifications
- Outline: Esscar (Active Alias Table: Default)
  - CALENDER PERIODS Time <2>
    - 2009 (+) <4>
      - QTR1 2009 (+) <3>
          JAN 2009 (+) (Alias: 200901)
          FEB 2009 (+) (Alias: 200902)
          MAR 2009 (+) (Alias: 200903)
      + QTR2 2009 (+) <3>
      + QTR3 2009 (+) <3>
      + QTR4 2009 (+) <3>
    + 2010 (+) <4>
  - TOTAL VEHICLES <4>
      2 DOOR SEDAN (+)
      4 DOOR SEDAN (+)
      4X2 PICKUP (+)
      4X4 PICKUP (+)
  + TOTAL MARKET <3>
  - MODEL YEAR <2>
      MYR 2009 (+)
      MYR 2010 (+)
  - METRIC or MEASURE Accounts <2>
```

Study carefully how the **MYR 2009** number can be easily added to the **MYR 2010** number to give us the `Total Model Year` number.

This is a highly simplified example of an Essbase database outline, its structure, and relationships. In the next chapter, we will go over the Essbase database outline much more thoroughly.

In the next section, we shall use what we have learned here to make decisions on the best methods to store data in our Essbase database.

Determine data storage options

Get ready to toss out everything you've ever learned about storing data in a typical relational database with tables, rows, and columns. Keeping the above example of the Essbase outline in mind, we will now begin covering how the data is stored in Essbase and the various options available to you (the Essbase programmer).

> An Essbase cube usually stores less physical data than a typical relational database must store to deliver the same results to the user. Usually, the greatest saving is in the expense of data retrieval times. The results returned from a typical Essbase database require less processing overhead than the similar results being delivered as the result of queries performed against relational database tables.

Essbase stores data in what is commonly referred to as a multidimensional array.

Inside the multidimensional array are the data cells. It is these data cells where the data is actually stored.

The smallest vehicle that Essbase uses to store data is a cell. A data cell however, cannot stand alone. The smallest *usable* vehicle to store data, contained in an Essbase database, is the data block (see the following figure). These data blocks are the building blocks of the Essbase cube:

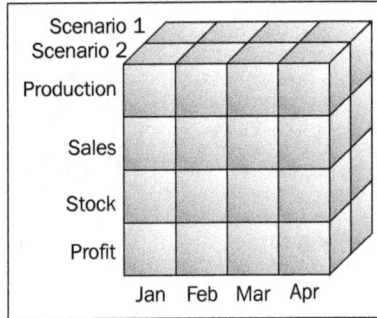

A simplified explanation is that the data blocks are made up of data cells. The number of data cells are, for the most part, in direct relation to the number of dimensions in the Essbase outline (the data attributes explained previously), and the number of possible data combinations or intersections that can be created.

Relational Sales Table					
Country	**Vehicle**	**Model Year**	**Retail**	**Fleet**	**Total**
US	Sedan	2010	50	200	250
US	4-Door	2010	33	67	100
Relational Stock Table					
Country	**Vehicle**	**Model Year**	**Retail**	**Fleet**	**Total**
US	Sedan	2010	75	75	150
US	4-Door	2010	45	155	200

In a traditional relational database, one new element of data may require an entire new row of data in *one to many* tables. Looking at the previous screenshot, you can see that if you need to add stock information on a vehicle, you will need to insert a new row in the Stock table of your relational database.

In Essbase, that same new piece of data is plugged into the waiting data cell that was created in the data block, when the database outline was structured or restructured. You can add a new dimension to the database outline or add new members to an existing dimension at any time. By adding dimensions to the database outline, you are actually increasing the size of the data block. When a data block is created by Essbase, it contains cells for all of the various dimensions whether you have the data at that point or not. In our example, the data block created by the database would already contain a cell for stock, even if you did not yet have a value to store there. When you have a value for stock, it just gets plugged into its data cell and the size of the database is unaffected.

When you add or remove information from the outline and save the outline, Essbase will automatically restructure the database and modify the data blocks (add/remove data cells) to incorporate the new outline information as necessary.

In Oracle Essbase there are two distinct storage options that can be used when creating a database. These storage options are known as the **Block Storage Option (BSO)** and the **Aggregate Storage Option (ASO)**. These storage options are discussed in greater detail later in this book. For most transactional Essbase applications, the more suitable of the two options is the BSO. For our example in this book, we will create an Application | Database using the BSO.

It should be mentioned that the size of the data blocks can have a dramatic effect on the performance of the system. It is always best to try and avoid extremely large and complex database outlines. As we explained previously, the data blocks are structured roughly in relation to the possible combinations of data based on the number of members in the database outline.

More members = larger data blocks.
Less members = smaller data blocks.

Oracle Essbase offers an extremely valuable option to help keep block sizes to a minimum in order to help keep your database running at peak performance. The dynamically calculated database member!

The dynamically calculated member is a measure typically derived from other data elements in the database. It is not physically stored in the database. Instead, it is only created (calculated) at the time you ask for it. There are three great benefits for building your database with dynamically calculated members:

1. There is a huge potential to create many new measures without adding new sources of data or writing expensive programs to derive the values.

2. While the dynamically calculated member occupies a place in the database outline, it does not affect the block size in the database, therefore, it does not affect performance.

3. The resultant measure is always accurate to the other measures in the database and will always **tally** (the derived number will always equal the result of the stored component numbers). There is never a question of "where did this number come from?".

Types of Essbase applications

A nice feature of Oracle Essbase is that it allows you to create high level umbrella applications under which you can group similar databases. The similarity in databases means they are either similar in function or purpose.

When we speak of an Essbase application, it must be noted that all databases are created under an umbrella application. You may have one or many databases under an application, but you cannot create a database without a parent application. Likewise, an application is virtually useless without dependent databases.

Oracle recommends that we have only one database for an application. The reason for this is that when you restructure a database, the entire application is locked and you will not be able to perform any other actions on the application or dependent databases.

This Application | Database structure allows for a more organized layout and design and also allows for better data and security management.

As mentioned, an Essbase application can be one of two types:

1. Aggregate Storage Option
2. Block Storage Option

Let's discuss them in detail.

Aggregate Storage Option (ASO)

In Essbase 9.x versions, the ASO is also called **Essbase analytics**. The ASO is most suitable for the sparser data sets of high dimensionality, allowing a greater number of dimensions and members. The ASO model is not a replacement for the BSO, but it is an alternative for the business users depending on the needs of the customer. In an Essbase Application | Database built using ASO, the data is loaded into the leaf nodes or lowest levels, but are not aggregated into the upper levels using typical Essbase `calc` and `store` methods. Rather, they are calculated dynamically on the fly (per user request).

It must also be mentioned that the ASO is best suited as a *Read Only* application. It is best used when analysis on large amounts of data is necessary for presentation, analysis, or reporting purposes.

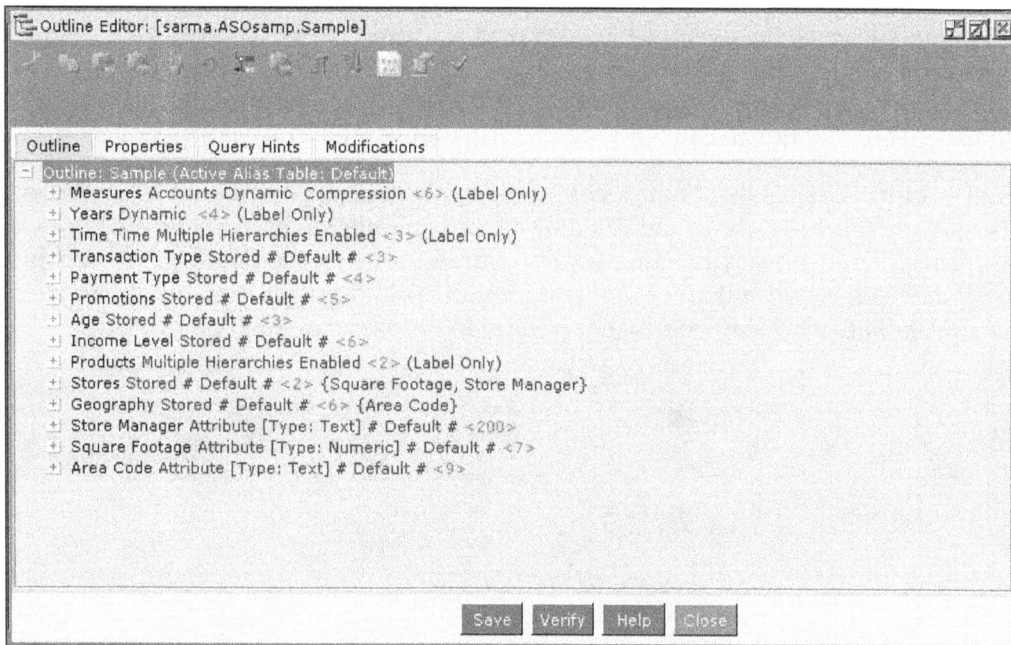

We will talk more about ASO, and the differences between ASO and BSO, in Chapter 10.

Block Storage Option (BSO)

The BSO is best suited for denser concentrations of data. The BSO also supports write back or update capabilities from Microsoft Excel using the "Lock and Send" method within the Essbase add-in or from automated batch data load operations. The Essbase add-in has built-in functionality that allows the user to update data directly in the database by simply selecting the *Lock* and then *Send* selections from the Essbase add-in menu. When selected, the Lock function will lock all the data blocks affected by the range of data contained in the Microsoft Excel spreadsheet. The Send function will then send the data values back to the database. After a successful update, the locked data is automatically unlocked. This database model is best suited for *Financial Applications* where the users can perform complex calculations. In BSO, each dimension is tagged as either a dense or sparse data concentration. In a dense dimension, the data cubes have the likelihood that *all* the cells in a data block will be populated with data. In a sparse setting, the opposite is true, there would likely be empty data cells. For example, in your database, the Calendar Periods dimension would most likely be a dense dimension, since there would be data for most items for each time period. The Market dimension would probably be sparse as chances are that not all of your products are sold in all of the countries.

Shown below is a snapshot of the sample BSO application provided with the Essbase installation. You will note (as indicated by the pink number in braces) that each dimension has a relatively low number of children. As mentioned in the ASO section, a BSO database is best suited for moderate amounts of data complexity where features like updatability tend to have a higher priority to the user than high performance.

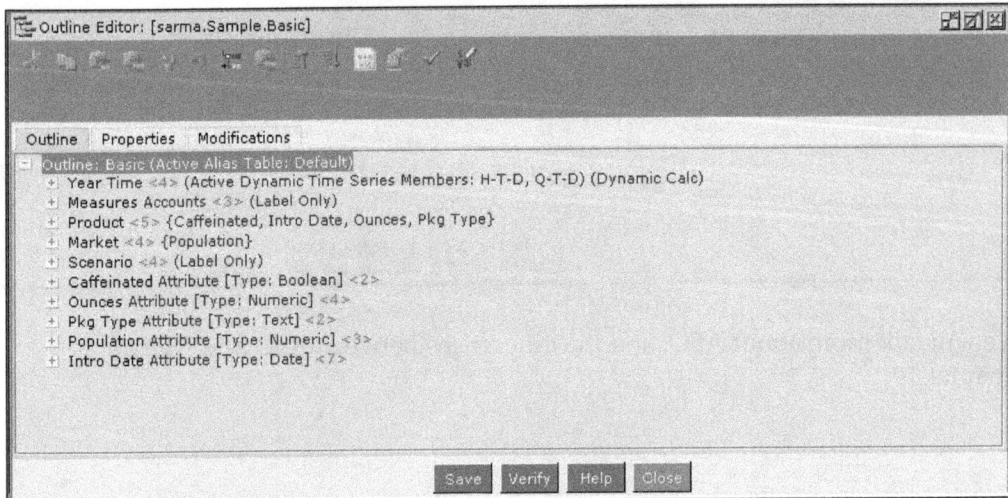

The Essbase server agent installation is equipped to handle multiple applications that can be all ASO, all BSO, or any mix of ASO and BSO applications.

When an Essbase application is started on the server, all the database objects pertaining to the application are loaded into the server's memory. For every Essbase application that is loaded, the server will launch a process named ESSSVR with a unique process ID. If a particular ESSSVR process agent is stopped, all the databases under the application will be stopped, and the memory that is being used by this process will be released.

> Typically, batch data load or cube build operations that use large amounts of resources are best performed during off-peak or even weekend hours. Wherever possible, we strongly recommend that all non-essential application and/or databases on the server be stopped during large processes to further increase performance.

We have just started an application and a snippet from the server log file can be seen below. Note the highlighted text below and how it depicts that Essbase has made a log entry for the application Demo being started. The process ID listed is the server operating system process ID.

```
[Thu Sep 11 00:40:44 2008]Local/ESSBASE0///Info(1051001)
Received client request: Get App and Database Status (from user
[hypuser])

[Thu Sep 11 00:40:44 2008]Local/ESSBASE0///Info(1051001)
Received client request: MaxL: Execute (from user [hypuser])

[Thu Sep 11 00:40:45 2008]Local/ESSBASE0///Info(1054014)
Database Basic loaded

[Thu Sep 11 00:40:45 2008]Local/ESSBASE0///Info(1051061)
Application Demo loaded - connection established
```

[Thu Sep 11 00:40:45 2008]Local/ESSBASE0///Info(1054027)
Application [Demo] started with process id [4744]

```
[Thu Sep 11 00:40:45 2008]Local/ESSBASE0///Info(1056090)
System altered

[Thu Sep 11 00:40:45 2008]Local/ESSBASE0///Info(1051001)
Received client request: MaxL: Execute (from user [hypuser])

[Thu Sep 11 00:40:45 2008]Local/ESSBASE0///Info(1051001)
Received client request: MaxL: Describe (from user [hypuser])
```

It should be noted that occasionally, when there is a disruption to an Essbase process (like an external database failure or a file server down), and the process has passed the point of no return (Essbase term), the instance of ESSSVR that was running the interrupted load process may place it into terminating mode. In spite of this, the process never really gets terminated.

To terminate this process, you either need to reboot the Essbase server causing interruption to the all other applications that reside on the server, or by using the above process ID, you can kill only the offending ESSSVR process on the Essbase server.

The following screenshot shows how to terminate the process in a Windows server environment. Highlight the process and click on the **End Process** button.

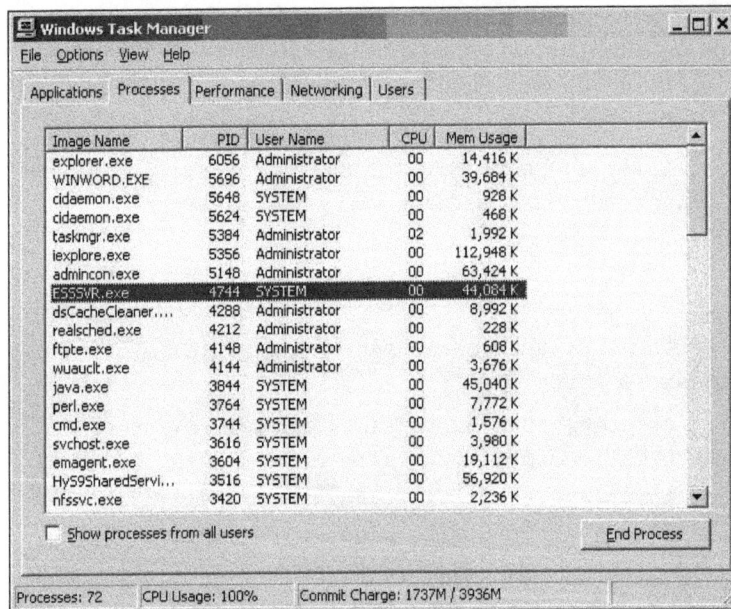

Unicode and Non-Unicode applications

Before we go further, let us explore the definition of Unicode. What is Unicode? According to http://unicode.org/, Unicode provides a unique number for every character, irrespective of the platform, the program, and the language used.

Essbase supports Unicode encoding. When you create an application, you define it as either a Unicode or Non-Unicode application. If you are dealing with customers across the globe and want to support different languages, then you would choose the Unicode setting for your application. The Unicode setting in Oracle Essbase uses the accepted standard UTF-8 character encoding.

Let us say our Esscar cube is being used by our *Financial Analysts* in the European Union and they want to see the sales information in their language, using Essbase's alias table ability you achieve this functionality.

The default Essbase setting is Non-Unicode for applications, databases, and related scripts, etc. Essbase Non-Unicode applications only support one character set which is defined by the **locale value** chosen at the time of installation. It must be the same across all Essbase components used in the installation.

> You cannot convert a Unicode application into a Non-Unicode application but you can convert Non-Unicode to a Unicode application.

Now that we have learned a little bit about Essbase applications, let's start building our first Essbase application.

Creating your first Essbase application

When viewing information in the EAS, you will notice that it is setup in a similar fashion to Windows Explorer, with a graphical hierarchical tree structure.

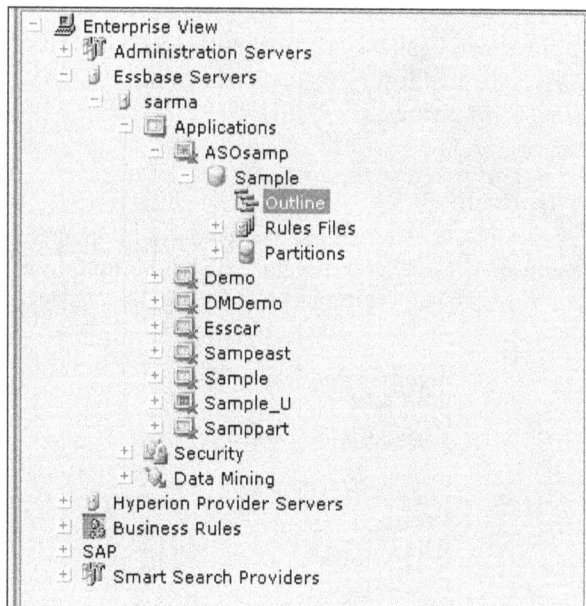

To create an Essbase application, click on the **File** menu in EAS and select **New**. You then have the choice of selecting either the **BSO** or the **ASO** storage options.

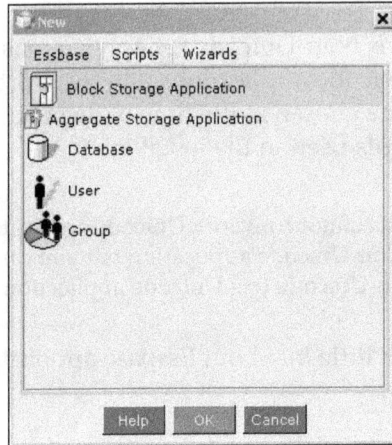

For our Esscar Motor Company example, we have selected BSO as our storage option. This is where you also have the option to choose either Unicode or Non-Unicode. We will be using Non-Unicode for our application. Now, give a name to your application, say, **ESSCAR**.

In a Non-Unicode application, Essbase supports upto 8 characters for the names of all Essbase objects like application names, database names, data load rules file names, and calculation script names.

> **Very important!**
> In Windows-based installations, using spaces in database object names and their associated directory paths should be avoided at all costs. Coding can sometimes be challenging when spaces are used.

Click **OK**. Hurray! you have now created your first Essbase application. Now that you have created your Essbase application, let us take a quick look into the Essbase application properties.

Essbase Application Properties

As the name suggests, Application Properties will allow you to set the properties for an application. You can update the name of your application, set the start up options, and also set the initial security levels. These properties can only be changed using the EAS by any user who at least has an access level of **Application Designer** to the application being updated and by automated scripts like Essbase command scripts or Essbase MaxL scripts. These scripts are explained completely later in this book.

There are two ways to get to the Application Properties:

1. Click on the name of the application to select it, then click on the **Action** menu on the EAS menu bar. Now, click on the **Edit Properties for "Esscar"**.

2. Click on the name of the application to select it and right-click over the application name. Here, you will also see **Edit Properties for "Esscar"** as one of your choices.

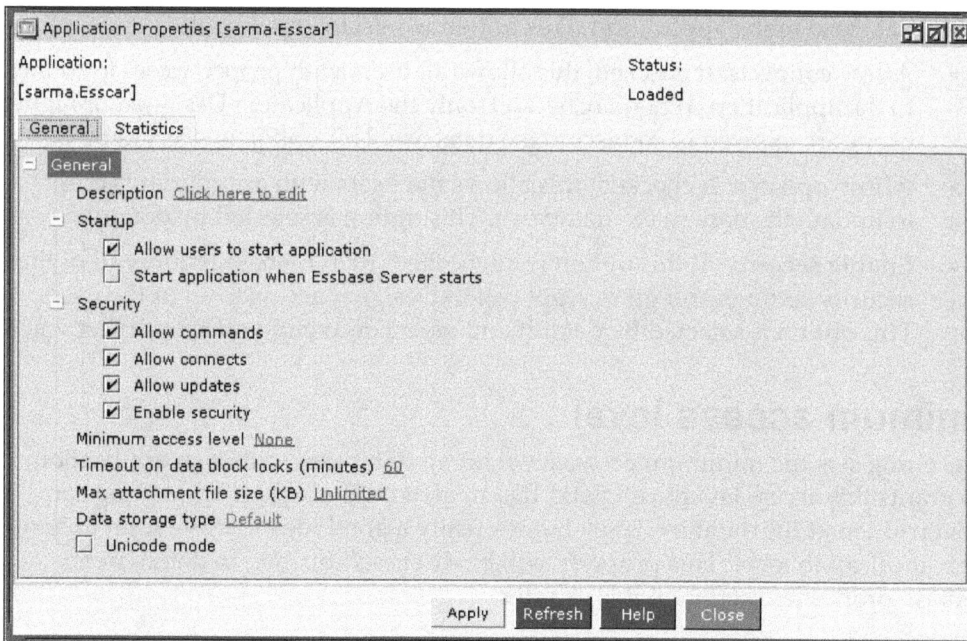

```
Application Properties [sarma.Esscar]

Application:                                    Status:
[sarma.Esscar]                                  Loaded

General    Statistics

General
       Description  Click here to edit
    Startup
          ☑  Allow users to start application
          ☐  Start application when Essbase Server starts
    Security
          ☑  Allow commands
          ☑  Allow connects
          ☑  Allow updates
          ☑  Enable security
       Minimum access level  None
       Timeout on data block locks (minutes)  60
       Max attachment file size (KB)  Unlimited
       Data storage type  Default
       ☐  Unicode mode

                                    Apply   Refresh   Help   Close
```

Startup section

This property is used to tell Essbase how to automatically start the application. There are two ways you can start an Essbase application:

- **Allow users to start application**
- **Start application when Essbase Server starts**

By default, **Allow users to start application** is selected and we advise you to leave it as it is. Only select the second option when it is absolutely necessary for the Essbase server to start your application. As you have previously learned, if an inactive application is started it will unnecessarily consume system memory. One of the only times it may be necessary to have an application start (when the Essbase server is started) is if you have an automated batch process which starts immediately following a server restart. This might be performed during routine server maintenance or housekeeping.

Security

There are several different types of security commands. They are listed as follows:

- **Allow commands**: If checked, this allows users to run commands on the database in the application. This option is selected by default.
- **Allow connects**: If checked, this allows all users with proper access to connect to the application. When unchecked, only the Application Designer, or higher users, are allowed to connect to the database. This option is selected by default.
- **Allow updates**: If checked, this allows the users with appropriate access to update the data in the databases. This option is selected by default.
- **Enable security**: If this option is unchecked, then Essbase ignores all of the security settings and gives Application Designer access to all of the users. This option is selected by default and we recommend you keep it that way.

Minimum access level

This setting sets the minimum access level for all databases within an application, and grants this access level to all valid IDs created on the server. The setting can be overridden at the database level, but it's really a good idea to leave it set to none at the application level. This property will be discussed further, in detail, in the database properties section of this chapter.

Types of Essbase databases

Essbase offers two types of databases that can be created. The first and most important choice is the normal or standard database. This database will be used in 100 percent of the applications you build in Essbase.

The normal (non-currency) database

The normal non-currency database is the cube you have heard so much about. All data dimensions and members are defined in the outline of this cube. The normal Essbase database is widely used for most data analysis where conversion of currency values is not required. In our Esscar Motor Company example, we could track and forecast vehicle production, sales volumes, trends, stocks, and all quite nicely with a simple to use non-currency database.

Essbase currency database

The currency conversion database is a great tool for analyzing data across international markets, which employ differing currencies. The currency conversion database stores the currency conversion values for each individual country. When currency data is requested by the user in his local currency, the normal cube will dynamically access the currency cube and convert the data on the fly.

> The symbiotic currency cube can be conceptually thought of as the currency dimension of the primary normal cube.

Database components

Let's now go through some of the most important components in every database.

- The database outline
- Linked Reporting Objects
- Partitions
- Calculation scripts
- Report scripts
- Rules files

The database outline

The database outline defines the structure of the multi-dimensional database, including its hierarchies, member formulas, and child to parent consolidations (data rollups).

Once a database is created, an Essbase outline is also created with the same name. This file is saved on the Essbase server with the .otl extension. In the next chapter, we talk in-depth about the Essbase outline.

Linked Reporting Objects

Using the **Linked Reporting Objects (LRO)**, you can attach an object to a cell. For instance, you could have a flowchart attached to a specific value in a cell alerting the user when the value was requested.

This object can be any of the following items:

- Cell note
- An externally created file like Microsoft Word, an image, or another Microsoft Excel file
- URL
- Another Essbase database

Partitions

Simply put, a partition is a slice of information from one database that is shared with another database. There are three options for partitioning data in Essbase.

- **Transparent partition**: Allows the users to access data from the source database as though it were stored in the target database. The source can be another database in another application or even on another Essbase server.
- **Replicated partition**: Is a copy of a slice of data from the source database that is stored in the target database.
- **Linked partition**: A linked partition points users from a cell in one database to a cell in another database. A linked partition can give users a different perspective of the data.

We will talk more about Essbase partitions in Chapter 8.

> Unless otherwise specified by you, the user, all Essbase file objects, including calculation scripts, report scripts, data load rules files, database index and page files, and database control files are stored on the Essbase analytic server using the server's own operating system's resident file system and are located in the default %Arborpath%/App/Database path.

When you install Oracle Essbase on your server and your client, the installation also creates new environment variables on your machines. The ARBORPATH environment variable is basically the path name all the way down to the Essbase folder itself. In the following screenshot, you can clearly see how the Essbase folder structure is laid out:

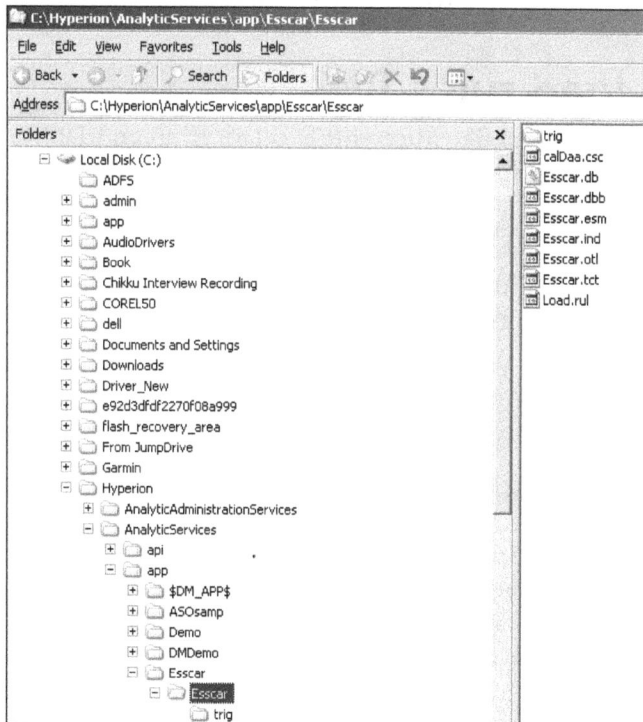

Calculation scripts

Essbase calculation scripts (Essbase file objects with the .csc extension) contain specific calculation instructions, written by you, that Essbase will use to perform specific calculations on the data. Essbase calculation scripts are actually ordinary ASCII text files which can be edited in a simple text editor, like Notepad, or which can be edited using the calculation script editor in the EAS. Essbase database calculation scripts are discussed in full detail in Chapter 4.

Report scripts

Essbase report scripts contain Essbase proprietary and cryptic instructions and commands. These are typically used in some sort of automated process to generate actual output reports which are extracted from the cube. Alternately, a report script can be used to extract data into a flat file, to export to a downstream system. These report scripts can be run manually from the EAS, or from an Essbase command script (MaxL script in later versions), or even from an API call inside a VB or COM+ application. Essbase report scripts are saved with the `.rep` file extension and they too are ASCII text files. Cursory knowledge is needed for creating or editing Essbase report scripts as they are actually coded in a symbolic Essbase pseudo-language. Essbase report scripts are discussed in detail in Chapter 6.

Database load rules files

Raw data from an ASCII text file, Microsoft Excel, or from an RDBMS database will be loaded into your Essbase cube using Essbase rules file objects.

Essbase rules files can be used in two ways:

- To dynamically build dimensions in the outline and add members (so you won't need to do it manually).
- To load data where you can define how the data is loaded, determine what data to skip or load, perform concatenations of separate columns into one, and even add business rules.

As with the Essbase report script objects, the rules file can be invoked from the EAS from an Essbase command script (MaxL script in later versions), or even from an API call inside a VB or COM+ application. The rules file objects are saved with the `.rul` extension and must be created, viewed, and edited through EAS. In Chapter 3, we will modify the Esscar database outline using the dimension build rules file functionality. In Chapter 4, we will discuss the data load rule file further.

Allowing duplicate member names

In Essbase 7.x and earlier versions, each outline member had a unique name and duplicate member names were not allowed. But in System 9, duplicate member names are allowed. If you want to have duplicate member names in your system, please make sure you check the **ALLOW DUPLICATE MEMBER NAMES** while creating the Essbase database.

Many people scratch their heads and wonder why you would want to allow duplicate member names in your database outline. Well, one example would be the city of New York and the state of New York. You may want to have New York in your outline as one state of the United States and then you may want to have New York in your outline as a city of New York state.

> A standard existing database outline can be converted to allow duplicate member names, but an outline that allows duplicate member names cannot be converted back to a standard outline.
>
> Exercise great care when using this option, as it is much like having data in a relational database table with a duplicate primary key.

Create your first Essbase database

You have your first Essbase application created and waiting. You have a good high level understanding of the types of Essbase databases that can be created. Let's now create your first database using EAS.

Select the Esscar application and right-click on it to bring up the application menu. From the menu, click on **Create Database** to bring up the following screen:

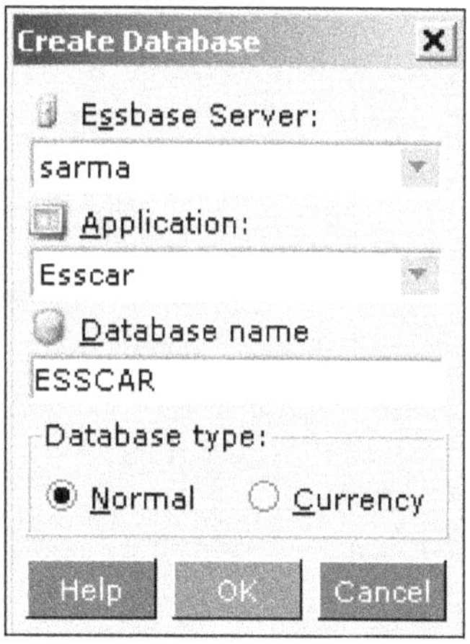

On the screen above, make sure you have the correct analytic server selected. Select the correct application (**Esscar**). Give a name to your database. In this case we will name the database **ESSCAR** (it's the same name used for the application).

[🔅 Remember, Oracle Essbase only supports object names upto 8 characters.]

Leave the default setting of **Normal** and do not check **Allow Duplicate Member Names**. Click **OK** and you now have a bouncing Essbase database. Congratulations!

Next, click on (expand) the **ESSCAR** database name shown under the **ESSCAR** application in EAS to reveal the database object selections that were added when the database was created.

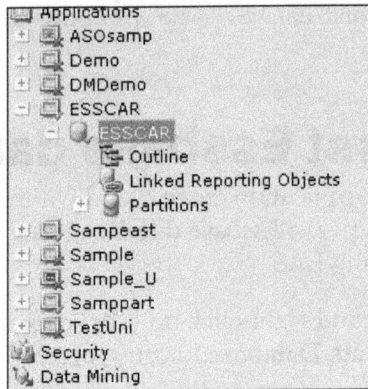

Right-clicking the **ESSCAR** database reveals several more menu options that are available to you. Click on the **Database Properties** selection to bring up the **Database Properties** screen shown as follows:

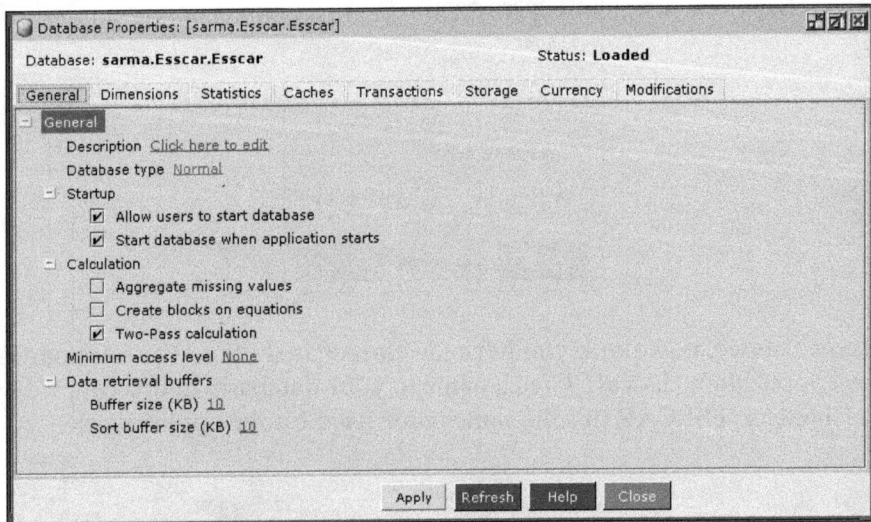

In the **Application Properties** screen as discussed previously, you see many database level options or properties that can be set or adjusted to suit your own computing or performance needs. We will take a moment to briefly discuss each available tabbed option on this screen, and the choices contained therein.

General tab

On this tab, the database name and description are displayed. Only the description field is editable and can be changed at will. The database name can be changed through another function not found on the properties screen (right-click on the database name in EAS and the **Rename Database** option will be available).

There is also startup information as shown on the **Application Properties** screen. In order to have optimal performance, leave the **Allow users to start database** checked and uncheck the **Start database when application starts** selection. There is usually no need to have a database start when its parent application starts.

The default calculation settings are best for now. The **Aggregate missing values** and **Create blocks on equations** both have database block size implications and should be used with extreme care. There will be much more on this topic in Chapter 5 on database calculation scripts. We leave the **Two-Pass calculation** option checked, because it allows you to code a member to use two-pass calculation functionality. You are not forced to use it just because the option is checked on this screen.

It is highly recommended you set **Minimum Access Level** to **None**, as all users must then be granted specific access to each database. The other choices are **Read, Write, Calculate,** and **Database Designer**.

Data retrieval buffers are settings that help with the performance of the spreadsheet add-in, and data being extracted with a report script object. More on these will be discussed in detail later.

Dimensions tab

In the **Dimensions** tab, you are presented with information on your database outline, with regard to the individual dimensions and their designation as either sparse or dense and the number of members contained. Much more about this is discussed in Chapter 3.

Database Properties: [sarma.Sampeast.East]

Database: **sarma.Sampeast.East** Status: **Loaded**

General Dimensions Statistics Caches Transactions Storage Currency Modifications

Number of dimensions 5

Dimension	Type	Members in Dimension	Members Stored
Year	Dense	17	16
Measures	Dense	16	13
Product	Sparse	22	19
Eastern Region	Sparse	6	6
Scenario	Dense	6	3

Apply Refresh Help Close

Statistics tab

The **Statistics** tab is a *Read-only* tab, but is very handy as it displays a wealth of useful information. The following screenshot illustrates this:

Database Properties: [sarma.Esscar.Esscar]

Database: **sarma.Esscar.Esscar** Status: **Loaded**

General Dimensions Statistics Caches Transactions Storage Currency Modifications

Statistics
- Database start time May 5, 2009 5:12:01 AM EDT
- Database elapsed time 1:15:14
- Number of connections 1
- Statistics last reset May 5, 2009 5:12:01 AM EDT

Blocks
- Number of existing blocks 0
- Block size (B) 16800
- Potential number of blocks 1
- Existing level 0 blocks 0
- Existing upper-level blocks 0
- Block density (%) 0.00
- Percentage of maximum blocks existing 0.00
- Compression ratio 0.00
- Average clustering ratio 1.00

Run-time
- Hit ratio on index cache 0.00
- Hit ratio on data cache 0.00
- Number of index page reads 0.00
- Number of index page writes 0.00
- Number of data block reads 0.00
- Number of data block writes 0.00
- Hit ratio on data file cache 0.00

Apply Refresh Help Close

Its better to look at the real screen for yourself through the EAS. When it comes to performance tuning, the settings on this screen will be invaluable!

Caches tab

Correctly set caches can make the difference between your business partner wanting to fire you or wanting to adopt you. We will discuss these important settings later on, but for now, just know that the default settings will be adequate for most moderate sized cubes with moderate sized calculation or reporting needs.

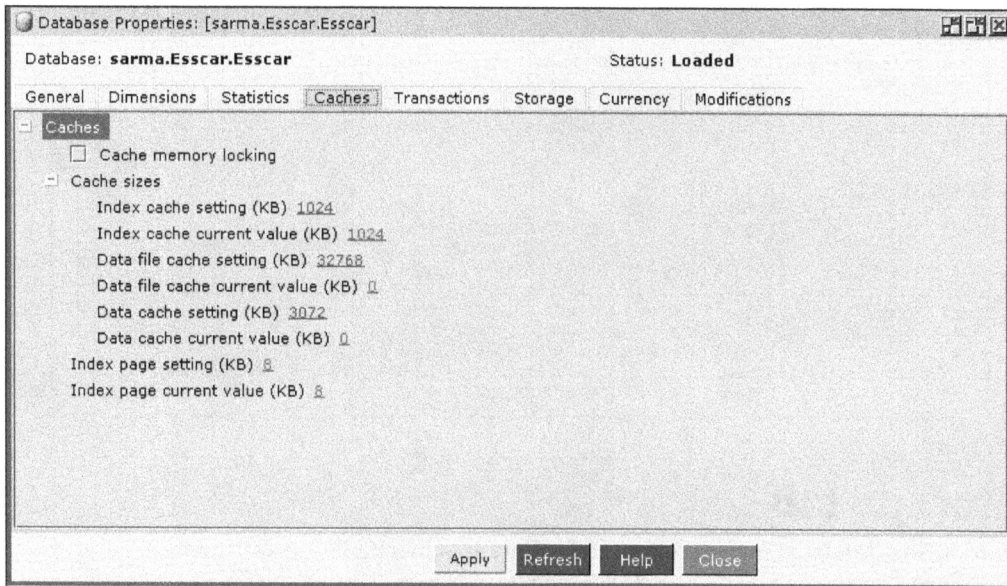

One suggestion on caches, unless you are using the direct I/O data load option which we will discuss in detail later, is to *never* check the **Cache memory locking** option . The **Cache memory locking** option locks the maximum amount of memory for each cache, whether the database uses it or not. If your system is running that close to maximum capacity, you better purchase some more memory in a hurry!

Transactions tab

Boring! Oh, sorry, this is a necessary option, but it's a setting that makes adjustments which never really help or hinder performance all that noticeably. Committing data after a certain number of transactions and not locking the entire database, when calculating does have merit. We have never really had to play with these settings on large or small databases. You would need to have some sort of extreme situation involving conflicting and concurrent processes to facilitate any adjustment to these settings.

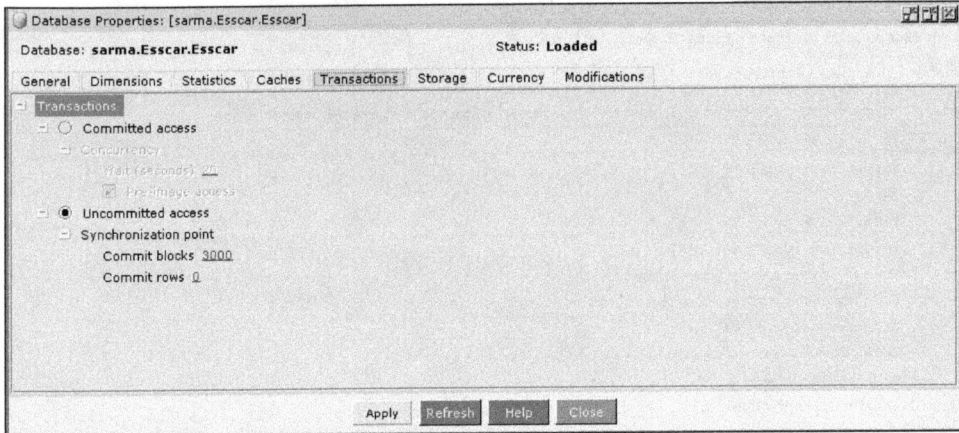

Storage tab

Here is one database property that definitely has merit! These settings affect how and where Essbase stores your database page and index files, the compression used, and the type of I/O used to read/write the data.

For starters, the I/O method can have a noticeable impact on performance when large data loads or transactions are involved. Buffered I/O uses the operating system's file system and is the default setting. When more performance is needed, the direct I/O setting can be used. The direct I/O setting provides asynchronous overlapped I/O that gives the user less waiting time.

Database Properties: [sarma.Esscar.Esscar]

Database: **sarma.Esscar.Esscar**　　　　　　　　　Status: **Loaded**

General　Dimensions　Statistics　Caches　Transactions　Storage　Currency　Modifications

Current I/O access mode: Buffered I/O
Pending I/O access mode: Buffered I... ▼
Data compression: Bitmap encoding ▼

Disk Volume	Partition Size	Unit	File Type	File Size	Unit

Set　Delete

Data/Index File Type	Size	Status	Name

Apply　Refresh　Help　Close

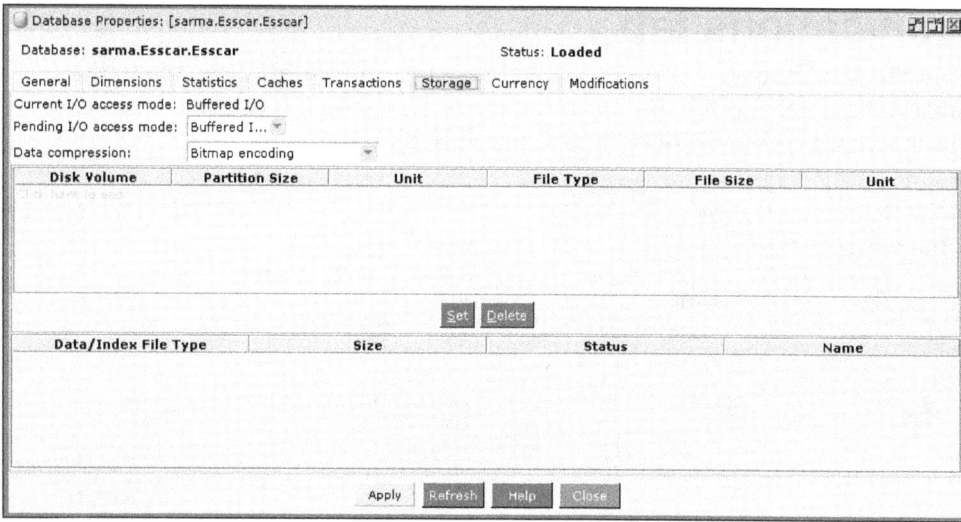

The **Storage** tab also has choices for data compression. The setting for bit-mapped compression is the default setting and is also the most efficient because it only stores cells that contain data. Any null values are not stored. There are several compression methods supported and Essbase can even run with no compression. However, it must be noted that Essbase will expand, to full uncompressed file size, any data page file it needs at the time of the request for data.

Currency tab

If you recall from the previous discussion on the normal and currency cubes and their uses, this tab is where you would create the symbiotic relationship by defining what currency cube the normal cube will be using for its currency conversions.

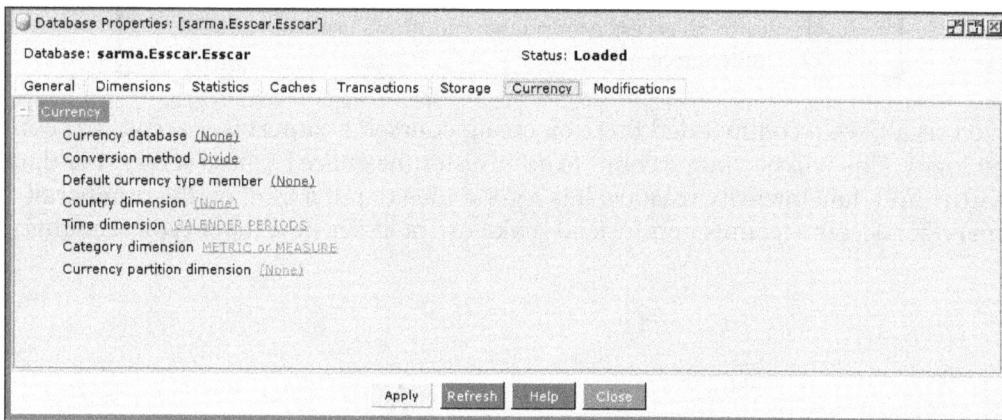

Database Properties: [sarma.Esscar.Esscar]

Database: **sarma.Esscar.Esscar**　　　　　　　　　Status: **Loaded**

General　Dimensions　Statistics　Caches　Transactions　Storage　Currency　Modifications

Currency
　　Currency database _(None)_
　　Conversion method _Divide_
　　Default currency type member _(None)_
　　Country dimension _(None)_
　　Time dimension _CALENDER PERIODS_
　　Category dimension _METRIC or MEASURE_
　　Currency partition dimension _(None)_

Apply　Refresh　Help　Close

Modifications tab

Within this tab, Essbase will record any changes or modifications made to the database, the data, and the outline in log form. This screen is useful if you need to check when a recent event occurred, possibly for debugging.

Operation	User	Start Time	End Time	Note
Outline update	sarma	May 5, 2009 5:12:00 AM EDT	May 5, 2009 5:12:01 AM EDT	

Database Properties: [sarma.Esscar.Esscar]
Database: **sarma.Esscar.Esscar**   Status: **Loaded**
General | Dimensions | Statistics | Caches | Transactions | Storage | Currency | Modifications
Apply | Refresh | Help | Close

Types of Essbase users

Yes, you'll meet all kinds of Essbase users. There are good Essbase users, and there are less than good Essbase users. The beauty is you get to control them.

Okay, so it's not a control issue, but at the same time you cannot have people in your databases running willy-nilly over anything they please. For starters, Essbase has some of the most comprehensive database access filters available. Each filter is completely customizable for a specific database.

> All access filters can be applied to either a single user or to an access group where multiple users are added when necessary.

If you recall, we recommended that you create yourself a **Supervisor** account at your first login. This will be your account to administer the entire Essbase server. For data security and data integrity reasons, it is a good idea to put a limit on the number of supervisor access accounts and instead make use of lesser **developer type** accounts.

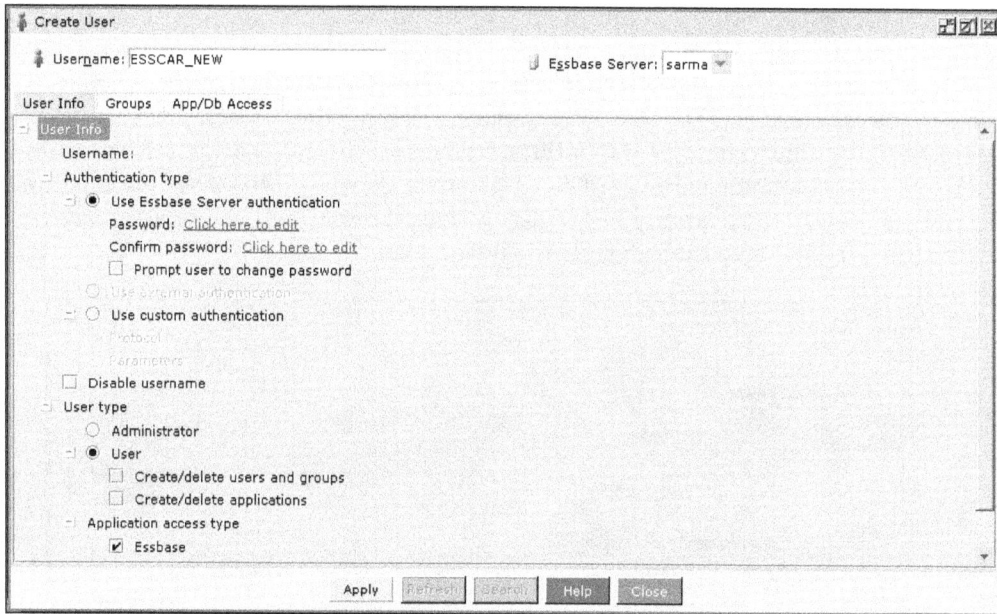

When you create a new user, you can also add the user into an already existing group by clicking on the **Groups** tab. In this way you do not need to set the Application | Database properties for each and every user. When you create a new user group you can select all the properties for that group.

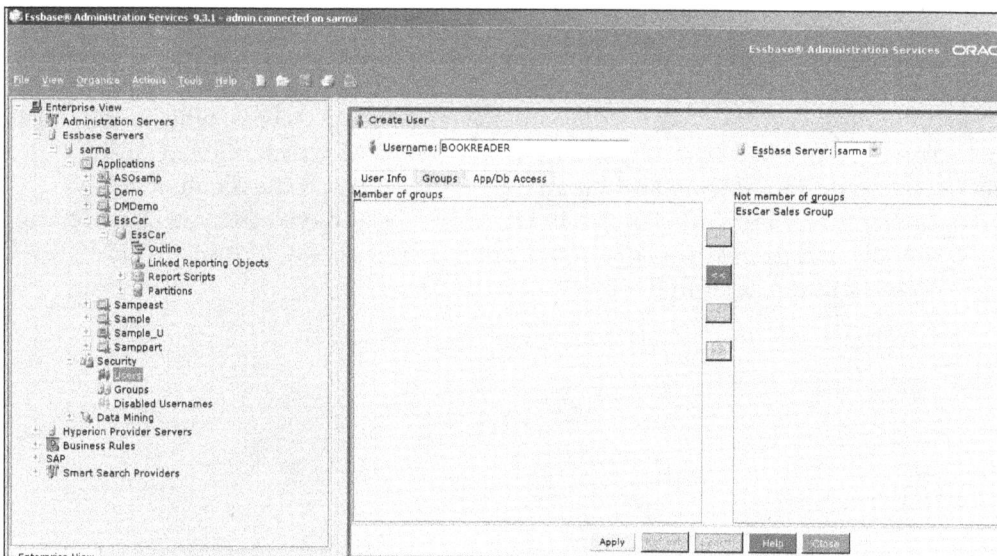

Developer access can easily be controlled with standard access level settings and a typical developer never needs access to more than the database he or she is working on at that time. The database designer level provides the developer with unrestricted access to the Application | Database you have created for the project. The database designer will be able to modify the outline, create and run calculation scripts, and create and run data loads using load rules. There is also an optional setting to allow the database designer the ability to grant new user accesses and reset passwords on the database(s) they have their designer privileges on.

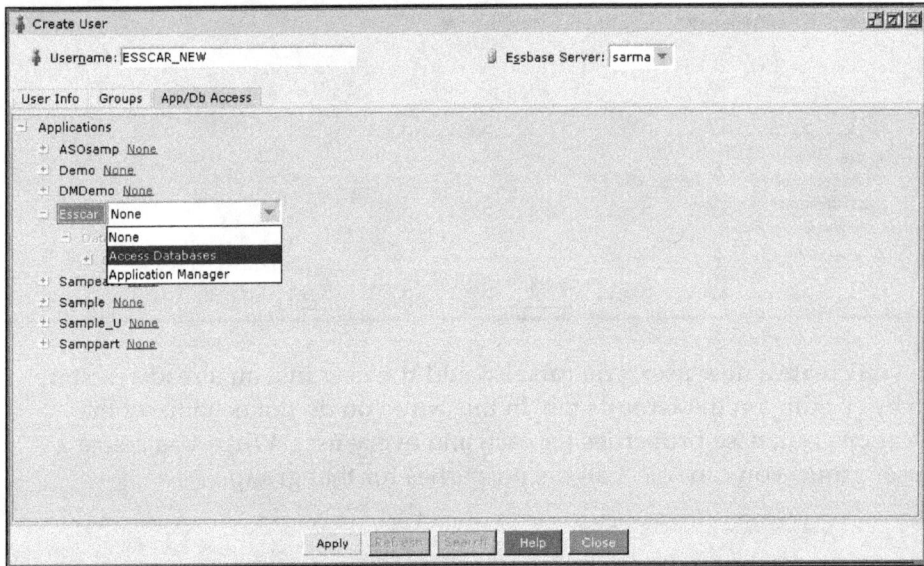

In the previous screenshot, we see the sub-screen **App/Db Access**, which is a tabbed screen selection reached from the **Create User** screen. As we mentioned earlier, this is where you can quickly add broad developer access at the database level. The options are few but sufficient for the type of user or developer you are granting access for. We will discuss in more detail, specific user access control, including the use of security filters, later in the book.

Summary

We made it this far and your head hasn't exploded, has it? Thank goodness! Oracle Essbase or for that matter, any OLAP or analytic application, seems to have a certain aura or mystique about them. Some people automatically shy away, thinking they're just beyond normal comprehension. This is just not true.

We're confident the information has been presented in a manner that allows you to grasp the concepts of Oracle Essbase and OLAP. We're also confident that you are beginning to think Oracle Essbase is no big deal and wondering what all the fuss is about.

It probably seems like this chapter has flown by. You have now built an Essbase application to house your newly built Essbase database. You've been given a high level view of some of the more important features and aspects of Essbase application and database properties. You've also created users for your databases.

In the next chapter, we go all out. We build a complete Essbase database outline for our Esscar Motor Company example, which we will use for the rest of this book. Starting with the base outline Essbase automatically creates when you build a database, we take you through adding data dimensions, adding data members to the dimensions, determining data storage options, loading data, and much more. A *veritable cornucopia* of Essbase database outline information awaits you!

3
Building the Essbase Outline

We know that any true technology geek gets impatient, at the very least, when made to suffer through too much reading and page turning. We too feel the same way, but it was absolutely necessary to give you everything we did in the previous two chapters. Likewise, it is also necessary to give you every detail in this chapter.

You are aware of the fact that the Esscar Motor Company is hunting for a new system to provide their production and sales planning department with the ability to quickly create sales and production forecasts, profit forecasts, scenario over scenario what-if analysis, and more.

Armed with what you have learned in the previous chapters and using the Oracle Essbase Esscar application and database you created in Chapter 2, we will now guide you through building an honest-to-goodness real and usable database outline.

We will show you how to build the dimensions necessary to describe the data using a step-by-step approach. We will add members to the dimensions that organize and store the data. We will also show you how to determine the best storage methods for the data. Finally, we will show you the different ways to load the data.

If you haven't done so yet, we recommend getting yourself near to a PC that has Essbase Administration Services (EAS) properly installed and connected to an active Essbase server. You'll want to perform the tasks we will be taking you through.

Before we begin

Before we get too deeply involved with the Essbase outline, we just wanted to be clear that the information and examples presented in this chapter assume that you have created your database using the BSO.

We devote most of the future chapter to explaining the BSO and the ASO options, both their similarities and their differences.

So remember, the BSO is the flavor of this chapter.

The Essbase outline—the foundation

Think of the Essbase database outline as the air traffic controller of the database or a planning and logistics manager or even a traffic cop. For those of you who are relational database fans, you can think of an Essbase database outline as a logical database model. It can be thought of as a tool that gives you a visual reference to how the data is stored in the database and how the different elements relate to each other. Think of the Essbase database outline as all of these things and more.

As the very foundation, the Essbase database outline is the framework or base platform, upon which the entire database is built. If you remember, when you created your first Essbase database in the previous chapter, a shell or empty Essbase database outline was automatically created.

This newly created shell outline has no dimensions or members, does not contain any data, and is just a place holder or starting point. Let us now learn about the various components and features that make up an Essbase database outline and then build one!

Dimensions and members

We have previously discussed that the Essbase database outline is comprised of components called dimensions and members. To quickly review, remember that the outline dimensions are best described as the categories of your data that is, model year, calendar periods, and so on. For you die-hard relational database types, dimensions loosely translate into the columns you use in your tables. Database outline members are the children of the dimensions. The database members and dimensions enjoy a hierarchical parent-child relationship with the dimensions at the highest level.

Dimensions are best used to describe the data in the data warehouse system. Dimensions are the top-most members in the hierarchy. A dimension can represent the summarized or consolidated data for all its children members. In the following screenshot **TOTAL VEHICLE** is the parent dimension.

Members are children of the parent dimensions. A parent dimension can have an infinite number of child members. The member can either store the data or dynamically calculate the data upon request.

The screenshot below shows the listing of the parent dimensions. The parent dimensions can be considered the root dimension members as there are no higher members in the hierarchical structure. The parent dimensions only have descendent or children members. Look closely, the number in the braces, like the **<4>** indicates the number of children under that dimension.

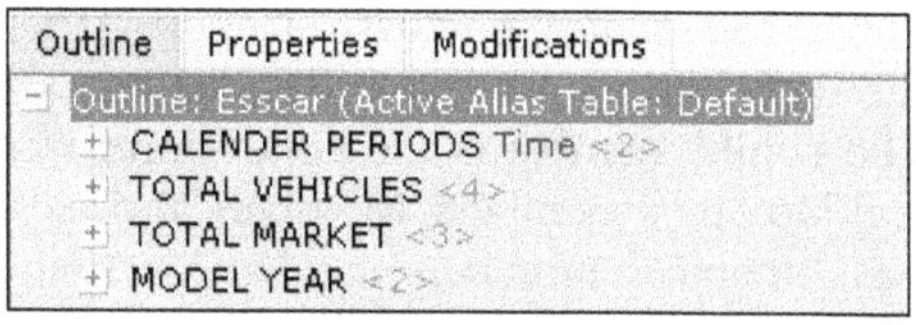

```
Outline    Properties    Modifications
- Outline: Esscar (Active Alias Table: Default)
  + CALENDER PERIODS Time <2>
  + TOTAL VEHICLES <4>
  + TOTAL MARKET <3>
  + MODEL YEAR <2>
```

Take a look as we expand the **TOTAL VEHICLE** dimension. In the following screenshot we see the **TOTAL VEHICLE** dimension expanded to reveal its four child members:

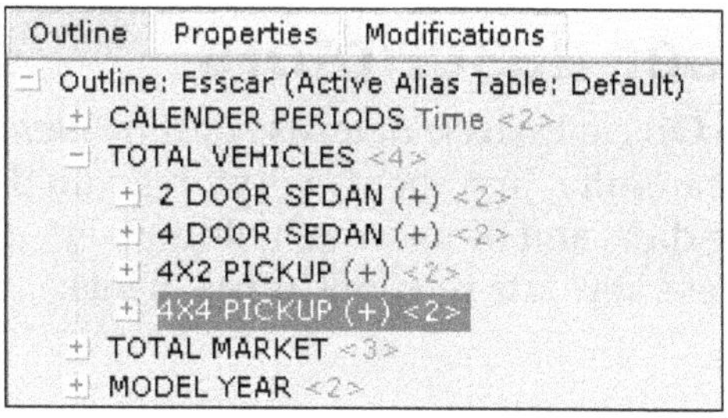

```
Outline    Properties    Modifications
- Outline: Esscar (Active Alias Table: Default)
  + CALENDER PERIODS Time <2>
  - TOTAL VEHICLES <4>
    + 2 DOOR SEDAN (+) <2>
    + 4 DOOR SEDAN (+) <2>
    + 4X2 PICKUP (+) <2>
    + 4X4 PICKUP (+) <2>
  + TOTAL MARKET <3>
  + MODEL YEAR <2>
```

Now you can clearly see the child members of the **TOTAL VEHICLE** dimension. Notice how each child member has two of its own children as evidenced by the **<2>** next to each member name.

In the following screenshot, you can see the **TOTAL VEHICLE** dimension expanded completely:

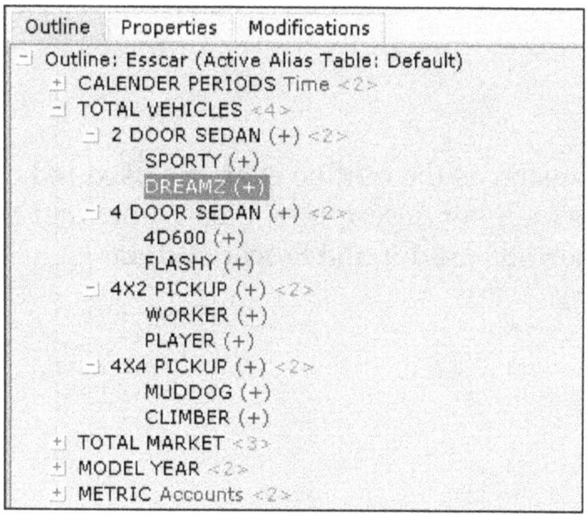

```
Outline    Properties    Modifications
- Outline: Esscar (Active Alias Table: Default)
  + CALENDER PERIODS Time <2>
  - TOTAL VEHICLES <4>
    - 2 DOOR SEDAN (+) <2>
        SPORTY (+)
        DREAMZ (+)
    - 4 DOOR SEDAN (+) <2>
        4D600 (+)
        FLASHY (+)
    - 4X2 PICKUP (+) <2>
        WORKER (+)
        PLAYER (+)
    - 4X4 PICKUP (+) <2>
        MUDDOG (+)
        CLIMBER (+)
  + TOTAL MARKET <3>
  + MODEL YEAR <2>
  + METRIC Accounts <2>
```

With the **Total Vehicles** dimension completely expanded, we see all of the child or descendent members. We now know that we have reached the bottom level of the dimension because there is no child indicator (**<n>**) next to the member names.

> An Essbase outline dimension is the upper-most member in the multidimensional hierarchical database structure. The dimension member can have unlimited child members but has no parent member. The child member can be a child member of the dimension parent and can also be a parent or child to other members. Members, those of which are not at the top level as dimension members, can have virtually unlimited child members while at the same time being a child member themselves.
>
> Outline members that share the same parent are called siblings. Essbase is just one big happy family!

Outline member descriptors

Here, we have listed the Oracle Essbase database outline members' descriptors. Please read this section carefully. Just about everything you do that pertains to loading data, calculating data, and dimension building with data will depend on your firm grasp of these key data relationship elements:

- Parent
- Child
- Siblings
- Ancestors
- Descendants
- Root
- Leaf
- Generation
- Level

Let's use the Time dimension as the outline example used to help in describing the definitions for these member descriptors. Please note that the Time dimension contains the calendar periods used in the Esscar system.

```
⊟ Year Time <4> (Alias: Period)
  ⊟ Qtr1 (+) <3> (Alias: Q1)
       Jan (+)
       Feb (+)
       Mar (+)
  ⊟ Qtr2 (+) <3> (Alias: Q2)
       Apr (+)
       May (+)
       Jun (+)
  ⊟ Qtr3 (+) <3> (Alias: Q3)
       Jul (+)
       Aug (+)
       Sep (+)
  ⊟ Qtr4 (+) <3> (Alias: Q4)
       Oct (+)
       Nov (+)
       Dec (+)
```

- **Parent**: A Parent is an outline member which has a child member or many children members below it. For example: **QUARTER 1** is a parent of **JAN**, **FEB**, and **MAR**.

- **Child**: A Child outline member is an outline member that has a parent. For example: **JAN, FEB,** and **MAR** are the children of **QUARTER 1**.

- **Siblings**: Sibling outline members are members that are at the same level in the outline and share the same parent. For example: **JAN, FEB,** and **MAR** are siblings.

- **Descendants**: Descendant outline members are all members below a parent, which include any children and their children. For example: **QUARTER 1**, **QUARTER 2, JAN,** and **APR** are the descendants of **YEAR**.

- **Ancestors**: Ancestor outline members are all members preceding a particular member, including the parent, the parent's parent, and so on. For example, **QUARTER 1** and **YEAR** are ancestors of **JAN**.

- **Root**: The Root outline member is the top-most branch of a member tree. For example, **YEAR** is the root member for **QUARTER 1, QUARTER 2, JAN** and **APR**. All upper-most outline members are the root members of their respective dimension. To put it another way, the root member has no parent.

- **Leaf**: Leaf is an outline member that has no children. The leaf member is also called the `Level 0` member. For example: **JAN, FEB, APR,** and **JUN** are the Leaf members or nodes or the lowest level member in its part of the outline.

Generations and Levels

Although the previous member descriptor definitions are very important, you will find that as you gain more experience, the use of the generation and level descriptors are by far the most commonly used and the most useful method of referring where a member is in the database outline. This is true for loading, calculating, and retrieving data.

Generation

The term Generation refers to the location of a member in a dimension relative to the root member. The upper-most generation is the outline itself which is Generation 0. Consider Generation 0 as the parent of the data dimensions. The root members are the actual dimensions and are called Generation 1.

> The Generation approach to traversing your database outline is a top-down approach. For example, Generation 1 is the highest level or the root level and the Generation 2 would be the next level down towards the leaf node or member which is the bottom member of the dimension.

Just like a family tree, the next level down in the outline from the Year level (the Quarter level) is Generation 2 in this example.

In the example below, YEAR is Generation 1 (also called GEN 1), and Quarter 1, Quarter 2, Quarter 3 and Quarter 4 are Generation 2 (GEN 2) whereas JAN, FEB, MAR, APR, and so on, are Generation 3.

```
GENERATION 1          Year
GENERATION 2          ↳ Quarter 1
GENERATION 3             ↳ JAN
GENERATION 3             ↳ FEB
GENERATION 3             ↳ MAR
GENERATION 2          ↳ QUARTER 2
GENERATION 3             ↳ APR
GENERATION 3             ↳ MAY
GENERATION 3             ↳ JUN
GENERATION 2          ↳ QUARTER 3
GENERATION 3             ↳ JUL
GENERATION 3             ↳ AUG
GENERATION 3             ↳ SEP
GENERATION 2          ↳ QUARTER 4
GENERATION 3             ↳ OCT
GENERATION 3             ↳ NOV
GENERATION 3             ↳ DEC
```

Level

Level also refers to the location of a member in the outline dimension, but it's counting starts from the leaf node all the way upto the root. The leaf node is called `Level 0`, the parent of the leaf node is `Level 1`, and its parent is `Level 2`, and so on until we reach the root member.

> Looking at the example above, you can ask the question, "In this outline, can the `Quarter 4` member be considered a `Generation 2` member and a `Level 1` member and can the DEC member be considered a `Generation 3` member and a `Level 0` member?" The answer is a resounding yes!

> The Level approach to traversing your database outline is a bottom-up approach. For example, the `Level 0` is the lowest level or the leaf node level. The `Level 1` would be the next level higher towards the root member.

In the example below, JAN, FEB, MAR, and APR are all `Level 0`. QUARTER 1, QUARTER 2, QUARTER 3, QUARTER 4 are `Level 1` members, and YEAR is a `Level 2` member.

```
LEVEL 2          Years
LEVEL 1          ↳ Quarter 1
LEVEL 0              ↳ JAN
LEVEL 0              ↳ FEB
LEVEL 0              ↳ MAR
LEVEL 1          ↳ QUARTER 2
LEVEL 0              ↳ APR
LEVEL 0              ↳ MAY
LEVEL 0              ↳ JUN
LEVEL 1          ↳ QUARTER 3
LEVEL 0              ↳ JUL
LEVEL 0              ↳ AUG
LEVEL 0              ↳ SEP
LEVEL 1          ↳ QUARTER 4
LEVEL 0              ↳ OCT
LEVEL 0              ↳ NOV
LEVEL 0              ↳ DEC
```

Types of dimensions

In Essbase, there are two types of dimensions, the first and most common dimension type is the **Standard dimension**. The other less common dimension type is called an **Attribute dimension**. Both are explained here.

Standard dimension

Standard dimensions are derived from the main business data components (or data categories we described earlier) and are then defined in a database cube. Some of the Standard dimensions in our example database are: TOTAL VEHICLES, MEASURES, CALENDER PERIODS, TOTAL MODEL YEARS, CUSTOMERS, MARKET, and SCENARIO. These dimensions can be tagged as Accounts, Time, and Country types. Some dimensions are not associated with any type of special dimension types and are considered general dimensions.

Briefly, let's explore the different ways you can tag a Standard dimension and their uses.

The Account dimension type

When you tag a dimension as an Account type, you are telling Essbase that this dimension will be used for your financial measures or metrics.

Available to the Account dimension are several accounting specific tags such as the **Time Balance** option that uses the Time dimension to calculate period specific data or the **Two Pass Calculation** option which will calculate the data in two passes when components of that data must be calculated first from the existing data.

The Time dimension type

The Time dimension type is the dimension where you define the periods used to calculate and report your data. This would typically be the dimension where you store calendar periods. The Time dimension also supports several of the Accounts dimension functions.

The Country dimension type

A dimension tagged as a Country dimension allows you to analyze your data across multiple countries, if you desire. You can also set the currency for each country to get true and current financial data analysis for each local market defined in your database.

No dimension type or general dimension

Not all dimensions need to have a specific identifier tag. You can always create a general dimension that you can use for any variety of data descriptor purposes. Most of your dimensions will be general dimensions.

The Currency Partition dimension type

This type of dimension is used for currency conversion in your database. The database would contain all financial data represented in a base currency. The `Currency Partition` dimension is used to allow local currencies from other regions to be brought in from a separate Essbase database.

The `Currency Partition` dimension is specifically designed for currency conversion applications and is not always necessary to achieve your desired results. Careful preparatory investigation upfront is always recommended.

Below is a sample screenshot showing an outline containing dimensions that are tagged with the various available dimension types. Once the dimensions are properly set, you will see the dimension type listed in the database outline next to the dimension name.

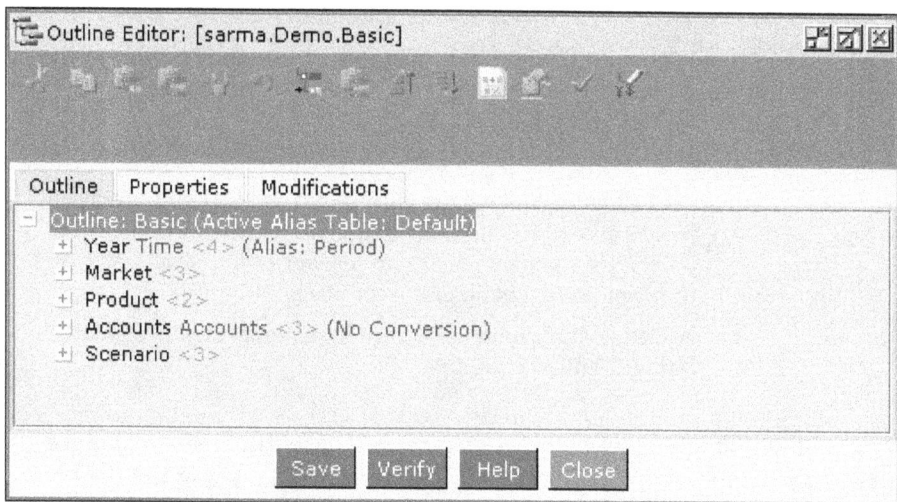

The specific dimension tags are for convenience and enhanced functionality. However, many of these options were not available in earlier versions of Essbase so you would have needed to code your own functionality.

The Attribute dimension

There is a dimension type known as an `Attribute` dimension type. The `Attribute` dimension is not a full blown standard dimension and in fact must be associated with a standard dimension. The `Attribute` dimension allows you to analyze your data with even finer granularity by adding data characteristics (for example, color) to your `Total Vehicle` dimension.

> If it is not an `Attribute` dimension type then it is some form of `Standard` dimension.

Dense and Sparse dimensions

As we described before, the data stored in an Essbase database is stored in a manner conceptually similar to that of a Rubik's Cube. Because of this structure, the folks at Oracle have devised a method of defining your outline dimensions and their data density to Essbase. Therefore, your database can be more efficient in the way it loads, stores, calculates, and retrieves your data.

The distinction between **Dense** and **Sparse** dimensions allows Essbase to efficiently handle large amounts of data that is not evenly spread across the data blocks. It is this efficiency that allows Essbase to offer the slice and dice style of data access, while still maintaining high performance for fast data processing and retrievals.

> Correctly set **Dense** and **Sparse** dimension attributes have a dramatic effect on overall memory usage and system performance!
> - In a **Sparse** dimension, the data does not exist for the better part of the member combinations. For example, all vehicles may not be sold in all of the countries
> - A **Dense** dimension has a very high percentage of available data cells filled with data.

First of all, you will need to consider whether a database dimension is **Dense** or **Sparse** in an Application | Database that has been created using the BSO. All dimensions in an ASO database are **Sparse** by default. When you have an Essbase database created using the BSO, Essbase allows you to describe your dimensions as either **Dense** or **Sparse** with the following understanding. Some data cubes, created roughly by dimension, are not fully populated with data. In fact, for the most part, the typical Essbase multidimensional database's cube always has a relatively **Sparse** concentration of data at the overall database level. It would be an extreme rarity to find your data densely populating every available cell with a stored value.

When you first start out, you can let Essbase automatically configure the **Dense** and **Sparse** dimension settings in your database. You do this using the EAS **Outline Properties** tab. Essbase will do this fairly well initially, based on the data already existing in the database.

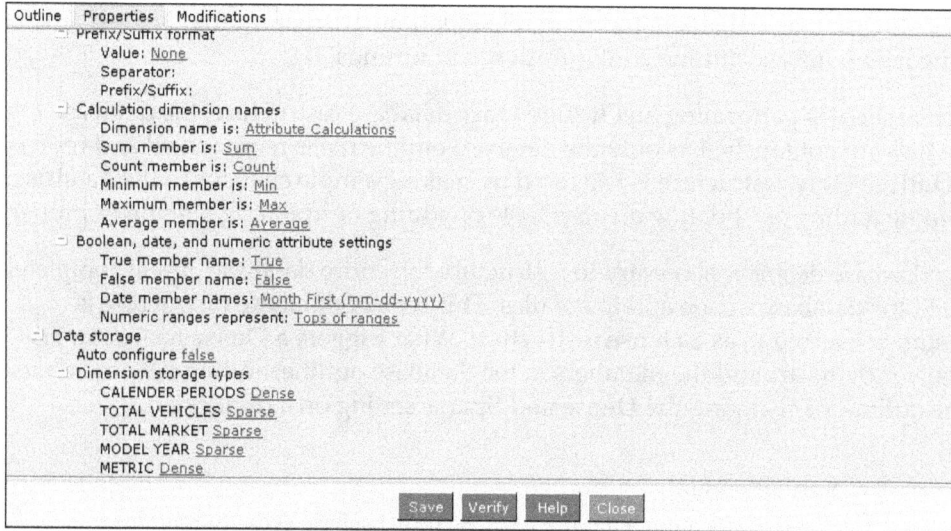

```
Outline   Properties   Modifications
       Prefix/Suffix format
           Value: None
           Separator:
           Prefix/Suffix:
     Calculation dimension names
           Dimension name is: Attribute Calculations
           Sum member is: Sum
           Count member is: Count
           Minimum member is: Min
           Maximum member is: Max
           Average member is: Average
     Boolean, date, and numeric attribute settings
           True member name: True
           False member name: False
           Date member names: Month First (mm-dd-yyyy)
           Numeric ranges represent: Tops of ranges
   Data storage
       Auto configure false
     Dimension storage types
           CALENDER PERIODS Dense
           TOTAL VEHICLES Sparse
           TOTAL MARKET Sparse
           MODEL YEAR Sparse
           METRIC Dense

                              Save   Verify   Help   Close
```

Notice in the preceding screenshot that there is an **Auto configure** option on the outline properties screen. If set to true, this option will let Essbase automatically set the **Dense/Sparse** settings of the dimensions in your database.

As time goes on and as both your knowledge of your system's data grows and your experience with Essbase increases, you will find that you can usually do a better job of configuring the **Dense** and **Sparse** settings yourself rather than let Essbase handle it.

You can, at any time, change the **Dense** and **Sparse** attribute of any dimension. You will do this using the EAS at the database properties screen.

One of the best features of Essbase is the outline or database restructure. Anytime you make a change to the database outline, you are offered the choice of saving the changes when you attempt to close the outline. The restructure choices available are **Outline Only** and **Outline and Data**.

When you make changes to your database outline, the changes may also affect the way the data itself is stored. Changes such as moving a member or changing a **Dense** setting to a **Sparse** setting will always require you to perform an **Outline and Data** restructure. When the restructure is called for, Essbase will actually perform what could be best compared to in the relational world as database reorganization. All of the existing data is unloaded and then reloaded into a structure that is most efficient for the new database outline configuration and settings.

When Essbase is performing an **Outline Only** database restructure, the database page files are not touched as only the database outline file is reorganized and resaved. An **Outline Only** restructure is triggered by making simple changes to the database, including adding or updating an alias table or adding or updating a member property.

When Essbase deems it necessary to restructure the entire database, it will completely rebuild the database's page and index files. This type of database restructure is sometimes referred to as a **Dense** restructure. What triggers a **Dense** restructure is actually moving around the members in the database outline, adding new members to the outline, or changing the **Dense** and **Sparse** setting on a dimension.

Very Important

When performing a database restructure, Essbase actually rebuilds new temporary database page files from the existing page files. When finished, Essbase will delete the old page files and rename the new ones.

Prior to any database restructure always make sure you have extra storage on your server. If the database you are restructuring is 30GB and you only have 20GB of space available Essbase will keep on going with the restructure until the disc space runs out and crashes the server!

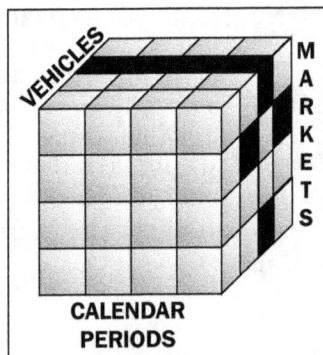

As you can see in the preceding screenshot, most of your data will have `Calendar Periods` associated with it, so it would most likely be tagged as a **Dense** dimension. The `Vehicles` dimension would more than likely be tagged as **Sparse**. You may want to tag the `Vehicles` dimension as **Sparse** because while you have vehicles for sale in all markets and probably have vehicle sales for all calendar periods, you will not have all vehicle models for sale in all markets. You may also not have sales for all vehicle models in all calendar periods.

For example, not all of Esscar's vehicles sell in all markets listed in the outline. The data is sparsely distributed across the data blocks. On the other hand, all of the data in your database ties to the `Scenario` dimension, so that data is densely populated across data blocks. You would set the `Market` dimension to **Sparse** and the `Scenario` dimension to **Dense**.

Build your first outline

That's it! Your brain is just chocked full of Essbase database outline knowledge. Let's build an Essbase database outline using the EAS.

Within EAS, perform the following tasks:

Double-click, to expand in the EAS, on **ESSBASE Severs** then **Applications** then **ESSCAR** (Application) then **ESSCAR** (database) and finally **Outline**. The ESSCAR database outline is opened in the Essbase Outline Editor as shown in screenshot below. Remember, as we said before, this is basically a placeholder outline created for you by Essbase when you created the new database.

Your job is to now build this outline into a fully functioning Essbase database outline that will support a real database.

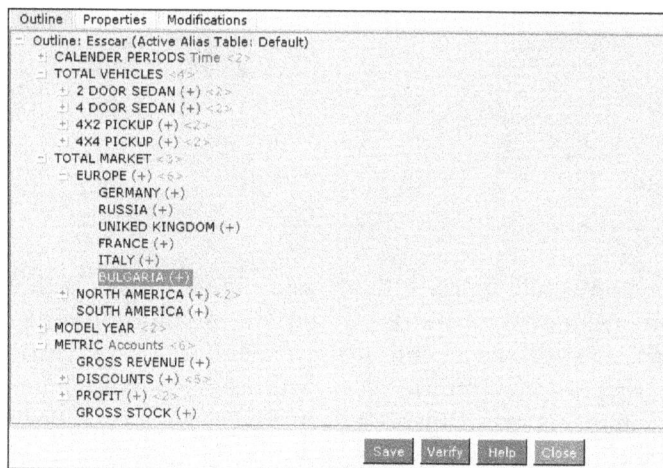

The steps to add dimensions and members to an Essbase database outline are:

1. Begin by right-clicking on **Outline,** and then click on **Add Child.**

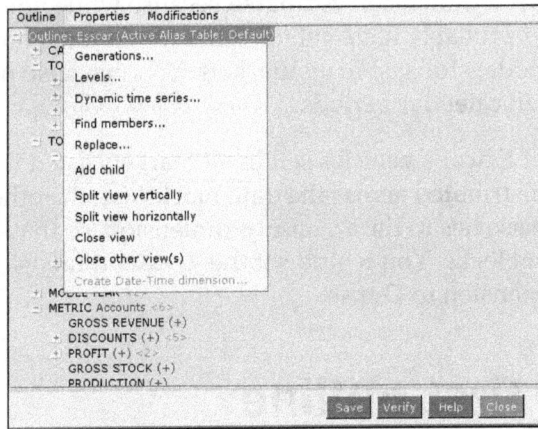

2. Enter **CALENDAR PERIODS** to name this new member and create your first Essbase database dimension.

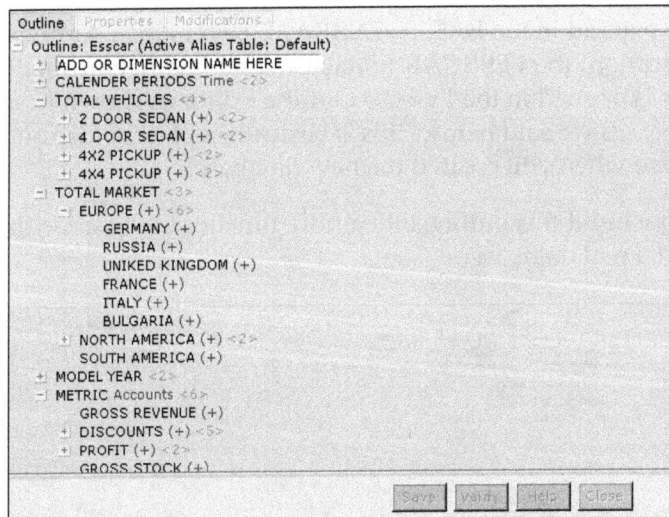

Remember, any child member that is added to the main outline is considered a data dimension in the Essbase outline. When you right-click on the data dimension, you will see an entirely new set of options. If your preference is to left-click (right and left mouse click, assumes right-handed mouse operation) you will activate an assortment of **Easy Access Menu** buttons where you can choose the types of dimensions as shown in the following screenshot:

Since **CALENDAR PERIODS** is supposed to be our time dimension, we will tag this dimension as the **Time** dimension type. Right-click on the **CALENDAR PERIODS**, click on **Add Children**, and enter **Year 2009**. To add another year, right-click on **Year 2009**, click on **Add Sibling**, and enter **Year 2008** and so on. Keep going until you add year members to **Year 2006**.

Following this same procedure, you can right-click on the year members you have just added and now add quarter periods as children to them. Once you have the quarter periods added (use the screenshot below as a guide) you will then add the month members to the quarters. While this may seem to be an inefficient and tedious task, it is necessary that you learn to be comfortable with manually editing an Essbase database outline.

Never fear! Editing a database outline manually is not the only way to update it. Shortly, we will explain the use of data **Load Rules** that can be used to load data into the database and automatically update the outline. These automated processes can be used for a variety of tasks from adding new members to the outline to performing database maintenance.

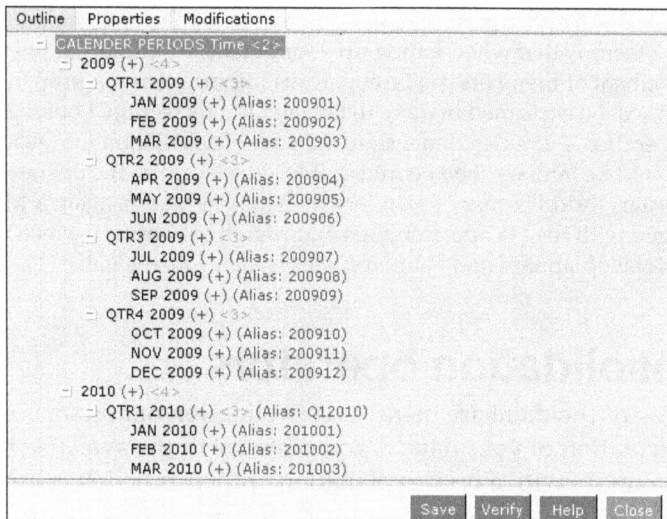

Member properties

Member properties are characteristics, set by you, that determine the behavior of the data stored in your database. For example, it is quite natural to want to know the value of sales for a quarter. If you set the consolidation property of each month member to (+) and calculate the database, the calendar quarter value will be the sum of the three child members under it which are the individual months. There is no need to load data at the calendar quarter's level since you can calculate it from the individual month's level.

There are also storage properties that Essbase uses to determine how the data is stored in the database. The following is a detailed explanation of member properties and their uses.

Member consolidations

When you define a new child member of a dimension, you need to tag that member with a consolidation operator. A consolidation operator will tell Essbase how this member will be calculated along with its sibling member(s) upto the parent member. Get familiar with the term *rolled up* because you will hear that term a lot when discussing how you are calculating your data. The term *rolled up* means summing children members to a parent member. When you sum the months of a quarter member, you are *rolling up* the months. Think of *rolling up* the same as adding up. The default property setting is the addition (+) operator.

Very important!

Depending on the dimension selected and the method of calculation, Essbase will either perform a top-down or a bottom-up calculation. What this means is that when setting up your database outline, the physical placement of members can be equally as important as the property settings. This will be explained in more detail later in this section. Looking at the `Calendar Periods` dimension, the path of calculation for **Quarter 1** would be January then February, if (+) is selected as the operator for February, add February to January then look at March, again if March is tagged with the (+) operator, then add March to February which is already the total of January and February. This is *rolling up* the data!

Valid consolidation operators

The proper setting of the database member consolidation operators is critical to the correct calculation of your data. A complete list of the available member consolidation operators with a brief explanation of their function is listed as follows:

- Addition (+) — adds this member to the result of the previously calculated sibling member calculation
- Subtraction (-) — multiplies the member by (-1) then adds the product to the result of the previously calculated member.
- Multiplication (*) — multiplies this member by the result of the previously calculated member
- Division (/) — divides the result of the previously calculated member by this member
- Percent (%) — divides the previously calculated member result by this member and multiples it by 100
- Exclude from consolidation (~) — do not consolidate (ignore) this member
- Never consolidate (^) — do not use this member in any consolidation in any dimension

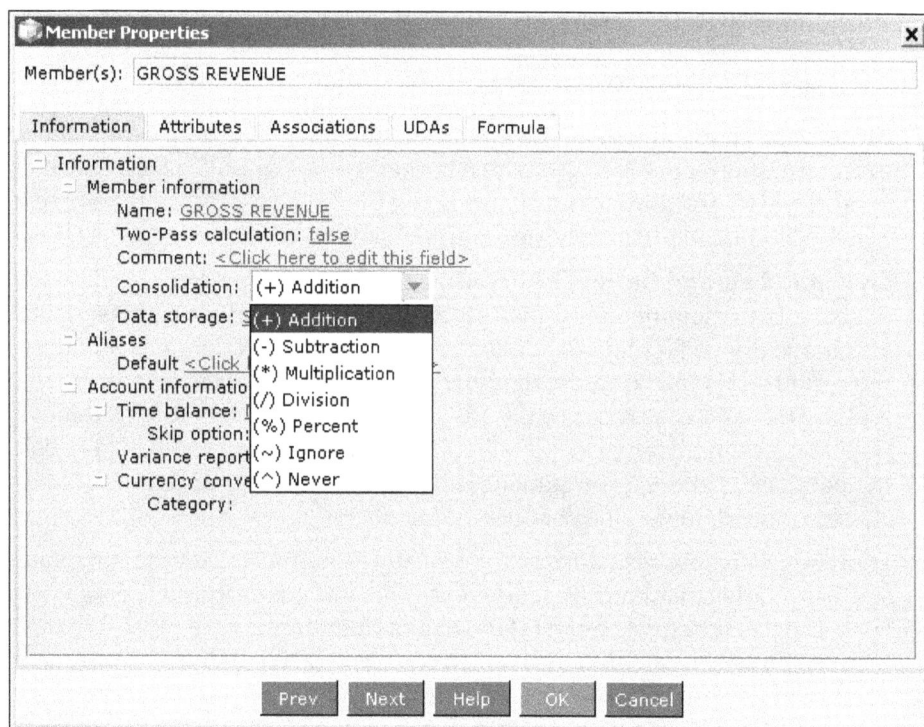

For example:

```
 -| TOTAL SALES (+) <2>
      SALES (+)
    DISCOUNTS (-)
```

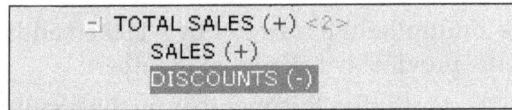

In the above formula:

```
TOTAL SALES = SALES + (DISCOUNTS * (-1))
```

Member storage

When you create a member in Essbase, you need to tag the member with a storage property on how the data is stored for this member. By default, when a member is created, it is tagged as **Store Data**. You can change the member storage option in **Member Properties | Data Storage**.

The different storage options available to you are explained as follows:

- **Store Data**: Stores the data value with the member. The data can be the result of a calculation, data load from an external source, or an Essbase "Lock and Send" directly from Microsoft Excel using the Essbase Add-in for Microsoft Excel. The data is physically stored in the database.

- **Dynamic Calc and Store**: The first time the data is requested, Essbase will dynamically calculate it and then store it with the member. Essbase will automatically recalculate the data and update the stored values on the next request for data if a component value used in the member formula changes. At the first call for a dynamically calculated and stored member's data value, the data is dynamically calculated and physically stored in its proper cell in the database. Unless a component value of the now stored data value has changed, the data is not dynamically calculated again.

- **Dynamic Calc**: Essbase does not physically store the calculated data value at all and only calculates it on demand. This is a good option if database size is an issue as it helps keep the database smaller. Some care must be exercised because dynamic calculations tend to consume large amounts of resources. Balance is the key here.

- **Never Share**: Does not allow Essbase to implicitly share this member. What this means in Essbase is when you have a member that only has one child member that member implicitly takes the value of the only child. There are times when you do not want this to occur. You can still share this member explicitly by creating another member of the same name and selecting **Shared Member** as its storage option.

- **Label Only**: Members you create as placeholders only. The **Label Only** option is a way to help organize your database outline without affecting database size. **Label Only** members do not contain any data. No data is physically stored in this member.

- **Shared Member**: For convenience, you may want to have a member appear in different groups take values from different groups or simply use a member's data somewhere else in the outline. The **Shared Member** allows you to do this with relative ease. Yes, the same effect could be achieved with specific calculation coding, but that can be complex and confusing. Look at the following screenshot to see how you would use a shared member:

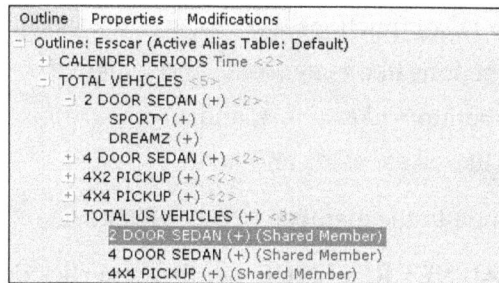

In the following screenshot you will see how easy it is to set the outline member properties using the EAS tool.

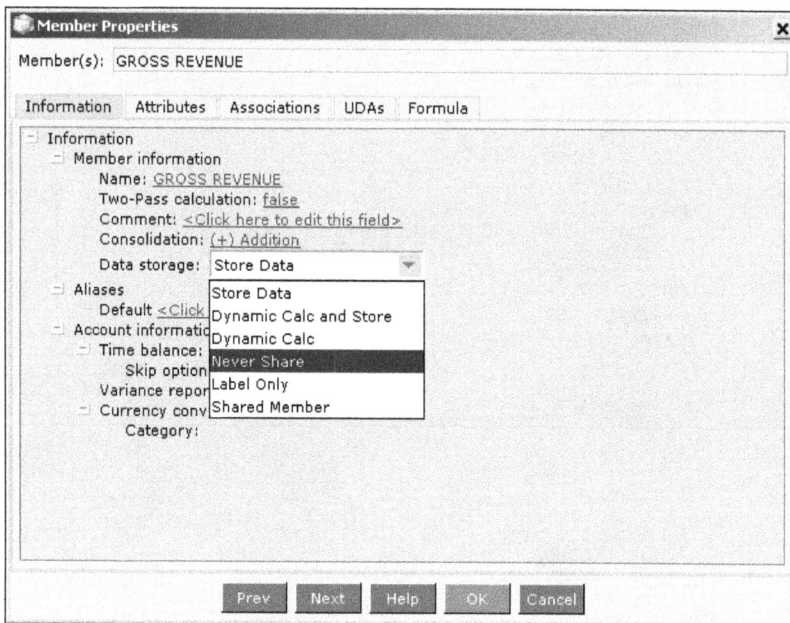

Member formulas

One of the coolest things in Essbase is that you can create a formula which will be attached to a member in the database outline. If the member is tagged as **Dynamic Calc**, the formula will execute when the user is trying to retrieve the data for that member. If the member is tagged as **Store Data**, the formula will execute when a calculation script is executed against that member.

Member formulas can be constructed by using some of the available *commands* and *functions* of which a few are listed here:

- Conditional coding functions like IF, ELSEIF, and ENDIF
- Boolean (true or false) functions like ISMBR, ISCHILD, and ISDESC
- Relationship functions like @LEV, @GEN, and @CURGEN
- Mathematical operators like +, -, *, and /
- Math functions like @ABS, @SUM, and @MOD

The steps to add a formula to the member TOTAL NET REVENUE are as follows:

1. Select the **TOTAL NET REVENUE** member and click on **Edit the formula for the selected member** as shown in the following screenshot:

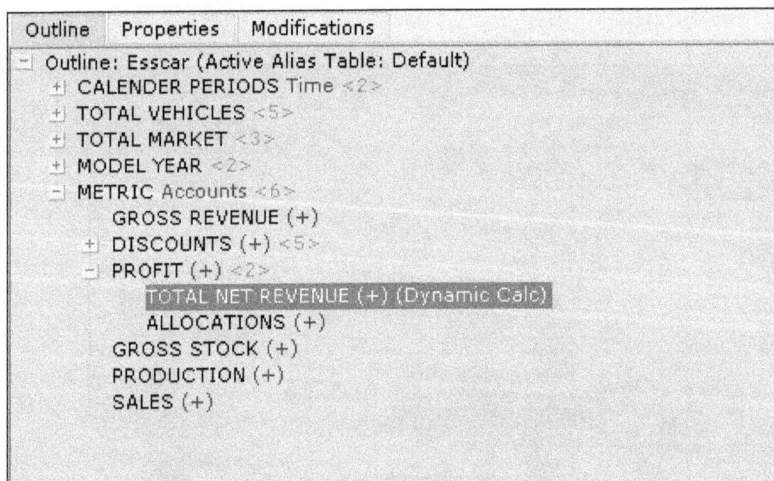

2. Enter the formula as shown below in the formula editor. The formula states that the member TOTAL NET REVENUE is calculated as GROSS REVENUE less DISCOUNTS

   "TOTAL NET REVENUE"="GROSS REVENUE" - "TOTAL DISCOUNTS";

   The member TOTAL NET REVENUE is tagged as **Dynamic Calc**. When a database user executes a retrieve for the data stored in the TOTAL NET REVENUE member, the TOTAL NET REVENUE value will be dynamically calculated as TOTAL NET REVENUE = TOTAL REVENUE - TOTAL DISCOUNTS.

3. As shown below in the **Formula** editor screen, once you have entered the formula, you can click on **Verify** to verify it and then click on **OK** to save the formula. It should be pointed out that the formula is only saved in a temporary buffer until the database outline has been saved.

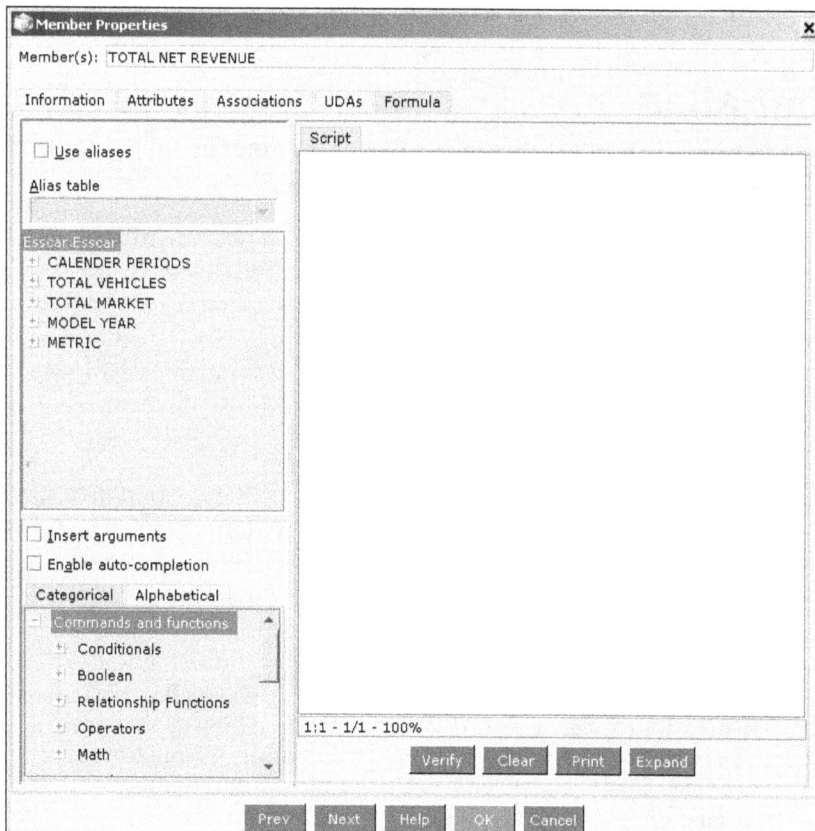

After you have clicked **OK** in the **Formula** editor, you can see the new formula in the Essbase outline next to the appropriate outline member. The following screenshot shows the formula attached to the outline member **TOTAL NET REVENUE**:

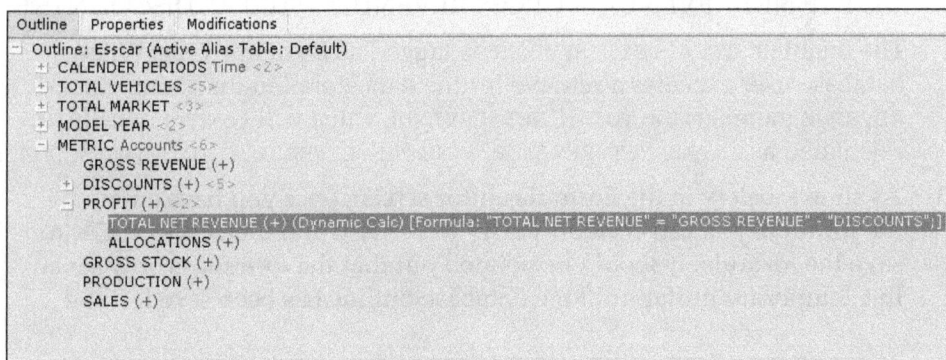

```
Outline    Properties   Modifications
  Outline: Esscar (Active Alias Table: Default)
   + CALENDER PERIODS Time <2>
   + TOTAL VEHICLES <5>
   + TOTAL MARKET <3>
   + MODEL YEAR <2>
   - METRIC Accounts <6>
        GROSS REVENUE (+)
   +   DISCOUNTS (+) <5>
   -   PROFIT (+) <2>
          TOTAL NET REVENUE (+) (Dynamic Calc) [Formula: "TOTAL NET REVENUE" = "GROSS REVENUE" - "DISCOUNTS";]
          ALLOCATIONS (+)
        GROSS STOCK (+)
        PRODUCTION (+)
        SALES (+)
```

Member alias

As the name implies, a member alias, is an alternate name for a database outline member. This is a very useful feature for several reasons.

For instance, let's say there is an Esscar car dealership whose member name in the database outline is Hood Esscar Best Dealers with the dealer ID code set up as an alias (03030-USA). The dealership is purchased by a person named Robin and he has decided to change the name of the dealership to Robin Hood Esscar Best Dealers. This dealership, for all Esscar purposes is the same dealership, so a simple outline change to the member name is all that is required while leaving the alias the same to identify the dealer to the system.

As a best practice, it is always advisable, wherever possible, to load data using the aliases and not the descriptions. If the aliases are left alone, any cosmetic naming changes to the database outline will only consist of the outline change. If the aliases are also changed, any special mappings must also be changed.

> When constructing an Essbase database, it is always advisable for you to plan appropriately and consistently. When setting up your outline, you must decide if the member names will reflect the full text name of the data element, or will you use alias tables for this purpose. Report generation, data loading, and data calculation can depend heavily on member names or aliases. To avoid confusion and simplify things, it is best to develop a strategy on how to use member's names and aliases and stick to it consistently!

The steps on how to add an alias name to the outline member TOTAL NET REVENUE properties are explained as follows:

1. From EAS, open the **Esscar** database outline.

2. Drill down to the member name **GROSS REVENUE.**

3. Right-click on the member name and click on **Edit Properties**, or click the button **Edit Properties** for the selected member in the outline editor.

4. Under **Aliases**, default alias table, add the code **TOTREV** as shown in the screenshot below.

5. Click **OK.**

6. That's it! You have just added an alias to the **GROSS REVENUE** member.

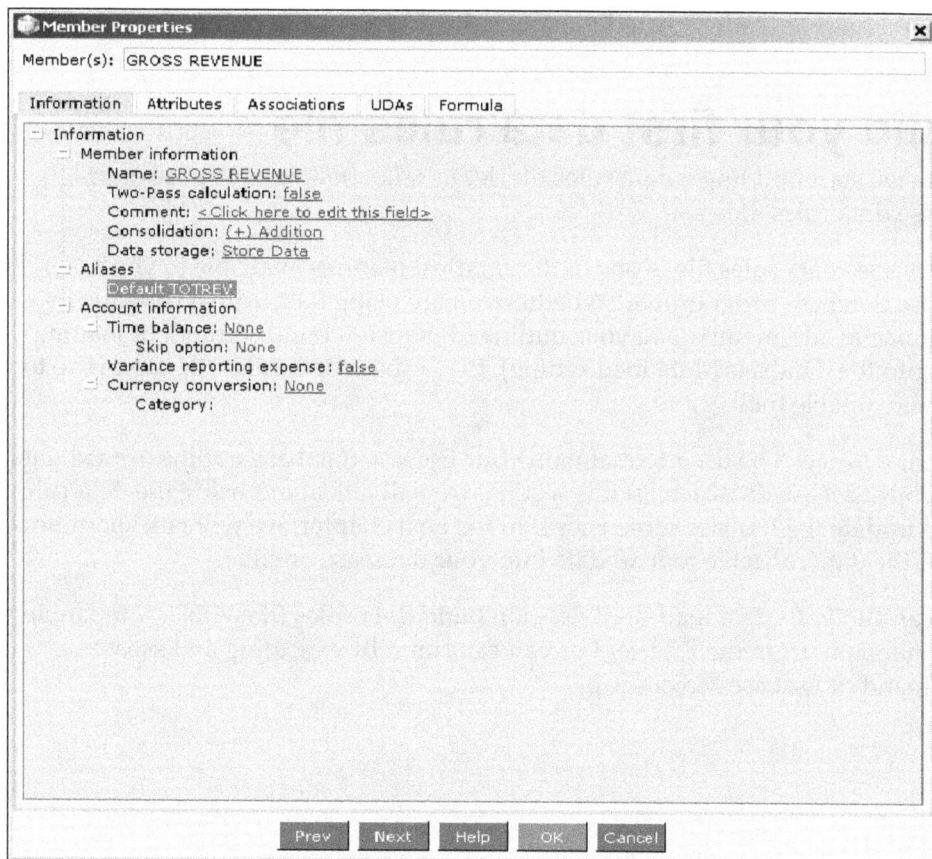

Alias table

Another use of an outline alias table is as a cross-reference table when interfacing with other systems. Experience has shown that even within the same company, but in different departmental activities, it is not uncommon for a different system to use a different name or code for the same model, unit, or part. Just like having a conversion or cross-reference table in a relational database, you can add a new alias table to your database outline any time.

A new alias table can contain the product names or codes as they are represented in another system, yet they are aligned to the correct members in your system. For example, if your system is part of the marketing activity and you receive data from the finance activity (who by the way calls everything by a different name than you do), you can execute a data load that specifically calls for and uses the Finance alias table you have specially created to handle the differences in product names.

Build your first data rules file

Before we start building a data rules file, let us talk about the purpose of the Essbase data rules file.

The Essbase data rules file is one of the smartest features available to you as an Essbase database programmer! Whether you are using data with a rules file to dynamically add members to your outline (dimension build setting), or loading data into the database (data load setting), the Essbase data rules file can prove to be an invaluable tool.

Data rule files can be used to maintain your Essbase database outline or load data into your Essbase database. In this section, we will talk about using the data rules file to update the Essbase dimensions. In the next chapter, we will talk about how to use the data rules file to load data into your database or cube.

You can run your data load or dimension build data rules file with accompanying data manually from the EAS tool or you can run it by executing an Essbase Command or Essbase MaxL script.

What are we talking about? Why use an Essbase data load rules file? Because we want to make input data Essbase-friendly, of course. Here are some the reasons why we use data rule files:

- Automatically cleanse the input data to filter out any errant values
- Remove the header and trailer from the input files
- Reject invalid data records
- Concatenate two fields into one field
- Dynamically add new members to the database outline
- Add aliases or update other member properties
- Transform or manipulate data
- Concatenate two fields or any other cleansing operations
- And many more

Data load rules files are something very special as you can see. You can practically build a complete Essbase database outline from scratch using nothing more than a properly configured data load rules file and your input data.

Next, we take you through the steps required to create a Dimension Build data rules file.

Step 1: Start the Data Prep Editor

The **Data Prep Editor** is the tool with which you will create your custom Essbase data load rules files. The tool is built right in to the already amazing Essbase Administration Services tool.

1. In EAS, click on the **File** menu pick.
2. Select **Editors** and click on the **Data Prep Editor** or Click on **New**, on the **New** dialog go to the **Scripts** tab and select **Rules File** and click on **OK**.
3. The **Data Prep Editor** will open as shown in the following figure.
4. The moment the **Data Prep Editor** is opened, the menu items in the EAS will change.

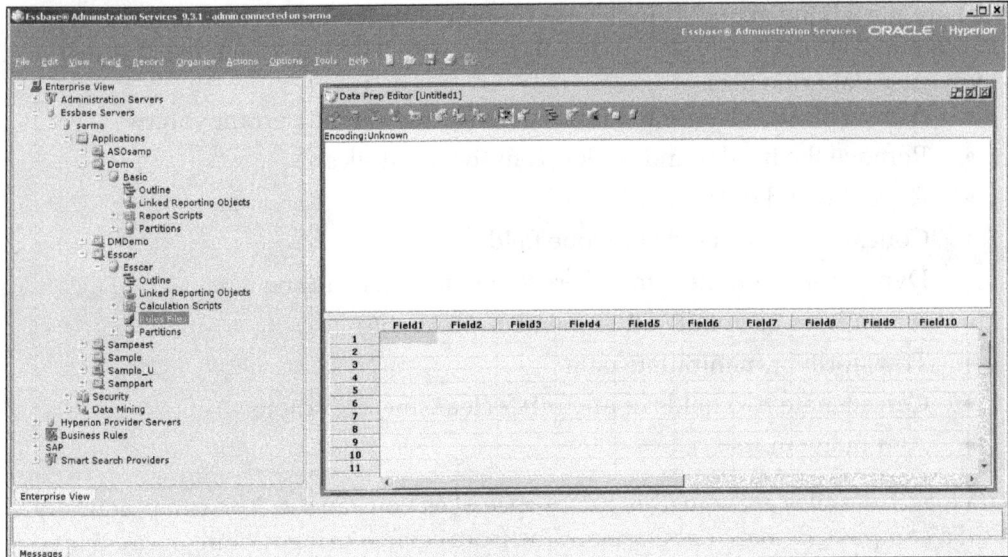

Step 2: Associate the Dimension Build Rules file

In order for you to successfully validate the rules file, you need to associate the rules to the database outline. This association of the rules file to the outline is saved, however, Essbase will ask you to associate the rules file again when you open this rules file the next time.

To associate an outline, open the **Data Prep Editor** again using EAS.

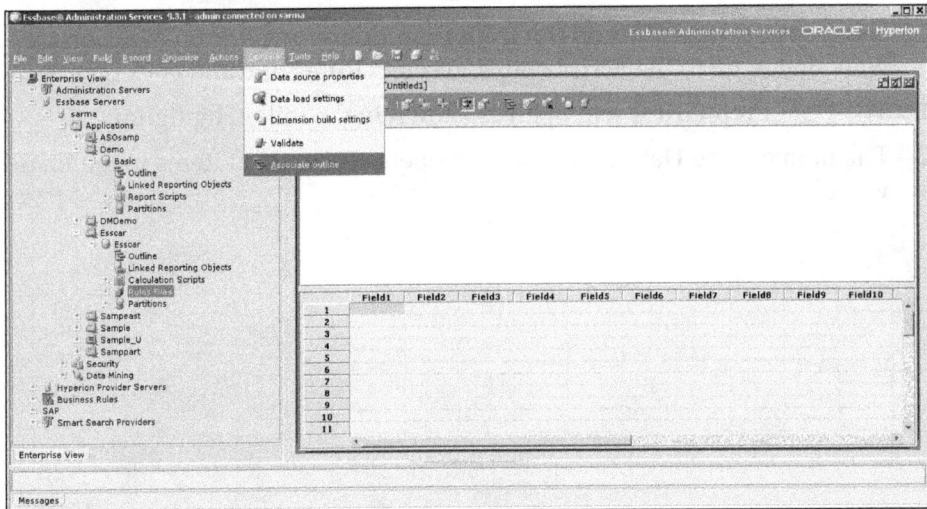

Click on **Options** and click on **Associate outline** or click on the **Associate** button in the **Data Prep Editor**.

Step 3: Open data load file or the SQL data source file

To update the database outline using the rules file, we need to have a data source file. To build a rules file, we need to acquire an exact representative sample of the actual data in order to map the data to our Essbase database outline.

The data sources can be files like text (`.txt`) files, Microsoft Excel spreadsheets, or from relational database sources using a SQL query defined in the load rule.

To open a data source file or SQL data source in EAS, with the **Data Prep Editor** open. After you've clicked on **File**, you should see the options **Open data file** or **Open SQL** shown as follows:

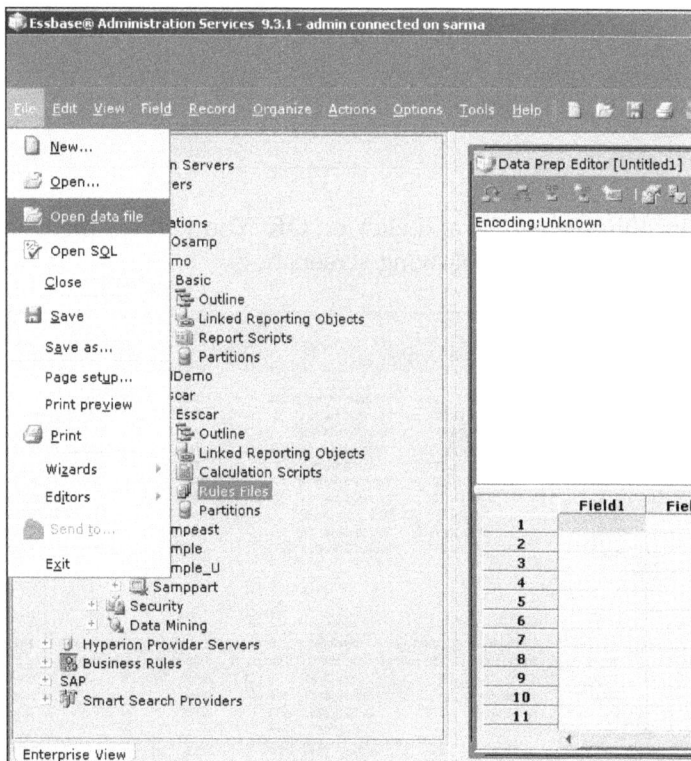

In our example, we choose a Microsoft Excel file as our data source.

1. Click on the **Open data file** option
2. Select the file system and browse to the file (for example: `c:\data\market .xls`) and the data in the excel file is as shown in the following screenshot:

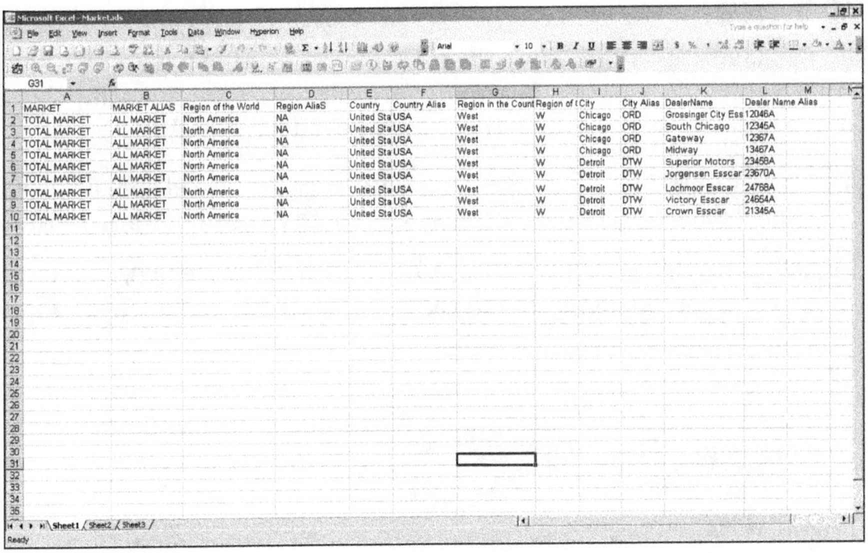

3. Select the above excel file and click on **OK**. You will see the **Data Prep Editor** as shown in the following screenshot:

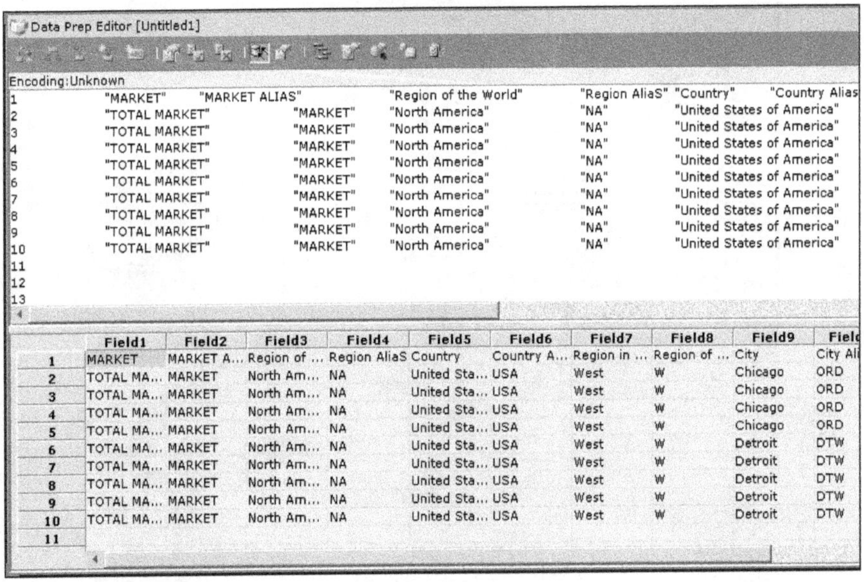

In this screenshot, the upper screen frame shows the data source file in its original form. The lower screen frame shows how Essbase will interpret the data before it gets loaded into your Essbase database.

In the example above, we discussed updating the outline from the input data source file. In the next chapter, we will talk about how to import data using the second method which is directly loaded from the RDBMS SQL Data Source.

Step 4: Set the Data Source Properties

While plenty of your data will be entered manually from user interaction, a good deal of it will likely come from external systems. Before Essbase can process any data file, we need to define the data to Essbase in the rules file.

Is the data in a comma separated file or tab delimited file? For some feeds, we need to ignore the header records which are usually the first row in the input file. These settings can be set in the **Data Source Properties**.

Delimiter: Data delimiters are used to separate individual fields in the data source. The types of delimiters available in Essbase are given as follows:

- **Comma**: This is for a comma separated data source file.
- **Tab**: This is for a tab delimited data source file.
- **All spaces**: The fields will be delimited by empty white spaces.
- **Custom**: The common delimiter which is agreed with the source systems. For example, colon (:) or any other single character.
- **Column width**: The data columns have specific widths. For example, the rules file will separate the data into columns based on all columns being ten characters in width.

To open an input data source file in EAS, with the **Data Prep Editor** open:

1. Click on **Options**, and then click on the **Data Source Properties**.
2. The first tab is the **Delimiter** tab as shown in the following screenshot:

3. Select or create the appropriate data delimiter. The appropriate delimiter is the character or set of characters that are used to separate the columns of your data. Essbase offers you a few of the most common delimiters and gives you the option of setting your own delimiters based on what is being used in your data file.

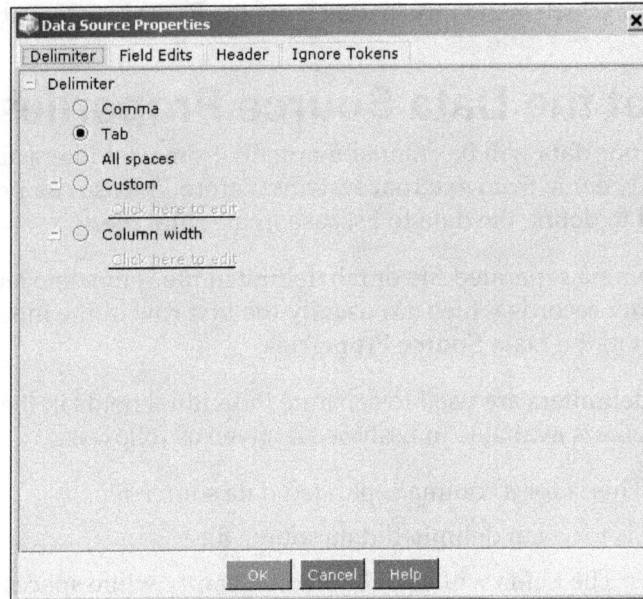

Step 5: Set the View to Dimension build fields

In this step, we need to define if this rule is used for **Dimension build fields** view or **Data load fields** view. By default, **Data load field** view is selected.

- **Dimension build field**: You will select this option when you are using the rules file with your data file to add new members to the outline or to update existing members in the outline.

- **Data load field**: This option is for loading data with a data load rules file and will be discussed in more detail later.

To set the **Dimension build fields** view in EAS, with the **Data Prep Editor** open:

- Click on **View** and then select the checkbox **Dimension build fields** as we are currently doing a dimension build. We will talk in-depth about the **Data load fields** view in the next chapter.

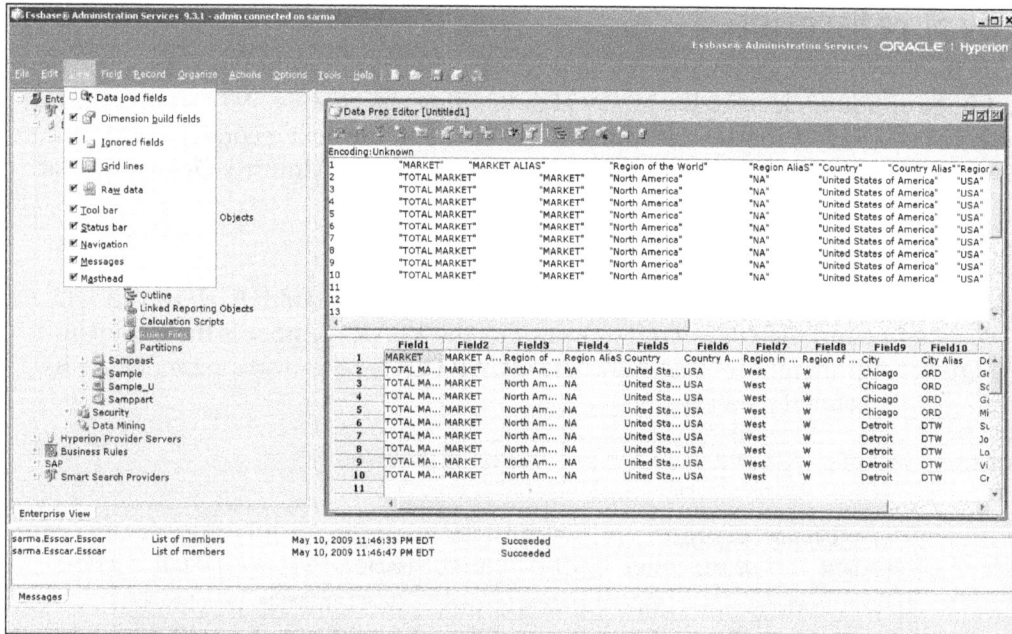

Step 6: Select Dimension build method

Build dimensions methods are basically used for adding, removing, or updating a member, an alias, or a property of an Essbase outline member. These are defined in the build rule files.

There are three ways you can build an Essbase outline:

- Generation reference
- Level reference
- Parent-child reference

Let us talk about how each method can be used to update the Essbase outline.

Generation reference

With the generation reference set, the data source should be arranged or organized from top to bottom as it pertains to the database outline structure. We consider the dimension name itself as `Generation 1`. Each record in the rules file contains the parent name as `Generation 1`, the child names are `Generation 2`, children of the child name are `Generation 3`, children of that child name are `Generation 4`, and so on. For example: **Year | Quarter | Month**.

Level reference

With the level reference set, the data source should be arranged or organized from the leaf node or bottom level to the top level or the dimension name. We consider the leaf node to be Level 0, the next record is called Level 1, the next record is Level 2, and so on, until we reach the top dimension level. For example: **Month | Quarter | Year**.

Parent-child reference

In the parent-child reference, the parent is followed by the child. Each record will have a parent and then its child. For example, the **YEAR** member is the parent and the **QUARTER** member is the child. The **QUARTER** level is also a parent since its child members are the months.

For this example, we have used the generation reference.

GEOGRAPHIC REGION	REGION ALIAS	HUB	CITY	CITY ALIAS	DEALER NAME	DEALER ALIAS
NorthAmerica	NA	Central	Detroit	DTW	Motor City EssCar	12045
NorthAmerica	NA	Central	Detroit	DTW	Motown EssCar	12046
NorthAmerica	NA	Central	Detroit	DTW	Phord City EssCar	12047
NorthAmerica	NA	Central	Detroit	DTW	East Side EssCar	12084
NorthAmerica	NA	Central	Chicago	ORD	Midwest EssCar	17801
NorthAmerica	NA	Central	Chicago	ORD	Soldier Field EssCar	17802
NorthAmerica	NA	Central	Chicago	ORD	Capone EssCar	17803
NorthAmerica	NA	Central	Chicago	ORD	St. Valentines EssCar	17804

As shown in the figure above, we can see two things:

- First, we see that the first record in the data file is a header record, which usually describes something about the data file itself such as the column names. This can be skipped by setting **1** in the **Number of lines to skip** in the **Header** section of the **Data Source Properties** as shown in the screenshot. Then click on **OK**.

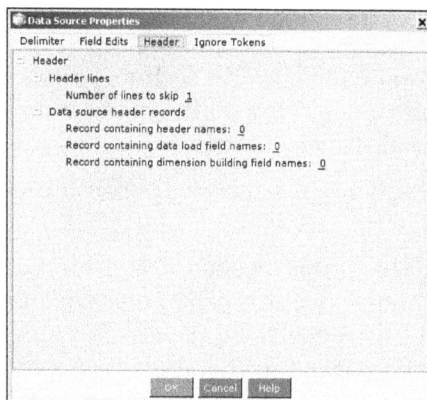

- Second, you can see that the data is starting from the top to the bottom, meaning we are going from the **Total Markets** to all the way down to the individual Dealer information. Remember, the best top-down data load method is the generations setting. We will need to choose the generation build method.

To choose the build dimension method, in EAS, with the **Data Prep Editor** open:

1. Click on **Options**, and then click on the **Dimension Build Settings**
2. Select the second tab which is the **Dimension Build Settings**, and you will see the **Dimension Build Settings** screen as shown in the following screenshot:

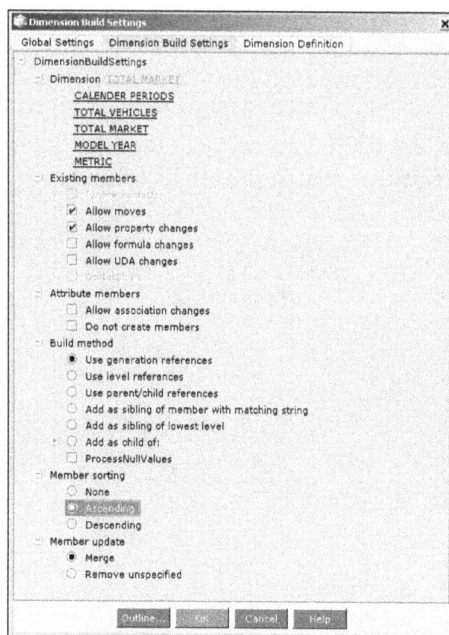

These are the actions you can do in the **Dimension Build Settings**:

- **Select the Dimension Name**: In this section, you can chose the dimension name for which this rule is being built—in our example, we have chosen **Total Market** as the dimension name

- **Existing Members**: If you are updating the outline quite often, you can chose these options.

  ○ **Allow Moves**: This property should be set to true if you think the member would move from one parent to another parent. When this move happens, the data will also move along with the member. If the parent of this member is a stored member, the roll up information will show the incorrect number.

  Let us say, in our example **INDIANA** is in the **EAST** region. Profit on **INDIANA** is 1 million dollars, profit on **EAST** is 5 million dollars and profit on **WEST** is 8 million dollars.

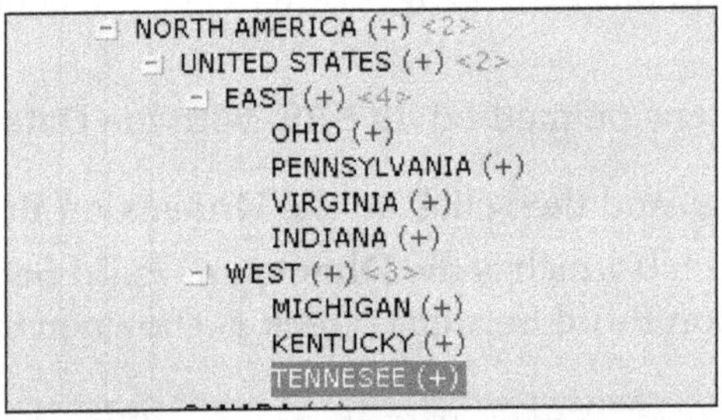

```
─  NORTH AMERICA (+) <2>
  ─  UNITED STATES (+) <2>
     ─  EAST (+) <4>
          OHIO (+)
          PENNSYLVANIA (+)
          VIRGINIA (+)
          INDIANA (+)
     ─  WEST (+) <3>
          MICHIGAN (+)
          KENTUCKY (+)
          TENNESEE (+)
```

During our market reorganizing the top management decides that **INDIANA** should be moved into the **WEST** region from the **EAST** region. After we run the Market rules file with the corrected data file, the `Market` dimension is updated with the new structure shown as follows:

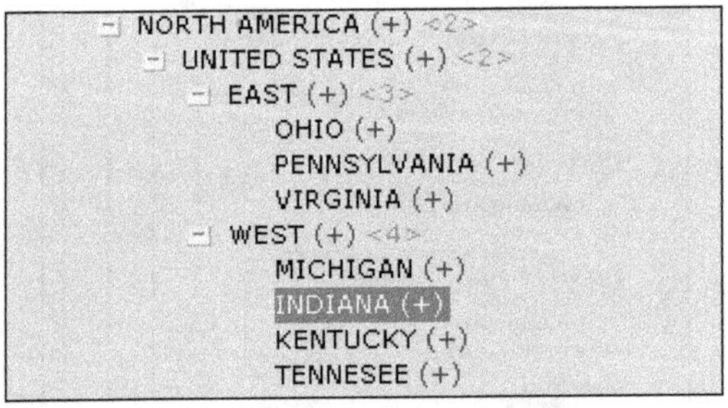

```
─  NORTH AMERICA (+) <2>
  ─  UNITED STATES (+) <2>
     ─  EAST (+) <3>
          OHIO (+)
          PENNSYLVANIA (+)
          VIRGINIA (+)
     ─  WEST (+) <4>
          MICHIGAN (+)
          INDIANA (+)
          KENTUCKY (+)
          TENNESEE (+)
```

INDIANA moves to **WEST** along with its profit, but the **EAST** still shows 5 million dollars, and **WEST** still shows 8 million dollars. In order to show the right numbers, the data needs to be recalculated as the parents WEST and EAST are stored data. In our example, we will enable this property for the **Total Market** member.

- ° Allow property changes: This allows the rules file to update the data storage properties, and consolidation operators. For example, changing the **Dynamic Calc** setting to **Dynamic Calc and Store**, or from (+) to (–) consolidation on a member. If this option is disabled, the rules will not allow the member properties to be updated. In our example, we will enable the **Allow property changes**. And yes, in your data file, the column that you designate as the member properties will actually contain the characters used in the database outline editor to indicate the specific properties. For example, if the member you are adding will have a consolidation of add, there will be a plus character (**+**) in the data. When this column is tagged as the member properties column during the build, Essbase will set the consolidation property to **+**.

- ° **Allow formula changes:** This allows the rule file to update the formula on a member, if a formula exists. If this property is disabled, you will not be allowed to change the formula from the rules file. In our example, we do not have a new property for **Total Market** so we are not enabling this property.

- **Select the Build method**: This is where you specify which method is used by this rules file to update the outline. There are three main methods in this section from which you can choose. We have previously chosen the Generation method as our source file is in the top to bottom hierarchical order.

- **Member sorting**: This property will set the sorting order while updating the outline using this rule. This sorting is applied to all of the members under this dimension.

These are the three sorting choices you can make:

- ° **None**: No sorting order is selected
- ° **Ascending**: Updates the outline in the ascending sort order
- ° **Descending**: Updates the outline in the descending sort order

For our example, let's select the **Ascending** order (A to Z).

- **Member Update**: There are two ways you can update members in the outline. Either adding a new member to the outline when a new member is included in the data file, or by completely replacing the outline with a new outline.
    - ○ **Merge**: This will add new members into the outline whenever a new member comes in with the data. New members are added in alongside existing members.
    - ○ **Remove unspecified**: This will delete all of the members in the outline and update the outline with the new members specified in the rules file and the accompanying data file.

Step 7: Format file

When necessary, Essbase allows you to manipulate or transform input data in order to make the data Essbase-friendly. To open an input source file in EAS, with the **Data Prep Editor** open:

1. Click on **Options** and then click on the **Data Source Properties**.
2. Go to second tab which is **File Edits** tab

These are things that you can edit in the input data file:

- **Move**: Changes the order of the fields in the input data. For example, if you want to move Field 3 into Field 2's place, you can click on the **Move** button and then move **Field 3** up as shown and click on **OK**. **Field 3** has now traded positions with **Field 2**. This is helpful when ordering data for dimension building purposes.

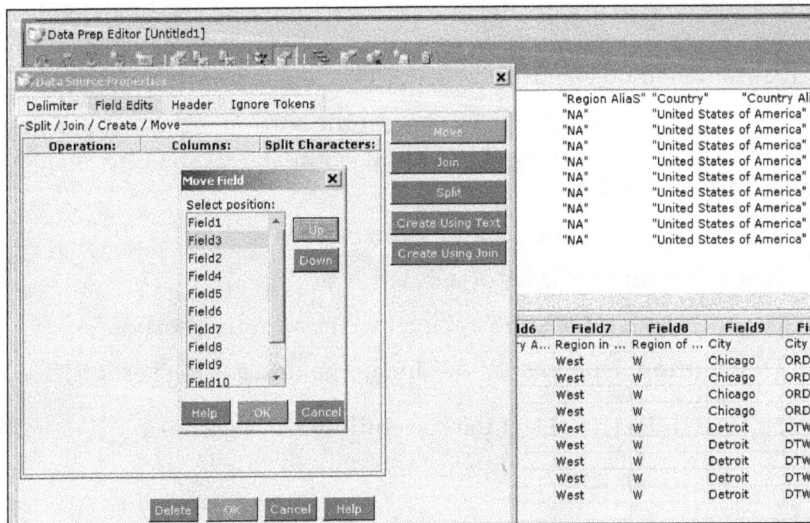

If you change your mind, you can always delete (undo) the column that was moved. Once you delete the moved column, it goes back to its original place.

- **Join**: Joins two or more fields to make a new unique column.

  In the example below, we have joined **Field 9** and **Field 10** together:

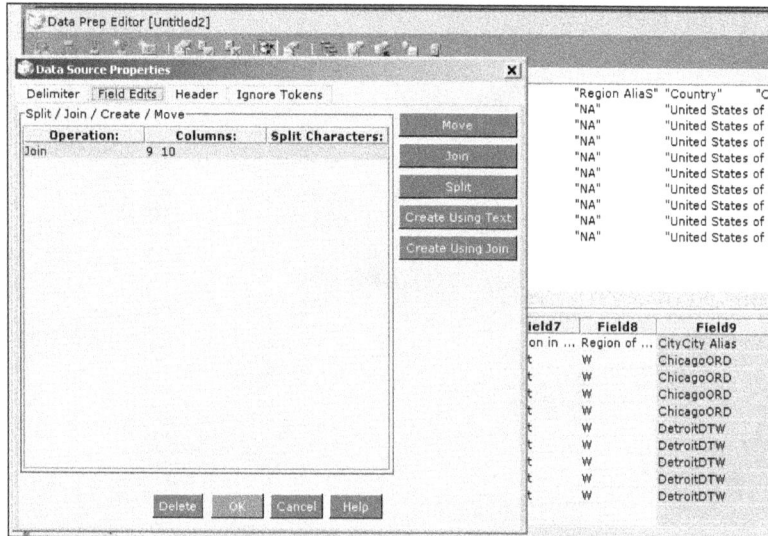

- **Split**: Splits the field at a given number of characters into two fields.

  In the following example, we split **Field 12**, which has the dealer code, into two fields as shown:

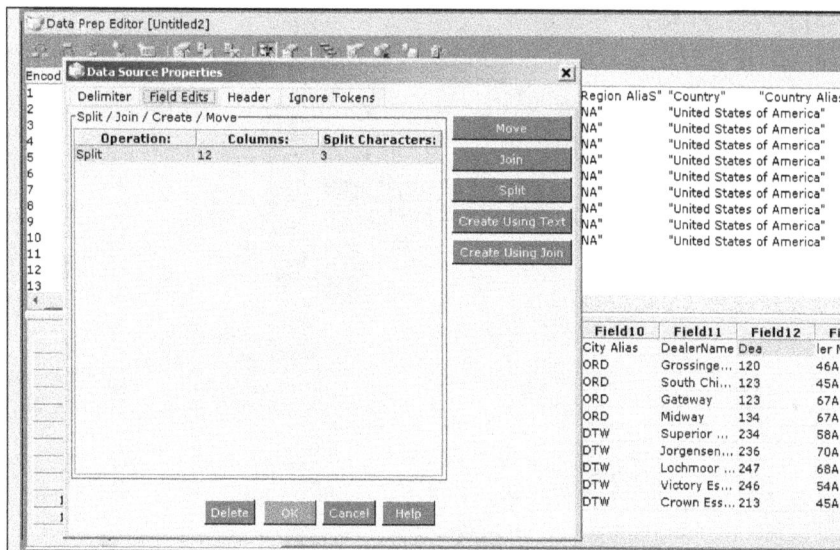

- **Create Using Join**: This function is used to join two or more fields to create a new field.

  In this example, we have joined the field containing the value of **United States of America** and the field containing the value **USA**, into a new field which looks like: **United States of AmericaUSA**, as shown in the following screenshot:

- **Create Using Text**: Creates a new field based on the text you have entered. This is particularly helpful when you need to make Essbase-friendly data that is repeatedly sent from the same source.

  As shown in the following example, a field is added between **Field 6** and **Field 7** called **US**:

Step 8: Associate fields with dimensions

Now that our source data file transformation is complete, we are ready to proceed with the outline update. Before we update the outline, we need to set the **Dimension Build Properties**, meaning we need to define the attributes of each column. In other words, how Essbase will interpret the data in each column.

Since our market data source is to be a generation build method, let us define each column and how the outline must be updated according to the data.

Open the **Dimension Build Properties** in EAS, with the **Data Prep Editor** open:

1. Click on **Fields** and then click on the **Field Properties**
2. Since this is Dimension build rule file, go to the tab **Dimension Build Properties**

    The following screenshot shows the **Dimension build** settings:

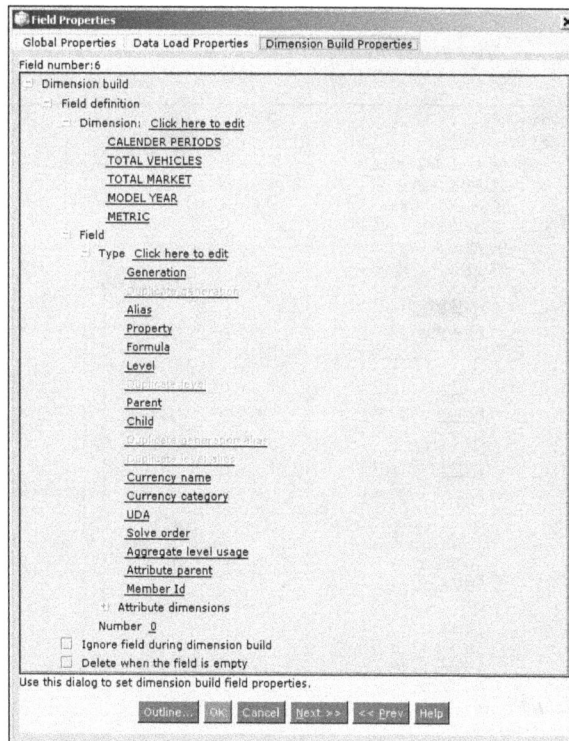

    In the **Dimension Build Properties** screen, you need to define the dimension name, and the corresponding field that the data will load to. Some of the available options are **Generation**, **Alias**, **Property**, **Level**, **Parent**, and **Child**.

You can also ignore a field by selecting the option **Ignore field during dimension build**. There may be times when an entire column or field is not needed for you to load the data into Essbase. For example, the file you are loading has a column for cities in it. Your database outline is only set up for countries and states. Cities are not needed so there is no need to even look at them.

In our example, the **Field 1** input data field is the Generation 2 member name (Generations always start from Generation 2 as the Generation 1 level is the dimension name itself) and the next field will be the member alias.

Click on **Field 1**, then assign the **Field Definition | Dimension** as TOTAL MARKET, in the **Field | Type** select **Generation** and in the **Field | Number** enter **2** and click **OK**. The input data **Field 1** is now set to load to Generation 2/Member Name. If you were finished, you could click **OK** now, with more fields to define, you can simply click on **Next**. Did you see how the cursor has automatically moved to **Field 2**. Select **TOTAL MARKET** as the dimension name and click on **Alias** field type. When you select **Alias** the **Field | Number** is set to Generation **2** as shown:

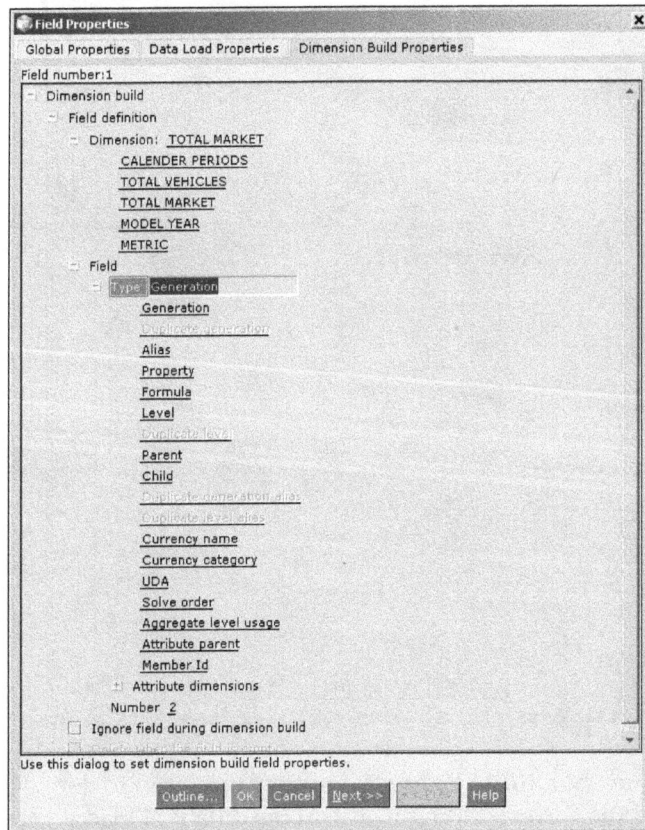

Repeat the above steps by clicking on **Next** and choosing the **Dimension** name and **Field | Type** until you reach the end of the file. The Generation number will be incremented by one for each new field in the data that you define as a new member.

Finally, all of the fields in the input data file are defined in the Essbase rules file. The rules file should look like this:

Step 9: Validate the Dimension Build rules file

Now that all of the input data fields are assigned to the appropriate outline members, we need to validate the rules file against the database outline. With the rules file open, click on the validate button (the quick select button says **Validate** when you hover over it). The validate function validates if the rules file is properly defined for the specific database outline. If the validate is successful, you will receive a validate successful message. If the rules file is not properly defined to the database outline, you will receive a message stating the validation was unsuccessful. One common example of a rules file validation failing is if you have two fields defined as building members in the same dimension. When you set the dimension build to use the generation method, you must be careful that you define the fields correctly. The field that is going to build `Generation 2` members must be the only field set upto do so.

Upon successful rules file validation, click on **File | Save** and give the rule file a name (preferably something meaningful but remember, upto 8 characters in the name). The rules file can be saved on either the Essbase server or as a local file. Where you save it depends on your specific architecture.

Update your outline using a rules file

Now that you have completed your first rule file, you need to update the outline using this rules file.

There are several ways you can update an outline using a data rules file and a data file:

- Updating the outline from the EAS Outline Editor
- Executing MaxL commands
- Making your own API calls
- Running Essbase command scripts

We will discuss the first and second points now, and the third and fourth points will be discussed with examples provided, in the next chapter.

Update your outline using the EAS Outline Editor

One of the easiest ways the outline can be updated is manually by using the EAS Outline Editor.

The steps to update the outline are:

1. In the EAS, open the **Application | Database** for which the outline needs to be updated.
2. Double-click on the **Outline**, the outline editor is opened for editing.
3. Or, you can click on the **Outline** in the **Menu** option and then click on the **Update outline**. The following screen will then be displayed:

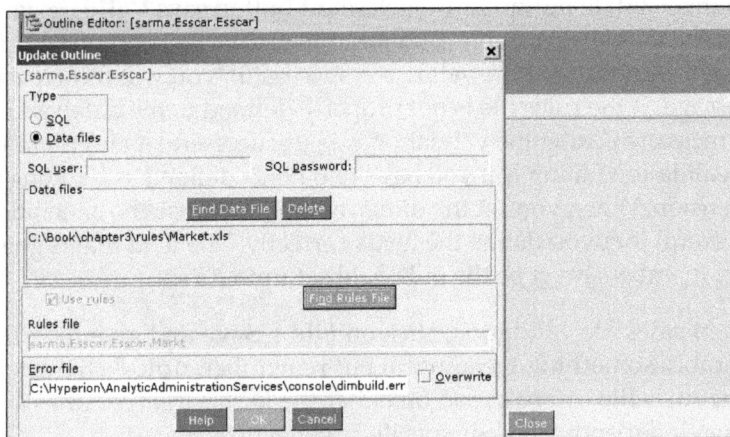

As you can see from the previous screen, you would be able to select either the **SQL** data source or the **Data Files**. If you choose to select **SQL**, then you will need to provide the **SQL user** name and **SQL password**.

1. We have a Microsoft Excel file as our data source so we have selected the **Data files** option.

2. Click on the **Find Data File**. Browse through the directory and select the data source file. You have the choice of a local file or a server file.

3. Click on the **Find Rules File** and select the rule file that you have built and saved on the server.

4. For the error file, you can give a different error file path and name, or you can use the default error file. If you think the error file already exists, please select the option **Overwrite**. If not, you will get an error message.

5. Click on **OK**.

6. Essbase will load the data per the instructions in the rules file you selected. If it is a dimension build rules file (as is this case), the outline itself will be updated.

7. The outline will be updated, saved, and restructured. The new outline is shown in the following screenshot:

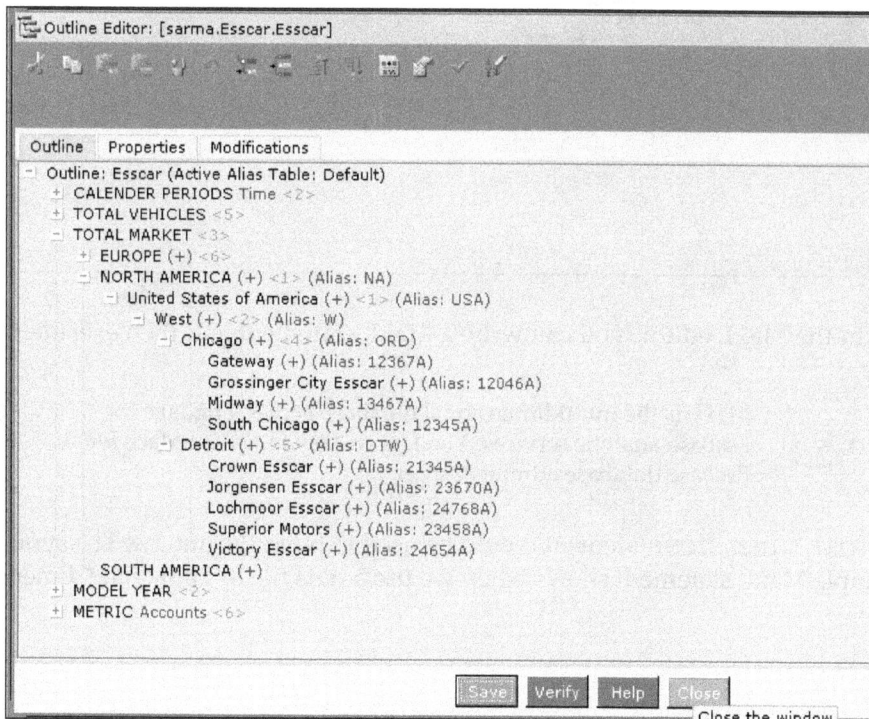

Update using MaxL Shell

In the earlier versions of Essbase, **EssCmd (Essbase Command Script)** was widely used as the shell script of choice. In the newer versions of Essbase, Oracle recommends using MaxL Shell scripts. Using the MaxL Shell statements, you will be able to perform most of the Essbase functions like dimension building, importing data, and calculating data.

A MaxL Shell script can be executed three different ways:

- Through the EAS editor
- From the DOS Command Line
- Shelled from within another scripting language

Executing MaxL from EAS editor

The steps to execute MaxL from EAS editor are:

1. Within EAS, click on **File | Editor | MaxL Script Editor**
2. The MaxL editor will be opened as shown in the screenshot below:

- In the MaxL editor, you can write a MaxL statement and then execute it.

> MaxL is the multidimensional database access language for Essbase analytic services. MaxL is an easy to use interface for Essbase database administration.

The IMPORT DIMENSION statement would be used to build the outline. The syntax in the example MaxL statement shows when we use a data file to update the dimension.

Syntax of Import Dimension statement

We will show you some actual code that can be used in the MaxL editor to execute database commands. As we will present in much greater detail later in this book, MaxL is a command-based scripting language that you can use for automating maintenance and routine tasks:

```
IMPORT DATABASE APPLICATION NAME.DATABASE NAME DIMENSIONS
FROM (input data file information)
LOCAL | SERVER /* Location of the data file
FILE TYPE /* Type of data source whether a Text files, Excel File,
            or Lotus File
DATA_FILE
FILE PATH ' Path of the file like c:/book/chapter3/rules/market.xls
USING (Information about the Rule File)
    LOCAL | SERVER ' Location of the rule file
    RULE_FILE
    RULE FILE NAME ' Name of the rule file like Markt
    ON ERROR APPEND TO (error File information)
    WRITE | APPEND
    ERROR File name ' Path for error file
                    ' c:/book/DimError.log
```

The following screenshot shows the code that was entered into the EAS MaxL editor and then executed by pressing the *F5* button or clicking on the **MaxL | Execute** button:

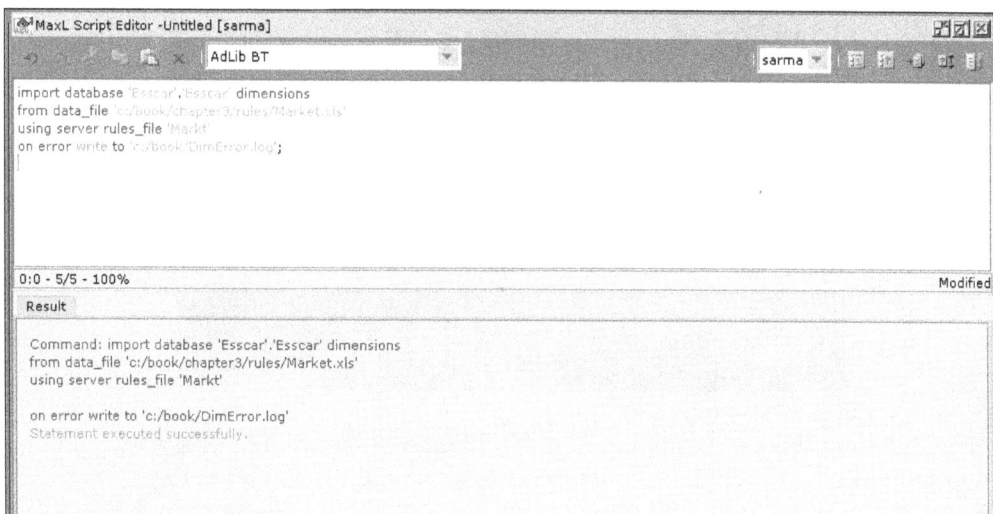

As shown in the previous screenshot, the script has executed without errors. Let's modify the script to force an error message.

We have changed the reserve word **database** to **data**. This is a glaring syntax error and will immediately generate an error message as shown in the following screenshot:

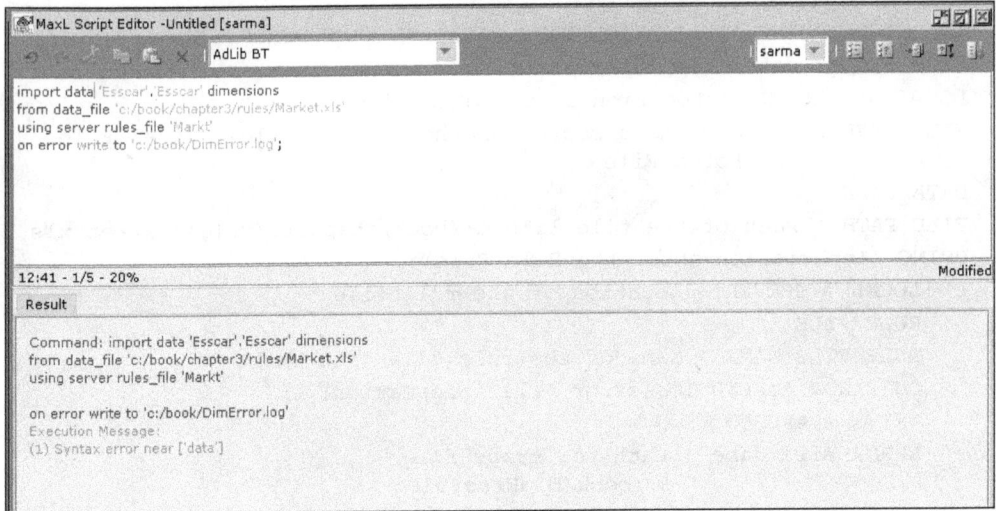

This script can also be saved with the extension .mxl for later use.

Executing MaxL from command prompt

You can use MaxL statements from the DOS command prompt as well. The essmsh.exe file is located in the $Arborpath/bin which, in our case, is C:\Oracle\AnalyticServices\bin.

From the command prompt, go to this directory and enter the word **ESSMSH** as shown:

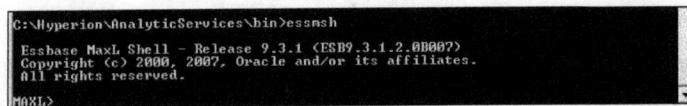

In the EAS editor, you need not log on to the Essbase server as EAS is already connected to Essbase. When using the command prompt, you need to log in to Essbase. Using the following syntax in a MaxL statement, you log in to the Essbase server:

```
Login 'UserID' 'Password' on 'ServerName';
```

The following is an example of logging in through the command line:

```
MAXL> login bookuser password on localhost;

OK/INFO - 1051034 - Logging in user [bookuser].
OK/INFO - 1051035 - Last login on Monday, May 11, 2009 11:17:29 PM.
OK/INFO - 1241001 - Logged in to Essbase.

MAXL> _
```

Now, that you are logged on to the Essbase server, you can execute any MaxL statement using the command line to update the Essbase outline. The following screenshot shows how you can achieve this. Notice how the syntax is very easy to read. Almost like a spoken sentence.

```
C:\WINDOWS\system32\cmd.exe - essmsh
OK/INFO - 1241001 - Logged in to Essbase.

MAXL> import database esscar.esscar dimensions
   2> from data_file 'c:/book/Chapter3/rules/Market.xls'
   3> using server rules_file 'Markt'
   4> on error write to 'c:/book/DimError.log';

OK/INFO - 1053012 - Object [esscar] is locked by user [bookuser].
OK/INFO - 1007132 - Building Dimensions Elapsed Time : [0.016] seconds.
OK/INFO - 1019017 - Reading Parameters For Database [Drxxxxxx].
OK/INFO - 1019012 - Reading Outline For Database [Drxxxxxx].
OK/INFO - 1019024 - Reading Outline Transaction For Database [Drxxxxxx].
OK/INFO - 1007043 - Declared Dimension Sizes = [35 17 23 3 14 ].
OK/INFO - 1007042 - Actual Dimension Sizes = [35 14 21 3 14 ].
OK/INFO - 1007125 - The number of Dynamic Calc Non-Store Members = [0 0 0 0 1 ]

OK/INFO - 1007126 - The number of Dynamic Calc Store Members = [0 0 0 0 0 ].
OK/INFO - 1007127 - The logical block size is [490].
OK/INFO - 1010008 - Maximum Declared Blocks is [1173] with data block size of [
490].
OK/INFO - 1010007 - Maximum Actual Possible Blocks is [882] with data block siz
e of [455].
OK/INFO - 1012710 - Essbase needs to retrieve [1] Essbase Kernel blocks in orde
r to calculate the top dynamically-calculated block..
OK/INFO - 1012736 - The Dyn.Calc.Cache for database [Drxxxxxx] can hold a maxim
um of [5349] blocks..
OK/INFO - 1012737 - The Dyn.Calc.Cache for database [Drxxxxxx], when full, will
result in [allocation from non-Dyn.Calc.Cache memory]..
OK/INFO - 1010008 - Maximum Declared Blocks is [1173] with data block size of [
490].
OK/INFO - 1010007 - Maximum Actual Possible Blocks is [882] with data block siz
e of [455].
OK/INFO - 1019020 - Writing Free Space Information For Database [Esscar].
OK/INFO - 1019017 - Reading Parameters For Database [Esscar].
OK/INFO - 1070013 - Index cache size ==> [1048576] bytes, [128] index pages..
OK/INFO - 1070014 - Index page size ==> [8192] bytes..
OK/INFO - 1070081 - Using buffered I/O for the index and data files..
OK/INFO - 1070083 - Using waited I/O for the index and data files..
OK/INFO - 1006025 - Data cache size ==> [3145728] bytes, [864] data pages.
OK/INFO - 1006026 - Data file cache size ==> [0] bytes, [0] data file pages.
OK/INFO - 1019017 - Reading Parameters For Database [Drxxxxxx].
OK/INFO - 1070013 - Index cache size ==> [1048576] bytes, [128] index pages..
OK/INFO - 1070014 - Index page size ==> [8192] bytes..
OK/INFO - 1070081 - Using buffered I/O for the index and data files..
OK/INFO - 1070083 - Using waited I/O for the index and data files..
OK/INFO - 1006025 - Data cache size ==> [3145728] bytes, [864] data pages.
OK/INFO - 1006026 - Data file cache size ==> [0] bytes, [0] data file pages.
```

Our Esscar outline is now updated with the new Market structure.

Hooray! You have built your first outline using an Essbase rules file and you have also learned how to execute the script manually and also by using MaxL to run a script that uses your load rule file.

Attribute dimensions

Attribute dimensions are dimensions associated with standard dimensions. Attribute dimensions are useful in describing a standard dimension member's attributes. For example, in our Esscar database, we have the `Vehicles` dimension. If we wanted to differentiate between a two or four door car of the same model, we could use an attribute dimension to accomplish this. We could also use an attribute dimension to track color.

Attribute dimensions are always dynamically calculated, which means they do not store the data. This is always a benefit as they do not affect the size or performance of the database.

Attribute dimensions must always be associated with a standard dimension.

Earlier, we briefly saw the differences between standard dimensions and attribute dimensions. Sometimes, your data has attributes that make it desirable to perform further analysis on it. In the case of the Esscar Motor Company, it may be desirable to track a certain vehicle model by its color. You may wish to compare how that model sells in markets based on population size. Essbase database attribute dimensions can help you with this type of analysis.

One of the most notable features of an attribute dimension is the fact that the entire dimension is a dynamically calculated dimension. Previously, we told you about dynamically calculated members in a standard outline. In an attribute dimension, all members are dynamically calculated. What this means is that Essbase does not need to store the data for an entire dimension! All of the data is calculated on the fly when requested and goes away when the user is finished. This, as previously mentioned, is a huge benefit when considering CPU performance and storage options.

Here are a few facts about attribute dimensions:

- An attribute dimension is a dimension that must be associated with a standard dimension.
- An attribute dimension can only be associated with one standard dimension, but a standard dimension can be associated with many attribute dimensions.
- An attribute dimension can only be associated with a **Sparse** standard dimension. This is an important point.

To create an attribute dimension and associate it to a standard dimension, you need to do the following:

1. Create a new dimension and tag it as an attribute dimension.
2. Next, create an association between this new attribute dimension and the standard dimension you wish to track attributes from.
3. Add the zero level members to the attribute dimension that correspond to the zero level members of the standard dimension.
4. Lastly, associate the members from the standard dimension to the zero level attribute dimension members.

As this is an advanced Essbase function, we have provided a high-level look at attribute dimensions and their set up and use. For complete details, please refer to the documentation which was provided when you purchased your version of software.

The following screenshot shows the **TOTAL VEHICLES** dimension with the new **COLORS** attribute dimension added:

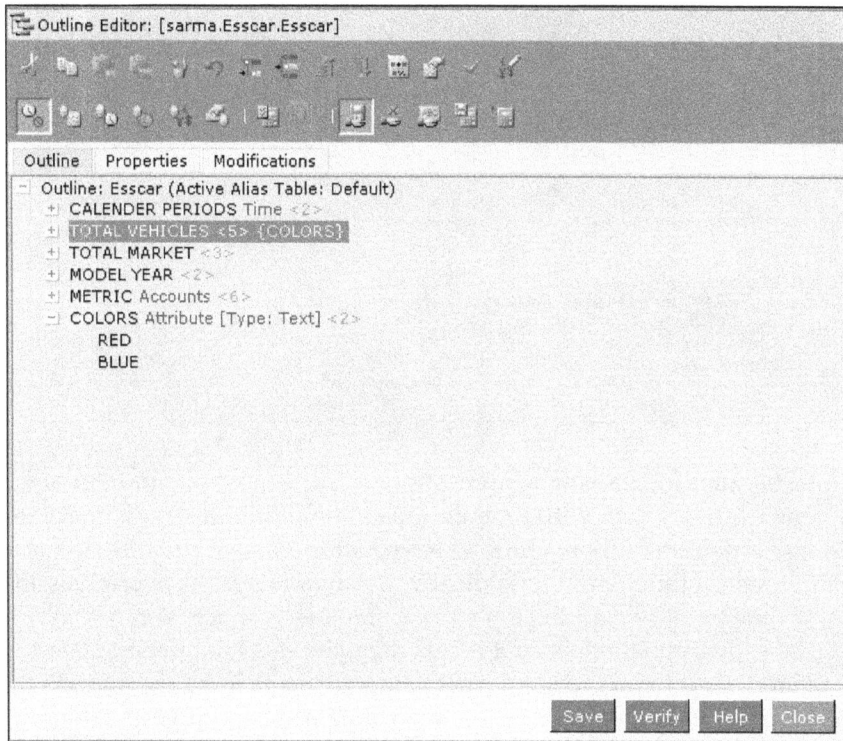

User Defined Attributes (UDA)

An Essbase UDA is a descriptive word or tag about an outline member. Similar to an alias, the main difference is that an alias may only be attached to one member. A UDA can be attached to many members.

What the UDA offers is a way to simplify and make the ongoing operations of your database more efficient.

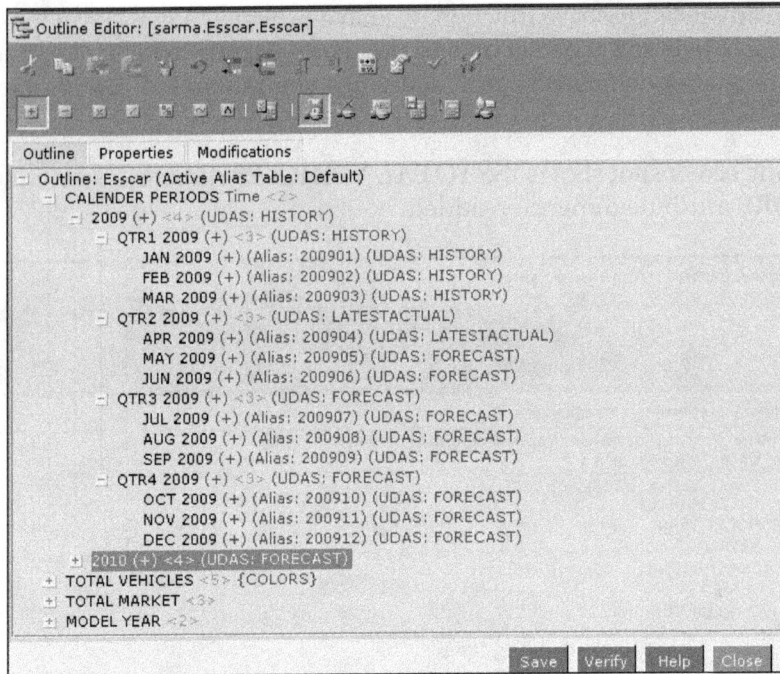

For example, because forecasting analytics is one of the most common uses for an OLAP system, the users deal with time periods that fall into three distinct categories. In any Essbase database outline, you will have historical time periods, actual time periods, and forecast time periods. Typically, the data you have previously loaded for historical time periods, and the data you just loaded for actual time periods, does not need to be fully calculated since it is real data and does not need to be derived or changed. On the other hand, your forecast data still needs to be calculated whenever you make a change to a component piece of data. If you tagged your calendar periods in the outline with UDAs of Forecast for the future periods, LatestActual for the first month back, and History for all historical periods in the outline. If you move the UDAs once a month to compensate for the new month in time, you could code a calculation script that would never need to be updated since you would write the script to calculate forecast periods by looking at the Forecast UDA.

Some UDA rules to keep in mind:

- You can assign many UDAs to a single member, but you cannot assign the same UDA to a member more than once.

- You can use the same UDA on many different members.

- A UDA cannot be the same name or word as a member name or alias name.

- UDAs cannot be used on Shared Members or members in an attribute dimension.

- UDAs run with the dimension they were created in and can only be assigned to other members in that same dimension.

- UDAs are member specific and only apply to the single member they are attached to. Parents, children, and so on, of a member assigned a UDA are not covered unless they also have the UDA assigned to them as well.

UDAs are added to the database outline members in much the same way as adding an alias or updating any other outline member property. When adding a UDA to an outline member, Essbase will display a list of UDAs available for the dimension in which the member resides. If the desired UDA does not exist, you may simply add it the first time.

Dynamic Time Series

Once again, Essbase gives us a feature so cool that it makes us wonder how we lived without it! The **Dynamic Time Series** function is one of those features.

We can't think of anyone who wouldn't use this functionality. Likewise, we can't think of anyone who wouldn't need this functionality.

What the **Dynamic Time Series** does for you is automatically calculate period-to-date data based on your Time dimension. Using our example database for the Esscar Motor Company, we see that it is probably a good idea to know our year-to-date vehicle production, by both calendar year and model year. The **Dynamic Time Series** function does this for you. You can easily calculate period-to-date data for any period as defined in your Time dimension.

In other words, Essbase can automatically calculate a cumulative number based on how you have the `Time` dimension set up. If you want to track how many vehicles you have built from the beginning of the year through the current month, the **Dynamic Time Series** can do this for you. If you were to build 1,000 units in January and 1,000 units in February, and 1,000 units in March, you would expect to see 1,000 units as your net number for each month's data pulled. But, if you want to know the total units through each month, you would expect to see 1,000 for January, 2,000 for February, and 3,000 through March. This is what a period-to-date calculation will give you.

The **Dynamic Time Series** member is actually created for you when you associate a predefined **Dynamic Time Series** member with the appropriate outline `Generation`. For example, to use the year-to-date **Dynamic Time Series** functionality, you would associate a year member with the `Generation 4` (month's level) `Calendar Periods` dimension. When you request the data at the **Dynamic Time Series** member, Essbase will automatically sum the `Generation 4` level members within the given year and return the results to you.

Essbase has provided the following predefined **Dynamic Time Series** functions. As always, if you have a special need, there are plenty of calculation functions available to allow you to code even the most complex custom calculation:

- **H-T-D** (History-to-date)
- **Y-T-D** (Year-to-date)
- **S-T-D** (Season-to-date)
- **P-T-D** (Period-to-date)
- **Q-T-D** (Quarter-to-date)
- **M-T-D** (Month-to-date)
- **W-T-D** (Week-to-date)
- **D-T-D** (Day-to-date)

Here is an important item to consider when coding **Dynamic Time Series** functionality. Your **Dynamic Time Series** member can be associated with any Generation in your time dimension, except the zero level Generation (you cannot have months adding upto a month-to-date value).

The steps to add a **Dynamic Time Series** member to the `Time` dimension of our Esscar database outline are:

1. In EAS, open the Esscar outline in the outline editor
2. Click on **Outline | Dynamic Time Series.**

3. On the **Dynamic Time Series** screen, select **Y-T-D** and **GEN 3** as shown in the following screenshot:

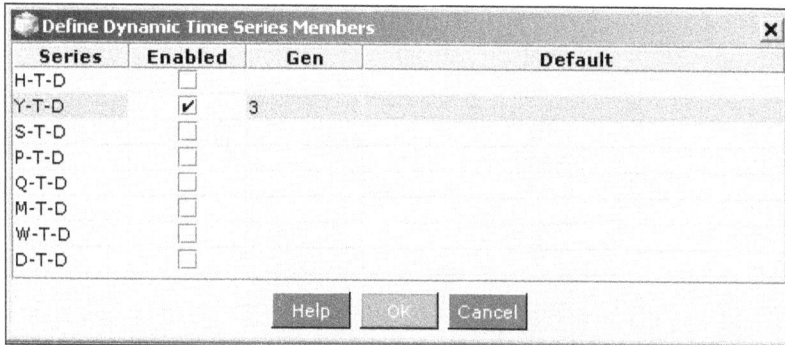

4. Once you click **OK**, the outline will be updated to reflect to the changes that you have made as shown in the following screenshot:

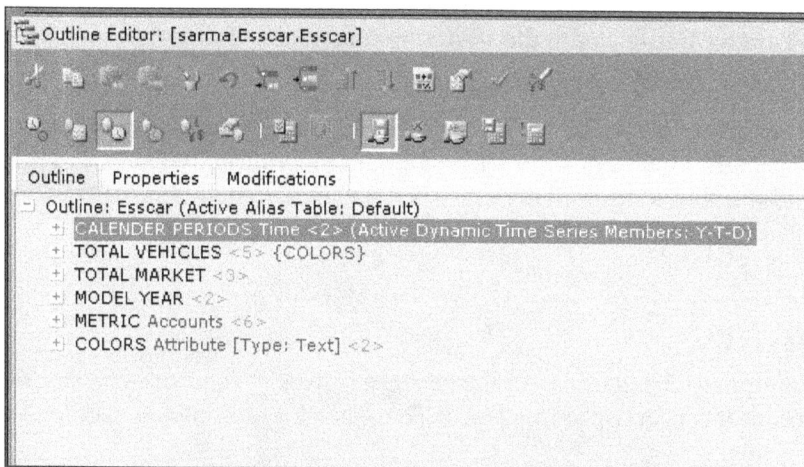

Shared members

Shared members are another great tool offered by Essbase to help you increase your data and reporting versatility in a simple and extremely efficient manner.

In a nutshell, a shared member is another occurrence of an already existing member in the outline. The shared member only stores a pointer to the existing outline member, thereby giving serious space and processing efficiencies in the database.

The benefits do not end there either. What you can do is have the shared member /original member be a child to many different parents. For example, if you have a product that is available in several markets, you can organize your outline with the child members as needed for each market. The shared member can appear in several places simultaneously and be selectively calculated with relative ease.

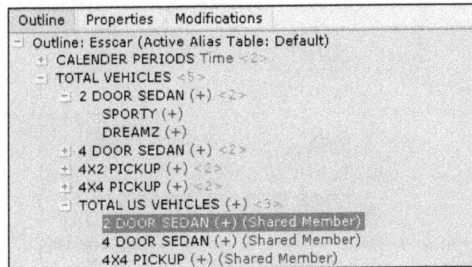

```
Outline    Properties    Modifications
Outline: Esscar (Active Alias Table: Default)
   CALENDER PERIODS Time <2>
   TOTAL VEHICLES <5>
      2 DOOR SEDAN (+) <2>
         SPORTY (+)
         DREAMZ (+)
      4 DOOR SEDAN (+) <2>
      4X2 PICKUP (+) <2>
      4X4 PICKUP (+) <2>
      TOTAL US VEHICLES (+) <3>
         2 DOOR SEDAN (+) (Shared Member)
         4 DOOR SEDAN (+) (Shared Member)
         4X4 PICKUP (+) (Shared Member)
```

In the preceding screenshot, notice how we have the individual vehicles located in three different groups in the database outline. The vehicles under the **Total Vehicles** parent are the original members and the vehicles located under **Total US Vehicles** and **Total Canada Vehicles** are the shared members. By doing this, we can create different group totals from the same pool of members in the outline.

There are only two main rules for Essbase shared members. You cannot tag a member as a shared member unless the same member already exists as a non-shared member and the shared members need to be the lowest members, or the Level 0 members, of their respective dimensions.

Summary

Well, that wraps up the chapter on the Essbase outline. We know you've been hit with a lot of information upto this point. There is a lot to know about the Essbase database outline.

You have learned how to add dimension level members to the database outline and you've learned how to make decisions on how to best determine what categories of your data best fit as Essbase database outline dimensions.

You have learned the myriad available properties that a database outline member can have. For instance, how the child members consolidate their values to the parent member, or do the individual members store data or have it dynamically calculated.

You have also learned that there are several ways to actually update an Essbase database outline. You can perform any necessary task manually by using the EAS, but you can also perform most routine tasks automatically by either using a dimension build load process or by executing a MaxL command script.

You are now at a point where you should have a good hold on Essbase applications, databases and outlines. You should also have a good understanding of multidimensionality as it pertains to Oracle Essbase.

Going forward the amount of information presented to you will not decrease but the use and/or purpose of the information will as what will be presented to you now will assume you have a good base to build on.

The coming chapters will now be your guide to enhancing what you know while at the same time enhancing your ability to efficiently maintain and support your Essbase database whether it be loading data (many different methods shown in next chapter), calculating data, or using your data.

In other words, by now, you know what to do. The rest of the book will show you how to do it better and with more options!

4
Loading Data into Essbase

You have learned how to perform an installation of Oracle Essbase on your server and client, and to install the Essbase Administration Services on your client as well. You have learned how to look at data in a multidimensional sense and make decisions on how to best build an Essbase database based on your data. You have also learned how to build an actual Essbase application and database, layout and build the database outline, and then experimented with some basic methods of data loading and outline building.

In this chapter you will learn, hands-on, how to perform several methods of loading data into your Essbase database. You will also learn how to use the many optional data load settings and attributes that assist you with loading data into your Essbase database. Along with manually loading data, you will also learn how to automate data loads for repeated data loading from interfacing systems.

Most importantly, you will learn that no matter how seemingly incompatible or dirty the input data is, Essbase provides many tools and utility option settings that allow you to convert, transform, filter, and clean your input data. Using these tools' functionality your data can quickly and easily be made ready to load into your Essbase database.

A term you will become very familiar with is Essbase-friendly. Essbase-friendly data or, making your data Essbase-friendly, simply means fixing up any data intended for loading into your Essbase database in such a way that you successfully load the maximum amount of data with the fewest number of rejections.

Let's start making your data Essbase-friendly and then loading your friendly data into your Essbase database.

Make your data Essbase-friendly

The reason this subject is something worth discussing here in Essbase is because unlike traditional relational database packages, Oracle Essbase includes many easy to use tools to quickly transform, alter, modify, or otherwise turn questionable data into good, usable data that can be fully and correctly loaded into your Essbase database. Creating Essbase-friendly data can be accomplished with a minimum amount of effort and expense, both on the Essbase side and the data source side, which is sure to please even the toughest business customer who no doubt is aware of how creating an extract of data from a traditional system sometimes means a lot of effort and even the writing of a complex program or two.

First, to make sure you understand, when loading data in Essbase the data must contain a representative element of data for each dimension in the target Essbase database's outline. For example, our Esscar database outline contains seven dimensions, so the data you intend to load must contain an element for each dimension plus the data value itself, for a total of eight elements of data. The following figure shows you how your data would look in a perfect world:

Measures	Calendar Periods	Vehicle	Model Year	Customer	Market	Scenario	Data Value
Production	Jan 2009	Hatchback	MYR 2009	Customer	Canada	June 2009	10,000
Sales	Jan 2009	Hatchback	MYR 2009	Retail	Canada	June 2009	12,500

Notice there are eight columns of data, one column for each dimension in the Esscar database outline and the data value itself. Now, as mentioned, this would be the perfect way to receive data from an outside source. It's too bad this is rarely the case when receiving data from another department or business activity, even within your own company. Heck, sometimes data from within the same company is the most inconsistent.

In the real world, you are lucky when you get the bare minimum of the data elements you need to satisfy your Essbase requirements from sources external to your Essbase database. This is not a great concern most of the time with Essbase and we'll tell you why, then we will take the rest of this chapter to show you how.

Essbase-friendly thoughts

Consider that you have constructed your Essbase database outline to be as flexible and detailed as possible for your business customer. You know very well that you won't always get clean data from an external system that will load right into your database.

There are many reasons why you may not get data sent to you just the way you would like it. First and foremost is the expense of writing a complex program to extract the data from one system and pretty it up for the receiving system. Second, it takes time to write such a program.

With Essbase, you have tools designed specifically to pretty up or make Essbase-friendly, even some of the most objectionable data.

In other words, with the tools that Essbase provides you and a little bit of your own creativity, there isn't much data out there that you would have a good reason to say no to making Essbase-friendly.

Here is a real world example of making your data Essbase-friendly that shows just what can be accomplished with very little effort. The data load rule you are about to see was developed in less than two hours.

Essbase-friendly example

The following screenshot shows an input data file that has been opened in the Essbase **Data Prep Editor**. The upper pane displays the data in its raw form and the lower pane shows you what the data will look like to Essbase during the actual data load.

The first column in the raw data view is the month column in numeric format. The second column in the raw data view is the calendar year in four digit format. Unfortunately, our month/year values in the database outline are formatted as MMM YYYY (for example, Jan 2009), with the month as a three character abbreviation then a space then the four digit year. You will also need them all in one column.

Next we join the month and year columns using the column join option in the
Data Source Properties screen as shown:

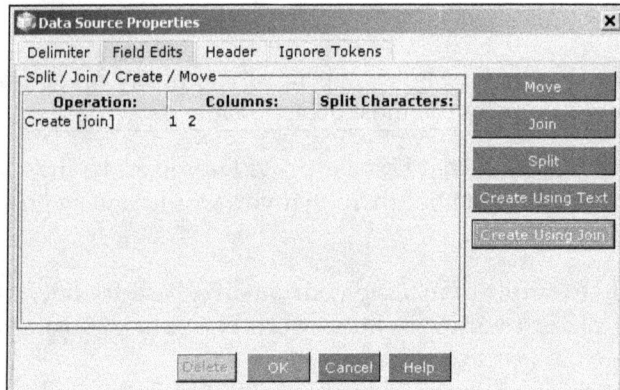

Observe how we told Essbase to join columns 1 and 2 into a new single column.
But wait, the date format is still wrong. What do we do next? Easy enough, all we
need to do now is set up the replace function to convert the date column into an
Essbase-friendly date format. Watch how easy it is:

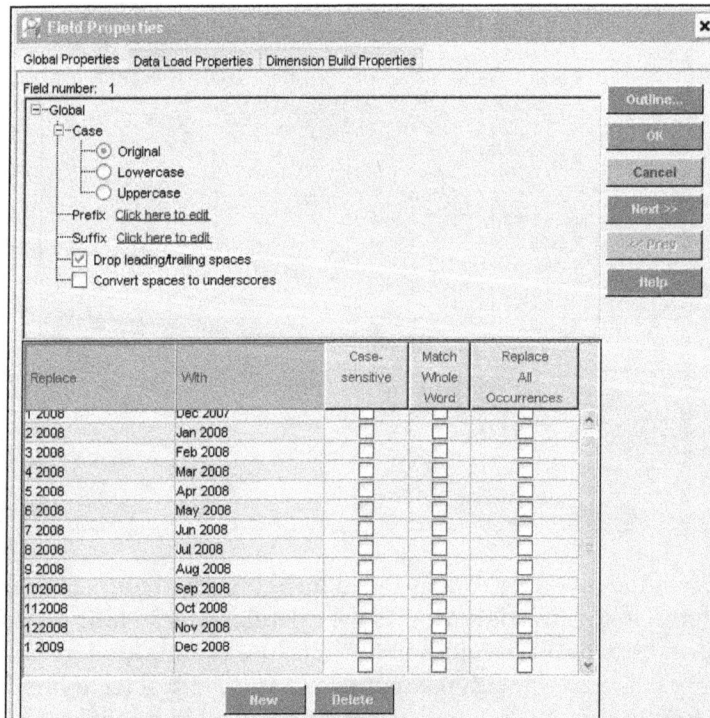

Replace	With	Case-sensitive	Match Whole Word	Replace All Occurrences
1 2008	Dec 2007			
2 2008	Jan 2008			
3 2008	Feb 2008			
4 2008	Mar 2008			
5 2008	Apr 2008			
6 2008	May 2008			
7 2008	Jun 2008			
8 2008	Jul 2008			
9 2008	Aug 2008			
102008	Sep 2008			
112008	Oct 2008			
122008	Nov 2008			
1 2009	Dec 2008			

Notice in the **Field Properties** screen how we replace the wrongly formatted date column with the correct format. There are other options as well depending on your specific needs.

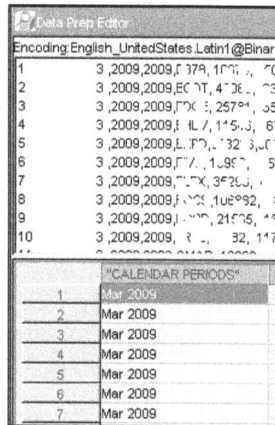

Finally, looking at the data in the first column, we see that what were once two separate columns with the wrong date format is now one column of correctly formatted data which will successfully load into our Esscar database. Total development time for this column was about 15 minutes. This is how you make your data Essbase-friendly!

Types of data sources

A typical data source for your Essbase database can contain many bits of information. Unlike traditional relational databases, Essbase data sources can be actual data values or they can be metadata. Because you can update your database outline dynamically with the same data that you ultimately load, data sources in Essbase take on a completely different meaning than in other types of systems. When talking about data sources in Essbase, any of the following can be considered.

Type of data

The data loaded into Essbase can be of two types, one is to load the data into the cube and the other is to update the outline of the cube:

- **Data loads**: These are the actual data values. This would be the numeric value of one of the existing measures in the database. This type of Essbase data source is usually the only usable type of data source in a traditional relational database.

- **Dimension build loads**: Information in the data that can actually be used to update the outline's member names, member aliases, member attributes, and more.

> The Essbase data rules file can be used both as a data load rules file, to load data values into the database and also as a dimension build rules file, to update or add new members to the database outline.

Types of files used for data loads

The data that is loaded into Essbase can come from different types of files like Microsoft Excel files, Text files, Comma Separated files or directly from a relational database. Let us talk about these file types and see how we can use each of them in Essbase.

Microsoft Excel files

Microsoft Excel files can be used as data sources in a couple of ways. First, they can be used to perform a "Lock and Send" of the data from the Microsoft Excel worksheet directly into the Essbase database. A Microsoft Excel workbook can also be used as an attached file or **Linked Reporting Object (LRO)**.

Text files

There are two types of text files:

- **Delimited text files**: Delimited text files are files that use a certain character, typically a comma or a semi-colon to delimit the data fields. This delimiter is used by the Essbase load rule to determine where one data field ends and another data field begins. Also, not all rows will be of the same length.
- **Fixed column width text files**: The fixed width type of text file has all rows of data the exact same length. Also, all of the data fields are the same length and in the same position and do not vary from row to row.

Essbase data export text files

One type of data source that loads without any intervention, in the form of data manipulation, or even without the aid of an Essbase data load rule is the Essbase database export text file. Essbase offers you the option of exporting the data from your database into text files (some do this for database backup purposes). When loading an Essbase exported file into an Essbase database with a similar outline, Essbase can automatically interpret the data fields and determine how to correctly load the data. This process is used in a database performance enhancing tip, which we will talk about later in this book.

Relational databases

We have saved the best for last! Without the time or expense of writing complicated interfacing programs, Essbase allows you to create a data load rule that automatically connects directly to an external relational database such as, Teradata or SQL Server, just to name a few. Using a load rule with connection information specified, you actually write an SQL query using the source database's own **Structured Query Language (SQL)** commands. You can use this data source to build the outline itself or to load the data values.

[By now, you should be telling yourself just how cool you think Essbase is and what did you ever do before you learned about it.]

Data load methods

We have discussed the types of data you can load into your Essbase database. We have also discussed how these types of data can be loaded as just the data values themselves, or that they can be used to build your Essbase database outline by dynamically adding dimension members and then loading the data values. Here, we will discuss some of the various methods you can use to load data into your Essbase database.

Data file freeform (no load rule)

This method is quite possibly the most worry free and easy way to load data into an Essbase database. When you have a properly formatted (Essbase-friendly) data file, all you need to do is drag-and-drop the file onto the EssCmd/MaxL executable files or their desktop shortcuts. Essbase will automatically determine what delimiter you are using and correctly load the data.

Here are just a few words of caution on using this data load method. The reason it is so easy at the load step is because the harder work has already been done at the front of this process to create an Essbase-friendly data source. If you were to create such a program, it would need to construct your data source file in such a way as to match the structure of the database outline. Each field, in every row of data in the file, would need to contain a representative member from every dimension in the Essbase database outline. The data in the file would also need to be ordered in the same order as the members in the outline from top to bottom.

Without a load rule, you do run the risk of either having an invalid character in one of your data fields or an incorrect or missing member name included in a row of data. When this happens, Essbase will successfully load the data file up until it reaches the invalid row. At this time, the load will halt without loading the remainder of the data, leaving you with an incomplete load.

To be honest, the best time to use this no load rule method of data loading is when your data source file is created from an Essbase database data export.

Essbase export and import (no load rule)

This method is fantastic for extracting data from your Essbase cube and loading it into another cube or just plain saving it off for backup. Start off with the EAS tool and right-click on your database and select the **Export...** option to begin the export of the desired data from the database.

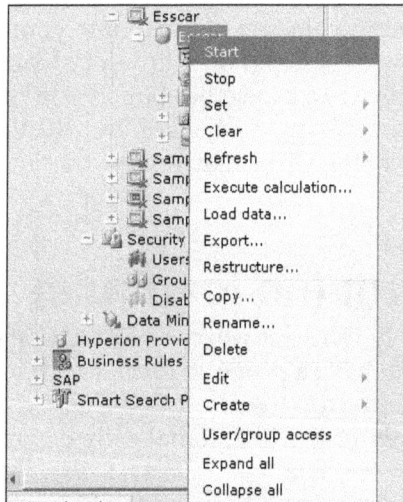

Upon selecting the **Export...** option, you will be presented with a small **Export Database** screen (seen in the next screenshot). On this screen, you have options on how you want to export your data from the database. There are many reasons why you will need to export data from your Essbase database (backup, send downstream). However, in this case, the data is exported so that you can import the data into another database or even into the same database at a later date.

Export Database   ✕

  ◯ [sarma.Esscar.Esscar]

Export to file:

  │

┌─ Export options ─────────────┐
│ ◉ All data
│ ◯ Level 0 data blocks
│ ◯ Input level data blocks
└──────────────────────────────┘

  ☐ Export in column format

  ☐ Execute in the background

  [Help]   [OK]   [Cancel]

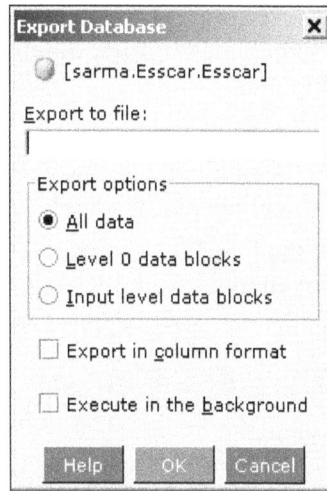

Because of this reason, you will do the following:

1. Give a name to your export file including an extension. When loading the data, Essbase will only look for a file with a `.txt` extension, so it is always best to add it now. Also, when exporting your data, Essbase will only build files upto 2GB each. If your database is larger than 2GB, Essbase will automatically create new files with the name you have chosen and append the number of the file to each one, for example, `EssCar01.txt`, `EssCar02.txt`, `EssCar03.txt`, and so on. Finally, very important, remember that Essbase object names must be upto 8 characters. This means your file name in this example must be upto 6 characters before Essbase appends the number to it.

2. Next, your export options are self explanatory. Select the level of the data you wish to export. If you are exporting the data for a complete restore, then obviously you will select the **All data** option.

3. Finally, the **Export in column format** option is very important. If you select this option, Essbase will export the data in a format compatible with spreadsheet applications using field delimiters. If you do not select this option, Essbase will export your data into a format that it will easily recognize and will be able to load back into the database without a rules file. The **Export in column format** is not supported in ASO cubes.

Okay, that should get your data exported quite nicely. When you are ready to import your data back into your database or into another database with a similar database outline you will do the following:

1. On the selection screen provided, when you right-click on the database in Essbase Administration Services, you will choose **Load data...** instead of the **Export...** option you were instructed to choose earlier.

2. Once you have selected the **Load data...** option, you will be presented with the following screen. It is in this screen that you define to Essbase how to load a particular data file.

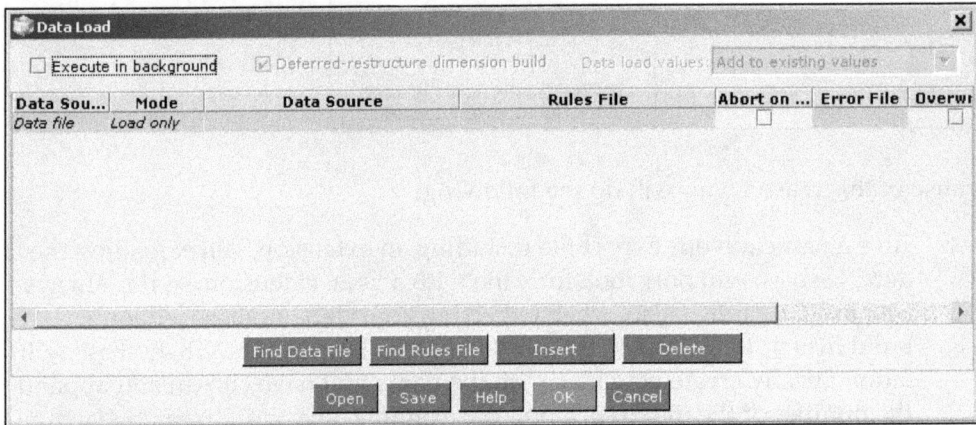

3. To load your newly exported data files, simply select the **Data files** radio button, then select the **Load data** and **Interactive** checkboxes.

4. Next, click on the **Find Data File** button which will open a file selection dialog box (seen in the following screenshot). Along the top, you will see tabs that allow you to choose from locating your file in the server file system or the analytic server file system. The data files can be on your local machine or on the Essbase server. If your file is on the server and it is stored in the Application | Database path, you should see this file in the **Essbase Server** tab. If the file is on your local PC, you need to click on the **File System** tab and search for the data file. Even if your data files are loaded onto the Analytic server (Essbase server), it is best to use the **File System** tab and select your data files through the operating systems file system.

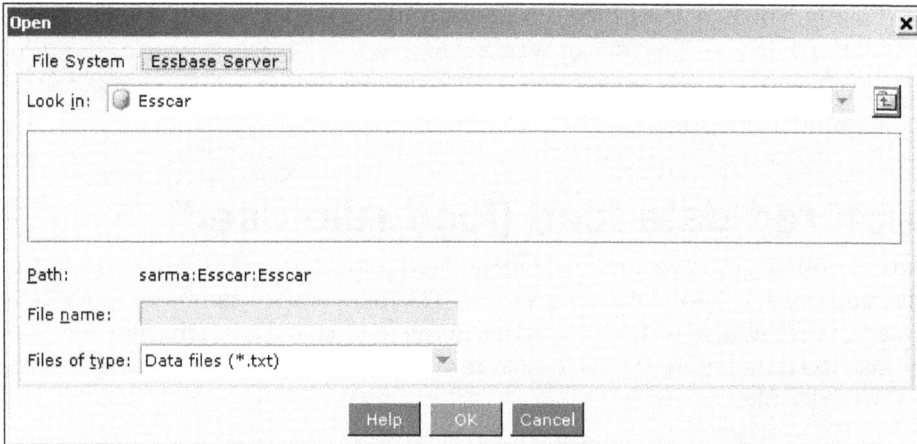

5. Once you have located and selected your file(s), you can click **OK** to return to the previous screen.

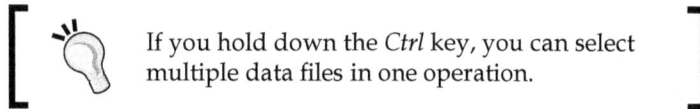

> If you hold down the *Ctrl* key, you can select multiple data files in one operation.

6. In this case, we are not using a rules file, so there is no need to select the **Use rules** checkbox. If you were to use a rules file (and this is a great method to manually test load rules files), you would check the **Use rules** checkbox. This in turn would allow you to click on the **Find Rules File** button, which will open another file selection dialog box exactly like the one for data files including the same choices and actions. You can add one or more data files at the same time. Simply click on the **Insert** button to add another row like the one shown here:

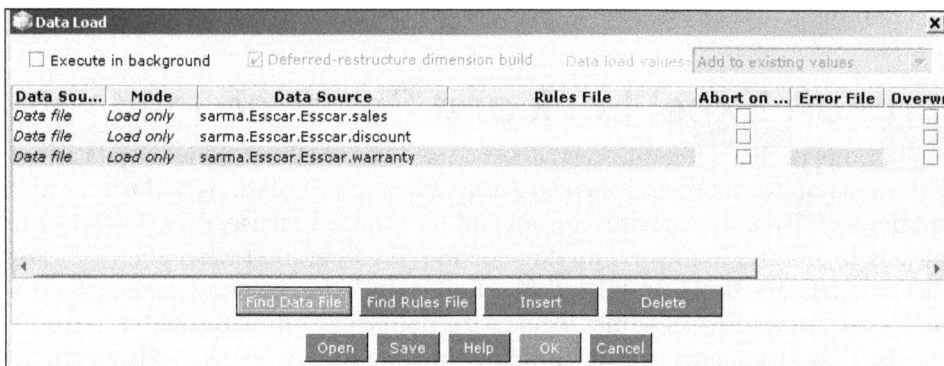

7. Finally, you can accept the default output for the log which will be generated by the data load or you can type a new path.

8. Click **OK** to load your data. There you have it! You have just loaded data without a rules file.

Structured data load (load rule used)

In Essbase, you can create a load rule file to load data into an Essbase cube. In this rule file, you need to define the data source. This data source can be a flat file or an SQL query, you can also write the queries in the load rule. Using the rule file, you can cleanse the data before it gets loaded into the cube. Let us quickly see the types of the load rules file:

- **Flat file load rule**: As explained earlier in this chapter, and will be demonstrated shortly, probably the most common method of loading data into your Essbase database is by a data flat file and Essbase data load rule method. Inside the data load rule, you define to Essbase what fields in the data file relate to what dimensions in the database outline. The database load rule is also where you can perform data transformations, data substitutions, data manipulations, or pretty much any other task you need to perform to get your data Essbase-friendly. Then either manually or automatically, you perform a data load into your Essbase database using the data file and the load rule created for it.

- **Relational database SQL load rule**: This data load method is essentially identical to the flat file load rule method, except for one huge difference. Instead of the input data contained in the form of a flat file, the data is being selected directly from a relational database's table or tables. Real SQL statements are used and an ODBC connection is used behind the scenes by the load rule to connect to the relational database. After this, the creation of the load rule is identical to the flat file method when it pertains to data handling, and so on.

Microsoft Excel Lock and Send (no load rule)

This method is perhaps the quickest, down and dirty, method of loading data into an Essbase database. While it is fast and easy, there are limitations and precautions. Since Microsoft Excel is the natural front end for Oracle Essbase, they do work rather seamlessly together. However, you do need to remember, that what you are doing with a spreadsheet's "Lock and Send" function is updating existing data as there are no provisions for adding new members to the database outline through Microsoft Excel. Also, Essbase seems to have difficulty locking too many data cells when asked by Microsoft Excel. Due to performance issues, you may want to consider splitting spreadsheets that contain a considerable amount of rows.

As this is typically how the business users will update the data, it is a more than acceptable method. This method is also ideal for tweaking specific data values prior to calculation.

Finally, this method is ideal for data validation when writing and executing new Essbase calculation scripts. You can retrieve data into your spreadsheet, execute your Essbase calculation script, and retrieve the data into another sheet to compare the changes. If the results are not what you expected, then simply "Lock and Send" the data in the first sheet back to the database, make adjustments to the calculation script, and run it again, then retrieve the data once more to validate. The "Lock and Send" method is explained in detail in the later chapters.

That was easy!

Building your first data load rules file

Actually, we should have said build your second data load rule file, as we have built one rules file already. The first one you built, in the previous chapter, is a dimension build rules file. Now, in this chapter, we are discussing how to load data into your Essbase cube so this is a data load rules file.

In the previous section, we talked about how to load data without a data load rules file. We will now learn how to cleanse the data, make the data Essbase-friendly and then load the data into the Essbase using an Essbase data load rules file.

Once you have created a data load rules file, just like the dimension build rules file, you can use it to manually load the data from the EAS or use EssCmd or MaxL (Essbase scripting languages), to load the data into your Essbase database. You can even write your own program that makes its own API call to load the data into Essbase.

Here are some of the advantages of using the data load rules files:

- Makes the data Essbase-friendly
- Ignores the data fields that do not need to be loaded into Essbase
- Specifies whether to overwrite the existing data, add to existing data, or subtract from existing data
- Trims out spaces
- Changes the scaling of decimal numbers
- Converts case from upper to lower and vice versa
- And much more

Next, we take you through the steps required to create a rules file you will use to load data into your Essbase database. Always remember, no matter how you load the data, through EAS, EssCmd or MaxL, or programmatically, you will always use the same rules file in your load process. That's simple and convenient!

Step 1: Starting the Data Prep Editor

Follow the given steps to start the Data Prep Editor:

1. In EAS, click on the **File** menu pick.

2. Select **Editors** and click on the **Data Prep Editor,** or click on **New**, and from the **New** dialog click the **Scripts** tab and select **Rules File**, then click on **OK.**

3. The **Data Prep Editor** will open as shown in the following screenshot.

4. Once the **Data Prep Editor** is opened, the menu items in EAS will change.

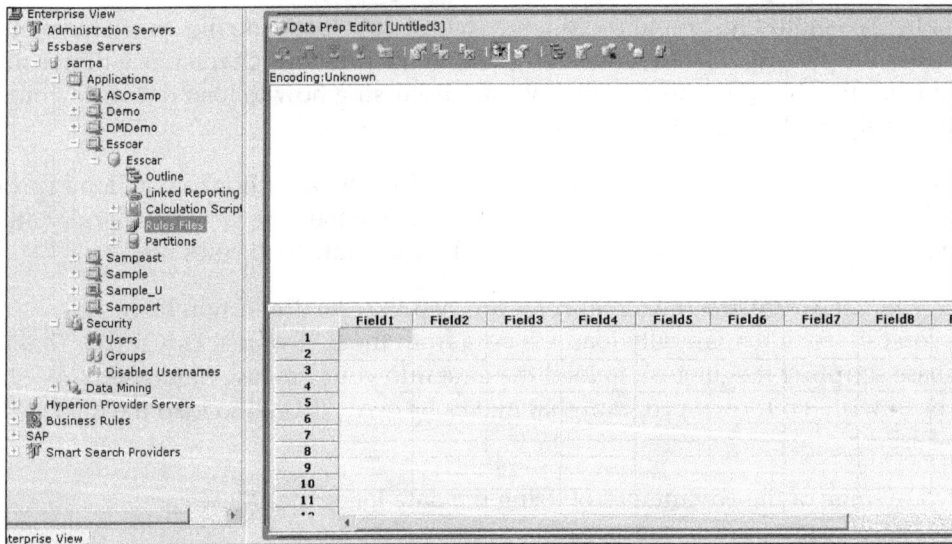

Step 2: Associating the data load rules file

In order for you to successfully validate the rules file to the database and outline for which it is intended, you will need to associate the rules file to the correct database outline. This association of the rules file to the database outline is saved the first time. However, Essbase will ask you to associate the rules file again to the proper database outline every time you reopen this rules file. You do not need to re-associate the database outline if you do not wish to as the rules file will remember the initial association.

To associate your data load rules file to a database outline:

1. Again, using EAS, open the **Data Prep Editor**.
2. Click on **Options** | **Associate Outline** or click on the **Associate** button in the **Data Prep Editor**.

Step 3: Opening data load file or the SQL data source file

The source data which needs to be loaded into the Essbase cube can be a data file (Comma separated files like a `.txt` file, or a `.dat` file) or a relational database which can be retrieved using the relational databases own SQL statements. The following screenshot shows the Esscar data in the relational database system (Oracle):

MARKET_ID	PRODUCT_ID	PERIOD	CUSTOMER	SCENARIO	MODELYEAR	REVENUE
12367A	ES440	200901	1	JUNE VERSION 1	MDL 2009	250000.00
12367A	ES440	200901	1	JUNE VERSION 1	MDL 2008	100000.00
12367A	ES440	200812	1	JUNE VERSION 1	MDL 2009	400000.00
12367A	ES440	200812	1	JUNE VERSION 1	MDL 2008	80000.00
12367A	ES440	200901	1	JUNE VERSION 1	MDL 2008	100000.00
12367A	ES440	200811	1	JUNE VERSION 1	MDL 2009	200000.00
12367A	ES440	200811	1	JUNE VERSION 1	MDL 2008	67980.00
12367A	ES440	200901	1	JUNE VERSION 1	MDL 2008	100000.00
12367A	ES440	200810	1	JUNE VERSION 1	MDL 2009	160000.00
12367A	ES440	200810	1	JUNE VERSION 1	MDL 2008	80000.00
12367A	ES440	200901	1	JUNE VERSION 1	MDL 2008	100000.00
12367A	ES440	200809	1	JUNE VERSION 1	MDL 2009	200000.00
12367A	ES440	200809	1	JUNE VERSION 1	MDL 2008	80000.00
12367A	ES440	200901	1	JUNE VERSION 1	MDL 2008	100000.00
12367A	ES440	200808	1	JUNE VERSION 1	MDL 2009	160000.00
12367A	ES440	200901	1	JUNE VERSION 1	MDL 2008	100000.00
12367A	ES460	200901	1	JUNE VERSION 1	MDL 2009	500000.00
12367A	ES460	200901	1	JUNE VERSION 1	MDL 2008	150000.00
12367A	ES460	200812	1	JUNE VERSION 1	MDL 2009	200000.00
12367A	ES460	200812	1	JUNE VERSION 1	MDL 2008	60000.00
12367A	ES460	200811	1	JUNE VERSION 1	MDL 2009	80000.00
12367A	ES460	200811	1	JUNE VERSION 1	MDL 2008	24000.00
12367A	ES460	200810	1	JUNE VERSION 1	MDL 2009	50000.00

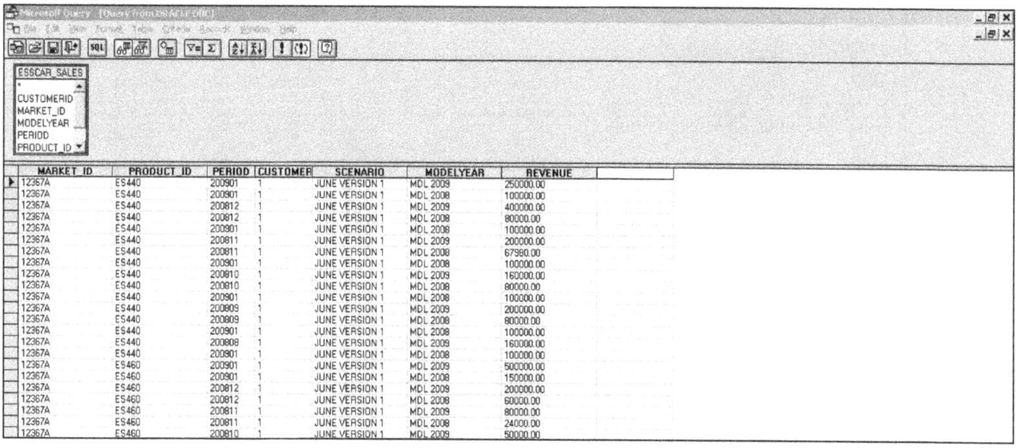

To open a data source file or SQL data source:

1. In EAS, open the **Data Prep Editor**.
2. Once you've clicked on **File** you should see the options **Open Data File** or **Open SQL**.

In the previous chapter, you saw how to use the Data File. In this chapter, we will see how we can achieve the same thing using the SQL data source:

1. Click on the **Open SQL** selection.
2. A new window will open asking you to select the **Server** name, **Application** name, and **Database** name. Please select the appropriate names and click **OK**.

3. You will see the **Open SQL Data Sources** window as shown in the following screenshot:

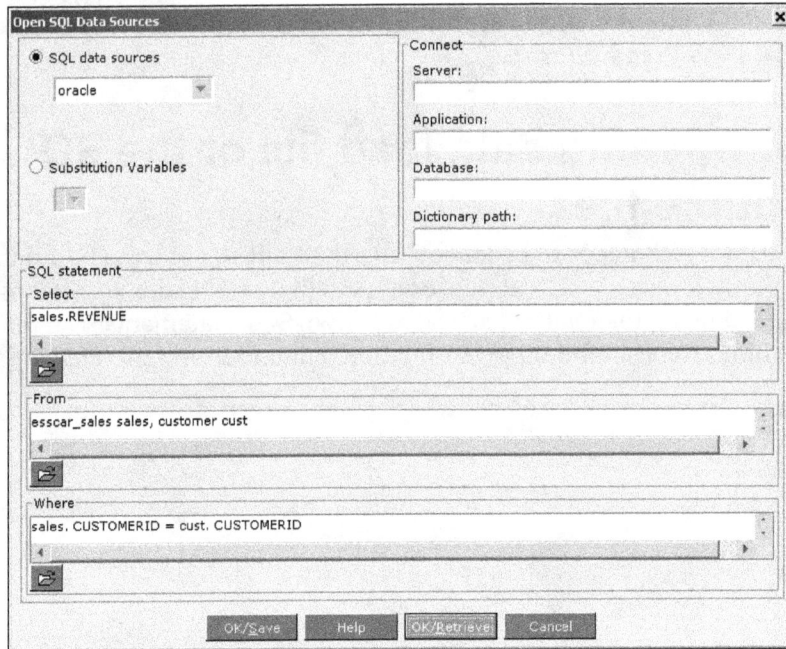

As shown in the previous screenshot, you can write your own SQL query. However, you are somewhat limited to what you can write. Here is how to write your own SQL query:

1. SELECT, FROM, and WHERE are already declared.

> This is a great feature for writing most queries, but if you are unable to write any particularly complex queries, you can always create an Essbase temporary table in your relational database that contains everything you need (data values, columns, and so on). Then, your data load rule SQL statement only needs to be a simple SELECT <column names> FROM, WHERE....

2. Write your query and click on **Retrieve**.
3. Enter the SQL user ID and password and click on **OK** and you should see the data populated as shown here:

	MARKET_ID	PRODUCT...	PERIOD	CUSTOME...	SCENARIO	MODELYE...	REVENUE
1	12367A	ES440	200901	RETAIL	JUNE VER...	MDL 2009	250000.00
2	12367A	ES440	200901	RETAIL	JUNE VER...	MDL 2008	100000.00
3	12367A	ES440	200812	RETAIL	JUNE VER...	MDL 2009	400000.00
4	12367A	ES440	200812	RETAIL	JUNE VER...	MDL 2008	80000.00
5	12367A	ES440	200901	RETAIL	JUNE VER...	MDL 2008	100000.00
6	12367A	ES440	200811	RETAIL	JUNE VER...	MDL 2009	200000.00
7	12367A	ES440	200811	RETAIL	JUNE VER...	MDL 2008	67980.00
8	12367A	ES440	200901	RETAIL	JUNE VER...	MDL 2008	100000.00
9	12367A	ES440	200810	RETAIL	JUNE VER...	MDL 2009	160000.00
10	12367A	ES440	200810	RETAIL	JUNE VER...	MDL 2008	80000.00
11	12367A	ES440	200901	RETAIL	JUNE VER...	MDL 2008	100000.00
12	12367A	ES440	200809	RETAIL	JUNE VER...	MDL 2009	200000.00

Step 4: Setting the View to Data Load Fields

As you recall, in the previous chapter we used the **Rules File** to update the database outline. In this chapter, we are using, but this time, we are using it for loading data into the Essbase database. Please select **Data Load Field View** in the **Rules File**. By default **Data Load Field View** is selected.

To set the Data Load Field:

1. In EAS, open the **Data Prep Editor**.
2. Click on **View** and then select the checkbox **Data Load Fields**.

Step 5: Setting the Data Source Properties

As discussed in the previous chapter, the **Data Source Properties** are also the same where you can set the column delimiter as Tab delimited or Comma delimited. The input columns from a relational database are Tab delimited which is selected by default.

To set the Data Source Properties:

1. In EAS, open the **Data Prep Editor**.
2. Click on **Options** and then click on **Data Source Properties**.

3. The first tab is the **Delimiter** tab.

4. Select or create the appropriate data delimiter.

Step 6: Updating the Data Load Settings

With this load rule setting, you can tell Essbase how to load the new data into the Essbase database and also, if necessary, how to load the new data in relation to the data that already exists in the database. In some cases, you need to load on a day-to-day basis. If there are adjustments to the data, how you will handle them?

In the rules file data load setting, you can tell Essbase how to load the data into the Essbase cube, define the headers, flipping of the numeric signs, clear specific data combinations, add to existing values, subtract from existing values, and so on.

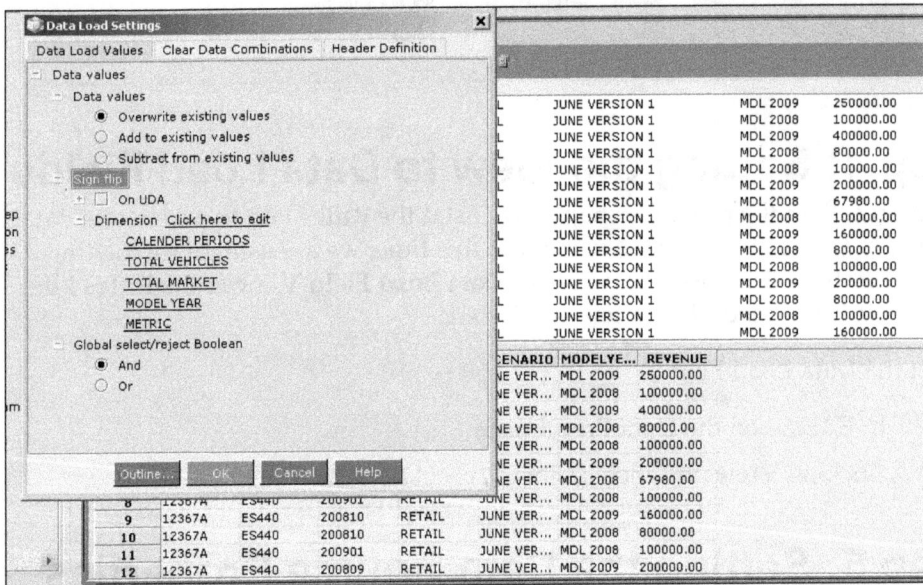

Step 7: Setting the Data Load Values

To set the Data Load Values:

1. In EAS, open the **Data Prep Editor**.

2. Click on **Options** and then click on the **Data Load Setting**.

3. The first tab is the **Data Load Values** tab.

4. There are three things that can be achieved in this tab setting: **Data values**, **Sign flip**, and **Global select/reject Boolean**.

Data values

There are three options you can choose from for loading data into an Essbase database as shown in the preceding screenshot.

- **Overwrite existing values**: Select this option if you want to load the new data completely and overwrite the existing data in the database.

> This will only overwrite the data included in the new feed. If there is an existing value that is not included in the new data, it will not be overwritten.

Let us say you are building or rebuilding your Essbase cube everyday. On Monday, you loaded data into the database that shows revenue generated as $40,000 and when you load new data on Tuesday the total revenue generated to date as $60,000. So, when you loaded the new data into the Essbase cube, the revenue from Monday's data feed is overwritten by Tuesday's revenue data. By default, in Essbase, the setting is set to **Overwrite existing values**.

- **Add to existing values**: Select this option if you want to add your data to the existing data.

> While this is a great feature, you must be very careful while using it. If you ever need to reload the same data, due to an interruption or some other issue, you need to restore the data to its original state before the first instance of the load. Otherwise, you will add to the values again resulting in erroneous data.

As in the example above, you are building data loads on a day-to-day basis. You have a TOTAL VEHICLES SOLD member in your database outline. The data load rules file you are using is set to **Add to existing values**. If the TOTAL VEHICLES SOLD member on Monday is 100 units and Tuesday's data shows 20 more units sold, when you load this data the TOTAL VEHICLES SOLD will get updated to 120 units (100 + 20) since you have set this data load rules setting to **Add to existing values**.

- **Subtract From existing values**: Select this option if you want to subtract the new data values from the existing data values.

Let us say you have a member called TOTAL VEHICLES IN STOCK and when you are loading data you need to subtract the daily sold quantity in the data feed from the quantity that already exists in the TOTAL VEHICLES IN STOCK member. If there are 1,000 units in the TOTAL VEHICLES IN STOCK member and you sold 100 vehicles today, when you load the daily data the 100 sold units will be subtracted from the 1,000 units in the TOTAL VEHICLES IN STOCK member. This will leave 900 as the new value in the TOTAL VEHICLES IN STOCK member.

Sign flip

Flipping the numeric sign is one of the features of the Essbase data load that can be accomplished in the data load rule. Sometimes it is necessary for us to flip the numeric sign of a set of values as they are being loaded into the database.

Consider that the basic profit calculation is Sales - Discounts = Profits. The data elements you receive from the corporate finance department are all in positive numbers. Sales and Costs are provided as positive numbers. Depending on how you have your database outline structured and to keep things simple (simple is good) for you to create a Profit member in your database outline, you would need it to have two children. One child would be Sales and other would be Costs. When you calculate the outline, the values would roll up correctly to a total Profit.

```
PROFIT (+) <3>
    NET REVENUE (+) /* LOADED AS POSITIVE VALUE */
    DISCOUNTS (+) (UDAS: NegSign) /* LOADED AS NEGATIVE VALUE */
```

Another way would be to just have a Profit member to load the data values to and use the **Add to existing values** setting so you would add a positive Sales value and a negative Costs value to the Profit member as the data is being loaded. The only drawback to this method is you would not have the component data handy and loaded into the database in the event there are issues or questions with the data. Debugging would also be more complicated as you would need to go back to the input data for any validations.

There are two ways, during a data load to flip a numeric sign on a data value. They are as follows:

1. Flip the numeric sign value based on an outline member UDA. For instance, you can only flip the numeric sign on members that are tagged with the UDA of Costs in the database outline. As you can see in the previous screenshot, there is a UDA called **NegSign**. While we are doing the **Dynamic Calc**, we check the UDA, if UDA is **NegSign**, we can do a negation. This is just an example.

2. Arbitrarily flip the numeric sign on all data values in a particular column or field by multiplying the number with a minus (-) sign.

Clearing Data Combinations

Depending on the circumstances, it may be necessary for you to clear the existing data values before loading the new data. To achieve this functionality you need to set all of the members that need to be cleared in **Clear Data Combinations** tab of the **Data Load Settings**.

> This can be an extremely valuable setting when loading data that may have holes in it. For example, you are loading data values for all months of a particular calendar year, but the new data load has no data values for the months of May and August, the result will be the old values mixing in with the newly loaded values. This happens because Essbase will only load or overwrite data values for specific values received in the data. If no new data is received for the months of May or August, the old data values will remain.

To set the **Clear Data Combinations**:

1. In EAS, open the **Data Prep Editor**.
2. Click on **Options** and then click on the **Data Load Setting**.
3. Click on the second tab, **Clear Data Combinations** tab.

In the **Dimension** list, double-click on the members you need to clear the data and they will appear in the **Combinations to clear** as shown here:

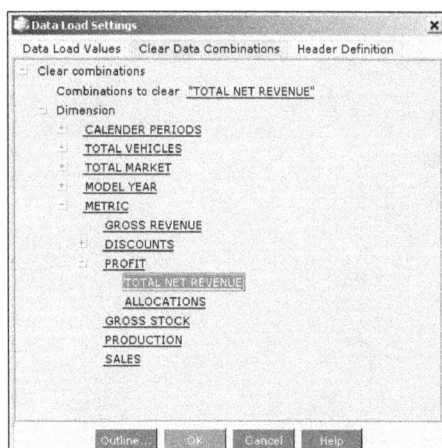

If you are using **Overwrite existing values,** then **Clear Data Combinations** may not be necessary as every time you load the data the old data will be cleared for the values you receive. However, if you are using **Add to existing values** or **Subtract from existing values**, you may need to clear the data values prior to the very first data load to this scenario just to make sure all of the data has been cleared.

Header Definition

As mentioned earlier, Essbase requires a representative of all of the dimensions in the database outline to be included in the data you are attempting to load. Obviously, this is not always possible or even practical. Never fear, the Essbase data load rules file once again has turned this potential issue into a non-issue!

While creating the data load rules file, one of the first things you do is map the different fields in the data to the appropriate dimensions the data will load to. If even one of the dimensions is missing, you will get an error when you try to validate the Essbase data load rules file. This is where the **Header Definition** function comes into play.

For example, the monthly file you receive from the marketing department contains sales information for the company. The data values are always in U.S. dollars, but there is no column or field in the data that specifically says **US DOLLAR** like you have defined in the database outline. All you need to do is quickly and easily add the **US DOLLAR** member in the **Header Definition** and Essbase will load data as if every record in the file contains **US DOLLAR** data values.

To set the **Header Definitions**:

1. In EAS, open the **Data Prep Editor**.
2. Click on **Options | Data Load Setting**.
3. Specify **US Dollar** in the **Header Definition** tab as shown here:

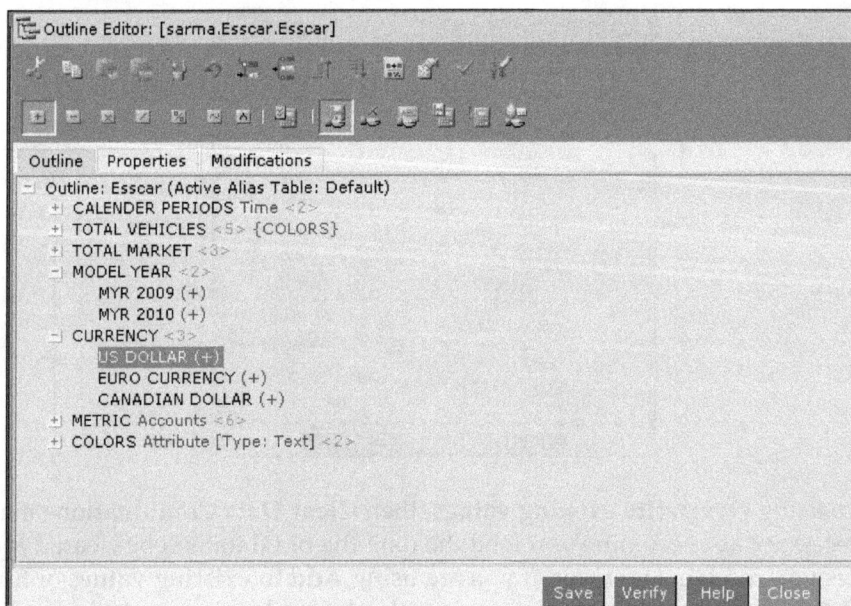

Step 8: Associating fields with Data Load Properties

In order to correctly load the data into the Essbase cube, we need to map each field in the data, using the data load rules file, to their specific database outline dimensions. This way, while Essbase is loading the data into the database, the data fields are correctly aligned to the right members in the database outline. Essbase will only use the fields you have mapped in your data load rules file. If the data file contains more fields than necessary, Essbase can simply ignore them if you have them tagged as **Ignore**.

This is the key step while setting up the data load rules file.

To open the Data Field Properties:

1. In EAS, open the **Data Prep Editor**.

2. Click on **Fields | Properties**.

3. As shown below, **Data Field Properties** option has three tabs: **Global Properties**, **Data Load Properties**, and **Dimension Build Properties**.

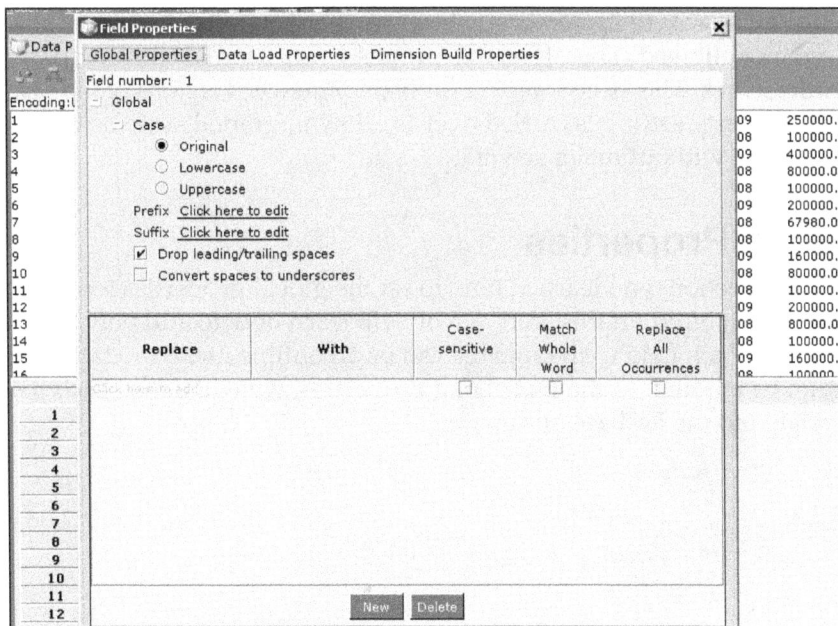

Let us talk about the **Global Properties** and **Data Load Properties** as **Dimension Build Properties** were already covered in an earlier chapter.

Global properties

As the term global applies to everything, in this context, global means both the Dimension Build Properties and Data Load Properties.

These are the settings that can be used in the **Global Properties** tab:

1. **Case**: There are three types of **Case** present: **Original, Lowercase,** and **UpperCase**. While updating the dimensions, you sometimes want all of the members to be upper case or lower case, or it can be left as originally sent in the data file. **Original** is selected by default. This is particularly important when you are working with Essbase installed on a Unix platform as it is case sensitive by default.

2. **Prefix** or **Suffix**: This is to add a prefix or suffix to the member so that the member name is unique. You can add your own prefix or suffix.

3. **Drop leading/trailing spaces**: This is used to trim the member before it gets loaded into database outline. This is selected by default.

4. **Convert spaces to underscores:** In the earlier versions of Essbase, spaces were not allowed. Therefore, this property was used to convert spaces to underscores. This is no longer a problem in newer versions of Essbase, but this property setting is carried over to allow upgraded systems to continue operation without major rework.

Data Load Properties

In the previous section, you learned how to set the global properties for your data load or dimension build. In this section, you will learn how to add only the data load field properties. Each field in the rule file can be an outline member, data member, or data that can be ignored. In the **Data Load Properties**, we will define each field and how it is related to the Essbase outline.

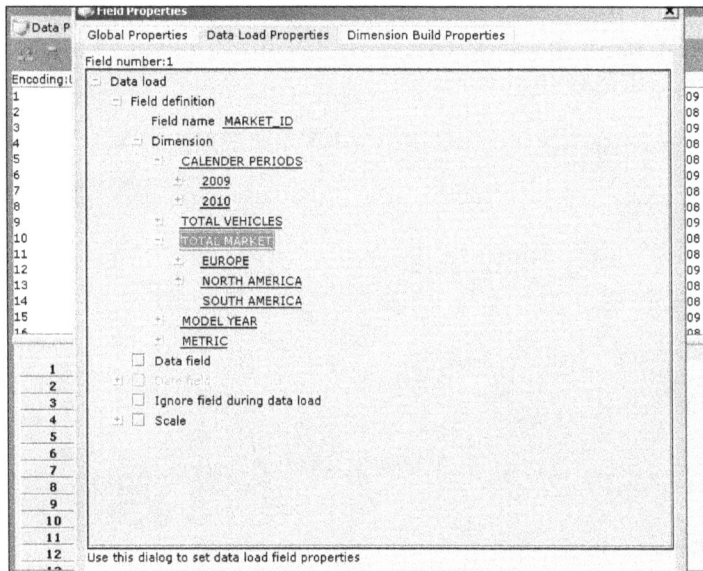

The settings that can be set in the **Data Load Properties** tab are as follows:

1. **Field name**: This is where you map your data element to the outline member. You are currently seeing **MARKET_ID**, which is the column name in the relational database where our data is coming from. The outline member name is different from this column name so you need to select the field name, clear the information that already exists, and then double-click on the correct outline dimension. You should then see the member name in the **Field name** (wrapped with double quotes if you have space in the member name). If you do not see the outline and its members, click on the **Outline...** button to associate this rule to the correct Essbase database. Click the **OK** button to complete this, or click the **Next** button to go to the next field.

2. **Data field**: The **Data field** can be defined in two ways, one is by defining the field name like in step 1. If all of the data you are loading is for the same value, Sales, then you can label this column as Sales. If this data value column will represent values for more than one member, that is Sales and Stocks, and the data source contains another column that identifies the data member, then the data values column can be named only Data.

As shown in the following screenshot, on field 7 we have defined the Account dimension name, Total Revenue, and on field 8 we have defined it as simply Data:

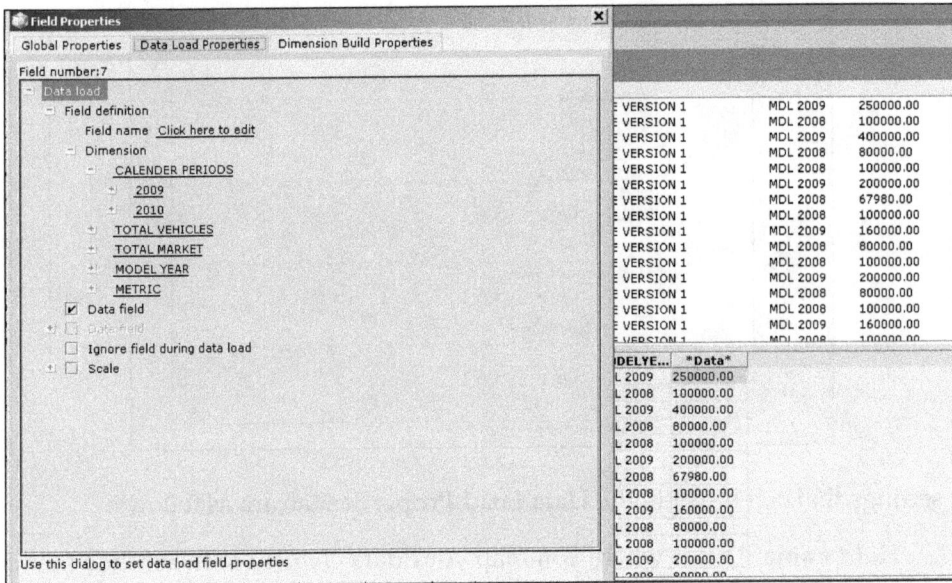

3. **Ignore field during data load**: For any fields that are not required to successfully load the data from the file you have received, all you need to do is check the **Ignore field during data load** option in the **Data Load Properties** tab.

4. **Scale**: Depending on the size of your company or the size of the egos of the company executives, you may find yourself gathering data that has been scaled to varying degrees. Because of this, Essbase offers you the option to scale your data as you load it. Typically, a busy executive may feel that the number 10,500,000 is too large and bothersome to look at. So, he will ask that his report have the data values scaled into the thousands ($1/1000^{th}$). This would give the report the presentation value of 10,500 which would represent 10,500,000. To do this, select the **Scale** option and enter the appropriate scaling value you wish to use on the data being loaded (10, 100, 1,000, and so on).

Repeat the steps above for all of the fields contained in the data source for which you are creating the data load rule, until all of the fields are defined to Essbase.

Now that you have updated the property settings on all of the fields, it would be a good idea to validate all of the field definitions and properties against your database outline. In the very next step, we will see how to validate the data load rule file.

Step 9: Validating the data load rules file

In this step, we will validate the correctness of the definition that you have provided to the rule file. Please make sure you validate after making changes to the rule file. If there is any error, you will get errors while loading the data.

To validate the data load rules file:

1. In EAS, open the **Data Prep Editor**.

2. Click on the **Validate** button (last button on the **Data Prep Editor** window), or you can click on **Options** and then click on **Validate**.

3. You should see a message, **The rules file is correct for data loading**, as shown here:

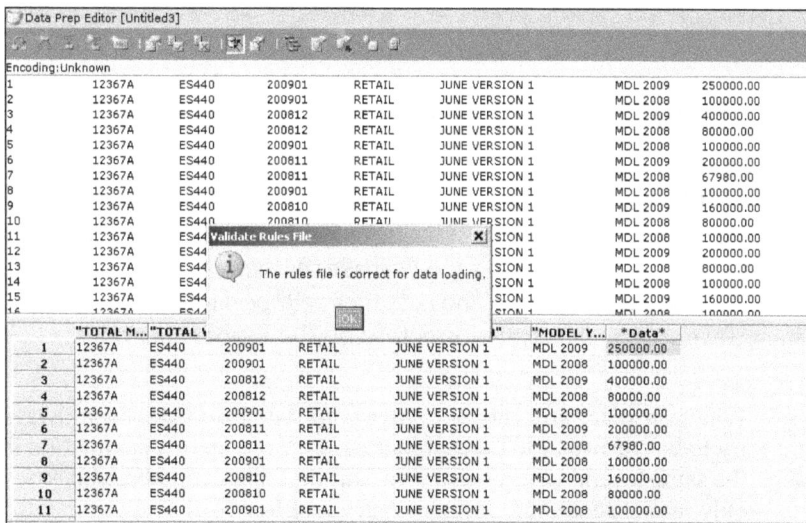

4. Let us actually remove the field definition for the **Field6** (go to **Field**, then **Properties**, then to Field 6 and remove the **Field name**) and now click on the **Validate** button. You should see an error message stating **Field6** is not defined as shown here:

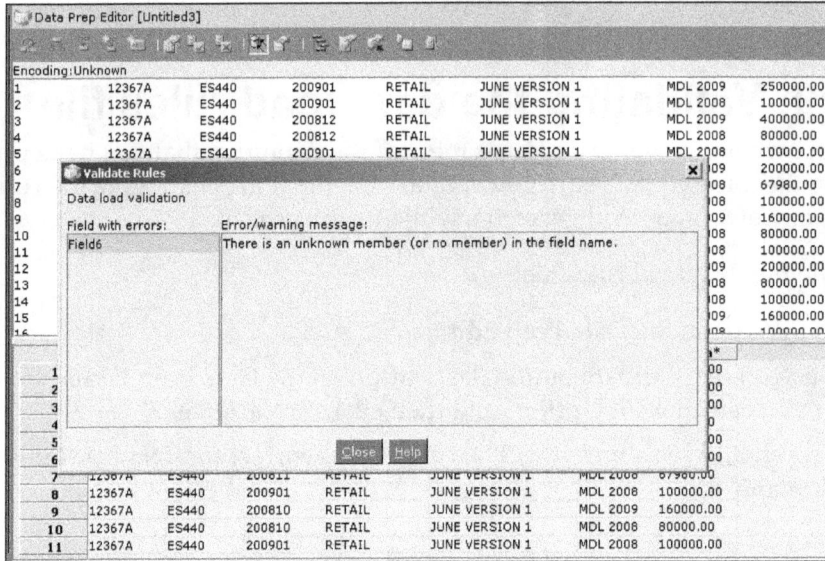

Step 10: Saving the data load rules file

Now that you have validated the data load rules file, and there are no errors, you can save the rules file. Remember to use the proper Essbase 8 character naming convention while saving the rules file. You can save the rules file in your local file system or on the Essbase server using the Essbase file system. We prefer to save all of the files on the Essbase server. The rule files will be saved with the .rul file extension in `Application|Database` directory on the Essbase server.

> Whatever place you choose to save your data load rules files, always try to be consistent to make things easier. Consistently saving files in the same location, or consistently naming Essbase database objects, only makes sense and provides easier and less costly support.

To save the data load rules file with the Essbase default extension of .rul:

1. In EAS, open the **Data Prep Editor.**
2. Click on **File | Save** button to save the file.

Loading data into your database

In the steps above, you learned how to create an Essbase data load rule. Now let us learn how to use this data load rules file to actually load data into your Essbase database. As with the Dimension Build, there are several ways to load data into an Essbase database.

A few of the ways you can load data into an Essbase cube:

- Using the EAS Outline Editor
- Using EssCmd or MaxL script commands
- Using your own API calls

In the next few sections, let us discuss how you can achieve it using the EAS and MaxL statements.

Using the EAS to load data into your Essbase cube

Using EAS is the manual way of loading data into the cube. This method will probably look very familiar because it is almost identical to the Import Data step of the Export/Import Data process, which we discussed earlier in this chapter.

To load data into an Essbase database, using EAS:

1. Navigate to your **Application | Database**.
2. Then click on **Actions | Load Data for "ESSCAR"**.
3. The **Data Load** screen will be opened as shown here:

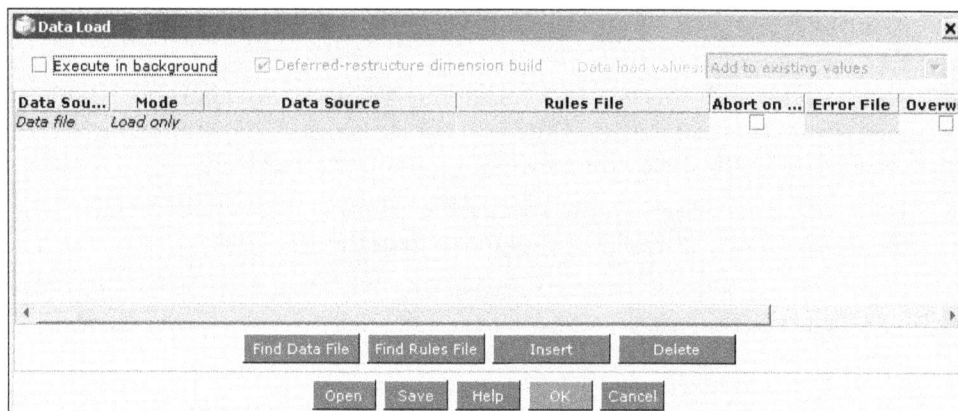

The different fields present on the previous screenshot are:

- **Data Source Type**: There are two types of data sources: **Data File** and **SQL**. If you have a comma or tab delimited data source file, you need to select **Data File**. If you are connecting to a relational database to use SQL statements, you need to select **SQL**. We will be selecting **SQL** as we will be loading the data from a relational database data source.

- **Mode:** There are three options in mode: **Load only, Build only,** or **Both**. Here, you need to mention what you are going to do with this data source. Whether it is used to load data only, update the database outline only, or used for both database outline updates and data loads. Occasionally, as per our business requirement, if a new member value arrives in the data file and does not already exist in the Essbase database outline, you can specify Essbase to update the outline with the new member value and then perform the data load. See how smart Essbase is! This scenario can be achieved by selecting **Both**. In the Esscar cube we want to load only the data, so we select **Load only**.

- **Data Source (Data File)**: If you are using a data file instead of a relational database data source, you may need to specify the location of the data source file. The data source file can be on your **Local System** or on the **Essbase Server**. To select a data file, click on the button **Find Data File** and follow the prompts.

> **Faster data loading**
>
> In case of extremely large data files, if possible, deliver the data file to the Essbase server so the data load will process faster, since you will eliminate the network response time from the load process.

- **Rules File**: If you have chosen the **SQL** option you must select a rules file name, as your SQL is embedded in the data load rules file. To select the data load rules file, click on the button **Find Rules File** and select the appropriate data load rules file.

- **Abort on Error**: If this box is checked, the data load will abort on any data load error. This is not always the best choice because, depending on where the error is in the data, you may end up with a partial load.

- **Error File**: This allows you to specify the error file location. Remember, there should not be any spaces in the path of the error file.

- **Overwrite**: When the checkbox is selected, the data load process will overwrite the existing error file if any. If the named error file does not already exist, Essbase will create a new error file.

- **SQL Username** and **Password**: Here, you need to enter a valid username and password for the relational database you will be connecting to. Since we are using a relational database in this example, we need to provide a valid username and password.

- **Insert**: This button in the data load form inserts another line so you can define one more set of data load rules. This allows you certain flexibility as it is sometimes necessary to load the same data source more than one time to get the desired load results.

- **Delete**: This button in the data load form deletes the line that you have selected. Remember, once you click on the **Delete** button, it will not prompt you for confirmation, it will delete the line. Use carefully!

- **Save**: It will save information you have for future use. The file will be saved in the standard XML format.

- **Open**: It will open the existing XML file.

- **Execute in background**: If this checkbox is selected, the data load will execute in the background and you can perform other tasks in EAS.

- **OK**: Once you click on the **OK** button, the data load will commence using data load rules file you selected. The data will be loaded into the Essbase cube. If there are any errors loading the data, a warning message is displayed in the **Data Load** pane that states the data was only partially loaded into your Essbase database. The error log you have defined will contain information on any rejected data values.

After you click on the **OK** button, the **Data Load Results** window will be opened as shown here:

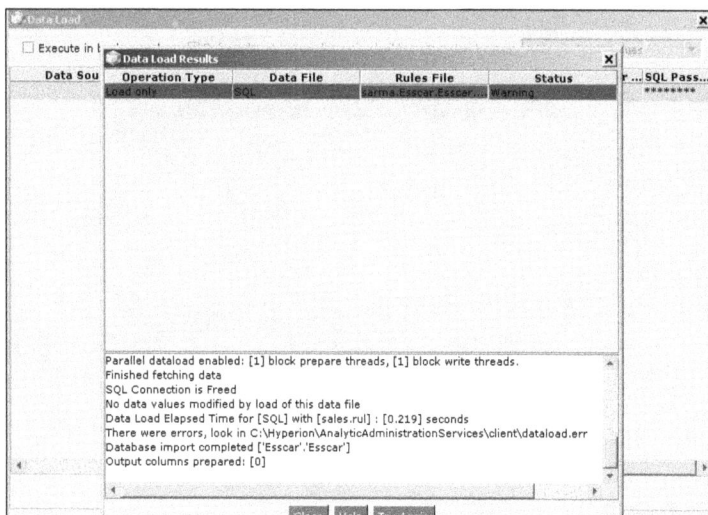

Oops! There is a warning message indicating there was an issue with some of the data and that some or all of the data did not load into your Essbase database. In order to debug the issue, you need to look into the error file generated by the data load process.

As you can see in the previous screenshot, the member name **ES440** is not found in the data base outline. This means this member does not exist in the database outline. Just to be sneaky, we removed the alias for the 4 X 4 PICKUP member from the outline on purpose to force this error. Essbase will attempt to load data into the database using the actual member names or aliases. You can even select a specific alias table to use.

Anytime if you see the *Member Not Found* in database message, it means this member does not exist in the Essbase outline.

Let us add the alias code **ES440** back into the outline and rerun the data load.

Hooray, we did it! As you can see in the following message, the data has successfully loaded into your Essbase database without any error messages:

Loading data using MaxL

By now, you must be familiar with the MaxL scripting language and its statements. We used MaxL to update the Essbase outline in the previous chapter. As you know, there are three ways you can execute a MaxL script. First, using EAS and the MaxL editor, second, you can execute MaxL scripts from the Command Prompt, and third, MaxL scripts can be executed from shell commands within another program.

Let's use the EAS and the MaxL editor to create a MaxL script and then execute the script to load data into the Essbase database.

Steps to execute MaxL from the EAS editor:

1. Within EAS, Click on **File | Editor | MaxL Script Editor.**

2. The MaxL editor will open.

3. Import Database MaxL statement should be used to load data.

Syntax for the Import Database MaxL statement:

```
IMPORT DATABASE APPLICATION NAME.DATABASE NAME
```

The various fields present in the MaxL statement are:

- DATA: We need to say data since we are loading data into the database.

- CONNECT AS <Database Username>: Please specify the user name here since we are loading the data from the relational database.

- IDENTIFIED BY <Database password>: Specifies your database password.

- USING <LOCAL SERVER NAME>: Location of the rules file.

- RULES_FILE <RULE FILE NAME>: Name of the rule file like dSales.

- ON ERROR WRITE TO <PATH FOR ERROR FILE>: Error file information. The Path for error file c:/book/dataload_chap4.err

The complete MaxL statement with correct syntax:

```
import database 'ESSCAR'.'ESSCAR' data
connect as 'hypuser' identified by 'password'
using server rules_file 'dSales'
on error write to c:/book/dataload_chap4.err
```

Move the above syntax into the MaxL editor, and execute the MaxL statement. The statement should run without any error messages being generated. The next screenshot shows that the data has loaded successfully into the Essbase cube using a MaxL script statement:

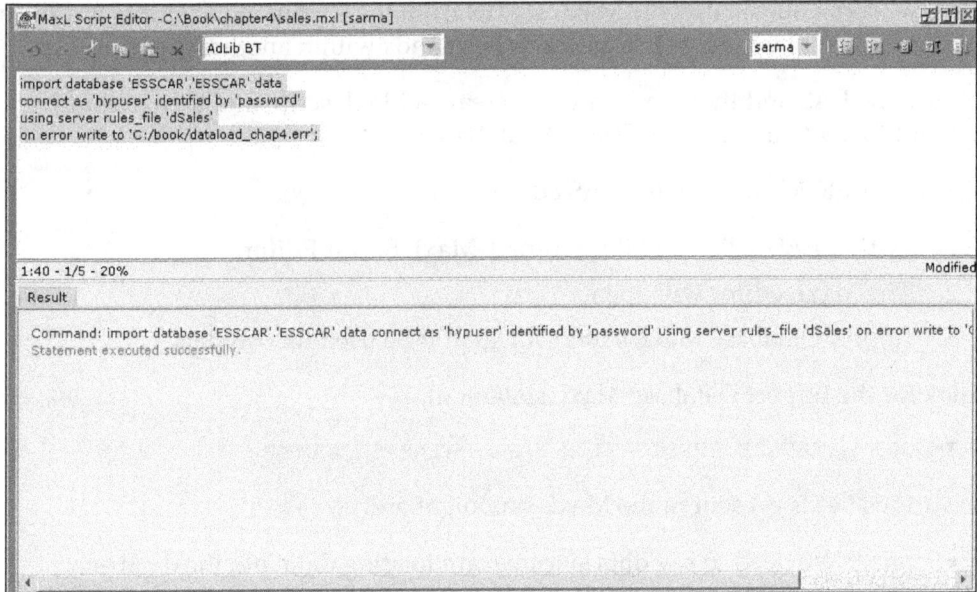

Now that you have successfully loaded the base data into your Essbase database, we now need to calculate the data in order for the data to be rolled up in the hierarchies described in the database outline. Parent values need to be summed from children values. Derived values need to be calculated from the newly loaded data component values.

All of this and more is performed using the Essbase calculation scripts, known simply as Calcs. Calcs will be discussed in much greater detail in the next chapter, but before we continue, let us quickly recap the differences between a Data Load and a Dimension Build.

Data Load vs. Dimension Build

First, an Essbase data load is very similar to an Essbase dimension build. Second, an Essbase data load is very different from an Essbase dimension build.

How can we make a contradictory statement like that? This is Essbase, that's how! Remember, Essbase is an art, not a science.

Loading data into an Essbase database is the process of loading specific data values into your Essbase database, based on a predefined database outline. This predefined database outline contains all of the necessary data attributes to organize the data into a logical and recognizable format.

Building dimensions in an Essbase database outline is the process of loading data as data attributes, instead of data values, into the database in the form of adding new dimension members to the database outline. The missing data attributes in the database outline that are contained in the data are added by the dimension build process so that the accompanying data values can be loaded and not rejected.

Summary

Wow, who knew Essbase was such an easy to use and versatile tool when it came to loading data and maintaining your outline?

Let's see, we have covered the how and why of making your data Essbase-friendly. We have also learned what it means to make data Essbase-friendly and what you need to do to make it so.

As if that wasn't enough, you've also learned all about what are referred to as data sources for Essbase. You now know that a data source can be merely data values you load into your Essbase database, based on a predefined database outline and data attributes accompanying the data values.

You have learned about the various types of data sources, how Essbase deals with them, and what you need to do to filter, manipulate, or cleanse them before use.

After all of that, we took all what you've learned about data and data sources and applied it by creating your first data load rules in Oracle Essbase. You then used that load rule to load some honest to goodness real data into your Esscar database. That was easy, wasn't it?

In the next chapter, we get into the handy dandy Essbase calculation script. This small tool is pretty much singularly responsible for the vast differences between Oracle Essbase and any typical relational database. Not only can you calculate data on the fly, you create new data elements that are derived from component data elements that exist in the database, without loading large amounts of data if the results you want can be derived from the data already existing in your database.

Turn the page and let's get started on calcs!

5

Calculating your Essbase Cube

Let's take a minute and review what we have completed so far. We now have a fully functioning Essbase operation set up. The server software is installed, the client software is installed, a real application and a database are built, and the database is loaded with data. It's all there and ready for the heart of the system. If the database outline is the foundation of an Essbase database then the calculation scripts are the heart of an Essbase database.

Although you can calculate both an ASO database and a BSO database, unless otherwise noted, the instructions in this chapter pertain primarily to the BSO.

In this chapter, you will learn about one of the most important pieces of functionality in Oracle Essbase. It is one of the main reasons why Oracle Essbase, with its cube technology is so vastly superior to any relational database when it comes to data analytics, analysis, and reporting. This important functionality is the Essbase database calculation.

To help you put the power of the Essbase database calculation to work for you, we will take you through the steps needed to be able to create and run an Essbase database calculation script. We will also show you the various types of database calculation scripts. Essbase database calculation scripts can be in the form of an Essbase database calculation script file, a database member formula written in the database outline and executed by a database calculation script, or a database outline member formula executed by Essbase only when the data is needed (dynamically calculated member).

One thing to keep in mind, some Oracle affiliates have offered a three day database calculation class that only covers how to write Essbase effective database calculation scripts. We have mixed feelings on the real value of such a class. With the information we provide in this chapter, combined with a little patience, practice, and common sense, there is absolutely no reason you cannot code your own robust database calculation scripts.

Read on, to continue this exciting calculation journey.

Calculating your database

In any Essbase database, the data can be grouped into two distinct categories. First, there is data that has been entered or loaded into the database. This data can be from some type of data load from an external source or from a Microsoft Excel spreadsheet with the Essbase add-in "Lock and Send" functionality.

Second, there is data that can be derived or calculated from the existing data elements which were entered, loaded, or input into the database. This data can be as simple as the total value at a parent level that has been added from the children values. It can also be the result of a complex calculation that has taken advantage of Essbase's extensive and powerful mathematical functions that are available to you in the calculation function library.

As we explained in the previous chapter, the input or loaded data that resides in your Essbase database can come from many and varied sources and, using the wide array of data load tools and options, can be quickly and easily prepared (made Essbase-friendly) and loaded into your Essbase database. This in itself is reason enough to become an Essbase believer.

The Essbase calculation script

The Essbase data calculation script has the same characteristics as any other Essbase file object. The script name can be no longer than eight characters and has a .csc extension. The calculation script file is actually an ASCII text format and can be opened and edited in any text editor.

The ideal way to create and edit an Essbase database calculation script is to use the built-in **Calculation Script Editor** found in the EAS tool. The benefits of using this provided tool includes reserve word coloring, much like the Microsoft Visual Basic editor, and a comprehensive syntax checker. These features make creating Essbase database calculation scripts a rather easy task.

To access the **Calculation Script Editor**, in EAS and with the tree structure expanded at the Application | Database you are working on, right-click on the **Calculation Scripts** heading and then click on **Create calculation script**. This will open the EAS database Calculation script editor. Follow these steps if you wish to create a new database calculation script from scratch. If you have already created one or more database calculation scripts and have stored them in the Essbase file system, they will be listed under the **Calculation Scripts** branch (shown below) and all you need to do to open the calculation script in the editor is to double-click the calculation script name. When asked if you want to lock the file object, select **Yes** to give yourself exclusive alter access to the script.

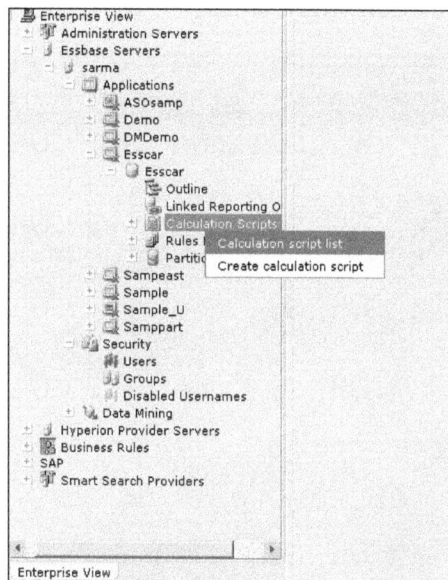

By default, Essbase will store your Essbase application file objects in the Application | Database path set up by Essbase, unless you specify otherwise.

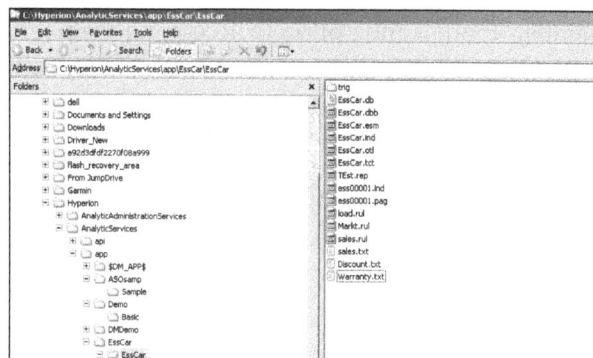

Looking at the preceding screenshot, you should notice two things. First, you can see how there are several different file types in the directory or folder and second, the path of the folder.

The files are placed by default into this folder by Essbase. It is not always practical to keep your calculation scripts, database page and index files, report scripts, and so on, all together in the same folder. Practicality aside, this arrangement may not even pass some installation's security and controls requirements. Luckily, Essbase allows you to save these files in any location that works for you.

The next screenshot shows the Essbase database calculation script editor opened to a blank and unsaved calculation script:

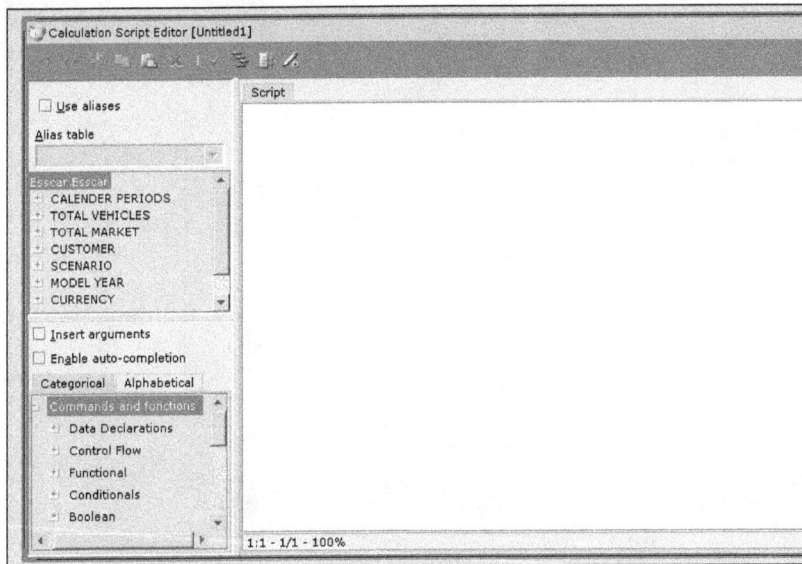

Essbase outline member formula

On any database member, there is the option to access the member's properties (as previously shown). One of the options on the **Member Properties** screen is the **Formula** tab. In the following screenshot, you will notice the member formula editor looks very much like the database **Calculation Script Editor**. Except for an occasional syntax difference, the member formulas you write for a database outline member are identical to the code used to write a database calculation script.

Member formulas can be written for all types of database outline members. The method used to execute a member formula is the only thing different. Member formulas can be executed when the database outline is calculated using the **Calc All** command or when attached to a dynamically calculated member and the user has requested data from that member.

For the script executed formula, you will set the **Data Storage** option to **Store Data**. For the dynamically calculated member, you will set the **Data Storage** option to **Dynamic Calc** or **Dynamic Calc and Store**.

Calculation types explained

As mentioned earlier in this chapter, there are three ways to calculate data in your Essbase database. There is the infamous Essbase database calculation script, the regular outline member formula, and the outline member formula written on a member tagged as **Dynamic Calc** or **Dynamic Calc and Store**. We will now give you an explanation of each calculation type along with its pros and cons.

Calculation Scripts

Mentioned already, but only briefly, was the venerable Essbase database calculation script. The database calculation script is an ASCII text file containing a series of precise commands and functions which are used by Essbase to perform calculations on the data stored in an Essbase database.

Essbase database calculation scripts are highly versatile and can be written, stored, and executed in a variety of ways.

To write an Essbase database calculation script, known as a calc script or calc, the easiest method is to use the **Calculation Script Editor** provided in EAS. This custom editor provides many features for coding database outline member selections, syntax checking, and function or command choices and their use.

The storing of an Essbase database calculation script is something that is entirely upto you—as the programmer/administrator. When you use the EAS Calculation script editor, it will default to saving the calculation script file object in the default Essbase database file structure, which is basically the database folder on the server.

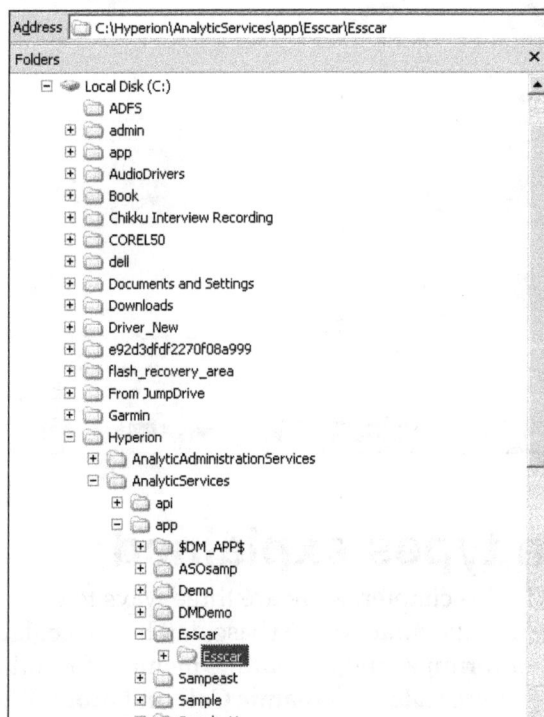

This is an acceptable place to leave the scripts, but it is not the best idea to allow access to a secure folder on a database server to too many people.

Again, executing an Essbase database calculation script can easily be performed from just about anywhere. You can execute a calculation script manually through the EAS tool, or through the Essbase Add-in for Microsoft Excel (provided your ID has calculation access), or programmatically using a shelled MaxL script or an API call.

The benefits of using a painstakingly written Essbase database calculation script are that you can specify the exact subset of data you wish to calculate.

Believe it or not, as amazing as an Essbase database calculation script is, there are a couple of drawbacks too. One drawback is that sometimes, because of all the power, an Essbase calculation script can be difficult to control. What we mean is that we can sometimes write a calc that will calculate too much data or take too long to execute. Also, when you create data using an Essbase database calculation script, the newly created data is created as stored data which can be a problem if you are creating too much of it. These are minor concerns which will be handled as you acquire more experience.

Stored data member formula

The outline member formula on a stored member is one way to create the data values you need in an Essbase database. It is very simple and easy to write, what can be thought of as a snippet of a full blown calculation script in the member formula editor located on the **Member Properties** screen.

Outline member formulas on stored members are also easy to execute as they may execute anytime when the dimension in which they reside is calculated.

Dynamic Calc and Dynamic Calc and Store

Dynamic Calc and Dynamic Calc and Store are database outline member property settings. Like we told you in the previous section, data created by an Essbase database calculation script is stored in the database. When you set the storage properties on a database member in the **Accounts** dimension to **Dynamic Calc** or **Dynamic Calc and Store**, the member formula will only execute when there is a request for the data.

In the case of a dynamically calculated member, the resultant data is not stored in the database, but is recreated every time there is another request for the data. With a dynamic calc and store member, the data is created the first time there is a request, then stored. On subsequent requests, the data will only be recreated if one of the component values has changed or has been updated.

These two data calculation options give you the benefit of always producing the freshest data based on the component values. They also help keep the database size small by not storing data or only small amounts of data. What we mean here is that with the use of dynamic calc and dynamic calc and store members you can help keep the size of your database smaller because you are not storing all of the possible data values for these members. A dynamic calc member stores no data in the database and a dynamic calc and store member only stores the data as it has been calculated. Stored members will store all data every time as it has been loaded or calculated, regardless of if anyone ever actually requests it from the database or not.

There are several ways to request data from an Essbase database which will trigger a dynamic calc member to create data. One is by performing a **Retrieve** of data using the Essbase Add-in for Microsoft Excel, another way is executing an Essbase report script.

Yes indeed, dynamically calculated data is a nice thing to have, but you must also be careful with its use. While dynamically calculated data offers greater accuracy, it can also be a performance hog depending on the amount of data being requested and the status of the component data involved in the calculation.

> A good rule of thumb for dynamically calculated data is to make sure you never calculate data whose component values are also dynamically calculated. This situation can cause drastic performance issues by hogging large amounts of memory to perform all of the necessary calculations.

Essbase calculation terminology

Yes, we're at it again! In the previous chapter, you learned a new term that was related to data intended for loading into an Essbase database. That term was Essbase-friendly.

In this chapter, there are more terms you need to learn so you can sound like an Essbase professional and also impress your co-workers. The new terms you will learn in this chapter are Essbase calculation-related terms.

In the following sections, we explain the Essbase calculation script commands so it will be helpful for you to become familiar with the calculation jargon first.

- **Calc**: You will use this word quite often. This is a very versatile word since you will use it as a noun as well as verb. Calc is Essbase lingo for any database calculation, but it can also describe a calculation action. For example, you could say, "I have written a new calc for gross stock." However, you could also say, "I need to calc the database." Both usages are correct.

- **Push down**: This term is used to describe what happens when you use a calculation function to populate the values of children members with the values of their parents. The time for doing this would be when your data is only loaded at the parent level but the same values should be applied to the children members.

- **Rollup**: This term is used to describe what happens when you add or sum the children members upto their parent level or it can mean the parent level of a group of children. As with calc, this term can be used as a noun or a verb. For example, "I'm writing a calc to rollup the regions to the Total Region level." You could also say, "Total Region is the rollup of the individual regions."

- **Stomp-on**: This is a good one and is mainly used to describe any data that you have unintentionally whacked or overwritten with a calc script. There are times when a parent member's value is not necessarily the rollup of its children. If you execute a calc that inadvertently rolls up the children to the parent, you have just stomped on the parent's data.

Because Essbase is an art and not a science and because this is a family book, there are several other terms you can frequently hear around an Essbase installation. We prefer that you learn these terms on your own.

Default database calculation script

While an Essbase database calculation script can be an extremely powerful tool, it can also be used for more routine database calculating. Whether you need complex calculations or outline rollups, a nice feature in your Essbase database toolbox is the ability to assign a default calculation script to each database.

A **Default Calc** is a database calculation script you would typically find yourself running repeatedly. To simplify your life, you set the script as the database's **Default Calc**. As you can imagine, you can set the **Default Calc** to any database calculation script you have created. By default, Essbase assigns the **Calc All** database function as the **Default Calc**. The **Calc All** function, in simple terms, calculates your database according to the outline member formulas and the consolidations you have specified in your parent-child relationships.

To set a calculation script to be your database's **Default Calc**, start by right-clicking on your database name in EAS and selecting the **Set | Default calculation...**.

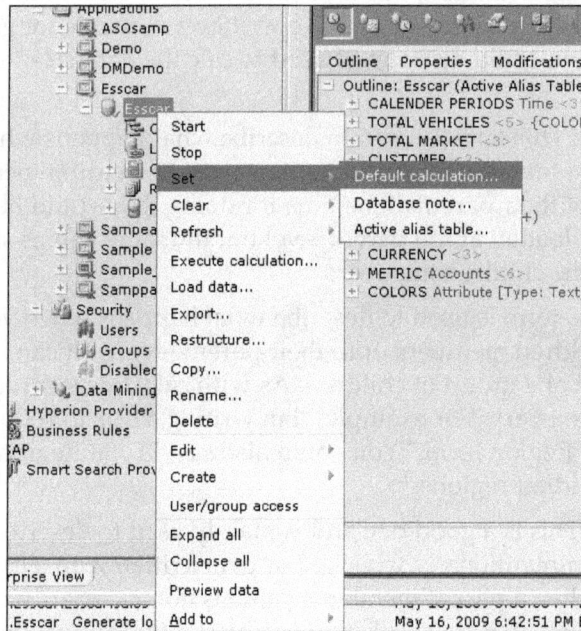

You should now see the screen depicted below. As you can see, this screen provides you with several choices regarding how to setting your database's default calculation script.

The first choice you have is a radio button which, when selected, allows you to choose any of the database calculation scripts you have written and stored with the database within the Essbase file structure on your server. Calculation scripts stored elsewhere cannot be chosen as the default calc.

If you select the second choice, **Use calculation string**, you can actually enter your own small set of calculation commands in the text box provided. This is where you will see the **Calc All** function set by Essbase as the database's **Default Calc** until you decide to change it.

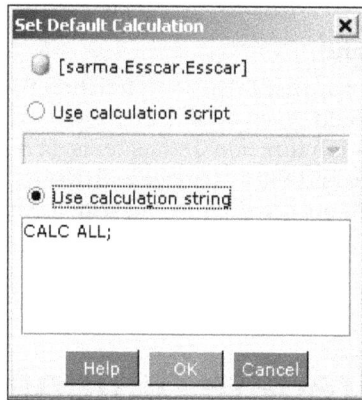

Your **Default Calc** can be executed manually by selecting it from the available choices on the screen that is displayed when you choose **Execute calculation...** from the list of choices that appear after right-clicking on your database name in EAS.

You can also programmatically execute your **Default Calc** using the appropriate command in your MaxL script or API call.

Calc All

The **Calc All** database calculation function can be executed in two different ways but will perform the same function. You can code the **Calc All** function in a database calculation script that is either executed manually or through a program. You can also set **Calc All** to be your database's default calculation string.

The **Calc All** command tells the Essbase to calculate the database according to the consolidations (parent-child rollups) and **Store Data** tagged member formulas that are set up in the database outline and members' properties.

There are occasions when you will create an Essbase database outline that is fairly simple and straight forward with regard to parent-child relationships. This database is more than likely used for presentation and reporting purposes only and the users' access is typically Read Only. With this type of arrangement, the only calculation that needs to be performed is usually after a data load or database/outline restructure. The **Calc All** command is perfect for this type of scenario.

When you initiate a **Calc All** function, Essbase attempts to determine the best order of calculation for the database, so you must be careful to verify the results of a **Calc All**. If your database requires complex or unusual calculations, you would be better served using a specifically written calculation script.

> **Very Important!**
>
> Since this is your first calculation function that you are learning about, we should give you this tip right now. The correct syntax for all calculation functional statements, in both scripts and formulas, is to end the statement with a semi-colon (;). Some statements are not required to end with a semi-colon, like conditional statements (if, else, endif), but all actionable statements are.

Calculate/Aggregate dimension

With an understanding of the **Calc All** function, we can now be comfortable describing the two very useful and related database calculation script functions.

Where the **Calc All** function is used to calculate the entire database based on the outline (consolidations and stored member formulas), the **CALC DIM** and **AGG** functions are used to perform almost the same function with dimension level precision.

The **CALC DIM** function performs exactly like the **Calc All** function in that it will execute calculations based on the database outline and **Store Data** tagged member formulas, with one huge difference. In calculating, functionality is constrained to only the database dimensions you list with this function. The following is an example of how you would code a CALC DIM statement to calculate only the Calendar Periods dimension.

To CALC DIM one dimension:

```
CALC DIM("Calendar Periods");
```

To CALC DIM more than one dimension in one command:

```
CALC DIM("Calendar Periods","Model Year","Market");
```

To make sure a specific order is followed:

```
CALC DIM("Market");
CALC DIM("Model Year");
CALC DIM("Calendar Periods");
```

The parameter section of this function can contain a comma separated list if you wish to calculate more than one dimension.

If you need to ensure a specific order of calculation for the dimensions, it is best to code individual CALC DIM statements containing only one dimension name in the order you need them to be calculated for each dimension.

Essbase Calc commands and functions

As discussed earlier, database calculations are very important features in the Essbase world. For some situations, you may need to write complicated calculation scripts, in other situations, they will be fairly simple. In order for you to become proficient in writing calculation scripts you need to have an understanding of some of the predefined commands and functions that can be used in an Essbase database calculation script. Let's discuss some of the more commonly used commands and functions in detail.

Data declarations

When you are writing some of the more complex calculation scripts, you will find it necessary to manipulate the data while calculating. For manipulating the data, you need to create variables.

In an Essbase calc, you can create temporary variables or global variables (also called substitution variables, which are discussed in greater detail later in this chapter).

The temporary variables are only available when the calculation script is running and they do not exist after the calculation script has completed. In order to use these variables in a calculation script, you need to declare them.

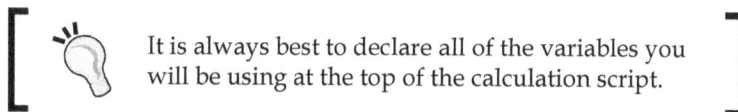

> It is always best to declare all of the variables you will be using at the top of the calculation script.

There are two types of temporary variables that can be used in an Essbase database calculation scripts:

- VAR: A variable containing only one value
- ARRAY: A one dimensional array declaration

The allowable naming convention for the VAR and ARRAY variables are similar to one another, you can use alpha characters "a through z", numbers "0 through 9", and special characters "$ (dollar sign), # (pound sign), and _ (underscore)". Remember, you cannot use the & (ampersand) as this is reserved for the substitution variables.

Example:

```
VAR cRevenue;
```

or

```
VAR cRevenue = 10,000;
ARRAY arrCust ["TOTAL CUSTOMER"];
```

The array size would be the total number of members in this dimension.

Control flow

Control functions control the flow of the data being calculated. As you will see, some functions help select the data while some help restrict the selected data. All in all, they are used to help you calculate your data quickly and efficiently.

FIX/ENDFIX

When we talked earlier about Essbase database calculation control, we meant the FIX/ENDFIX command. These are the control gate keepers of the database calculation script.

The FIX/ENDFIX commands are for use only in an Essbase database calculation script. When you code a member formula, the formula only applies to the member in which it is coded, hence, there is no need for FIX/ENDFIX commands.

Using Essbase's full complement of calculation functions and commands, for precise calculation purposes, it hardly matters what your outline looks like, or how it is laid out. In terms of dimension order, **Sparse** or **Dense** settings, whether or not you have an **Accounts** or **Time** dimension, or pretty much any other way you have your database set upto fit your own needs, the calculation script can be coded to do exactly as you wish. With the FIX/ENDFIX command, you can zero in with razor sharp precision on only the data values you wish to calculate.

When you employ a FIX/ENDFIX command you are telling Essbase to select a subset of data from the database for calculating. In this way, you will not calculate too much data at any given time. You also will not calculate data that you do not intend to (the definition of Stomp-on).

What you will realize by using the FIX/ENDFIX command, besides the benefits described above, is keeping your database calculation scripts running at peak performance.

The FIX command selects data from the database by blocks. Due to this fact, and also because you want to ensure the highest possible performance while executing calculation scripts, it is recommended that wherever possible, you FIX only on members that are in Sparse Dimension. When you FIX on a Dense Dimension, Essbase needs to pull all of the data blocks affected by the FIX statement into the system's memory, thus potentially affecting performance. This is because dense members have a greater potential to populate across more blocks.

Of course, you can fix on any database member(s) you wish, and sometimes you will have no choice. However, if calculation script performance becomes an issue, this is one of the first places to look to make improvements.

For example:

```
FIX(Sparse Dimension)
    IF(Dense Dimension)
        Any Calculation Function;
    ENDIF
ENDFIX
```

> There is one caveat to this. Essbase will only FIX on members in blocks that have been previously created. You can solve this by using the CREATEBLOCKONEQ command in your calculation script. This command will create the necessary missing blocks for your sparse members.

When you use the FIX/ENDFIX command, you are basically turning on, and then off, the data filtering that you incorporated using the FIX/ENDFIX command in the first place. In a typical calculation script, you may have many separate instances of FIX/ENDFIX commands that enclose a wide variety of calculation functions. The FIX/ENDFIX commands can also be nested inside one another, much like nested IF/ENDIF statements. For every FIX statement, there must be a matching ENDFIX.

> There is one critical thing you must know about nesting FIX/ENDFIX commands. Never fix on one level of a dimension, then fix again on a different level of that same dimension in a nested FIX command.

Always attempt to FIX to the specific level you intend to for a dimension in one FIX command. The reason for this is because even though the next FIX command is nested within the first FIX command it will still pull the entire dimension into the calc pool for filtering. In the example of a bad implementation below, the first FIX command will select all members from the Calendar Periods dimension. The second FIX command will select all of the zero level members from the Calendar Periods dimension. This will actually result in all members of the Calendar Periods dimension being calculated.

Do *not* do this:

```
FIX("Calendar Periods")
    FIX(@LEVMBRS("Calendar Periods",0))
        Any Calculation Function;
    ENDFIX
ENDFIX
```

Do this instead:

```
FIX(@IDESCENDANTS("Calendar Periods" AND
                  @LEVMBRS("Calendar Periods",0))
      Any Calculation Function;
ENDFIX
```

In the following examples, we will show you how to narrow down the amount of data you will calculate in your database for various scenarios.

Basic FIX and ENDFIX examples

To begin with, as mentioned earlier, FIX and ENDFIX commands can be nested. We have also given you some tips regarding when to use the FIX and ENDFIX commands and what to avoid when nesting them, like the same dimensions named in separate FIX commands.

For starters, this is how you would code the simplest of FIX and ENDFIX commands:

```
FIX(@IDESCENDENTS("Calendar Periods"))
    "Gross Stock" = "Production" - "Sales";
ENDFIX
```

Notice how the FIX command has an area to list selection dimensions. Within the parenthesis you can list multiple dimension names separated by commas, member names, or a list of member functions that returns member names. There are also functions that return members at specific levels in the outline. You can even use basic structuring similar to a mathematical formula with AND/OR statements bracketed by extra parenthesis.

In the example immediately above, notice how we are calculating the value for Gross Stock for all Calendar Periods. If your database was extremely large, with several years of historical data in it, this would be inefficient to always calculate the entire **Time** dimension.

Now, suppose you added **User Defined Attributes (UDAs)** to the periods in the time dimension and only wanted to calculate current periods? Here is what you would do:

1. Add UDAs of **Historical, Current**, and **Forecast** to the individual year members and their children in the database outline. For example, if the current calendar year is 2009, then 2009 and all of its children would have the UDA of **Current** added to them in the outline. All years and their children prior to 2009 would get the UDA of **Historical**. All years and their children later than 2009 would get the UDA of **Forecast** added in the outline:

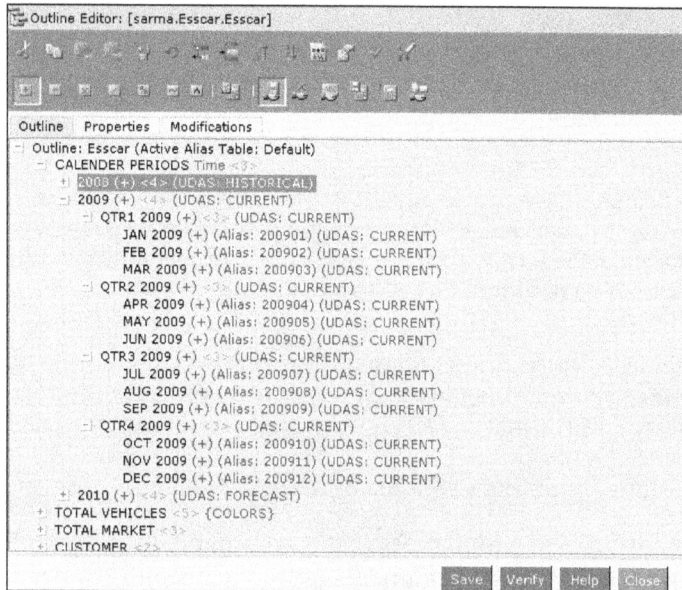

2. Decide that you only want to calculate Gross Stock for the Current and Forecast time periods.

3. Recode your FIX and ENDFIX command statements to look like this:

```
FIX(@UDA("Calendar Periods","Current") OR
        @UDA("Calendar Periods","Forecast"))
    "Gross Stock" = "Production" - "Sales";
ENDFIX
```

Aren't FIX and ENDFIX commands the greatest?

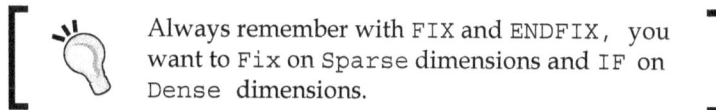

> Always remember with FIX and ENDFIX, you want to Fix on Sparse dimensions and IF on Dense dimensions.

EXCLUDE/ENDEXCLUDE

Well there you have it! With the release of Essbase version 9.x we now have EXCLUDE and ENDEXCLUDE commands to compliment the FIX and ENDFIX commands.

Now, without confusing you, we can tell you to consider the FIX and ENDFIX commands as an include statement that tells Essbase what data to keep for calculating. And, if including data proves difficult (and there are times it will), then you now have the EXCLUDE and ENDEXCLUDE commands to tell Essbase what data to leave out when selecting data for calculating. See examples in the next section.

When we talked earlier about Essbase database calculation control, we meant the FIX and ENDFIX commands. Well, we also mean the EXCLUDE and ENDEXCLUDE commands. These commands complete the data control gate keeper job in the Essbase database calculation script.

> The EXCLUDE and ENDEXCLUDE command is only for use in an Essbase database calculation script. When you code a member formula, the formula applies only to the member in which it is coded, there is no need for EXCLUDE and ENDEXCLUDE commands.

Because these database calculation commands are coded exactly like the FIX and ENDFIX commands, we do not believe that we need to spend a great deal of time explaining what should be obvious as far as the syntax is concerned.

Remember the following points while using the EXCLUDE/ENDEXCLUDE command:

- You can nest EXCLUDE and ENDEXCLUDE command statements. However, make sure you only code arguments for a dimension in one EXCLUDE statement no matter how many nested levels you have similar to the FIX command.
- You can code many instances of EXCLUDE and ENDEXCLUDE commands in the same calc script.
- You must have an ENDEXCLUDE for every occurrence of the EXCLUDE command.
- You do not need to end an EXCLUDE or ENDEXCLUDE statement with a semi-colon.
- You code a comma separated list of members or functions that return a list of members between the parentheses on the EXCLUDE command.
- The EXCLUDE statement tells Essbase what data to leave out of the calculation.

Basic EXCLUDE/ENDEXCLUDE examples

To begin with, as mentioned earlier, EXCLUDE and ENDEXCLUDE commands can be nested. We have also given you tips regarding when to use the EXCLUDE and ENDEXCLUDE commands and what to avoid when nesting them, like the same dimensions named in separate EXCLUDE commands.

For starters, this is how you would code the simplest of EXCLUDE/ENDEXCLUDE commands:

```
EXCLUDE("Canada")
    "Gross Stock" = "Production" - "Sales";
ENDEXCLUDE
```

Notice how the EXCLUDE command has an area to list dimensions. Within the parenthesis you can list dimension names separated by commas, member names, or a list of member functions that return member names. There are also functions that return members at specific levels in the outline. You can even use basic structuring similar to a mathematical formula with AND/OR statements bracketed by extra parenthesis.

In the example immediately above, notice how we are calculating the value for Gross Stock for all markets except Canada.

> There has not been a tremendous amount of feedback regarding the use and performance of EXCLUDE and ENDEXCLUDE as they are new in version 9.x. We can only assume that the EXCLUDE and ENDEXCLUDE commands function exactly like the FIX and ENDFIX commands, except to exclude the referenced data instead of including the referenced data.

Aren't EXCLUDE and ENDEXCLUDE commands the greatest as well?

Functional

In Essbase database calculation scripts, you may be required to perform certain functional commands like Set functions, Cleardata functions, or the Datacopy function that is used to copy data from one member to another member, all before you start the execution of your database calculation.

SET command functions

SET command functions are used to tune the calculation and database factors that affect calculation performance and are initially coded at the beginning of a calculation script. SET commands stay in effect for the duration of the calc script unless coded again mid-script.

Let's take a look at some of the widely used SET command functions:

- SET AGGMISSING ON/OFF: This command specifies if Essbase should turn the consolidation of the # missing values ON or OFF. This is only applicable to Sparse dimensions.

  Example:
  ```
  SET AGGMISSING ON;
  SET AGGMISSING OFF;
  ```

- `SET CACHE HIGH/DEFAULT/LOW/OFF/ALL`: In the Essbase configuration file, if you have specified values for the `CALCCACHELOW`, `CALCCACHEHIGH`, and `CALCCACHEDEFAULT`, then when you run a database calculation script you set the calculator memory cache to `HIGH`, `LOW`, or `DEFAULT`. When you preset these values in the script (as needed), you can realize a better performance while the script is executing.

  The Essbase configuration file is stored in the Essbase program directory on the server. This file can contain many entries for tweaks and adjustments that help your Essbase system perform better. The Essbase Configuration file is explained in more detail in Chapter 9 of this book.

  Let us say the following are the settings for the calc cache in the Essbase configuration file. Oops! We introduced a new term here. The Essbase configuration file is new and we have not talked about it yet. Well, we will discuss the configuration file in the coming chapters. However, for now know that it is a file where you can set up your server settings and adjustments which improve the overall performance of data loads and data calcs.

  Now, where were we? Oh yes, the server calc cache settings:

  ```
  CALCCACHEHIGH 150000000
  CALCCACHEDEFAULT 100000000
  CALCCACHELOW 50000000
  ```

  In the Calculation Script you have defined:

  ```
  SET CACHE HIGH;
  ```

  This command sets the calculator cache to 150,000,000 bytes.

  ```
  SET CACHE DEFAULT;
  ```

  This command sets the calculator cache to 100,000,000 bytes.

  ```
  SET CACHE LOW;
  ```

  This command sets the calculator cache to 50,000,000 bytes.

- `SET CALCTASKDIMS n`: Specifies the number of `Sparse` dimensions that can run in parallel, where n is maximum number of `Sparse` dimensions. This command can help speed up the performance of a calculation script by identifying tasks or transactions that can be run in parallel instead of serially.

  ```
  SET CALCTASKDIMS 1
  ```

  In the above command, the last `Sparse` dimension is identified as the task that can run in parallel.

- `SET CALCPARALLEL n`: Enables the calculation tasks to run in parallel, where n is number of threads. The value of n can be 1 to 4 for 32 bit and 1 to 8 for 64 bit servers.

  ```
  SET CALCPARALLEL 4
  ```

The command above enables four threads to run in parallel. This means that upto four threads can be used by the system to calculate the data instead of the default one thread.

- SET FRMLBOTTOMUP ON/OFF: This command enables you to do bottom-up calculation on the formulas. The command can help speed up the processing of complex formulas on Sparse Dimensions when the associations and dependencies are straight forward. When there are a lot of range type functions used, there may be inconsistent results achieved.

  ```
  SET FRMLBOTTOMUP ON;
  SET FRMLBOTTOMUP OFF;
  ```

- DATACOPY membername1 to membername2: This command copies data from one member to another member.

  ```
  DATACOPY "TOTAL REVENUE" to "BILLED REVENUE";
  ```

  This example above will copy the values in TOTAL REVENUE to BILLED REVENUE across all levels.

  ```
  DATACOPY "TOTAL REVENUE"->@LEVMBRS("Calendar Periods", 3) to
           "BILLED REVENUE"->@LEVMBRS("Calendar Periods", 0);
  ```

  This example above will copy TOTAL REVENUE from the YEARS level to BILLED REVENUE at the month level.

  > In a database calculation script, member names which have a space in them must be in double quotes. If there is no space in a member name, there is no need to have a double quote.
  >
  > It is not a bad idea to always wrap member names in double quotes, whether they contain spaces or not. This makes them easily identifiable when reading a calc script.

- CLEARBLOCK ALL/UPPER/NONINPUT/DYNAMIC/EMPTY: This command clears the blocks and sets "#missing" in the blocks. You need to clear blocks before data refreshes to clear off all of the old data. Remember, this is not entirely removing the blocks, these blocks still exist and when you do a data load it will be a little slower. If a block had no data already, meaning it is already #missing, it will be removed.

  - ALL: Clears and sets "#missing" to all data blocks.
  - UPPER: Clears and sets "#missing" to all of the consolidated level blocks.
  - NON INPUT: Clears and sets "#missing" to all of the non-input members, the members to which data is not directly loaded.

- ○ DYNAMIC: Clears and sets "#missing" to all of the data which has been created by a Dynamic Calc and Store member.
- ○ EMPTY: Removes all of the blocks which are already "#missing" blocks.

Examples:

```
CLEARBLOCK ALL;
CLEARBLOCK UPPER;
```

- CLEARDATA MemberName: Removes all of the data for the member name specified, replacing it with "#missing". The "#missing" symbol is Essbase speak for null values.

Example:

```
CLEARDATA "TOTAL REVENUE";
```

The functions discussed above are just some of the more widely used calculation script functions available to you. We will discuss more functions in the coming chapters.

Conditionals

In the Essbase database calculation script, like most other programming languages, you can test data situations with conditional statements. Without a doubt, the IF and ENDIF statements are the most common.

IF/ENDIF

Ah yes, the IF and ENDIF commands, the partners to the FIX and ENDFIX commands. As stated earlier in this chapter, these tools have been provided to allow you to write high performing and efficient calculation scripts and to precisely calculate your data without stomping on other data.

If the FIX and ENDFIX commands are the gate keeper of the data, the IF and ENDIF commands are the ushers directing you (your data) to the correct seat. Just like the IF and ENDIF commands in any programming language, the IF and ENDIF commands you use in Essbase for calculating, perform conditional checking or testing of the data to help decide if or how it gets calculated.

Remember the `FIX` and `ENDFIX` commands are best used on `Sparse Dimension` due to the physical construction of the Essbase cube. Well, the opposite is recommended for the `IF` and `ENDIF` commands. Because the `IF` statement needs to test every occurrence of the data brought to it, it is best to use the `IF` and `ENDIF` commands against a `Dense Dimension` because there will be fewer cells of data that need to be tested since the original subset of data was pulled in as a `Sparse Dimension`.

For example:

```
FIX(Sparse Dimension)
    IF(Dense Dimension)
        Any Calculation Function;
    ENDIF
ENDFIX
```

Again, while this is not always possible, it is a good idea to follow this recommendation whenever possible.

Just like the `FIX` and `ENDFIX` commands, the `IF` and `ENDIF` commands can be nested. We have never been able to determine if there is a limit, but we have also never hit a limit when coding either. For every `IF` statement, there must be a matching `ENDIF` statement. When using `ELSE` or `ELSEIF`, you will still need one `ENDIF` for every `IF` statement.

For example:

```
IF(Conditional Argument)
    Any Calculation Function;
ENDIF
```

Or this:

```
IF(Conditional Argument)
    IF(Conditional Argument)
        Any Calculation Function;
    ELSEIF(Conditional Argument)
        Any Calculation Function;
    ELSE
        Any Calculation Function;
    ENDIF
ENDIF
```

Also, like the `FIX` and `ENDFIX` commands, the `IF` and `ENDIF` command statements do not need to be terminated with a semi-colon. Only the actionable calculation function statements need to be terminated by a semi-colon.

Unlike the FIX and ENDFIX commands, the IF and ENDIF commands can be used in Essbase calculation scripts as well as database outline member formulas.

Much like the FIX command, the IF command accepts a comma separated list of conditional arguments, of which a full compliment is included in Essbase.

> Always remember with IF and ENDIF, you want to Fix on Sparse and IF on Dense.

Boolean

As you know, Boolean tests are used to check for either a true or false condition. In an Essbase calc script, you can make good use of the Boolean test functions. Some of the more widely used Boolean functions are @ISUDA, @ISMBR, @ISLEV, @ISGEN, @ISPARENT, @ISCHILD, and many more.

Some of the most widely used Boolean functions are discussed here:

- @ISMBR: This function is used to test if the current member being calculated is a member specified by the parameter(s) entered into the function.

  Syntax:

  `@ISMBR (membername, rangelist, mbrlist)`

  ○ `membername` — a single member name

  ○ `rangelist` — a range of members returned by a member function

  ○ `mbrlist` — a comma separated list of members

  Example:

  `@ISMBR("DETROIT")` — returns true if the current member is DETROIT.

- @ISLEV: Returns true if the current member being calculated is in the same level as the member specified in the @ISLEV parameter.

  Syntax:

  `@ISLEV(dimname, levelname, level number)`

  Example:

  `@ISLEV("TOTAL CUSTOMER",0)` — returns true if the current member is in the zero level in the database outline.

- `@ISCHILD(mbrname)`: Returns true if the current member is child of the member specified in the @ISCHILD parameter.

  Syntax:

  `@ISCHILD(mbrname)`

Example:

@ISCHILD("DETROIT") — returns true for all members that are children of the DETROIT member.

These are just a few of the many Boolean functions that Essbase has provided to you to allow for the increased performance of customized database calculations. You should now have a good understanding on their use and the parameters required to make them perform as designed.

Relationship functions

As you know, an Essbase cube is lot like a family. In fact, this is a family that has a lot of relationships. The relationship functions are used to fetch data for the current member position from a different member's position. The most widely used relationship functions are @PARENTVAL and @ANCESTVAL.

- @PARENTVAL (dimension, membername): This function returns the value of the parent of the current member being calculated for the listed member.

  Example:

  @PARENTVAL("TOTAL VEHICLE","TOTAL SALES"): This returns the TOTAL SALES for the parent of the current member.

  This is the product structure of our Esscar Database:

  ```
  -| TOTAL VEHICLES <5> {COLORS}
     -| 2 DOOR SEDAN (+) <3>
          ES460 (+)
          SPORTY (+)
          DREAMZ (+)
     -| 4 DOOR SEDAN (+) <3>
          ES440 (+)
          4D600 (+)
          FLASHY (+)
     -| 4X2 PICKUP (+) <2>
          WORKER (+)
  ```

  If the current product member being calculated is "2 DOOR SEDAN", then the output of this:

  @PARENTVAL ("TOTAL VEHICLE","TOTAL SALES") is **TOTAL SALES** for the **CARS** outline member which is the parent of "2 DOOR SEDAN".

- @ANCESTVAL (dimension, genlevNum, [membername]): This function returns the value of the parents, grandparents, great grandparents using either the generation or level reference from the current member selected.

If `GenlevNum` (the specific generation or level number) **is:**

- ° > 0 then it is using Generation reference
- ° <+ 0 then it is using Level reference

Example:

`@ANCESTVAL ("TOTAL VEHICLE",2,"TOTAL SALES")`: If current member being calculated is the STINGER COUPE, then the returned member is `TOTAL SALES` at the `CARS` level.

`@PARENTVAL` and `@ANCESTVAL` are used for one dimensional value swapping. If you want to return values from another member based on multiple dimensions, then you will use the `@MDPARENTVAL` and `@MDANCSETVAL` functions. For more information, refer to the online technical reference included with your EAS software.

`@XREF`: This function is used to reference data in another Essbase database. The XREF requires you to define a location alias to another database. The other database can be similar to the original database or should at least have some similar dimensions.

`@XREF(LOCATION ALIAS, [MEMBERLIST])`: For more information, refer to the online technical reference included with your EAS software.

`LOCATION ALIAS` — you need to set a location alias as shown in the steps below.

`MEMBER LIST` — this is optional, you can give the list of the member names for which you need the data.

The following are the easy steps required to create the very useful location alias:

1. In EAS, select your application and click on **Action.**

2. Select **Edit** and click on the **Location Alias for "ESSCAR" (Your Application).**

3. In the **Location Aliases** screen, give an **Alias name.** Select the **Essbase Server, Application, Database, User name,** and **Password** and click on the **Test** button.

4. Once you click on the **Test** button, it will verify your existence on that Server or Application and the **verified** checkbox will be checked. Now, click on the **SET** button to save the information as shown in the following screenshot.

5. You can click on the **Delete** button to delete an existing Location Alias.

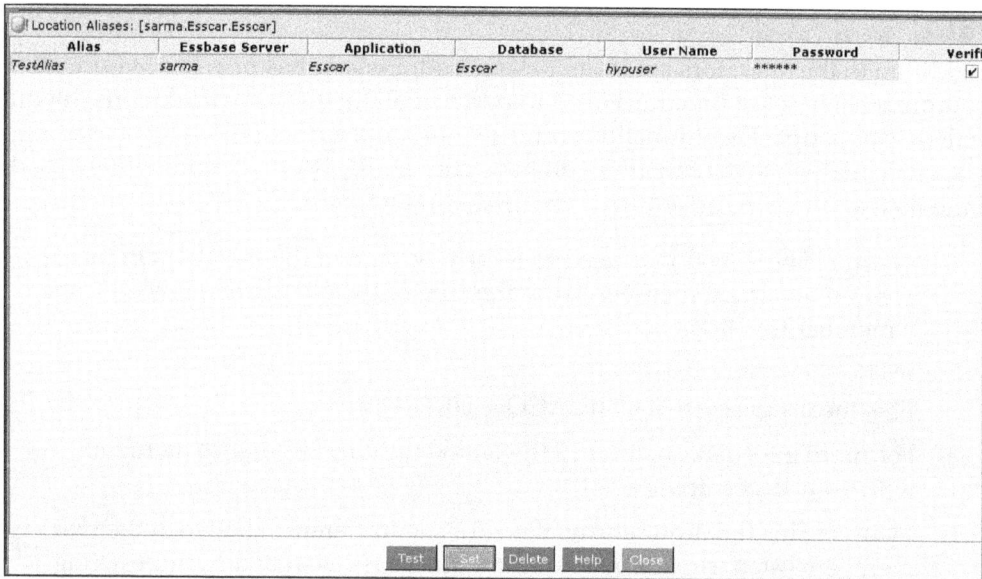

Alias	Essbase Server	Application	Database	User Name	Password	Verifi
TestAlias	sarma	Esscar	Esscar	hypuser	******	✔

Location Aliases: [sarma.Esscar.Esscar]

Test Set Delete Help Close

Operators

In calc scripts, you can use all of the routine arithmetic operators like +, -, *, /, logical operators like =, >, >=, <=, ==, <>, !=, and cross dimensional operators -> (minus sign with Greater than symbol). Since you are reading this book, we assume that you are very familiar with Arithmetic and logical operators. Of course, probably much better than we are!

Cross Dimensional Operator: This operator fetches the data by joining members of different dimensions. You should only pick one member from each dimension. This formula can be used in calc scripts and can also be used in outline member formulas.

For example:

"TOTAL REVENUE" -> "TOTAL VEHICLE" ->"YEAR 2009" – The output of this command returns the Total Revenue for all Vehicles sold in the year 2009.

Basically, you have said, "Give me the TOTAL REVENUE value at the TOTAL VEHICLE level at the YEAR 2009 level." All in one statement!

Math

In addition to the operators previously described, Essbase has provided you with a comprehensive set of functions used to perform mathematical calculations in your database calc script. These functions return values to the calculation data based upon the specific mathematical function you have chosen. Some of the more widely used mathematical functions are @SUM(), @AVERAGE(), and @VAR().

- @SUM(): This function is used to return the sum of the members in the comma separated member list or the sum of the members returned from a member function.

  @SUM("CHICAGO","DETROIT");

  This means the sum of CHICAGO + DETROIT.

  For more information, refer to the online technical reference included with your EAS software.

- @VAR(): This function returns the variance (difference) between the two members listed as parameters. The variance is calculated by subtracting the first member from the second member.

  @VAR(ACTUAL,BUDGET);

- @VARPER(): This function is used to return the percent variance (percent difference) between the two members listed. The percent values are calculated by dividing the first member by the second member.

  @VARPER(ACTUAL,BUDGET);

- @ROUND(): This function will round the value of the **expression** parameter to the number specified by the NUMDIGITS parameter to the right of the decimal.

  @ROUND(EXPRESSION, NUMDIGITS)

  @ROUND(SALES,2)

  If the Sales value = 1000.926, then after rounding, it would be 1000.93.

Member set

Member set functions typically return a list of database outline members. Depending on the function you have selected for use, it can dynamically generate a list of members that are needed in the calculation. Member set functions are widely used in conjunction with the FIX() statement to help specify a list of outline members for calculation.

Let's take a look at some of the commonly used member set functions:

- `@CHILDREN()`: Returns the list of all of the children of the member named in the parameter.

  Syntax:

  `@CHILDREN(mbrname)`

  Example:

  `@CHILDREN("Detroit");`

  Returns all members that are children of the member `Detroit`.

- `@SIBLINGS()`: Returns the list of all siblings (members at the same level and with the same parent) for the member specified in the parameter.

  Syntax:

  `@SIBLINGS(mbrname)`

  Example:

  `@SIBLINGS("Illinois");`

  Returns all siblings of the member `Illinois`.

Range (Financial)

In the Range functions, you can code a range of members as an argument. You can then SUM or AVERAGE the range for a new value.

- `@SUMRANGE()`: Used to sum the values for a given range of members where `mbrname` is the member which will contain the summed values.

  Syntax :

  `@SUMRANGE(mbrname, Rangelist)`

  Example:

  `@SUMRANGE(Sales, @DESCENDANTS(2009));`

  Returns the sum of Sales for all descendants of the year = 2009.

- `@AVGRANGE()`: Used to calculate the average values for a specified range. As you remember in the `@AVG` function, we talked about `SKIPNONE`, `SKIPMISSING`, `SKIPZERO`, and `SKIPBOTH` parameters and their purpose holds true for the `@AVGRANGE()` function as well.

  Syntax:

  `@AVGRANGE( SKIPNONE | SKIPMISSING | SKIPZERO | SKIPBOTH , MBRNAME, [RANGELIST] )`

  Example:

  `@AVGRANGE(SKIPMISSING, Sales, @DESCENDANTS(2009));`

Returns average `Sales` value for all sales in the 2009 periods. SKIPMISSING will exclude any periods that contains a #missing (NULL) value.

- `@NEXT()` and `@PRIOR()`: As the functions' names imply, their use will either the PRIOR value from a specified dimension or the NEXT value from a specified dimension.

Syntax:

```
@NEXT(mbrname[, n, Rangelist])
@PRIOR(mbrname[, n, Rangelist])
```

Example:

```
@NEXT(Sales,2,Years);
@PRIOR(Sales,2,Years);
```

For the `@NEXT()` function, the example returns `Sales` for the year member 2 periods ahead of the member currently being calculated. Likewise, for the `@PRIOR()` function, it returns the `Sales` for the year member 2 periods ahead of the member currently being calculated.

Forecasting

Forecasting functions can be used to estimate values for a certain period of time. A couple of the forecasting functions available to you are `@MOVAVG()` and the `@MOVSUM()` functions.

- `@MOVAVG()`: This function applies a moving n-term mean to an input data set. Each term in the set is replaced by a trailing mean of n terms. `@MOVAVG()` modifies a data set for smoothing purposes.

Syntax:

```
@MOVAVG(mbrName [, n [, XrangeList]])
```

Example:

```
@MOVAVG(Sales,3,Jan:Jun);
```

In this example, the `@MOVAVG()` function smoothes sales data for the first six months of the year on a three month term.

- `@MOVSUM()`: This function applies a moving sum to the specified number of values in an input data set. `@MOVSUM()` modifies a data set for smoothing purposes.

Syntax:

```
@MOVSUM (mbrName [, n [, XrangeList]])
```

Example:

```
@MOVSUM(Sales,3,Jan:Jun);
```

In this example, the @MOVSUM() function smoothes sales data for the first six months of the year on a three month term.

Statistical

Statistical functions are used to compute descriptive statistics. Some of the statistical functions are @COUNT(), @RANK(), and @MEDIAN(), just to name a few.

- @COUNT: Returns the number of values available in the specified member list. You have the option to exclude the #MISSING, ZEROS, BOTH, or NONE.

  Syntax:

  ```
  @COUNT(SKIPNONE | SKIPMISSING | SKIPZEROS | SKIPBOTH , MEMBERLIST);
  ```

  MEMBERLIST is a comma separated list of members or you can use any of the provided member set functions.

  Example:

  ```
  @COUNT(SKIPBOTH,@RANGE("TOTAL REVENEUE",@CHILDREN("CARS")));
  ```

  This example will return the number of children of the CARS member that have a value in the TOTAL REVENUE member.

- @RANK(): This function returns the rank of a specified member. The rank of a value is equivalent to its position (its rank) in the sorted data set.

  Syntax:

  ```
  @RANK (SKIPNONE | SKIPMISSING | SKIPZERO | SKIPBOTH, value,
  expList);
  ```

  value is the position (rank) of the member who's value you wish to return from expList.

  Example:

  ```
  @RANK(SKIPBOTH,Sales,@RANGE(Sales,@LEVMBRS(Product,1)));
  ```

  In this example, we return the rank of products based on Sales as Essbase loops through the member list returned by the @RANGE() function.

- @MEDIAN(): Returns the median (middle number) of the specified data set (expList). Half of the numbers in the data set are larger than the median, and half are smaller.

  Syntax:

  ```
  @MEDIAN (SKIPNONE | SKIPMISSING | SKIPZERO | SKIPBOTH, expList);
  ```

Example:

```
@MEDIAN(SKIPBOTH,@RANGE(Sales,@CHILDREN(Product)));
```

This example returns the median (middle value) of the Product dimension based on the value of Sales.

Date and Time

The date and time category only has one function, and it is new for Essbase version 9.x. That function is called @TODATE().

@TODATE(): Coverts a date string into numbers of seconds elapsed since midnight, January 1, 1970.

Syntax:

```
@TODATE (FormatString, date)
```

Format of String can either be "mm-dd-yyyy" or "dd-mm-yyyy".

Example:

```
@TODATE("mm-dd-yyyy","12-12-2008");
```

Miscellaneous

Finally, we have a few miscellaneous calculation functions which do not belong in any of the other categories. There are only three miscellaneous functions which are @CALCMODE(), @CONCATENATION(), and @SUBSTRING().

- @CALCMODE(): This function tells the calc script how the formulas need to be calculated. The @CALCMODE() function can tell Essbase to toggle between two different calculation modes. First, you can toggle between CELL and BLOCK modes, then, in a second statement, you can toggle between formulas being calculated in TOPDOWN or BOTTOMUP modes.

  What a handy function!

  Syntax:

  ```
  @CALCMODE(CELL | BLOCK | TOPDOWN | BOTTOMUP);
  ```

  Example:

  ```
  @CALCMODE(CELL);
  @CALCMODE(BOTTOMUP);
  ```

  The two statements above will place Essbase in the CELL mode for calculating and also calculate member formulas from the bottom up.

- @CONCATENATE() and @SUBSTRING(): These functions are used to manipulate the string values in member names as the calculation script is running.

  ° @CONCATENATE(): This is used to concatenate to two given strings. These strings can also be member names.

Syntax:

```
@CONCATENATE(STRING1, STRING2)
```

Example:

```
@CONCATENATE("a","West");
```

This example returns a string value of aWest which can be used elsewhere for testing member names.

@SUBSTRING(): This is used to return string characters from the specified string from given starting and ending positions.

Syntax:

```
@SUBSTRING(STRING, STARTING POSITION, ENDING POSITION)
```

° STRING: Can be a String or a member name.

° STARTING POSITION: The position from where you want to select the first character of the substring. The first position in the string is zero (0).

° ENDING POSITION: The last position you wish to select for your substring. If omitted, @SUBSTRING() will stop at the last character in the string being evaluated.

Example:

```
@SUBSTRING("TOTAL MARKET",0,4);
```

In this example, the function returns the string value of TOTAL.

Order of calculation

By now, you have a good understanding of what an Essbase calculation is. You have learned about a head-spinning number of database calculation functions and commands. We now need to describe for you another one of those conceptual ideas that Essbase is famous for.

As we've said many times before, Essbase is an art, not a science! The idea of how to determine the order of calculation is made up of equal parts of scientific blah, blah, blah about, "Well this is how Essbase is written so this is how it works", and generous portions of, "I kept tweaking the script or the outline until I got the results I needed."

Isn't that great? How do I figure out something like that? Well, here is how it's supposed to work:

1. During a CALC ALL database calculation, Essbase will calculate your dimension tagged as Accounts first.

2. Next will be the dimension you have tagged as Time.

3. Then, Essbase will calculate the remaining Dense dimensions in the order they appear in the EAS outline viewer (top to bottom).

4. Finally, Essbase will calculate the remaining Sparse dimensions again, in the order they appear in the EAS outline viewer (top to bottom).

5. If you do not have a Time dimension or an Accounts dimension, Essbase seems to calculate the Dense Dimension (top to bottom) first.

6. Then, Essbase will finish up with the Sparse dimensions (top to bottom).

Now, within each dimension, the order of calculation is supposed to work like this:

1. First, consolidations are performed as per the **Member Properties** settings (formulas and rollups) for the level zero members of all of the branches in the dimension currently being calculated.

2. The calculations continue rolling up the data to Level 1, then to Level 2, and so on, until the entire dimension has been calculated.

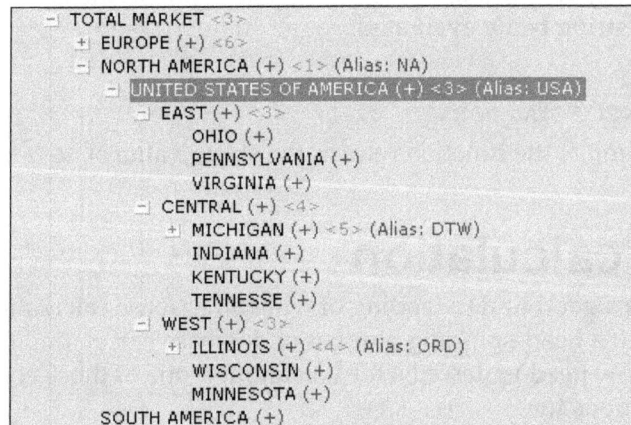

```
─ TOTAL MARKET <3>
  + EUROPE (+) <6>
  ─ NORTH AMERICA (+) <1> (Alias: NA)
    ─ UNITED STATES OF AMERICA (+) <3> (Alias: USA)
      ─ EAST (+) <3>
          OHIO (+)
          PENNSYLVANIA (+)
          VIRGINIA (+)
      ─ CENTRAL (+) <4>
        + MICHIGAN (+) <5> (Alias: DTW)
          INDIANA (+)
          KENTUCKY (+)
          TENNESSE (+)
      ─ WEST (+) <3>
        + ILLINOIS (+) <4> (Alias: ORD)
          WISCONSIN (+)
          MINNESOTA (+)
    SOUTH AMERICA (+)
```

Notice the different levels in the **TOTAL MARKET** dimension in the preceding screenshot. On expanding the **UNITED STATES OF AMERICA** market, you see the lowest or zero level members appear to be states. Then, next up are regions, and finally the United States market itself. When we talk of rolling up data, this is what we mean. The database outline is set up so the states add up into the regions and the regions add upto the market.

What's that you say? This ordering of calculation will never work for us because we need to have the **Model Year** dimension and the **Market** dimension rolled up first before we calculate the **Accounts** dimension. Plus we do not want to mess with the ordering of the dimensions in the outline! What do we do?

Well, that is why you write yourself a custom Essbase database calculation script and control the order of calculation exactly the way you want it.

Two-Pass Calc

Because of how Essbase stores the data and the order it is calculated, there is an occasional need for this cool function.

You see, sometimes, a data component in the calculation of one data value has not been calculated at the time the system needs it. This is because some component pieces of data are dependent on other data values being calculated prior to their use in another calculation. Essbase has recognized that the data may need to be calculated once to produce the correct values at one level, and then the component data is calculated again to produce the correct values at another level.

The option to set the **Two-Pass** attribute is only available on **Outline** members in the **Accounts** dimension that are tagged as **Dynamic Calc** or **Dynamic Calc and Store**.

As usual, Essbase has a good reason why this is available on Dynamic Calc and Dynamic Calc and Store members. It is because when you write your own custom database calculation script, you are in complete control of the order of calculation.

Dynamic calculation members also follow a slightly different methodology when calculating than calculation scripts and database calculations. Dynamic calculation members, in general, do not follow the dimension order of the outline as non-dynamic database members do.

> A good tip to remember when writing calcs is to pay close attention to, and code for, the correct order the data needs to be calculated in.
>
> For example, if you want to see how many total vehicles were sold in a given market and across time (months, quarters, years), you want to make sure you have rolled up sales across the **Vehicles** dimension as well as the **Market** dimension, before you rollup the Calendar Periods dimension. See how easy that is?

In the following screenshot you can see how the vehicle totals are correct because the vehicle dimension has already been calculated:

	Jan 2009	Feb 2009	Mar 2009	Qtr 1 2009
Sporty	4000	300	4000	0
Reserved	5000	7800	5000	0
2 Door Sedan	**9000**	**8100**	**9000**	**0**
Functional	750	4000	750	0
Flashy	1350	5000	1350	0
4 Door Sedan	**2100**	**9000**	**2100**	**0**
Worker	12500	750	12500	0
Player	350	1350	350	0
4X2 Pickup	**12850**	**2100**	**12850**	**0**
Muddog	300	4000	300	0
Climber	7800	5000	7800	0
4X4 Pickup	**8100**	**9000**	**8100**	**0**
Total Vehicles	**32050**	**28200**	**32050**	**0**

Now that we have the sales rolled up in the vehicle dimension, we can now calculate the Calendar Periods dimension which will roll up the values of the months to the quarters, and then to the years. Can you imagine how the numbers would look if we rolled up the Calendar Periods dimension first?

	Jan 2009	Feb 2009	Mar 2009	Qtr 1 2009
Sporty	4000	300	4000	8300
Reserved	5000	7800	5000	17800
2 Door Sedan	**9000**	**8100**	**9000**	**26100**
Functional	750	4000	750	5500
Flashy	1350	5000	1350	7700
4 Door Sedan	**2100**	**9000**	**2100**	**13200**
Worker	12500	750	12500	25750
Player	350	1350	350	2050
4X2 Pickup	**12850**	**2100**	**12850**	**27800**
Muddog	300	4000	300	4600
Climber	7800	5000	7800	20600
4X4 Pickup	**8100**	**9000**	**8100**	**25200**
Total Vehicles	**32050**	**28200**	**32050**	**92300**

Looking at these examples can also give you a good idea of why it is so important to correctly set up your dimensions with regards to the **Dense** and **Sparse** settings. You can take solace in the fact that this only applies to BSO databases and there are *no* **Dense** or **Sparse** considerations for ASO databases. ASO databases only contain `Sparse` dimensions.

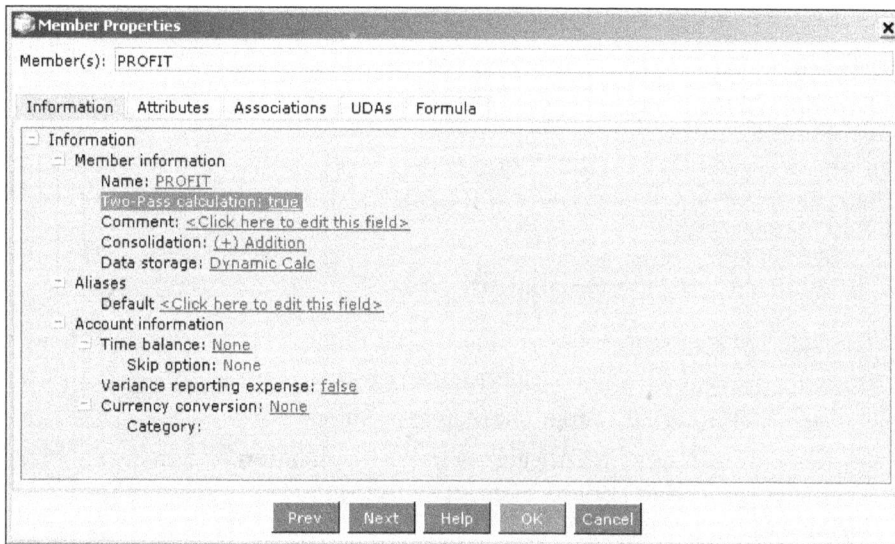

Using Substitution Variables

One of the coolest things in Essbase is the substitution variable. Substitution variables are like global variables that can be defined once and then used anywhere in Essbase you want to. The main use for substitution variables is to create a dynamic, easy to use variable which will change with time. Each variable name will have a value associated with it which can be changed (recreated), displayed or deleted.

For example, let's say you have a batch job that runs every day. In this daily job you are loading data, calculating it, and creating a unit report for the current month. Now, can you guess what should be the value of the substitution variable? You got it, it is the `Month` value from the database time dimension. You set the value of the time variable once and you can use it in the SQL statement in your data load rule file. You can also use its value in the `FIX` statement in a calc script, and in an Essbase database report script. When you code any one of these scripts, you use the name of the substitution variable in the statement in place of the actual value.

In Essbase, you can use substitution variables in the following places:

- Dimension Build or Data load Rules File (used in the SQL interface)
- Calculation Scripts
- Report Scripts
- Outline Formulas
- MDX Queries
- Partition Definitions

Substitution variables can be defined on a server level, application level, or database level. These variables can be created using EAS, MaxL scripts, or using API calls and Essbase EssCmd scripts.

Some rules while creating the variables are:

- The value of a substitution variable should not exceed 256 bytes or characters.
- The substitution variable value should not begin with the ampersand [&] character, although all other characters are allowed.
- The user should have *READ* access to the application or database which has the variable and should have ADMINISTRATOR access to read a variable at the server level.

Substitution Variables using EAS

We have talked a lot about the substitution variable, let us now see how to create a substitution variable using the EAS.

1. In EAS, scroll down to your **Essbase server** and select it.
2. Click on **Actions | Variables | Variable for** <YOUR SERVER NAME>.
3. You should see the **New Variable** screen as shown:

4. For a Server level variable you need to select All Apps from the Application drop box and **all dbs** from the database drop box.

5. For an Application Level variable you need to select your application from the **Application** drop box.

6. For a Database Level variable, you first need to select your application from the **Application** drop box and then select your database from the **Database** drop box.

7. To give a **Name** to the variable, enter **sCurMonth** and set the **Value** to **200801**. Click **OK**.

8. The substitution variable is now created on the server. In order to view the substitution variable, select your **Server**, Click on **Actions | Edit | Variables**. You will see the **Substitution Variables** screen as shown:

9. To edit a variable which is already created, on the **Substitution Variables** screen, select the value on the variable you want to change, update the **Value** and then click on the **Set** button.

10. To copy a variable, click on the **Copy** button and the **Copy Substitution Variables** screen will be displayed (shown below). Select your **Application** then **Database** from their respective drop-down boxes. Next, select the **Variable** name checkbox, check on the **Overwrite Exiting value** and click **OK**.

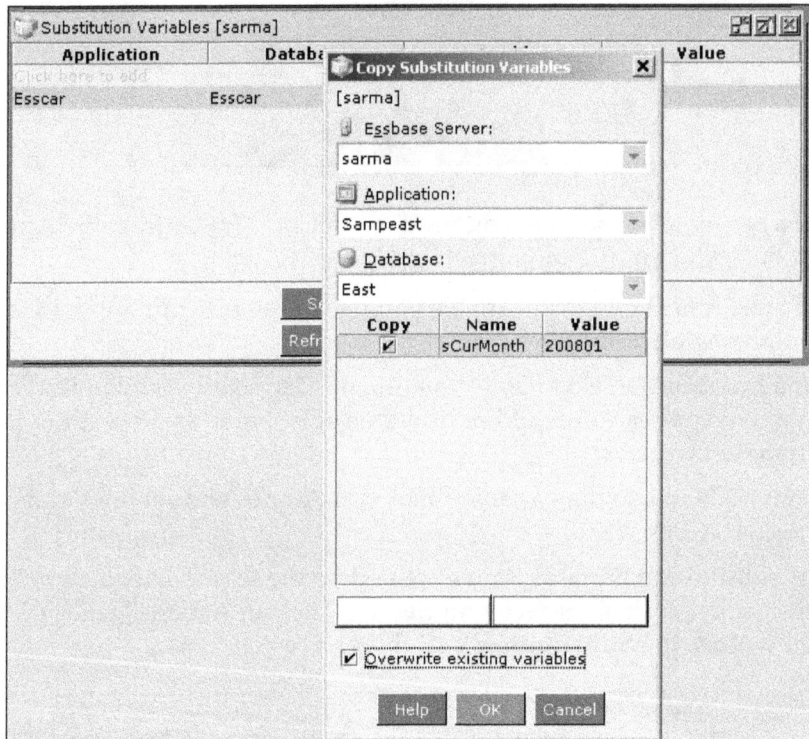

To reference a substitution variable from your calc script, you must use the substitution variable's name preceded by an ampersand (&).

Substitution Variables using MaxL

Now that you are familiar with how to create, drop, and copy a substitution variable using the EAS, let us learn how we can set up a substitution variable at Application, Database, and Server level using the MaxL statement.

Steps to Execute MaxL from the EAS Editor:

1. Within EAS, click on **File | Editor | MaxL Script Editor.**
2. The MaxL editor will be opened.
3. Variables can be defined at the Server, Database, and Application level.

Create variables at the server level

Server level variables can be created by the use of ALTER statement.

Syntax:

```
ALTER SYSTEM ADD/SET/DROP VARIABLE
```

- VARIABLE-NAME: Name of the variable
- STRING: Value for the variable

Example:

- Create Variable: `alter system add variable 'varSystem' '200801';`
- Edit Variable: `alter system set variable 'varSystem' '200802';`
- Delete Variable: `alter system drop variable 'varSystem';`

Create variables at the application level

Using the ALTER command at the application level, we can create, edit, or delete a substitution variable.

Syntax:

```
ALTER APPLICATION [APPLICATION-NAME] ADD/SET/DROP VARIABLE
```

- VARIABLE-NAME: Name of the variable
- STRING: Value for the variable

Example:

- Create Variable: `alter application ESSCAR add variable 'varAppl' 'ESSCAR1';`
- Edit Variable: `alter application ESSCAR set variable 'varAppl' 'ESSCAR';`
- Delete Variable: `alter application ESSCAR drop variable 'varAppl';`

Create variables at the database level

Using the ALTER command at the database level, we can create, edit, or delete a variable.

Syntax:

```
ALTER DATABASE APPLICATION-NAME.DATABASE-NAME ADD/SET/DROP
VARIABLE
```

- VARIABLE-NAME: Name of the variable
- STRING: Value for the variable

Example:

- Create Variable: `alter database ESSCAR.ESSCAR add variable 'varAppDB''ESSCAR1';`
- Edit Variable: `alter application ESSCAR set variable 'varAppDB''ESSCAR';`
- Delete Variable: `alter application ESSCAR drop variable 'varAppDB';`

> Using Maxl, if you want to create a variable which has a double quote in it, define it as shown below:
> ```
> alter database 'ESSCAR'.'ESSCAR' add variable 'varDQ' '"TestDQ"';
> ```

Displaying the Substitution Variable and its value

To display a substitution variable, the display MaxL statement will be used.

Syntax:

```
display variable

    all
    variable name
    on application APPLICATION-NAME
    on database DATABASE-NAME
    on system
```

all: Displays all existing substitution variables on the server.

Example:

```
display variable all;
```

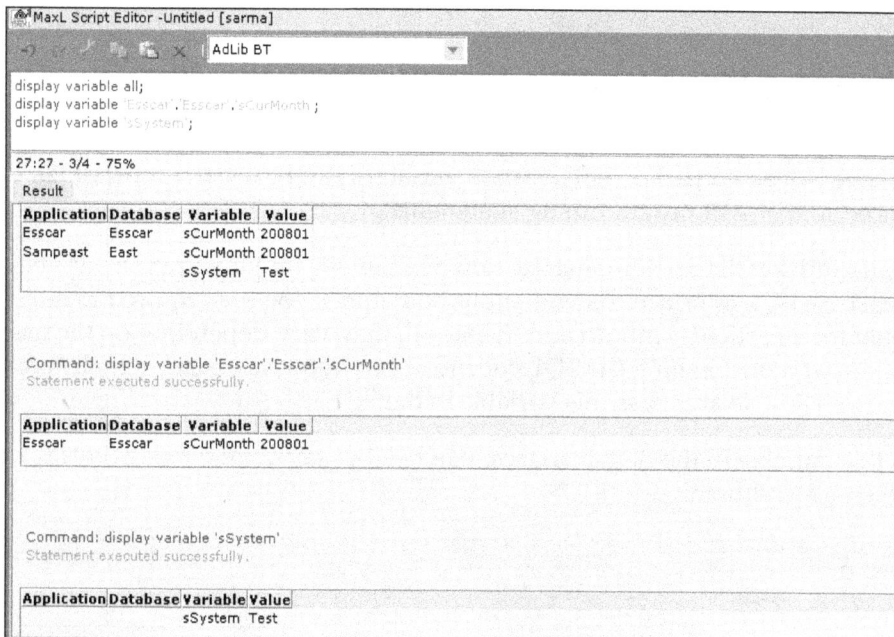

- `variable name`: Displays the variable with the Variable Name statement. For Server level Variables, you should just give the `Variable-Name` statement, for Application level variables, you should code `Application-Name.Variable-Name` and for variables declared at the database level only, you should code `Application-Name.Database-Name.Variable-Name`.

  Example:

  ```
  display variable 'VARSYSTEM';
  display variable 'ESSCAR'.'ESSCAR'.'VARAppDB';
  display variable 'ESSCAR'.'varAppl';
  ```

- `on application`: Displays all of the variables which are defined for that application.

  Example:

  ```
  display variable on application 'ESSCAR';
  ```

- on database: Displays all of the variables which are defined on the Database.

  Example:

  ```
  display variable on database 'ESSCAR'.'ESSCAR';
  ```

Displaying the Substitution Variable in the SQL editor

As we have discussed earlier, substitution variables can be used in most of the Essbase editors or API programming statements.

We would quickly like to demonstrate how we can use the substitution variable in the Essbase SQL interface. As you know, sometimes you are required to build a cube only for a particular month and the month may vary depending on the user's request. Instead of changing the SQL code for every request we can actually create a varMonth variable and pass this variable in the SQL.

To call this variable in the SQL interface, you need to say &Substitution-variable (@VarMonth) as shown:

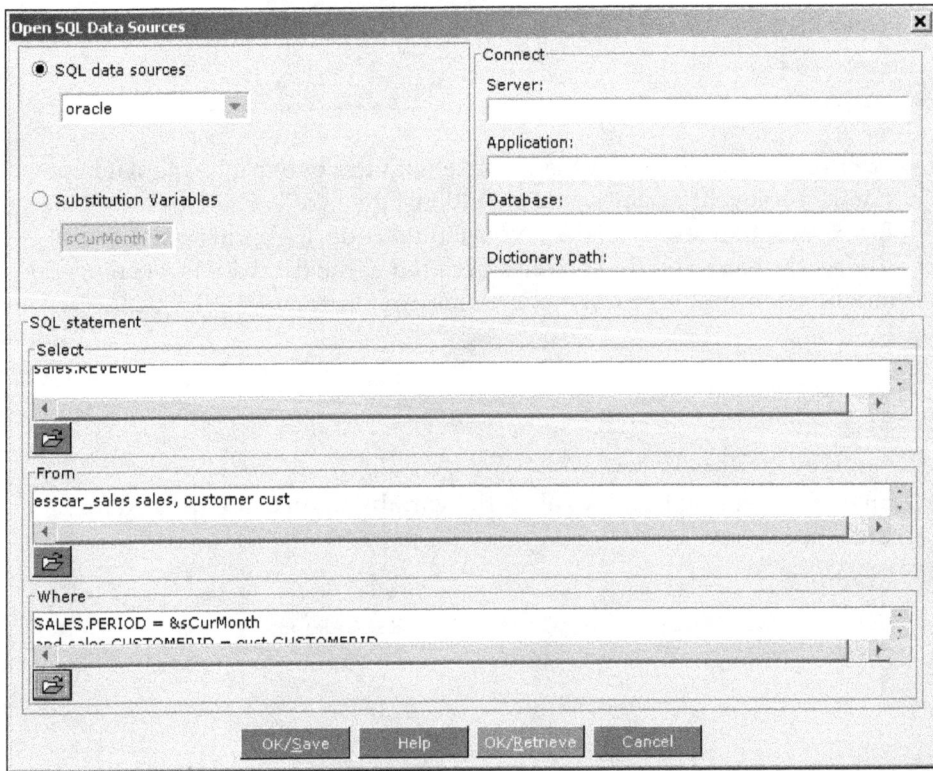

Check it out, you can use the substitution variable from the **Calculation Script Editor**, or any other script or object that executes in Essbase.

Building your first Calculation Script

The name of this section gives you the impression that we will be discussing Essbase database calculation scripts, exclusively. What you learn here is also about 95% applicable to coding database outline member formulas as well. As mentioned earlier in this chapter, aside from a few member set functions and the FIX and EXCLUDE commands, almost everything that you can code in a database calculation script can be coded in a database outline member formula.

To begin with, open the **Calculation Script Editor** in EAS by drilling down to your Essbase database like **Essbase Server | Application | Database**, then right-clicking on **Calculation Scripts** and then selecting the **Create calculation script** option. You will now see the **Calculation Script Editor** as shown earlier in this chapter.

Take a close look at the editor itself. Notice the various options that help simplify the calculation script writing process on the left side. First up is a checkbox allowing you to view the database outline using the database outline member aliases instead of the database outline member names. There is also a list box that allows you to select the outline alias table, should you have more than one created for your database outline.

The next feature is a great help when writing a calculation script. What you see under the alias table selection area is a simplified representation of the database outline. When you click on an outline member, its name is placed in the script wherever you placed the cursor.

Underneath the outline feature are two check boxes. If you check **Insert arguments**, when you click on an argument, listed near the bottom it will place the calculation argument into the calculation script wherever you place the cursor. If you check the **Enable Auto-completion**, the editor will offer you the choice of automatically completing the statements you are typing, much like a Microsoft Visual Basic editor.

Finally, at the bottom is a visual tree representation of all of the available database calculation functions and commands. If you have the **Insert arguments** checkbox checked, the editor will place the argument you click into your calculation script wherever you have placed your cursor.

Writing and saving a Calculation Script

For starters, we will begin by entering the example code we used earlier to demonstrate the FIX and ENDFIX command. We will then save the file (Essbase calculation script object).

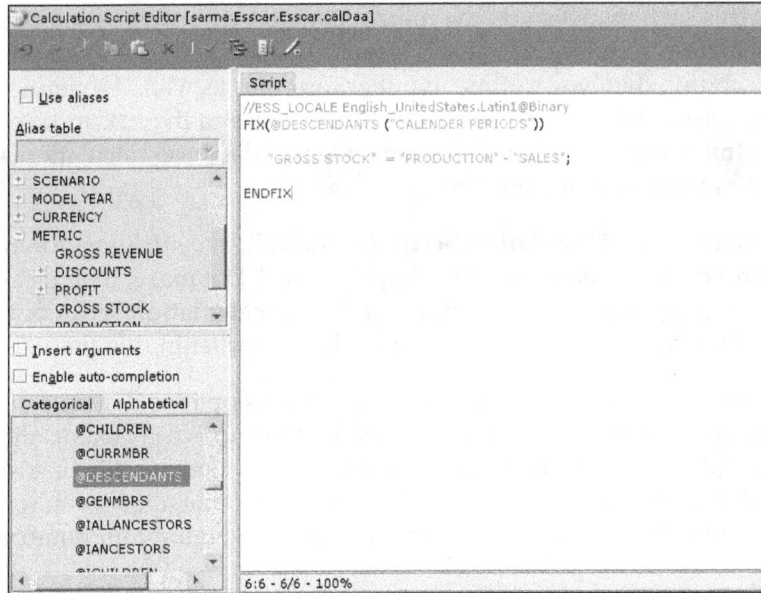

As you can see above, we have entered a basic **FIX** statement wrapped around a simple **GROSS STOCK** calculation where **GROSS STOCK = PRODUCTION – SALES**. The way this calculation script is written, Essbase will calculate a value for GROSS STOCK at descendents of the Calendar Periods level (all child members of the Calendar Periods member). This is an actual executable database calculation script which will really calculate a value for the GROSS STOCK member. It is also an excellent calculation script that is perfect for illustrative purposes.

Members not selected by the FIX command are not included in the calculation.

Although very brief and simple, it is a valid and executable Essbase database calculation script. We can now save this script to the server.

To save your database calculation script, do the following:

1. Make sure you are in EAS, then, simply click on **File | Save**.
2. A standard file save dialog box will open.

3. You are given the option of selecting a file system to save your script to or letting Essbase save the file in its own file system. EAS defaults to the Essbase file system and for this and future examples, please allow Essbase to choose the location of the file.

> For most Essbase functionality including EssCmd, MaxL, and so on, the Essbase command or function will look in the default location, which is the Application or Database folder located on your analytic server for the named calculation script. In most cases, all you need to provide is the name of the calculation script instead of the complete location (path) of the object.

4. Give your calculation script a name, but remember, no more than eight characters!
5. Click **Save** and your Essbase database calculation script is now saved to the Essbase analytic server. Congratulations!

Now, get ready as we take this script and use it as an example of the many different ways you can execute an Essbase database calculation script.

Executing your Calculation Scripts

After all that work, you do you would want to actually run your database calculation script, don't you? Ha, of course you do!

Because the database calculation is such an important part of the entire Essbase experience, Essbase provides you with many different methods for executing a database calculation script. As you will learn, there are coding options that give you great flexibility when you are automating the database calculation process. There is also generous flexibility given too which allows users to execute database calculation scripts without the time and expense of coding some elaborate process. The best part is that you, the Essbase database administrator/programmer, can make the determination as to the best method to employ for you particular situation.

Running Calculation Scripts manually using EAS

EAS should be your best friend by now. This tool is your one-stop source of Essbase administration tools. This is why it should be no surprise that after you have coded your new Essbase database calculation script using the EAS tool, you can also execute the script using the EAS tool. This ability facilitates effortless testing of database calculation scripts or easy running of maintenance calculation scripts.

There are several ways to execute a database calculation script from EAS.

For starters, if you have a script to run that you already know is ready to go without changes, all you need to do is drill-down to the calculation script name and right-click on it then select **Execute....**

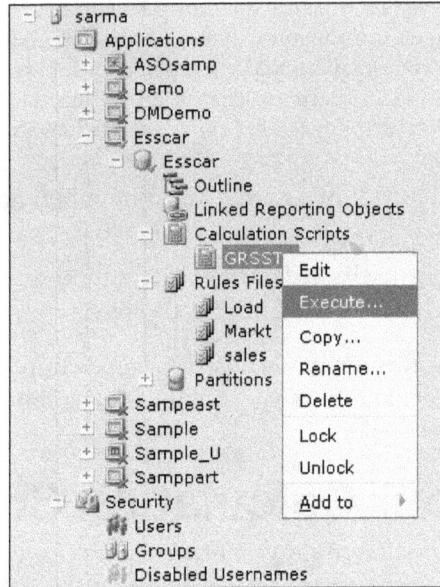

A small dialog box will open which will contain the name of the script you have selected with buttons to **Cancel**, get **Help**, or click **OK** to execute.

This dialog box will also offer you the choice to select **Execute in the background**. If you select the **Execute in the background** option, Essbase will run the calculation script in the background, thus freeing up the EAS tool and allowing you to work on something else while the calculation script is running.

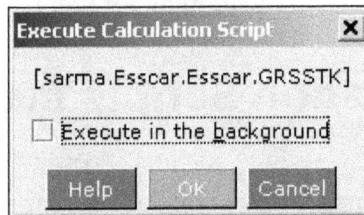

If you do not select the **Execute in the background** option, the EAS tool it will continue to display the small **Execute Calculation Script** screen while the calculation script is running and you will not be able to perform any tasks in this session of EAS until the calculation script completes.

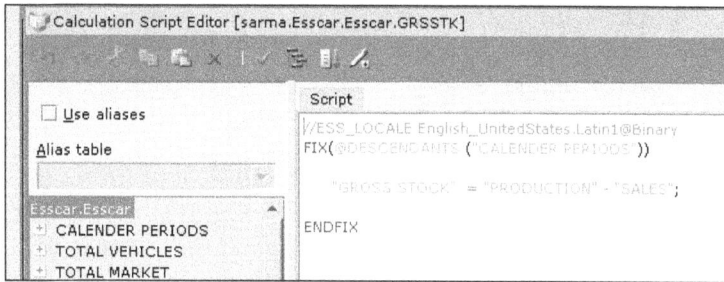

The other method of executing a database calculation script through the EAS tool is when you have the script itself opened in the **Calculation Script Editor** (shown above). By opening the database calculation script in the editor you activate three more ways to execute an Essbase database calculation script:

1. Click on the menu pick, **Options | Execute Script**.
2. Click on the button on the EAS toolbar that has the small downward pointing arrow.
3. Press the *F5* function key on your keyboard.

All three of these options perform the exact same task of executing the active database calculation script currently opened in the **Calculation Script Editor** of your EAS tool.

Something you must consider is when a calculation script is running against a database, it is a good idea to refrain from attempting to perform database maintenance or update tasks to the database itself. For example, if you make changes to the outline and attempt to save the outline while a calc script is running, the outline save will fail due to portions of the database being locked by the calculation process.

Running a Calculation Script using an Essbase Command Script (EssCmd)

As discussed in previous chapters, Essbase offers you several coding options that you can use to automate many Essbase tasks and functions. The Essbase Command Script, or EssCmd, is one of these options.

The EssCmd is an ASCII text file that contains Essbase-specific commands. The EssCmd database command script, like all Essbase objects, must be named using no more than eight characters. The extension used is `.scr`.

The EAS tool does not provide an official editor for writing EssCmd scripts so in Windows for example, you would use any text editor such as Notepad.

We discuss in-depth task automation for your Essbase system in future chapters. Here, we will show what a basic EssCmd script should look like to execute your Gross Stock database calculation script.

What the EssCmd script looks like

The basic coding of an Essbase Command Script (EssCmd) is shown below. We would enter the code for the EssCmd as shown and then save it as `GrsStk.scr` on the Essbase analytic server in the Application or Database folder:

```
OUTPUT 1 "c:\Esscmd.log";
LOGIN "EssServerID" "EssID" "EssPass" "ESSCAR" "ESSCAR";
RUNCALC 2 GRSSTK;
OUTPUT 3;
LOGOUT;
EXIT;
```

We will cover in-depth Essbase command scripts and how to write and use them in a future chapter. In the meantime, for more information, refer to the online technical reference included with your EAS software.

- The first command statement you see is the OUTPUT statement. This statement, followed by the number 1 and a path and filename, tells Essbase to begin logging the execution of this script and where to put the log.

- Next, the LOGIN statement, followed by a space separated list, will remotely connect to the Essbase server. The list includes the server name or IP Address, the Essbase ID, the password for the Essbase ID, the application name you want to connect to, and the Essbase database name.

- Here is the command we are now using! The RUNCALC command statement is followed by a number and the calculation script name. In this case, the number 2 tells Essbase that the calculation script is an analytic server stored Essbase object. The calc type is followed by the calculation script name.

- Next up is the OUTPUT statement again. This time, we have coded a 3 after the command which tells Essbase to turn off the logging output.

- Finally, we code the LOGOUT and EXIT commands. The LOGOUT statement disconnects the script from Essbase and the EXIT command exits the script from the Essbase session.

Well, now that you know how to code a basic Essbase Command Script, we will describe the various methods for executing it. They are as follows:

1. **EssCmd Drag and Drop**: Your client software should have come with a file called `Esscmd.exe`. If you have this file, it will be located wherever your Essbase client software was installed. On a Windows machine, the path is typically `C:\Hyperion\AnalyticServices\bin`. All you need to do is create a desktop shortcut to this executable file, then drag any `EssCmd.scr` file onto the shortcut and the script will execute. If you do not have the `EssCmd.exe` file on your machine, you can always get it from the `*\Essbase\Bin` folder on your Essbase analytic server.

2. **DOS Command Line**: All you need to do is navigate to the DOS command prompt from your desktop. Then, type in a typical command line action at the command prompt. This will tell Windows to run the `EssCmd.exe` with the Gross Stock EssCmd script:

   ```
   "esscmd.exe  EssCmd.scr"
   ```

3. **Shell Command in Code**: You can easily use the Shell function in code to run your EssCmd Essbase Command Scripts. The Shell function can be used in languages like Microsoft Visual Basic or Microsoft Visual Basic for Applications to name a few:

   ```
   Shell "esscmd.exe  EssCmd.scr", vbNormalFocus
   ```

> If you register the `EssCmd.exe` on your PC, like you would register any DLL using the `regsvr32` function, you will be able to call the `EssCmd.exe` in a command line or shell command without having to include the entire path in the command.
>
> This is particularly useful to know because the `EssCmd.exe` itself only accepts paths with a length of upto 128 characters.

Running a Calculation Script using a MaxL Script

Here we have another command scripting facility for you to use to automate functionality in Essbase. The MaxL command script operates in much the same way as the EssCmd script, although MaxL is supposed to be a much easier and more efficient scripting language.

While the EssCmd scripting language has been around since the earliest versions of Essbase, the MaxL scripting language was introduced in Essbase version 7.x.

Running a calculation script using MaxL can be accomplished in three different ways. The first method is through the EAS tool, from the **MaxL Script Editor**. The second method is from the DOS command prompt, or command line execution. The third method is to use the Shell command from a coding language like Microsoft Visual Basic or Microsoft Visual Basic for Applications.

While we will explain how to use MaxL in-depth in a later chapter, we will give you a basic explanation here. The code for a basic MaxL command script to run a calculation looks like the following:

```
login 'UserID' 'Password' on 'ServerName';
execute calculation 'ESSCAR'.'ESSCAR'.'GRSSTK';
```

This code, when run from MaxL, will login to the Essbase server and then execute the GRSSTK.csc against the ESSCAR application/ESSCAR database.

To create a MaxL script file object, simply open the **MaxL Script Editor** in the EAS tool by clicking the **EDITORS** menu pick, then clicking on **MaxL Script Editor**. The **MaxL Script Editor** is shown as follows:

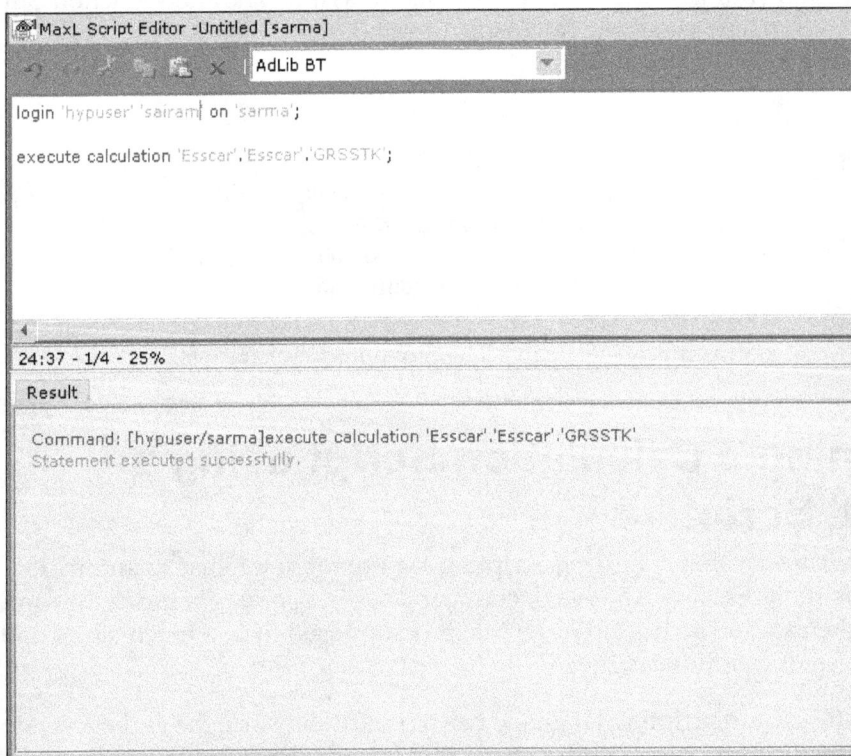

After you enter the appropriate commands to execute your database calculation script, you can save the MaxL script by clicking **File | Save** and giving a name to your file object. Just like with the **Calculation Script Editor**, the default location the EAS saves your MaxL file to is the **Analytic Server | Application | Database** folder. Consequently, this is where the MaxL function will look for the file when you call it.

The MaxL command script file object is saved with an .mxl extension.

Now that you know how to code a basic MaxL Command Script, we will describe the various methods for executing it:

- **Through the EAS Tool**: Just like executing a calculation script from the EAS tool, you have virtually identical options for executing a MaxL script through the EAS tool when the MaxL script editor is open.

    i) Click the menu pick **MAXL** and then click **Execute** to run the MaxL script currently open in the editor.

    ii) Click on the button on the EAS toolbar that has the small downward pointing arrow.

    iii) Press the *F5* function key on your keyboard.

- **DOS Command Line**: All you need to do is navigate to the DOS command prompt from your desktop. The next step is to type in a typical command line action at the command prompt. This will tell windows to run the essmsh.exe with the Gross Stock MaxL script:

    ```
    "essmsh.exe  MaxL.mxl"
    ```

- **Shell Command in Code**: You can easily use the Shell function in code to run your EssCmd. The Shell function can be used in languages like Microsoft Visual Basic or Microsoft Visual Basic for Applications to name a few.

    ```
    Shell "essmsh.exe  MaxL.mxl", vbNormalFocus
    ```

> If you register the essmsh.exe on your PC, like you would register any DLL using the regsvr32 function, you will be able to call the essmsh.exe in a command line or shell command without having to include the entire path in the command.
>
> This is particularly useful to know because the essmsh.exe itself only accepts paths with a length of upto 128 characters.

Running a Calculation Script using the Essbase API

The Essbase API is a comprehensive set of tools that allow you, the Essbase programmer/database administrator, to automate many Essbase tasks and functions through code in several popular languages.

For the sake of consistency, our examples in this book will mainly focus on the use of Microsoft Visual Basic, or COM+, in a Microsoft Windows environment. The following is an example of the code required to execute the GRSSTK.csc database calculation script using a call to the Essbase API from Microsoft Visual Basic.

In your program, your typical Essbase calculation call would be in a sub-routine like the following:

```
Declare Function EsbCalc Lib "ESBAPIN" (ByVal hCtx As Long, ByVal
Calculate As Integer, ByVal Script As String) As Long
Sub ESB_Calc ()
    Dim sts As Long 'Essbase process return code
    Dim Script As String 'Variable to hold calc script
    Dim Calculate As Integer '1 = Yes, 0 = No
    Dim ProcState As ESB_PROCSTATE_T ' Test if calc still running
    Script = "CALC ALL;" 'Calculation script passed as a string up to
                        '64 KB in length
    Calculate = ESB_YES 'Set API calc function to Yes meaning to
                        'Execute the calc script
    sts = EsbCalc (hCtx, Calculate, Script) 'Actual call to the
                                            'calculation function
    sts = EsbGetProcessState (hCtx, ProcState) 'Test the process
                                                'state
    Do Until ProcState.State = ESB_STATE_DONE
    sts = EsbGetProcessState (hCtx, ProcState)
    Loop 'Perform this loop until the calc script has completed
End Sub
```

What you see here is a basic VB sub-routine. We will explain it using the Essbase API in greater detail later in this book, but to demonstrate the many ways to execute a database calculation script it is necessary to go over this briefly:

- You will notice how the first task performed is to declare the API function in the program.

- Next, the variables are dimensioned.

- Set the **Script** variable to contain the actual calculation script. To simplify matters, you can use the program to open your existing calculation script and read it into the **Script** variable. A maximum length of 64KB is allowed.

- Set the **Calculate** variable to **Yes,** which for this command means to actually calculate the data. Setting this variable to **No** would have Essbase validate the calc script instead.

- Execute the **EsbCalc** function passing it the **hCtx** variable (context variable explained later), the **Calculate** variable, and the **Script** variable. At the same time placing the Essbase process return code into the **sts** variable.

- Finally, perform a loop that checks the state of the process until the calculation script process has completed. This loop will hold up further program executions until the calculation script has completed. The benefit of this is that another routine in your program will not inadvertently grab data that has not been calculated yet.

Running a Calculation Script from Microsoft Excel

Yes, after all that, there are still a couple of ways to execute a calculation script against your Essbase database!

Of course you would have had to assume that since Microsoft Excel is the natural front end for an Essbase database, that there would be a way to fire off a calculation script from it. Well, honestly, there are a couple ways you can do it.

Running a Calculation Script through the Essbase Add-In

When you install the Essbase Add-In for Microsoft Excel on your PC you get a new menu pick on the standard menu bar called **Essbase** (you knew this already).

Provided your ID has Calculate access to the database you login to all you need to do from Microsoft Excel is click on **Essbase | Calculation....**

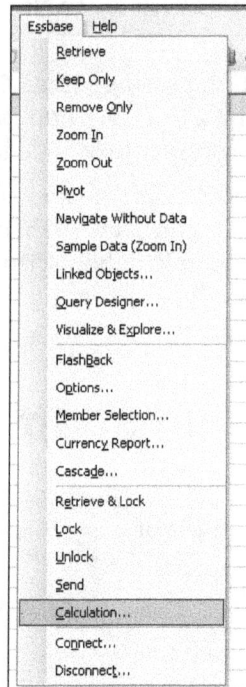

Once you click on the **Calculation...** option from the Essbase menu, you will see the following screen:

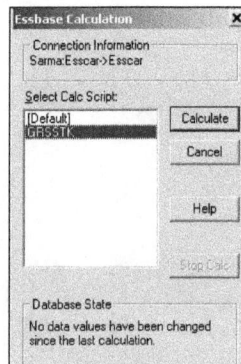

On this screen, you are presented with a list of database calculation scripts that your ID has access to run. You are also presented with buttons for the options to **Calculate**, **Cancel**, and the option to access **Help**. It should be pretty obvious to you, what each of these buttons will do when clicked!

Finally, there is a **Stop** button on this screen. While we never recommend stopping a database calculation script, doing so by letting Essbase determine when it is safe, is at least the best way. Keep in mind that Essbase will interrupt the calculation script when it deems it is safe and this could leave your data partially calculated. Also, Essbase has what is known as the **point of no return** where it will decide to let the process complete rather than interrupt it.

Running a Calculation Script using Microsoft Excel VBA

This example is only for Microsoft Excel **Visual Basic for Applications (VBA)**. Yes, it's true, you can code functionality in VBA almost exactly how it would be done in Microsoft **Visual Basic (VB)**, and if that is what you want to do, then see the VB example.

The reason we get excited about this is because Essbase provides a full library of functions for Microsoft Excel's VBA, including specific macro functions that automate all of the menu choices contained in the Essbase Add-In for Microsoft Excel.

This is a nice feature is because the macros can quickly and easily be coded to allow for **RAD (Rapid Application Development)** on your Essbase/Microsoft Excel project.

To begin with, much like declaring an API function in VB, you will need to declare the macro function using the example below. This declaration statement can be anywhere in your project:

```
Declare Function EssVCalculate Lib "essexcln.xll" (ByVal SheetName
    As Variant, ByVal calcScript As Variant, ByVal synchronous As
    Variant) As Long
```

The actual command you code in your sub-routine looks like the following statement:

```
Application.Run macro:=EssVCalculate(SheetName, calcScript,
synchronous)
```

This command can be run at any time from your VBA program. The following parameters are used by passing them to the function:

- **SheetName**: This is supposed to be the Microsoft Excel workbook worksheet that was active at the time the `EssVCalculate` command was executed. Essbase does not require the sheet name for this function, so you can simply enter the **vbEmpty** verb.

- **calcScript**: This variable is the name of the database calculation script you wish to run. If there is a drawback to using this function, it is that the calculation script must reside in the default Application | Database folder location on the analytic server. To run the default database calculation script, assign the value of **[Default]** to the **calcScript** variable.

- **synchronous**: This tells Microsoft Excel whether to wait for the calculation script to finish or not, before executing the next line of code in your program. It is always a good idea to wait for the calc to complete, if you may need the calculated data elsewhere in the program. Running a calc with **synchronous = True** means the program will wait for the calc script to complete before it resumes execution.

Whew! Knowing that the Essbase database calculation script (calc) is such an integral part of the Essbase machine, are you surprised there are so many ways to execute it?

We didn't think so!

Summary

Yes, there was a lot to digest in this chapter! Essbase database calculations are very complex and powerful tools. It takes time and experience to really get good at writing a database calculation script and you may never meet someone who has the nerve to introduce himself as an Essbase database calculation expert.

Like anything else, you now have a good foundation to build on. You know the differences between member formulas and calc script functionality. You've learned about the various ways you can accomplish a database calculation. You've also been provided with some insights into the calc topic that can only be gotten from someone who has laughed and cried over Essbase database calculations.

So go ahead and start building. Try to remember, at first, baby steps are good!

Up next, we cover actually using your Essbase database or cube for the purpose which it was intended for; data analysis and reporting. What are you waiting for?!

6

Using your Essbase Cube

Wow, after that last chapter on database calculation scripts, who could blame you if you wanted to take a break and try to fully digest just what it is that you learned back there!

Do you ever get the feeling that the information in this book is coming at you like a snowball rolling down a hill, with every chapter building onto the previous chapter, and your Essbase knowledge growing ever larger? Well, you're right! That is exactly what it is like.

After your little rest and once you realize that you are now proficient in writing and executing Essbase database calculation scripts, it's time to learn how to actually use your Essbase cube to present your data for analysis, report your data, and extract your data for export to downstream users and systems.

Using your Essbase database

So, here you have this nice Essbase database that you know how to load with data. You also know several different ways to calculate the data in the database once it has been loaded.

Okay, what do you do with your Essbase database now? You can't cook dinner on it, can you? Maybe you can cook dinner on your Essbase database after all. It does have plenty of delicious ingredients. We're pretty sure though, that that's not what you really want to do with it.

There are lots of ways to use your Essbase database and the data contained in it. When we talk about using your Essbase database, we are talking about the real life uses for which it was intended. The Essbase database or cube, itself is just the vehicle used to collect, organize, and deliver the actual data. The data is the cargo in the cube that you've taken all this time upto now to handle properly.

How do you use your data in the real world

In the real world, you will have many different people using your Essbase database and its accompanying data for many different reasons or purposes. Whether the users of the database and its data are big shot executives, data analysts, or simply an IT support person charged with ensuring a consistent and reliable feed of data to a downstream system, they all require a smooth running system that delivers the data as needed.

Ad hoc data

As the name implies, ad hoc data is your on the fly retrieval and interpretation of the data in your Essbase database. This type of data usage is one of Essbase's biggest strengths. As we will explain in greater detail in Chapter 7, the Essbase Add-in for Microsoft Excel can and will be one of your most useful and used Essbase tools.

By simply starting the Microsoft Excel program on your PC, with the Essbase add-in installed, you have the ability to quickly and easily create useful and informative spreadsheets. With a little more experience, there is no reason why you wouldn't be able to also create very professional looking reports quickly and easily.

No matter the Essbase add-in skill level, you can be assured that at any given time someone, somewhere, may need to quickly pull some data from your Essbase cube. This simply cannot be done with traditional databases.

Canned reporting

Canned reports are used with a little more forethought than ad hoc reports are however, they can be pulled anytime the user decides they need to be refreshed.

When we talk of canned reports, we mean pre-created reports or system generated report templates, usually in Microsoft Excel worksheet format, that the user can refresh with new data whenever they see fit.

One thing you'll never get tired of seeing in this book is the fact that a system created with Oracle Essbase and Microsoft Excel is an amazingly easy to use and equally easy to develop system. You can use the superb programming abilities already included in Microsoft Excel VBA to develop easy to use, yet powerful, reporting functionality. One method of this is the canned reports method. Another method is the Essbase report script.

The Essbase report script is a script that is generated as a by-product of the Essbase Query Designer which you access through the Essbase add-in. This script can be pasted into a Microsoft Excel worksheet and retrieved to populate the data into a respectable looking report.

Another method is the reporting of your data using the MDX query language that has been included with Oracle Essbase since version 7.x. MDX queries can be written in a similar way to an SQL query and executed in batch or through the EAS MDX query editor screens.

Export data

What always happens when you have a good system with good data, which is in demand by other departments in your company? Why, it seems as though everybody has to get some of it loaded into their own system, that's what happens.

If there is anything that could be remotely described as a drawback to an Essbase system, it would be the data exporting functionality. Where traditional RDBMS systems allow the selection of data for export to meet almost limitless criteria, the Essbase method is a bit less robust.

First of all, instead of an interfacing system establishing a connection with your database and fetching data into something like a recordset or a cursor, with Essbase, you are limited to using an Essbase report script and extracting the required data into a flat file. The flat file can then be sent to the downstream system so they can load it into their tables as needed. Unfortunately, the selection arguments available when building an Essbase report script are somewhat limited. We'll get more into report scripts in a moment!

Forecast analysts

The forecast analyst is one person who takes full advantage of Essbase's unique data calculating abilities. For starters, a forecast analyst wants to see what the data looks like out into the future. When we say "future" we mean future periods based on what is most commonly tagged as the **Time** dimension in the database outline.

The forecast analyst has data which, on a period to period basis, is dependent on the previous period's numbers. Consider that a Gross Stock number for the current month is the result of the prior month's Gross Stock number, plus the current month's production (units produced), less the current month's sales (units sold). If we would like to know the resulting Gross Stock numbers for the next six months, all we need to do is update the forecasted sales numbers and the forecasted production numbers in the database, run a small database calculation script, and we now have forecasted Gross Stock numbers.

		MYR 2009	US Market				
		July 2009	August 2009	September 2009	October 2009	November 2009	December 2009
4 Door Sedan	Sales	2850	1800	2275	3250	3800	3200
	Production	3000	3500	3200	3500	3200	3000
	Gross Stock	1650	3350	4275	4525	3925	3725

This type of data analysis can be performed over and over with the results repeatedly retrieved into the same Microsoft Excel worksheet until the forecast analyst is satisfied with the resulting data.

		MYR 2009	US Market					
		July 2009	August 2009	September 2009	October 2009	November 2009	December 2009
4 Door Sedan	Sales	2850	1700	2275	3250	3800	3200
	Production	3000	3500	3200	3500	3200	3000
	Gross Stock	1650	3450	4375	4625	4025	3825

In the preceding screenshot, notice how changing just one **Sales** value has affected all of the future **Gross Stock** values. All you had to do was send back the new value, calculate your data, and then retrieve into your worksheet. You literally get your results immediately. Just try that with a typical relational database.

> Better still, you could add a member formula to the **Gross Stock** member and tag it as a **Dynamic Calc** member. Then all you would need to do is send the data back and retrieve the new values.

Planning analysts

Planning analysts perform many of the same data analysis tasks as forecasting analysts, but there are some noticeable differences.

Because of Essbase's dynamic data calculating abilities, Essbase is the perfect tool for planning analysts who not only need to look at forecasted data like a forecast analyst, but also need to look at several versions of forecasted data and the variances between them. With a **Scenario** dimension in your Essbase database outline, you can enter different forecast data for the same time periods at the same time. You can then calculate the data and almost immediately look at several different strategies for your business' planning activity.

			MYR 2009	US Market					
			July 2009	August 2009	September 2009	October 2009	November 2009	December 2009
4 Door Sedan	Scenario 1	Sales	2850	1700	2275	3250	3800	3200
		Production	3000	3500	3200	3500	3200	3000
		Gross Stock	1650	3450	4375	4625	4025	3825
	Scenario 2	Sales	4200	1700	2275	3250	3800	3200
		Production	3000	3500	3200	3500	3200	3000
		Gross Stock	300	2100	3025	3275	2675	2475
	Scenario 3	Sales	2850	1700	2275	3250	3800	3200
		Production	2800	3500	3200	3500	3200	3000
		Gross Stock	1450	3250	4175	4425	3825	3625

How is that for results? As you can see in the previous figure, a planning analyst can easily see three or more different scenarios that represent the same market conditions, yet allow differing factors to display long term effects.

Budget analysts

Yes, most of these different analysts seem like they perform somewhat similar tasks. That is true for the most part and budget analysts are not very different from the others, at least in terms of procedure.

An Essbase database is ideal for a budget analyst, as it is for most any type of data analyst. Essbase's ability to dynamically calculate large amounts of data is a key factor in the successful budget analyst's job to provide the company's decision makers with powerful, accurate data. It is this data that helps them make intelligent business decisions.

The primary job of the budget analyst is to combine the data created by the planning and forecast analysts with actual historical data to establish baseline data. This baseline data will be used to gauge the company's performance going forward against the actual data as it occurs and the forecasted data as planned.

		MYR 2009		US Market			
		January 2009	February 2009	March 2009	April 2009	May 2009	June 2009
4 Door Sedan	Current Scenario	7250	9650	12100	14000	14750	13100
	Budget Scenario	19850	22750	23500	21000	21100	17100
	Variance to Budget	(12600)	(13100)	(11400)	(7000)	(6350)	(4000)
2 Door Sedan	Current Scenario	7875	7375	10950	9850	8575	4100
	Budget Scenario	13100	9050	7050	5075	3100	1910
	Variance to Budget	(5225)	(1675)	3900	4775	5475	2190

Good, accurate data can have an effect on the very course a company travels. By using the wide assortment of analytical calculation commands in conjunction with the unparalleled flexibility of the Essbase database outline, a good budget analyst can create reports that show:

- How the company actually performed compared to the long range budget forecast
- How the company continues to perform compared to the monthly revised forecast and the long term budget forecast
- How the company needs to perform to meet its goals and objectives

Hey, they don't call it business intelligence for nothing!

Financial analysts

Okay, these are the guys you need to watch out for. What the financial analyst does is take in everything all of the other analysts do and crunch it into money numbers. It seems as though a financial analyst in a company typically carries a lot of weight. Well, lucky for you and for your programming in Essbase.

Once again, Essbase comes through for you and your customer. Essbase provides a full complement of financial calculation functions which will satisfy the most discriminating number cruncher. From such computations as compound interest, discounts, and growth, you can be sure that the financial picture of your company is in good hands.

The real target users of your Essbase data

As an IT person you may ask, "Why do I need to know who the Essbase data user is?" Well, because of the usefulness and versatility of your Essbase data to the decision makers in the company, the real end-user of your Essbase data is usually an executive or some other big shot. In fact, you may not even know it, but the data in a typical Essbase database system usually shows up in reports that are used at the highest levels of the company.

Your job is to make these people happy. Thankfully, Essbase makes your job easy in so many ways.

Ways to extract your Essbase data

There are many different ways to extract data from an Essbase database. We have described several of them at different times in this book, depending on the topic being covered. For the sake of organization, we will list the various methods of extracting data from your Essbase database here:

- **Essbase Add-in for Microsoft Excel:** It seems like we can't say enough about this particular tool. Designed to work seamlessly with the world's most popular spreadsheet program, the Essbase add-in is the tool of choice of data analysts everywhere. Yes, you can pull data out of your Essbase database with the add-in and load up an Excel worksheet. Even though Microsoft Excel has a limit of 65,536 rows through the 2003 version and many more rows available in Microsoft Excel 2007, it seems that Essbase can have a hard time handling spreadsheets that contain more than 1,000 rows. Performance rapidly degrades and you can even experience timeouts. We highly recommend that you pay attention to this and at the first signs of trouble with large spreadsheets, you split them into smaller subset spreadsheets.

- **Oracle Smart View:** This tool is separate from the Essbase add-in and in fact, must be purchased as a separate component to be used with the Essbase suite of applications. As will be discussed at great length in the *Appendix*, Smart View is a dynamic data retrieval tool that allows the user to pull data directly from an Essbase database into any of the Microsoft Office components. This allows for the creation of Microsoft PowerPoint presentations that never need data updating as fresh data can be retrieved in real time into the slides. The same holds true for Microsoft Outlook emails and Microsoft Word documents. Oh yes, and it also works with Microsoft Excel.

- **Essbase Query Designer:** This tool is a part of the Essbase add-in and is a menu pick from the Essbase menu in Microsoft Excel. The Essbase Query Designer tool allows you to create simple to complex Essbase queries. This is accomplished through the use of an easy to use visual query wizard. The saved query can be opened and retrieved in Microsoft Excel to return your data.

- **Essbase Report Script:** The Essbase report script will be discussed in great detail in the next section. An Essbase report script can be created from scratch as an ASCII text file or conveniently, a report script can be created by Essbase, as a by-product of the Query Designer function. Essbase report scripts can be executed within a Microsoft Excel worksheet, Essbase command script or MaxL script, or from an Essbase API call.

- **Essbase MDX Query Language:** Essbase MDX can be easily described as a structured query language for multidimensional databases. MDX queries for the most part use simple and easy to understand statements to extract data from your Essbase database. MDX queries can be executed in much the same manner as Essbase report scripts or MaxL scripts.

All of the above mentioned methods are used to report or extract the data that is in your Essbase database or cube. Some of the above mentioned tools go beyond the scope of the Microsoft Excel add-in and can be used by the other Microsoft Office products as well like Oracle Smart View. The Essbase add-in is the most complete tool in terms of functionality and ease of use. Included with the Essbase Add-in for Microsoft Excel is the **Essbase Query Designer (EQD)**, which allows you to visually design custom reports from Essbase. The downside to the EQD is that the reports are only usable in Microsoft Excel.

The Essbase report script can be used to run reports from a batch program and automatically send a morning report to key persons. While the formatting can be orderly, the report is still an ASCII based report without the pretty colors or graphs.

And then there's MDX, which is a nice option, but the scripts do tend to require a bit of maintenance. However, the resultant output is in a very usable format.

The Essbase Report Script

Just like other Essbase file objects, Essbase database report scripts are actually ASCII text file objects with an extension of `.rep`. As with other similar Essbase file objects, they must also follow the same naming convention of upto 8 characters, and the directory path must not contain any spaces.

An Essbase report script may be stored anywhere in the file system, but is considered to be in its default location when saved into the database folder on the analytic server, much the same as a database calculation script. The benefit of storing the report script file objects in their default location comes when you are coding an API or EssCmd function, you only need to mention the name of the report script and not the fully qualified path to that particular object.

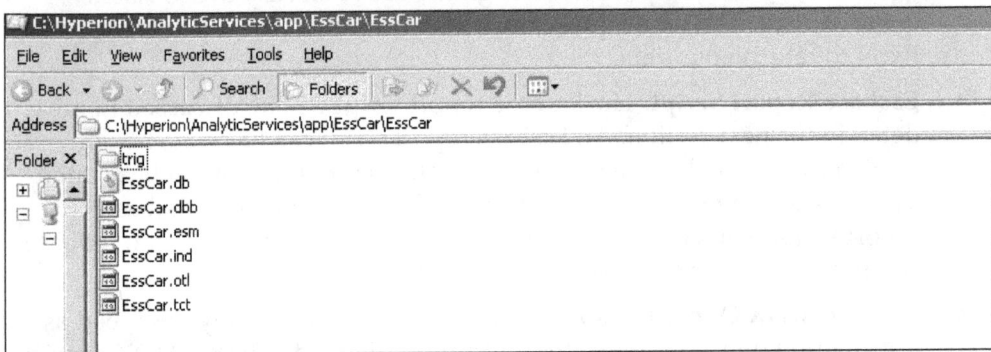

Okay, so what exactly is an Essbase report script? Well, an Essbase report script is an ASCII text file that contains commands or instructions for data retrieval, formatting, and output that Essbase uses to extract data from an Essbase cube into either a formatted report or an ASCII text flat file that can be sent to downstream systems as a data feed.

While report scripts are certainly capable of creating reports, hence the name, an Essbase report script is more than likely used to extract data into flat files. Most Essbase users seem to prefer reports created in Microsoft Excel as opposed to free standing plain paper reports.

> Although most report scripts are created to extract data from a database for export to other systems, a properly written Essbase report script can be pasted into a blank Microsoft Excel worksheet and then retrieved. Essbase will interpret the commands and dump the data into the worksheet.

How to create an Essbase Report Script

There are three ways to create an Essbase report script. Because a report script is really an ASCII text file with a .rep extension, the first way to create one would be to open a new text file in any text editor and begin typing the report script commands. We really do not recommend this method as you would have to be highly skilled in the Essbase report script area. A text editor like Notepad that is included with Windows, is best suited for editing an already existing report script.

To access a complete listing of all available Report Writer commands, get to your EAS screen and click **Help | Information Map | Technical Reference | Report Writer Commands**. Here you will find an overview as well as each report writer command function explained with coding examples. This information is included with your EAS installation.

The second way to create an Essbase report script is to use the Essbase report script editor supplied with the EAS. The report script editor can be accessed in much the same way as accessing the calculation script editor.

You should know this drill by now. In EAS, drill-down to the database for which you wish to create an Essbase report script.

Double-click on the database name to expand the selections and right-click on the **report scripts** heading. The set of options displayed will offer you the choice of editing an existing report script or creating a new one. Selecting either choice will open the Essbase report script editor.

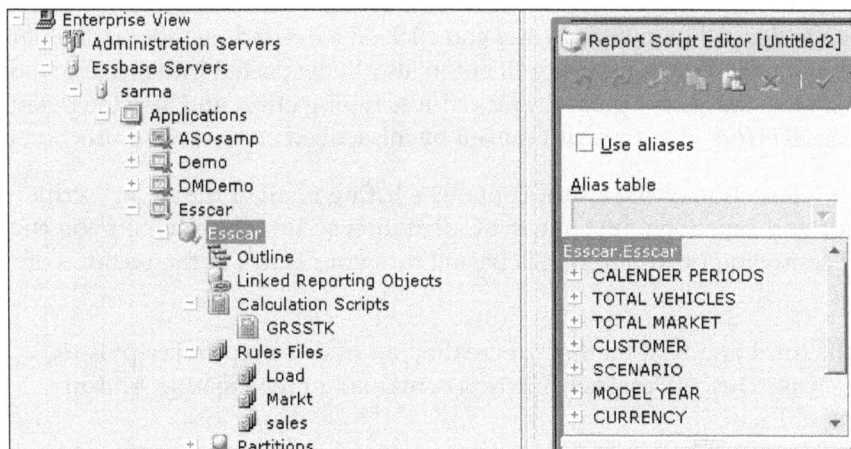

The use of the built-in **Report Script Editor** is exactly like the **Calculation Script Editor** described in detail in Chapter 5. As shown in the following screenshot, the **Report Script Editor** window is divided into three basic sections:

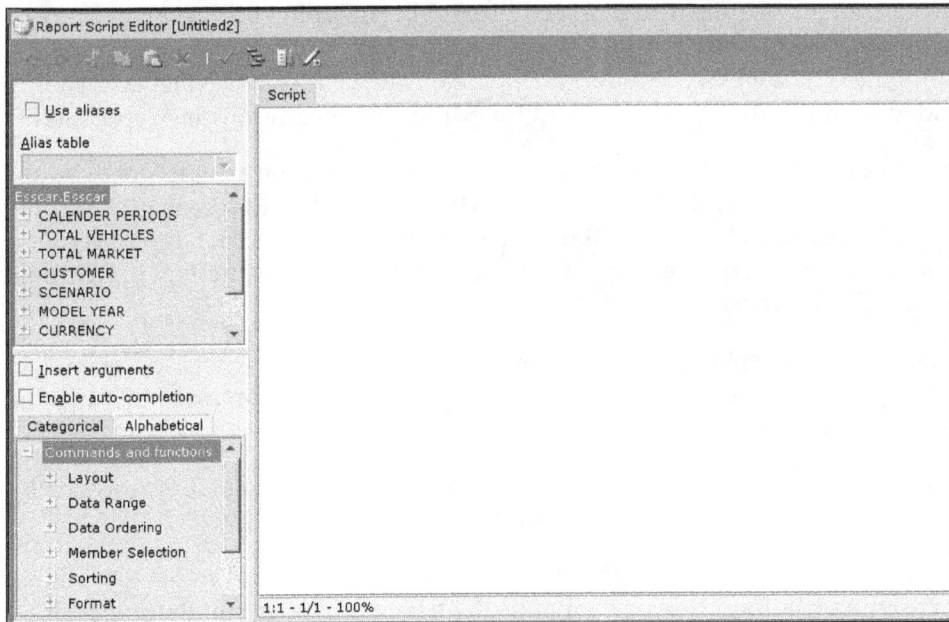

Just like the **Calculation Script Editor**, the upper left section of the **Report Script Editor** contains a smaller version of the outline editor. This section allows you to drill-down to desired members. When you click on a desired member in the outline representation, the member name will automatically be pasted into the script editor where you have the cursor placed. This reduces typing effort and also the potential for typographical errors in your script caused by misspelled command or function names.

The lower left section of the editor contains a listing of all of the report script commands and functions. Just like the Calculation script editor, when you click a desired command or function, it is pasted into your script at the position of the cursor.

Finally, the third and best method of creating an Essbase report script is to use the Essbase Query Designer function contained in the Essbase Add-in for Microsoft Excel.

We actually recommend this as the primary method of report script creation while keeping the other two methods for editing existing scripts.

We will discuss the Essbase Query Designer in-depth in the next chapter. So, for now, we will go over just briefly why we like this method.

For starters, the Essbase Query Designer allows you to visually select database outline members you wish to include in your report or extract. It also allows you to decide the placement of the column members and the row members. While the resultant query is designed to be used with a Microsoft Excel worksheet, when you save the query, you also have the option of having Query Designer create an Essbase report script from the parameters and selection criteria you specified in your query.

With very little modification, an automatically generated Essbase report script can be executed from EssCmd scripts, API calls, or MaxL command scripts.

Another benefit of using the Query Designer to generate a report script is that it will properly code complex functionality for you. Therefore, there are no elusive syntax errors for you to debug.

Report script commands and functions

Well, just like the calculation scripts, there are several different categories of Essbase report script commands and instructions. Unlike the calculation commands and functions, the report script commands and instructions basically deal with data selection and formatting.

As we said earlier, the arsenal of data selection commands and instructions is perhaps not the most robust when compared to the specific commands available to a user of SQL for instance. This can occasionally result in more data than is required being returned. This is hardly an issue that is worth fretting over.

We will list for you here the complete report script command and instruction categories. For each category, we will give examples of a couple of the most commonly used commands or instructions. For a complete list of all Essbase report script commands and instructions, please refer to the EAS Online Help that is supplied with each installation of EAS.

Report layout commands

The report layout commands tell Essbase how you are setting up your report page with regards to what members will be row members and what members will be column members. Some members will also be page members, where their attribute applies to all of the data selected and does not need to be represented in either a row or column.

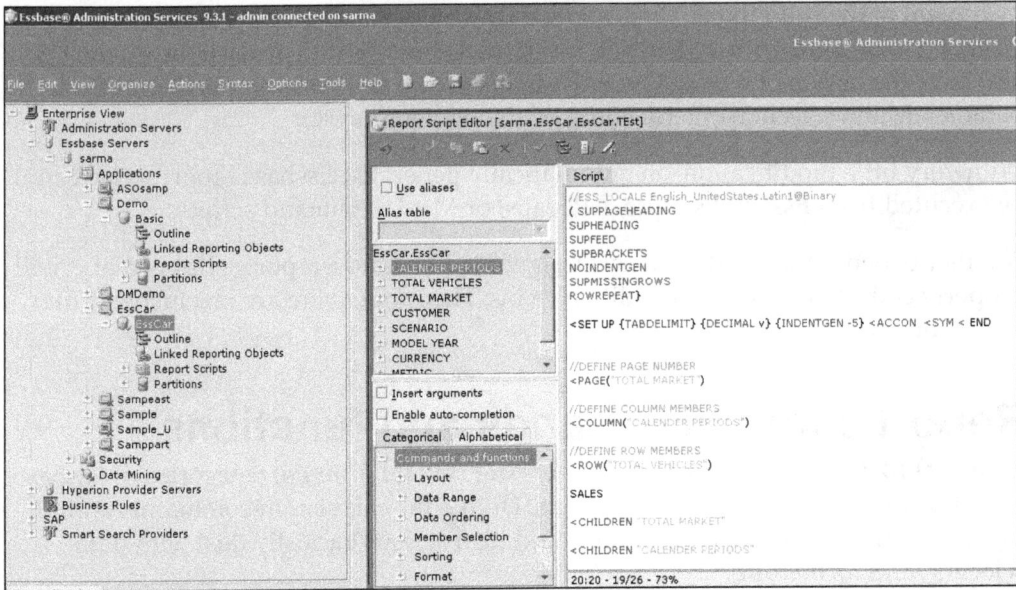

The syntax of these members is discussed below:

- **COLUMN**

  Syntax:

  ```
  <COLUMN(comma separated dimension list)
  ```

  Example:

  ```
  <COLUMN("Calendar Periods", "Scenario")
  ```

  This example will place members from the `Calendar Periods` and `Scenario` dimensions into the report output as column members.

- **ROW**

  Syntax:

  ```
  <ROW(comma separated dimension list)
  ```

Example:

```
<ROW("Total Vehicles", "Model Year")
```

This example will place members from the `Total Vehicles` and `Model Year` dimensions into the report output as row members.

- **PAGE**

  Syntax:

  ```
  <PAGE(comma separated dimension list)
  ```

  Example:

  ```
  <PAGE (Market)
  ```

  This example will place members from the `Market` dimension into the report output as page members.

Data range commands

The data range commands are a good example of the limitations in data selection we mentioned earlier. As of this writing, there are only three commands available to you. After you look at the coding examples, you will see why we spoke of limitations.

BOTTOM

Syntax:

```
<BOTTOM ([<rowgroupDimension>,]<rows>, <column>)
```

Example:

```
<BOTTOM (100, @DATACOL(2))
```

With the `BOTTOM` command, the returned data is sorted in descending order by the data values and the bottom number of rows, as specified by parameter two for the column specified in parameter three is returned.

In the example, the bottom 100 rows of data would be sorted according to the values in data column number two.

The `TOP` command is identical, but returns the top number of rows specified.

Data ordering command

Yes, it says data ordering command because there is only one command. Although this command has a name similar to a command used in relational databases, the difference, and to some a limitation, is that the data returned by the Essbase report script is ordered by data value columns only. Columns that contain metadata or member names, cannot be sorted using this command, since only columns containing numeric data values are considered for ordering.

ORDERBY

Syntax:

```
<ORDERBY ( [<rowgroupDimension>,] <column> [<direction>]{,<column>
     [<direction>]})
```

Example:

```
<ORDERBY (Sales, @DATACOL(1) DESC)
```

This example will sort the rows of data returned with the member name of **Sales** on data column one in descending order (data value order):

DECEMBER 2009	UNITED STATES	MYR 2009	2 DOOR SEDAN	SALES	120
NOVEMBER 2009	UNITED STATES	MYR 2009	2 DOOR SEDAN	SALES	1150
OCTOBER 2009	UNITED STATES	MYR 2009	2 DOOR SEDAN	SALES	1100
SEPTEMBER 2009	UNITED STATES	MYR 2009	2 DOOR SEDAN	SALES	1000
AUGUST 2009	UNITED STATES	MYR 2009	2 DOOR SEDAN	SALES	950
JULY 2009	UNITED STATES	MYR 2009	2 DOOR SEDAN	SALES	900
JUNE 2009	UNITED STATES	MYR 2009	2 DOOR SEDAN	SALES	800
MAY 2009	UNITED STATES	MYR 2009	2 DOOR SEDAN	SALES	750
APRIL 2009	UNITED STATES	MYR 2009	2 DOOR SEDAN	SALES	700
MARCH 2009	UNITED STATES	MYR 2009	2 DOOR SEDAN	SALES	600
FEBRUARY 2009	UNITED STATES	MYR 2009	2 DOOR SEDAN	SALES	550
JANUARY 2009	UNITED STATES	MYR 2009	2 DOOR SEDAN	SALES	500

Member selection and sorting commands

To compensate for the limitations we mentioned previously, Essbase provides us with several dozen member selection and sorting commands. You have already seen many of these commands in the previous chapter on calculation scripts and they perform the same functions. The only difference is that the syntax for the report script commands is different than it is for the calculation and member formula commands. Here are a few examples so you can get the idea.

CHILDREN

Syntax:

```
<CHILDREN mbrName
```

Example:

```
<CHILDREN "Calendar Periods"
```

This example will return data rows for all children of the `Calendar Periods` member, but no data for the `Calendar Periods` member itself. Notice we said member when `Calendar Periods` is actually a dimension too. We did this to show you that in this command, you can enter any member name that has its own children and want only to return its children.

Keep in mind that Essbase will do exactly as you instruct it to do. When you say to return the children of the `Calendar Periods` dimension, you will get the **Quarter** values. Other dimensions not mentioned will be at the highest level unless specified.

ICHILDREN

Syntax:

```
<ICHILDREN mbrName
```

Example:

```
<ICHILDREN "Calendar Periods"
```

This example will return data rows for all of the children of the `Calendar Periods` member and for the `Calendar Periods` member itself. Notice that here too we said member when `Calendar Periods` is actually a dimension as well. We did this to show you that in this command, you can enter any member name that has its own children and want to return those children and their parent.

Format commands

The format commands tell Essbase how your report output will look. Unless otherwise specified in the command itself, these commands can be used multiple times in a script, and will only affect the rows of data returned by other commands that are written after the format commands in the script.

There are many more of these formatting commands available to you. Some have almost overlapping abilities, so they can be somewhat confusing. If you are using your report script to extract data for a flat file, you will not need too many of these formatting commands. If you are trying to create really fancy looking reports, you will need plenty of practice and patience.

SUPCOMMAS

Syntax:

```
{ SUPCOMMAS }
```

Example:

```
{ SUPCOMMAS }
```

This example will return numeric data rows with no commas delineating the numbers for values over 999.

COMMAS

Syntax:

```
{ COMMAS }
```

Example:

```
{ COMMAS }
```

This example will return numeric data rows with commas delineating the numbers for values over 999.

WIDTH

Syntax:

```
{ WIDTH number [ column1 [ column2 [ columnN ] ] ] }
```

Example:

```
{ WIDTH 20 }
```

This example will truncate all column widths to 20 spaces wide, regardless of their actual width.

Column or row calculation

While these are some pretty cool commands, we recommend that you be very careful with their use. As you must know by now, we have repeatedly stated the benefits of Essbase's dynamic data calculating abilities and there is no arguing that.

When you use these row and column calculation commands, you are artificially creating data that does not actually exist in the Essbase database.

We say to be cautious because if there is ever a question about the report script generated data, it will not always be the easiest to track down or debug. Again, nice functionality, but use it very carefully.

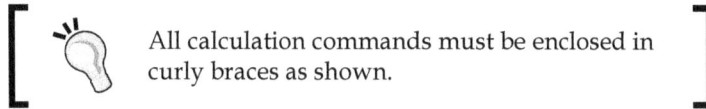

> All calculation commands must be enclosed in curly braces as shown.

CALCULATE COLUMN

Syntax:

```
{CALCULATE COLUMN "newColumn" = expression }
```

Example:

```
{CALCULATE COLUMN "Actual YTD" = 1 + 2}
```

This example will create a new column called `Actual YTD` which will be the sum across of columns 1 and 2. Again, if the `Actual YTD` value does not exist in Essbase, it may be difficult to debug the data displayed on the report, unless you are intimately familiar with the report script itself.

ONCOLCALCS

Syntax:

```
{ ONCOLCALCS }
```

Example:

```
{ ONCOLCALCS }
```

This command must be used in the script prior to coding the `CALCULATE COLUMN` command to turn **on** the column's calculating ability.

OFFCOLCALCS

Syntax:

```
{ OFFCOLCALCS }
```

Example:

```
{ OFFCOLCALCS }
```

This command must be used in the script after coding the `CALCULATE COLUMN` command to turn **off** the column's calculating ability.

Member names and aliases

This set of commands allows you to pick and choose what member alias tables to use for the display of member names. Again, if you are extracting the data from Essbase with your report script simply for flat file export purposes, you do not need to worry much about member names.

OUTALTSELECT

Syntax:

```
<OUTALTSELECT AliasTableName
```

Example:

```
<OUTALTSELECT Display
```

This command tells Essbase to output the data from this point forward in the script using the member names from the **Display** alias table. All rows of data returned will have member alias names that are stored in the **Display** alias table.

Building your first Essbase report script

Hopefully your brain hasn't fallen out yet. There's still so much to do. We are now going to build a simple Essbase report script from scratch. As described previously, navigate your way to the **Essbase Report Script Editor** in your EAS console.

Go ahead and open a new and empty **Report Script**. Click on **File | Save** and let Essbase save your report script in the default location with the name of test.rep.

The first thing we need to know is the comment identifier. In any Essbase report script, a double forward slash // tells Essbase to ignore that line. This is how you begin a comment line. The double forward slash must begin in column 1 of the file with multiple rows all beginning with the //.

For example, a single line comment would look like this:

```
// This is a comment line.
```

A comment block with multiple lines would look like this:

```
// This is a comment block.
// It has several lines in it
```

Also, it must be noted that if you are using a report script to create an actual report which will be printed and viewed by others, then your report script can be long and complicated and perform several tasks at once. If you recall, we mentioned earlier that some types of commands can be used more than once is a script. Well, the exclamation point is the delimiter that tells Essbase that a series of commands is over, and the next set of commands begins a new part of the report. You also end a report script with !, also known as a bang. This lets Essbase know it has finished.

Of course, if you're using the report script to generate a flat file extract to ship downstream somewhere, then you will only use ! once and only at the end of the report script.

Let's begin writing our simple Essbase report script. If you have your Esscar database outline set up the way we instructed you earlier in this book, you should be able to code the test.rep report script exactly as shown. Please enter into the report script editor the following code and comments:

```
//Define page members
<PAGE ("Total Market","METRIC")
//Define column members
<COLUMN ("Calendar Periods")
//Define row members
<ROW ("Total Vehicles")
//Select specific members to include in report Sales
<CHILDREN "Total Market"
<CHILDREN "Calendar Periods"
<CHILDREN "Total Vehicles"
// Always end your script with a !
!
```

Now, if you execute this simple script, you will get a report file that when opened looks like this:

United States Sales Model Year

	2009	2010
	========	========
2 Door Sedan	20,400	40,800
4 Door Sedan	20,400	40,800
4X2 Pickup	20,400	40,800
4X4 Pickup	20,400	40,800

Canada Sales Model Year

	2009	2010
	========	========
2 Door Sedan	20,400	40,800
4 Door Sedan	20,400	40,800
4X2 Pickup	20,400	40,800
4X4 Pickup	20,400	40,800

Mexico Sales Model Year

	2009	2010
	========	========
2 Door Sedan	20,400	40,800
4 Door Sedan	20,400	40,800
4X2 Pickup	20,400	40,800
4X4 Pickup	20,400	40,800

Not too shabby for an amateur, eh? Notice that the output actually looks fairly presentable and professional and we haven't even taken advantage of any of the real report script functionality. Now look at what happens to the output when we add a few commands to the same report script that turns it from a report file into a flat file.

First, you will notice this line added to the top of the report script file:

```
//ESS_LOCALE English_UnitedStates.Latin1@Binary
```

It is just a comment line added by Essbase to identify what language setting is being used by the system so you do not attempt to run with the wrong setting. You can delete the line, but Essbase will put it back again the next time you open and save the report script through the Essbase report script editor.

```
//ESS_LOCALE English_UnitedStates.Latin1@Binary
//This block of commands will turn a report script that create a
//report into a report script that creates an ASCII text flat file.
//If you look closely you should be able to recognize what some of
//the commands will do. For instance, the first one will suppress
//the page heading if any. The second command will suppress any
//column headings. The third command will suppress any page feeds that
//would have been sent to the printer had this been a multiple
//page report
{SUPPAGEHEADING
 SUPHEADING
 SUPFEED
 SUPCOMMA
 SUPBRACKETS
 NOINDENTGEN
 SUPMISSINGROWS
 ROWREPEAT}
//This line tells Essbase how to set up the output data. For example,
//the first command tells Essbase to Tab delimit the output data
//columns.
<SETUP {TabDelimit} {decimal v} {IndentGen -5} <ACCON <SYM <END
//Define page members
<PAGE ("Total Market","METRIC")
//Define column members
<COLUMN ("Calendar Periods")
//Define row members
<ROW ("Total Vehicles")
//Select specific members to include in report
Sales
<CHILDREN "Total Market"
<CHILDREN "Calendar Periods"
<CHILDREN "Total Vehicles"
//Always end your script with a !
!
```

We have not altered the original script in any way except to add the commands we explained at the top of the script. When we execute the same script now, we get vastly different output results that are more suitable for a data extract than a report.

2 Door Sedan	20400	40800
4 Door Sedan	20400	40800
4X2 Pickup	20400	40800
4X4 Pickup	20400	40800
2 Door Sedan	20400	40800
4 Door Sedan	20400	40800
4X2 Pickup	20400	40800
4X4 Pickup	20400	40800
2 Door Sedan	20400	40800
4 Door Sedan	20400	40800
4X2 Pickup	20400	40800
4X4 Pickup	20400	40800

With a little rearranging of the row and column commands, we could easily add the **Model Year**, **Market**, and **Sales** member names to the rows of data, so each row in the output file would contain all of the necessary data attributes.

Yes, there is a lot to learn when it comes to Essbase but it doesn't need to frighten you. Like we said about the calculation scripts in the previous chapter, take baby steps, and practice.

Executing your report scripts

Now that you have created your own report script, pat yourself on the back and tell yourself that you are going to be a good and successful Essbase administrator/developer. You have overcome the difficult part which is creating the report script. Now comes the easy part, running the report script.

Just like executing an Essbase database calculation script, Essbase offers several methods for executing a database report script.

Some of the ways that you can run Essbase database report scripts are:

- Run reports from EAS

- Run reports using EssCmd

- Run reports using MaxL

- Run reports using API calls (as discussed in Chapter 8)

Run reports using EAS

Upto now you have learned many tasks that an Essbase developer or administrator can do through EAS. Running report scripts is just one more better example of how you can effectively use EAS. Like we discussed running calc scripts from EAS before, there are also many ways to execute report scripts from EAS.

From EAS, drill-down to your **Application** | **Database** | **Report Scripts** and you will see your report script **test**. Right-click on the **test** report script and then click on the **Execute** button as shown:

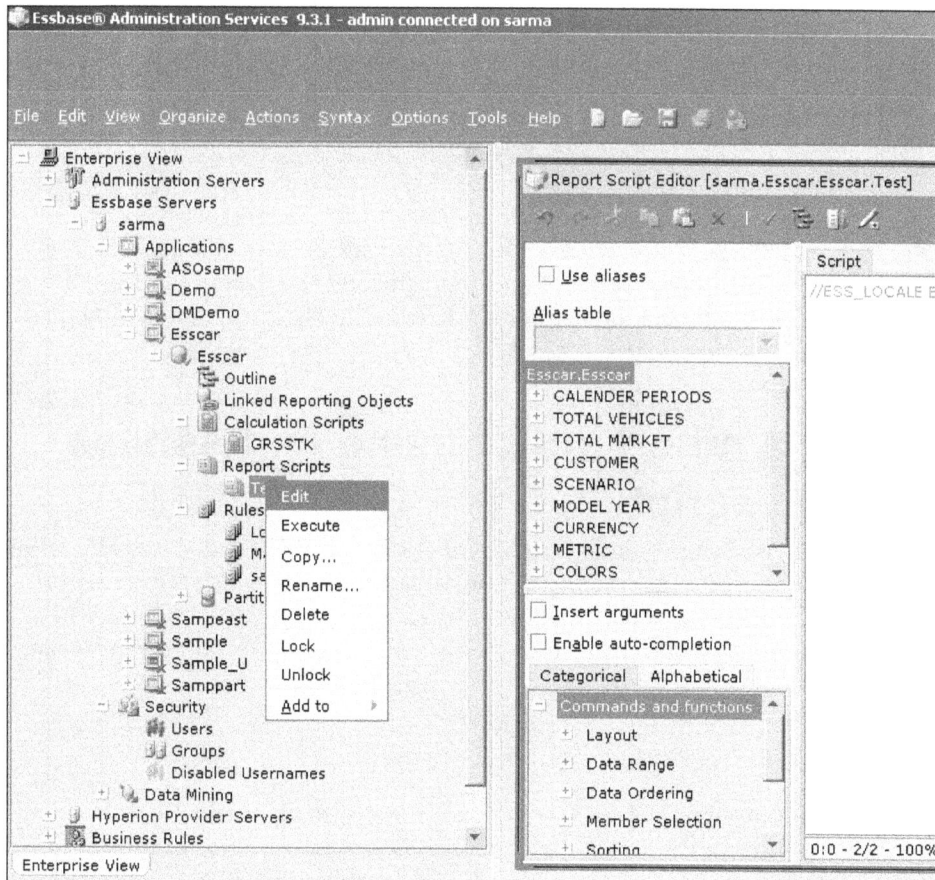

Once you click the **Execute** button a dialog box will open which asks if you want to execute the script in the background and send the results to the **Console** or to the **Printer**. You can also specify if you want to send the retrieved results to an output file. Isn't this the coolest feature? You can then send this output file to your customers to tell them that your data load and calc are completed and here is what your data now looks like. The output file can be .rpt or .txt file. These are the two options that are provided through EAS. If you wish to save an output file, just provide an output file path and file name and click **OK**, as shown and the report will then be executed:

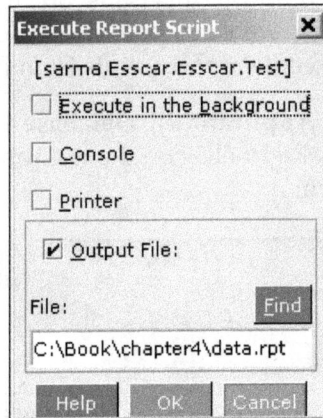

```
Execute Report Script                    ✕

  [sarma.Esscar.Esscar.Test]
  ☐ Execute in the background

  ☐ Console

  ☐ Printer

  ┌─────────────────────────────────┐
  │ ✔ Output File:                  │
  │                                 │
  │ File:                   Find    │
  │ C:\Book\chapter4\data.rpt       │
  └─────────────────────────────────┘

     Help        OK       Cancel
```

There are also other ways you can execute a report script from within EAS. For instance, you can open a report script and then click on the **Execute** button of the **Report** menu or you can click on **Options | Execute** in the EAS menu or by pressing the *F5* button on your keyboard.

Running a report script using an Essbase command script

As we have discussed in previous chapters about being able to execute calculation scripts using Essbase command scripts, you are also able to run database report scripts from an EssCmd as well. When you run a report from an EssCmd, you have the option to save the output in an ASCII text file or a formatted report file.

EssCmd Syntax:

```
RUNREPT numeric reportscript outputfile
```

- `numeric` (possible 1, 2, or 3) – specifies the physical location of the report script.

i)   Local/Client based report script.

ii) Remote/Server report script.

iii) Specifies that the file is not an Essbase default object and you need to provide the fully qualified path with the name of the report script.

- `reportscript` — name of the report script. This parameter will depend on the numeric value chosen for the first parameter.

- `Outputfile` — fully qualified name and path for the output file. If no path is specified, Essbase will place the file in the default database folder.

```
OUTPUT 1 "c:\EsscmdReport.log";
LOGIN "EssServerID" "EssID" "EssPass" "ESSCAR" "ESSCAR";
SELECT "ESSCAR" "ESSCAR"
RUNREPT 2 "test" "c:/book/test.dat"
LOGOUT;
EXIT;
```

Once you have executed the above EssCmd at the DOS prompt (as shown in the following screenshot), the output data will be saved in the text file called `test.dat`, which will be created in the path described. As you can see, we have created a file with a `.dat` extension, instead of creating an `.rpt` or `.txt` file. We just want to make you aware that when you are saving an output file from an EssCmd, you are not obligated to use any particular file extension and may choose any one you wish.

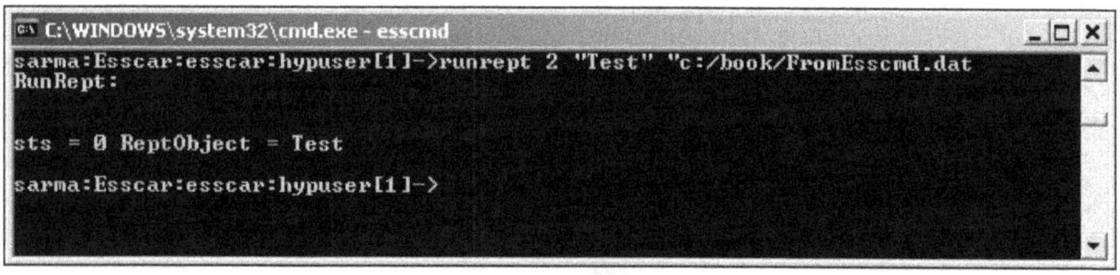

Upon the execution of the command, you will see the return code in the form of **sts** (Status code). If **sts** is **0**, that means there is no error. If the return code is not zero, it will provide you an error message as shown:

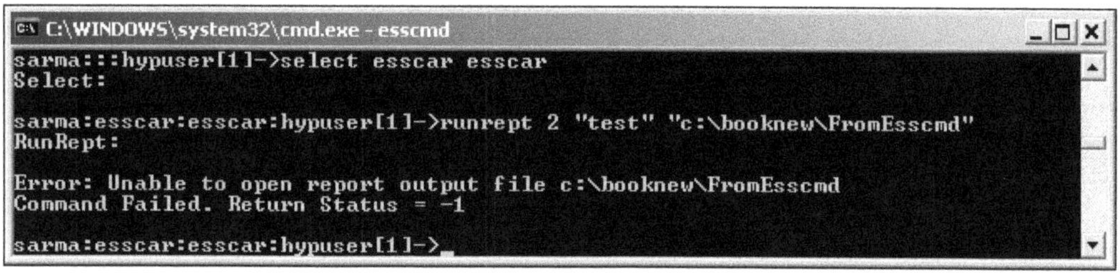

Running calc using a MaxL script

How can we forget MaxL? There is no way we can forget MaxL. MaxL is the new generation of command scripting language used by Essbase. If you look closely at the MaxL statements, you will see that they are very close to your typical SQL statements. Since you will be exporting data, you will use the EXPORT MaxL statement to run the report script.

Syntax:

```
EXPORT DATABASE database name USING LOCAL/SERVER REPORT_FILE report
script name TO DATA_FILE output data file name.
```

Code:

```
export database 'ESSCAR'.'ESSCAR' using server report_file 'Test' to
data_file 'c:/book/test.rpt';
```

This code, when executed from MaxL, will execute the Test.rep against the ESSCAR application/ESSCAR database.

To create a MaxL script file object, simply open the **MaxL Script Editor** in the EAS tool by clicking the **Editors** menu pick, then click on **MaxL Script Editor**. The **MaxL Script Editor** is shown in the following screenshot:

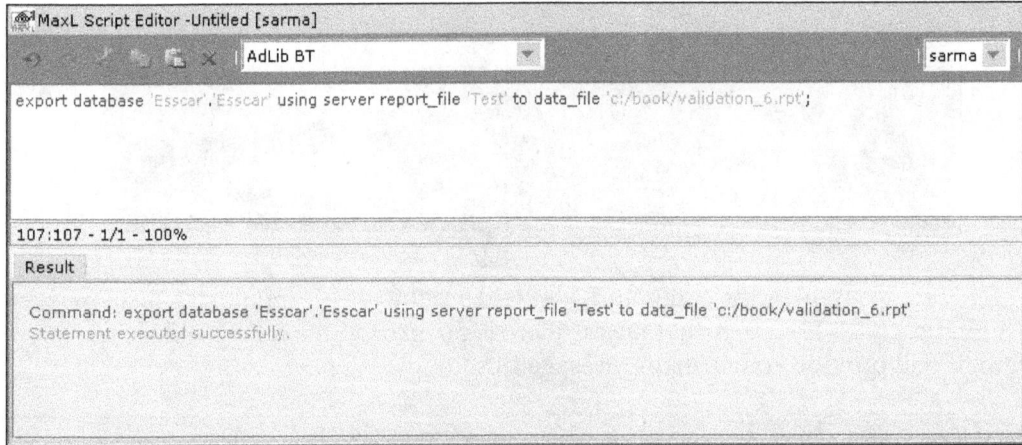

You can execute the script by clicking on the **Execute Script** button on the MaxL menu or on the **EAS | Execute** on the EAS menu or press *F5* to execute the script. Once the script is executed, you will see the validation_6.rpt file in the location specified.

Previewing data in EAS

Until now you have used EAS to create users, update the outline, load data, calculate the data, and so forth. You will now see how EAS can also be used to preview the data in an Essbase cube. You can preview data for both aggregate storage and block storage databases. You can preview the data in spreadsheet format or in HTML format.

Here are the steps to preview data in EAS:

1. In EAS, select the database and click on **Actions | Preview data** or right-click on the database and select **Preview data**.

2. On the right side of the EAS frame, you will see the **Data Preview Grid** screen with two tabs, a **Cubeview** tab and a **Properties** tab as shown here:

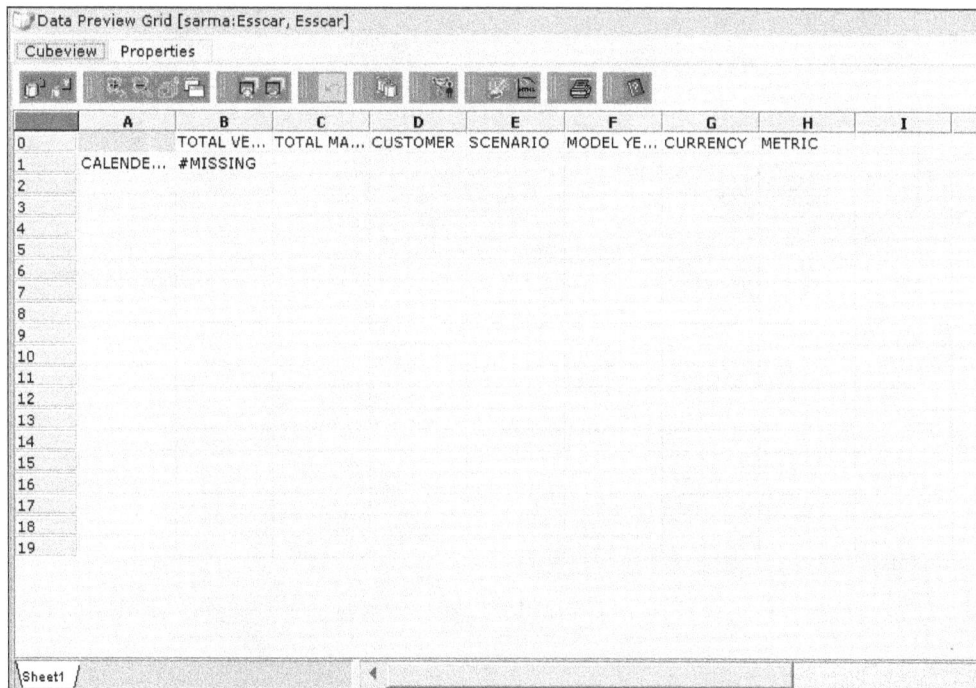

Here, you can see there are two tabs, one is for the **Cubeview** and other tab is for the **Properties**. The **Cubeview** is the view that shows the data and is always defaulted to the Dimension level view. In order for you to look at the lower levels, you will need to drill-down. The properties for the **Cubeview** can be set in the **Properties** tab.

Cubeview

In the **Cubeview**, you are provided with a Tool bar which allows you to drill-down, retrieve data, and have an HTML view of data. The following is an example of the tool bar. For an explanation of each button available to you, simply hover over the button with the mouse.

When the member selection button is clicked, the standard member selection screen will be displayed as shown in the following screenshot:

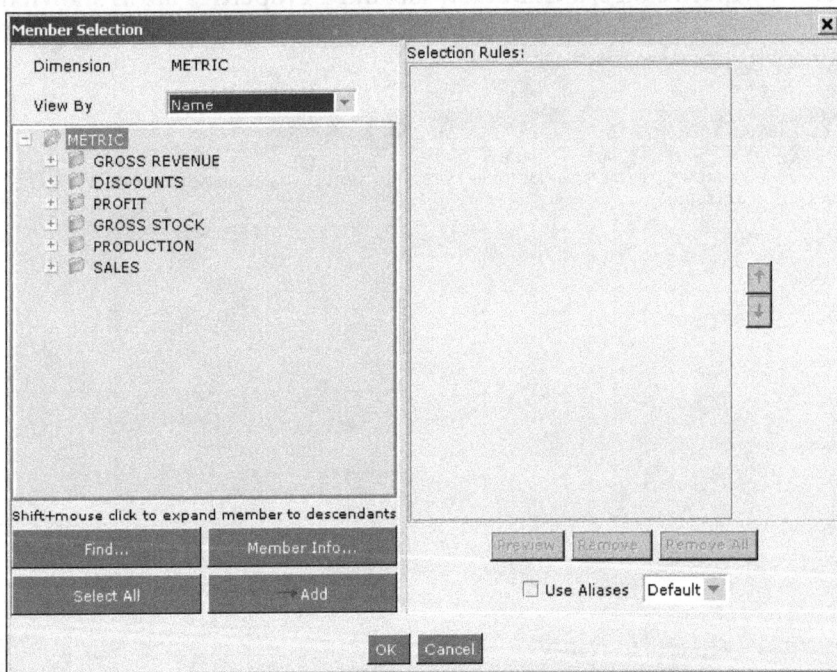

In the **Member Selection** screen (shown above), you can see that all of the members are in the usual tree format. You also have the ability to **Find...** the members and also to see the **Member Info...** for a selected member. There are options for you to **Select All** of the members at one time and to **Add** specific members to your selection rules. Using **Member Info...**, you will get the dimension name of the member, the **Generation number** and **Level number** of the selected member and you can also see the **Member Formula** if any. You can also view the member names by alias by checking the **Use Aliases** checkbox.

When you click the **Preferences** button, you open the **Preferences** screen. In the **Preferences** screen (shown below), you can set the preferences for the current cube view. You can set up the number of **Undo** steps and also format the **Member cells** and **Data cells** by clicking on the **Format Cells** tab. The **Format Cells** checkbox is checked by default.

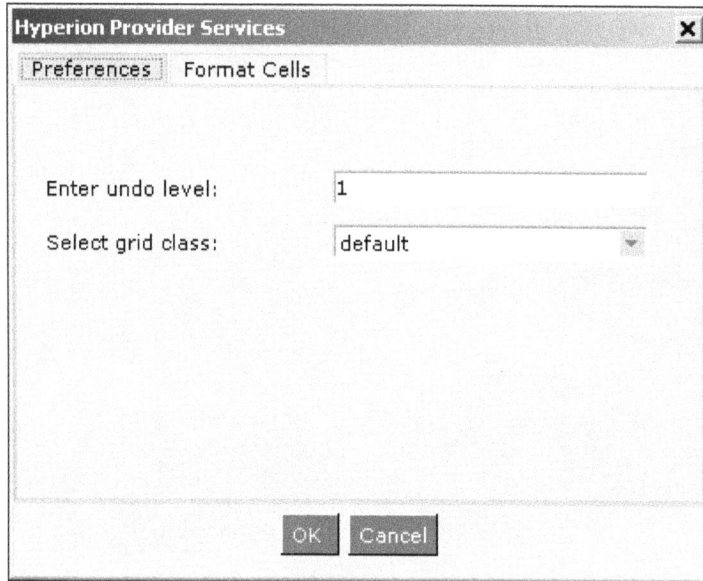

Properties

Selecting this tab in the **Cubeview** screen allows you to set up the data formatting properties for the current cube view grid. These properties are only applicable to the current session and cannot be saved. Some of the properties that can be set are as follows:

- **Drill level**: When you perform a drill-down on the data, you can choose whether you want to do a drill-down to the **Next level, Bottom level,** or **Sibling Level**. By default, the drill level is set to **Next level.**

- You can choose to **Suppress Zeros, Suppress Missing** and **Suppress Underscores** from being displayed in your report.

- Selecting **Display Alias Names** will display member names using the alias table selected by you.

- On the bottom of the **Properties** screen you will see two buttons, **Refresh** and **Save**. The **Refresh** button retrieves the last saved properties and refreshes the **Properties** screen with them, and the **Save** button will save the properties you have updated for this session. The next screenshot shows the **Properties** screen:

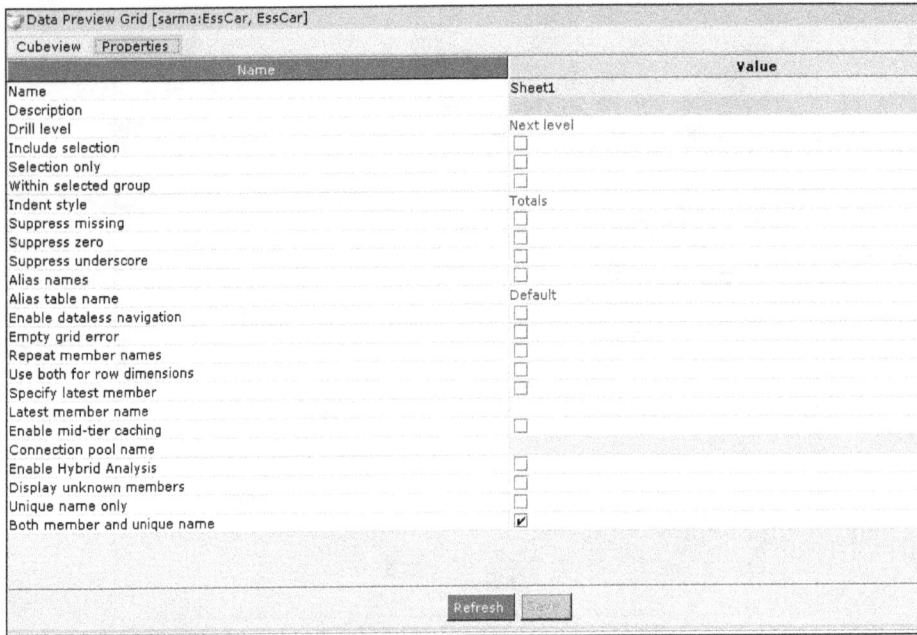

Summary

Well, we have certainly covered a lot of ground, especially in the last couple of chapters. By now you should have a good understanding of the what, when, how, and who, when it comes to installing, designing, building, loading, and now using an Essbase database system.

Next up, we cover the incredible Oracle Essbase Add-in for Microsoft Excel. If ever there was a super tool, this is it! The Essbase add-in, seamlessly installed in your Microsoft Excel spreadsheet program, gives the user one of the most powerful tools for data analytics available today. Nowhere else can you start with a blank spreadsheet and end up creating, updating, calculating, analyzing, and reporting data. All of this in just minutes, without ever leaving your seat. Wow!

Oh, and because we want you to be right there on top of the world of Essbase, we are also including a full section in the *Appendix* on Oracle Smart View. Although not a replacement for the Essbase add-in, Smart View has many similar qualities, as well as many new and exciting features.

7

Getting the most out of the Microsoft Excel Add-in

In the real world it is no secret that a very large percentage of data and financial analysts do their jobs using Microsoft Excel. It is also no secret that a very large percentage of these same analysts actually like Microsoft Excel very much and enjoy using it.

This is probably why, after you tell them that they can continue to use Microsoft Excel to do their jobs even with the addition of Essbase, you will see a large smile spread across their faces. Just wait until you tell them they can continue to use Microsoft Excel but can now perform complex data analytics and create professional looking reports by taking advantage of the easy to install and use Essbase add-in. Our guess is that you will be peeling them off of the ceiling.

Get ready, because after all of the prior instruction, it is now time to actually learn how to use Essbase and the Essbase add-in to connect to the Essbase database, analyze data, modify or create data, create reports, run database calculation scripts, use the really cool Query Designer function included in the add-in, and a whole lot more.

Reporting with the Microsoft Excel Add-in

Assuming you have the Essbase Add-in for Microsoft Excel installed on your PC you will see the **Essbase** menu pick available on the main Microsoft Excel menu toolbar.

If you read how to install the add-in but did not do it, please install it now for you will need it in this chapter.

If you have installed the add-in but do not see the **Essbase** menu pick there is no need to re-install the add-in. Occasionally the Essbase add-in will not load when you open a new instance of Microsoft Excel. If this happens you can simply re-load the add-in by following the steps below.

Steps to reload the Essbase Add-in into Microsoft Excel:

1. In Microsoft Excel, with at least the default blank workbook open, navigate to the **Add-Ins** screen by clicking on **Tools | Add-Ins** in Microsoft Excel version 2003 and earlier or by clicking **Add-Ins** directly in Microsoft Excel version 2007.

2. From the **Add-Ins** screen select the **Hyperion Essbase OLAP Server DLL (non-Unicode)** by checking it's box and click on **OK**.

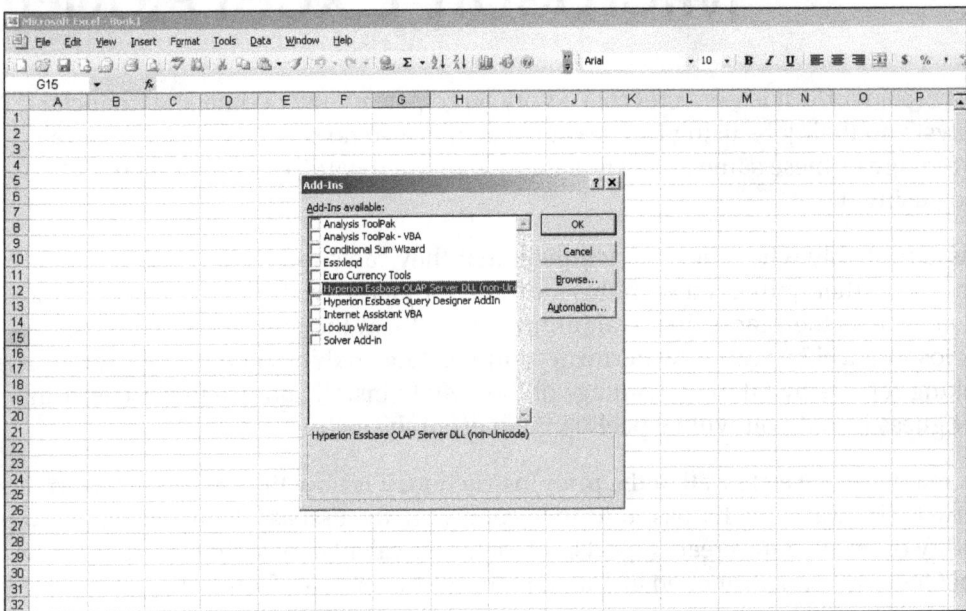

3. You should see the **Essbase** menu pick as the add-in loads and now you are again ready to use Microsoft Excel for Essbase reporting.

If, in the **Add-In** selection screen, you do not see the **Hyperion Essbase OLAP Server DLL(non Unicode)** add-in, then follow these steps to locate the add-in xll file:

1. Click on the **Browse** button on the **Add-Ins** screen.

2. Browse to where you have the Essbase add-in installed. Typically this file will be in your local drive in a path similar to: `C:\Hyperion\AnalyticServices\bin\`

3. Select the `essexcln.xll` file and click **OK**.

4. In the **Add-Ins** screen you should see the **Hyperion Essbase OLAP Server DLL(non Unicode)** selected. Now click **OK** on the **Add-Ins** screen.

5. You should see **Essbase** menu in Microsoft Excel as shown in the following screenshot:

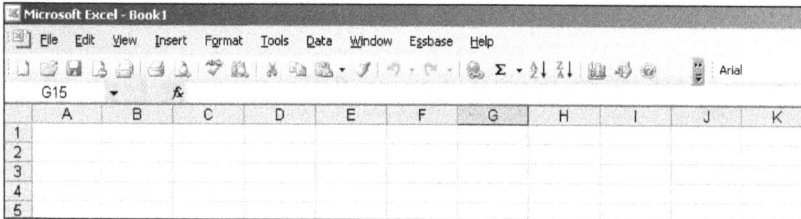

That's it! You now have the Essbase Add-in for Microsoft Excel installed, loaded, and ready to use.

When you click on the **Essbase** menu pick from Microsoft Excel's main toolbar you will have approximately two dozen choices. There are a couple of choices that we feel must be explained without regard to the order of their appearance on the menu. However, for the most part we will be starting at the top and working our way to the bottom of the menu.

The Essbase menu looks like the following screenshot with all of the choices available. Please note that the order in which they appear is somewhat different than the order in which we will be discussing them.

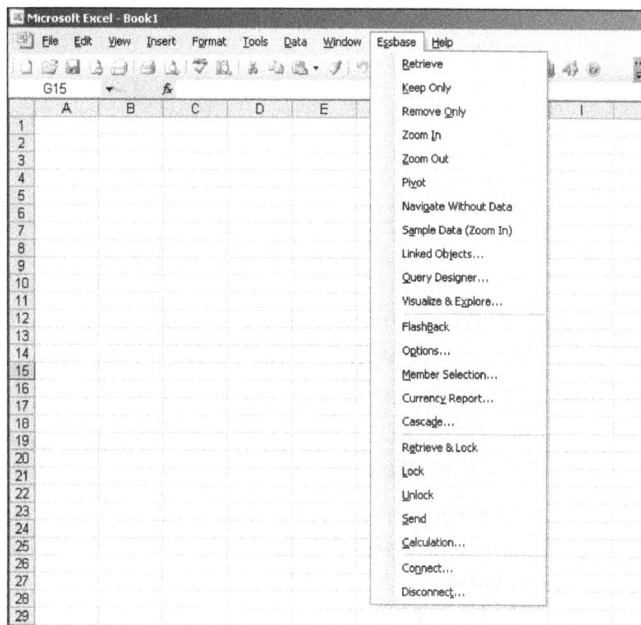

Connecting to Essbase

Obviously, connecting to the Essbase database is one of the first tasks you should perform. Otherwise there isn't much you can do, except the regular old, boring Microsoft Excel tasks. To establish a connection to the appropriate Essbase database, simply follow the steps here.

Connecting to Essbase from Microsoft Excel

What could be easier than connecting to your Essbase database right from your favorite data analysis tool? Does it get any better? Once you become familiar with the Essbase Add-in for Microsoft Excel and all of its myriad features, we just know you will agree.

1. From the Microsoft Excel main menu bar click on **Essbase | Connect....**

2. The **Essbase System Login** screen will appear as shown:

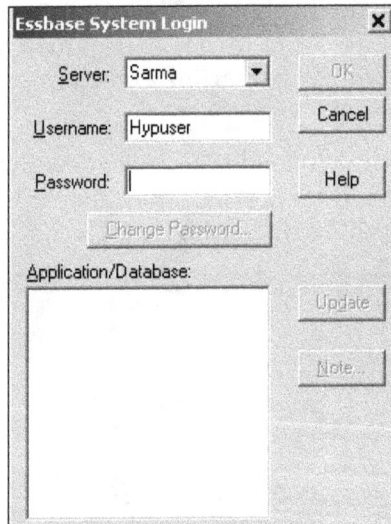

3. Enter the appropriate **Server** name, your **Username,** and the **Password** assigned to your ID. Once completed, click **OK**.

4. If your password has expired, the system will inform you of that fact and allow you to choose a new password. You may also change your password at any time by clicking on the **Change Password** button after any successful login.

5. Once you have entered the correct password, you will then be shown the list of Essbase **Application/Database** that your ID login has access to on the server you selected.

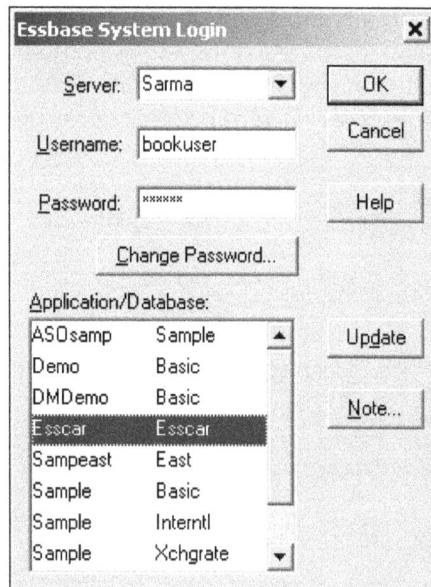

6. Select the **Application/Database** you wish to work with and click on **OK**. The active Microsoft Excel worksheet is now connected to the **Application/ Database** you selected. You are ready to go to work with Essbase on this worksheet.

> In Microsoft Excel, once you have logged into an **Application | Database**, Essbase will automatically connect any other worksheets in the same Microsoft Excel workbook to the **Application | Database** you logged into, on the first worksheet.
>
> If you need to connect different sheets in the same workbook to different Application | Databases, you will need to activate those sheets and perform another **Essbase | Connect...** as needed.

Some of the buttons present in the previous screenshot are explained as follows:

- **Change Password**: Allows you to change your password whenever you deem necessary. After entering a valid user ID and password, the button will become active and allow you to use this function.

- **Update**: Refreshes the database list in your login screen. If for some reason a database was offline when you first connected you would not see it in the login screen. Use the **Update** button to refresh the list.

- **Note**: This is a note that resides with the Essbase database and is also called a **Database Note**. This note can contain information left by the administrator about the current state of the database and its data. This can be a very useful feature for the end-users or current production support staff.

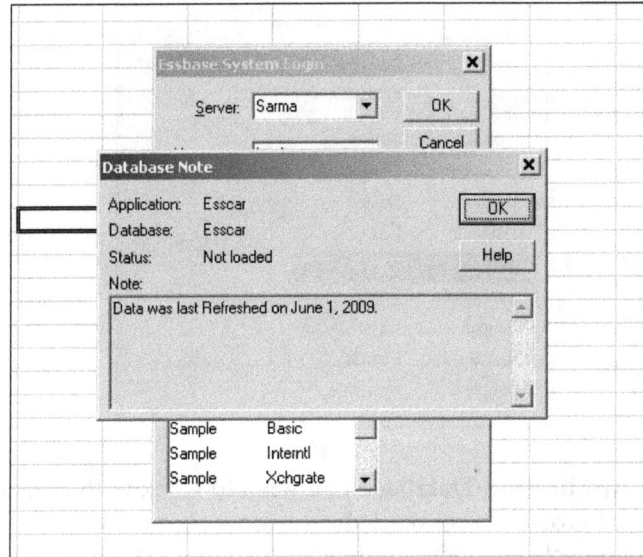

Disconnecting from Essbase

There are three main reasons to get very familiar with this function:

1. Once you are working with Essbase, your connections will remain open, even if you close the Microsoft Excel workbook. The connections to the Essbase server are only terminated when you close Microsoft Excel or explicitly disconnecting each sheet manually or with code. To avoid potential connection issues, it is always advisable to disconnect all Microsoft Excel worksheets when you are finished with them.

2. If you need to retrieve data into the same sheet from a different database, it is good to disconnect it first before you connect it to another database.

3. The **Essbase Disconnect** screen is the best way to monitor what sheets are connected to what Application | Databases and even servers. It is not uncommon to have multiple sheets in the same workbook connected to databases from different applications across different servers.

To disconnect a worksheet from a database perform the following steps:

1. From the Microsoft Excel main menu click on **Essbase | Disconnect...**.

2. At the disconnect screen you will see a listing of all of the Microsoft Excel worksheets that have active connections to Essbase Application|Databases.

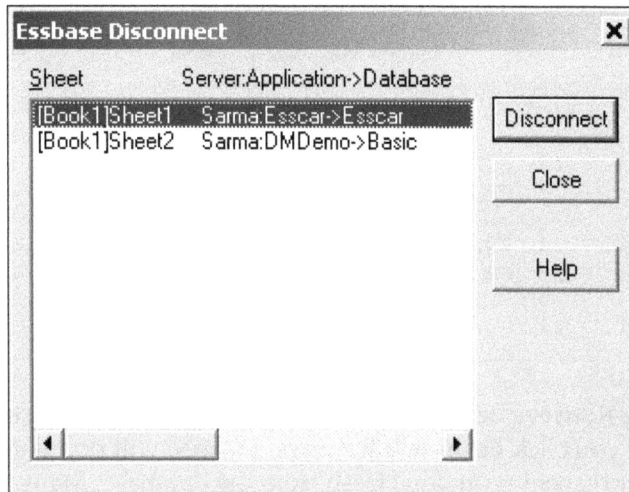

3. Select the sheet which you want to disconnect and click on the **Disconnect** button. The connection for that worksheet will be terminated.

4. Click on the **Close** button to close the **Essbase Disconnect** screen.

5. As with any Essbase screen, the **Help** button when clicked, will provide help information about the current screen and its functions.

Launching the Essbase Query Designer

Although included in the Essbase add-in, this menu choice almost qualifies as its own reporting tool. The **Essbase Query Designer (EQD)** is quite powerful, therefore we have dedicated a full section to it later in this chapter.

To launch the EQD, simply click **Essbase | Query Designer...**.

Retrieving data from Essbase

In one way this can be a dual function task. If you perform an **Essbase | Retrieve** and are not logged into a database, Essbase will automatically bring up the Essbase login screen and allow you to connect to an Application|Database of your choice before you continue.

Also, if you perform a retrieve on an empty worksheet, Essbase will do a generic retrieve that brings in all of the high level database dimensions and drops them on the Microsoft Excel worksheet (as shown in the following screenshot). You can now take this generic retrieve and by performing various Essbase spreadsheet functions, like the Zoom In or the Pivot, you will have yourself a fine looking report in no time.

	A	B	C	D	E	F	G	H	I
1		TOTAL VEHICLES	TOTAL MARKET	CUSTOMER	SCENARIO	MODEL YEAR	US DOLLAR	GROSS REVENUE	
2	JUNE 2008	0							
3	JULY 2008	#Missing							
4	AUGUST 2008	500000							
5	SEPTEMBER 2008	1400000							
6	QUARTER3 OF 2008	1900000							
7	OCTOBER 2008	620000							
8	NOVEMBER 2008	743960							
9	DECEMBER 2008	1480000							
10	QUARTER4 OF 2008	2843960							
11	YEAR 2008	4743960							
12									
13									
14									
15									
16									

Quite possibly the **Retrieve** add-in function will be the Essbase function you use most often. When you click **Essbase | Retrieve**, Essbase will populate the active Microsoft Excel worksheet with data, fresh from the database. Many times there will be data loads or database calculations occurring throughout the day and you will always want to make sure you are looking at the latest and greatest version of the data. A simple **Essbase | Retrieve** takes care of it for you.

Setting the add-in spreadsheet options

Here is a vital piece of the Essbase add-in. Setting the Essbase add-in options correctly can dramatically affect how you and the add-in perform. The options screen contains four tabs containing user settable options that affect the add-in's behavior at the individual worksheet level and also global options, which affect the add-in's behavior at the Microsoft Excel level. Access these screens by clicking **Essbase | Options....**

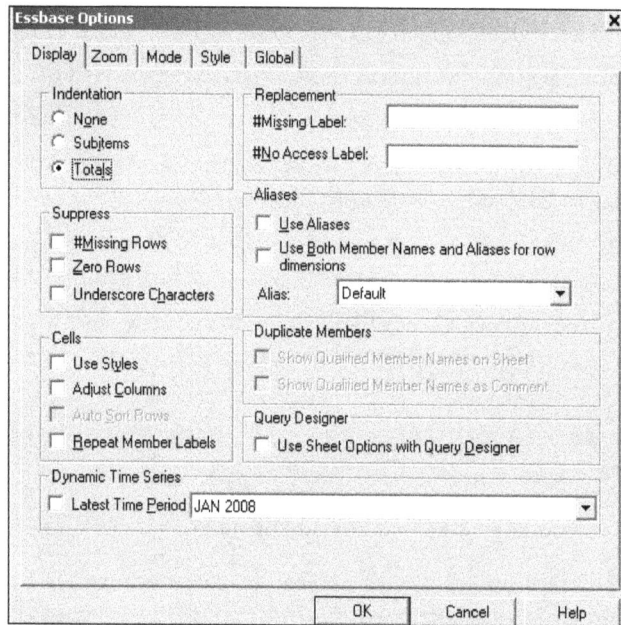

As shown in the previous screenshot, the **Essbase Options** screen on the **Display** tab contains settings that affect how Essbase will display your data. The settings on this tab are sheet level settings and only affect the Microsoft Excel worksheet that was active when the options screen was opened and the settings applied. You can select a different sheet in the workbook and set different options for it.

Display tab

The first group of available options is the **Indentation** setting. The **Indentation** setting is a row heading setting and only affects how the row members' names are justified in their rows. The available settings are explained here:

- **None**: All data retrieved will maintain the same column justification
- **Subitems:** The children members of a parent would indent on the report
- **Totals**: Parent members would be indented

Only one of these options can be selected at a time.

The next option group is the **Suppress** options. Here you can tell Essbase what values or lack of values you wish to prevent from showing up on the report:

- **#Missing Rows:** These are Essbase NULL values
- **Zero Rows:** This means the entire row of data has zero values
- **Underscore Characters:** This could be rows that contain invalid data values

You can choose one, all, or none of the **Suppress** options.

Next up are the **Cells** options. Here you have four choices that you can choose between:

1. **Use Styles:** This option will use any styles that have been defined for this member in Essbase

2. **Adjust Columns:** This option when checked, will automatically adjust the Microsoft Excel columns to fit the member names being retrieved

3. **Auto Sort Row:** This option tells Essbase to sort the member data according to the structure of the database outline and is only available if you have the **Free Form** setting checked

4. **Repeat Member Labels:** This setting will populate every row of the retrieved data with the member name or label

In the **Replacement** section of the **Essbase Options** screen, you have two choices:

1. **#Missing Label:** This allows you to tell Essbase what value to substitute for null values that are returned in your report

2. **#No Access Label:** This allows you to substitute a value in cells that you do not have the proper access to view

In the **Aliases** section, you have the choices of:

1. **Use Aliases:** This option will return the data using the member names stored in an alias table. If you select this option, the **Alias** table combo-box is available for you to choose the alias table from.

2. **Use Both Member Names and Aliases for Row Dimensions**: This setting will fill two columns as row headers with both the member names and the names stored in the selected alias table.

The **Query Designer** option will only affect you if you are using EQD. If checked, it will apply the sheet options to the resultant report created from an Essbase query.

Lastly, the **Dynamic Time Series** option, when checked, allows you to choose the last date from the time dimension to be used in dynamic time calculations.

As you can see in the next screenshot, we have indented the sub or children items by checking the **Indent SubItems** selection, the columns are automatically adjusted to fit the column names by checking the **Adjust Columns** checkbox, and the #Missing and Zero values have been suppressed because only the calendar periods with data have been displayed. You can tell this because the value for Quarter 1 is the same as the value to 2009. If there were values for the subsequent calendar periods, the total for 2009 would be different than the Quarter 1 2009 value.

	A	B	C	D	E	F	G	H	I
1		TOTAL VEHICLES	TOTAL MARKET	CUSTOMER	SCENARIO	MODEL YEAR	US DOLLAR	GROSS REVENUE	
2	AUGUST 2008	500000							
3	SEPTEMBER 2008	1400000							
4	QUARTER3 OF 2008	1900000							
5	OCTOBER 2008	620000							
6	NOVEMBER 2008	743960							
7	DECEMBER 2008	1480000							
8	QUARTER4 OF 2008	2843960							
9	YEAR 2008	4743960							
10									
11									
12									
13									

Zoom tab

The functions found on this tab are page or sheet level options that aid the user in quickly drilling up or down to desired levels of data.

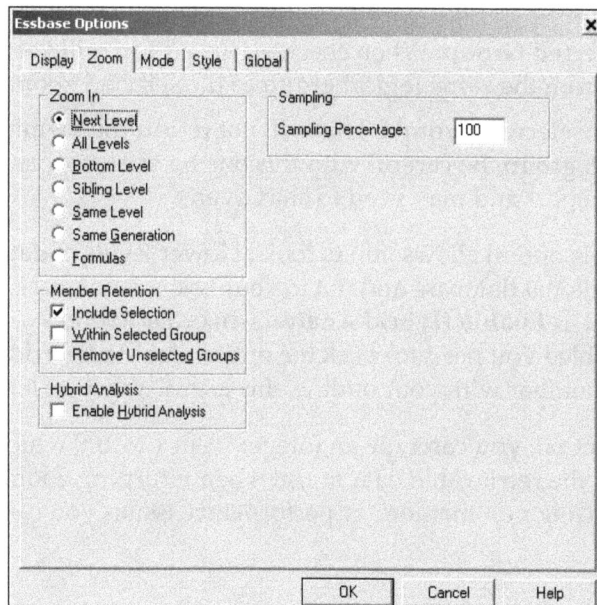

The first section on the **Zoom** tab allows you to control how the add-in reacts when you use the **Zoom In** function. You may be wondering what zoom in and zoom out means? As you all know, on a camera there is a function that allows you to zoom in on your subject. What does it do? It will give you a closer look at the object for which you are trying to take a picture. In a similar way, when we use the **Zoom In** function in Essbase, its gives you a closer look at the data by drilling down either one level down or several levels down. There is an entire range of choices but you are allowed only one at a time.

Your **Zoom In** choices are explained as follows:

- **Next Level**: The zoom will go to the next level down from the selected member from which you zoomed.

- **All Levels**: The zoom will go all the way down to the bottom of the dimension and include all of the levels in-between.

- **Bottom Level**: This option will skip all intermediate levels and return only the lowest level from the dimension that was zoomed on.

The rest of the choices are self-explanatory here and perform similarly.

The **Member Retention** section gives you options that tell Essbase what to do with the member(s) that you selected for your zoom:

- **Include Selection**: This will zoom from the selected member to the level determined by the previous set of options and also include the selected member.

- **Within Selected Group**: When checked, the add-in will keep all members if they are from the same logical group as the selected zoom member.

- **Remove Unselected Groups**: This will not return the members that are not in a selected group. Be careful with this one because you can lose members from your report and may need to start over.

The **Hybrid Analysis** option allows you to look at lower levels of data that is available in the back-end relational database and not in your Essbase database. The outline members are tagged as **Enable Hybrid Analysis**. In order to know which members are hybrid analysis enabled you need to check the option **Enable Hybrid Analysis**. Unless you are intimately familiar with your outline, this is probably best left unchecked.

In the **Sampling** section, you can type an integer from 1 to 100 which will tell Essbase what percentage of the retrievable data to use when returning zoom data. Unless your zooms are causing you memory or performance issues you can leave this at **100**.

Mode tab

The **Mode** tab allows the user to select the mode that Essbase will use to deliver the data to the Microsoft Excel worksheet. There is also an option on this tab that allows the user to control the read access mode that Essbase will use against the data while a user is connected to a database and is actively retrieving data.

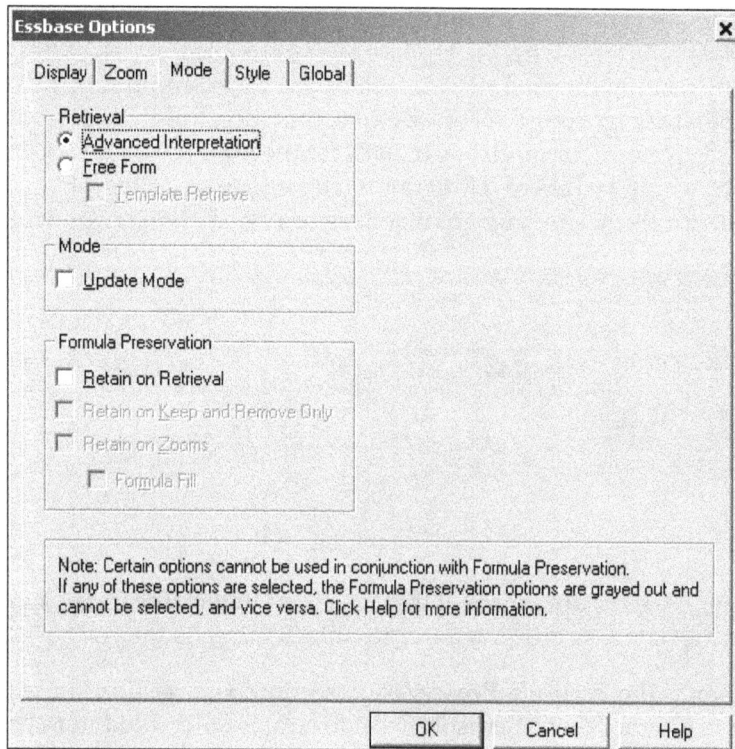

The **Retrieval** section of this tab allows you to tell Essbase how you want to configure your Microsoft Excel worksheet for retrieves:

- **Advanced Interpretation**: This choice allows you to layout your spreadsheet any way you like, as long as you are following the basic Essbase rules for report formatting with regard to row and column member placement.

- **Free Form**: This option will try to determine the best way to layout your report and it may not be the format you like. Also, this option allows you to check the **Template Retrieve** option, which will allow you to enter Essbase report script commands directly onto the spreadsheet for retrieval.

The center section is the **Update Mode** option. Be careful with this option because when checked, if you have the proper database permissions, Essbase will exclusively lock all of the data cells and/or blocks that contain the data represented in your spreadsheet, whether you used it for data **Retrieves** or data **Sends**. The blocks will remain locked by you until you perform an **Essbase | Unlock** using the spreadsheet you originally locked the cells with. When the cells or blocks are exclusively locked by you, other users or processes cannot access the locked data and will fail.

In the next screenshot you see a spreadsheet with data from an Essbase database. If you perform a data retrieve with the **Update Mode** box checked, all of the data blocks that contain any piece of the data represented by the sheet would remain exclusively locked in the database by your ID. For example, the Sales, Production, and Gross Stock for the U.S. market, for model year 2009, for the months of July 2009 through December 2009, would be locked. Until unlocked by you, any attempts to read or update these data values, either by another user or a calculation script, would fail.

		TOTAL MARKET	CUSTOMER	SCENARIO	US DOLLAR	MYR 2009		
		JULY 2009	AUGUST 2009	SEPTEMBER 2009	OCTOBER 2009	NOVEMBER 2009	DECEMBER 2009	
4 DOOR SEDAN	SALES	2850	1800	2275	3250	3800	3200	
	PRODUCTION	3000	3500	3200	3500	3200	3000	
	GROSS STOCK	1650	3350	4275	4525	3925	3725	

If you no longer have the spreadsheet that you used to lock the data blocks and cells, you will need the database administrator to unlock the cells for you.

The third section is the **Formula Preservation** section. This section contains options that tell Essbase how to treat Microsoft Excel formulas embedded in the cells of the spreadsheet:

- **Retain on Retrieval**: If checked Essbase will keep the formula, even if there is data available in the database for this cell
- **Retain on Keep and Remove Only**: This setting tells Essbase to keep any Microsoft Excel formulas that are included during the use of a **Keep Only** or **Remove Only** function.

> The **Mode** tab contains options that are worksheet level and may not apply across all open workbooks.

Global tab

As the name of this tab implies, the options set here apply globally to all Essbase related activity within Microsoft Excel on the current machine. There is an assortment of option types here, from mouse button control to error messaging and Essbase session logging.

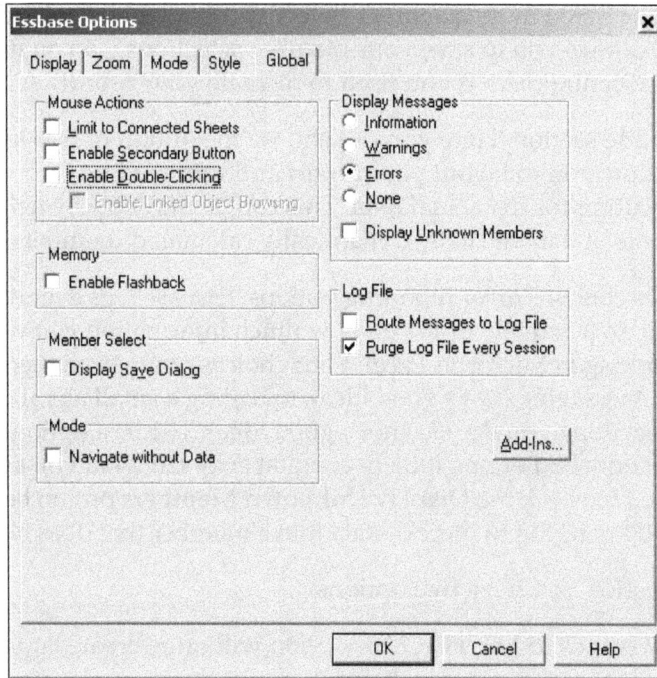

It is always good to check your **Essbase Options** before beginning any serious work just to make sure they are set the way you like them.

The first section on this tab is the **Mouse Actions** option:

- **Limit to Connected Sheets**: Will tell Essbase to apply the **Mouse Actions** option settings to only the Microsoft Excel worksheets that are connected to an Essbase database.

- **Enable Secondary Button**: Gives your mouse Essbase functionality options while right-clicking.

- **Enable Double-Clicking**: This gives you Essbase drill-down capability right in the Microsoft Excel spreadsheet cell. You simply double-click a member and it will perform a **Zoom In**. If you also check the **Enable Linked Object Browsing** option, Essbase will open a **Linked Object** dialog box, if a cell you double-click has a linked object.

The **Memory** section allows you to enable the **Flashback** function. This performs exactly like an undo. You only get one **Flashback** but it can be a lifesaver. You will want to keep this option checked.

The **Display Save Dialog** in the **Member Select** section, when checked, will open a dialog box that allows you to save your member selections, so you do not need to go through reselecting them if you need to recreate your report.

Next up is the **Mode** section. Here you can choose the option of **Navigate without Data**. This will allow you to layout your report and retrieve into it to see how it works without waiting for the actual data. This can be particularly helpful if you have large amounts of data or many dynamically calculated members.

Display Messages contains error reporting options. Essbase logs everything you do in the system logs, so it is really upto you how much information you wish to receive while you are working in Microsoft Excel. Your choices range from there being virtually no error messaging (not a good idea), to having a small alert box appear with a message for everything you do (also not a good idea). The best option is the **Errors** option which will only bother you if there are fatal errors in what you are trying to do. Also, there no need to check the **Display Unknown Members** option because Essbase will tell you if you are trying to retrieve data into a member that does not exist.

In the **Log File** section you have two options:

- **Route Messages to Log File**: This option will often create large log files on your client and is not very helpful or necessary
- **Purge Log File Every Session**: A good idea so you do not create huge, system slowing log files on your client.

Lastly, the **Add-Ins** button allows you to load custom Essbase add-ins. These can be API calls, custom coded functions, or any other repeated functionality that has an add-in format.

Selecting Essbase members for your query

This menu pick is probably the next most used tool after the options screens. The **Essbase Member Selection** screen allows you to quickly and easily set up and populate Microsoft Excel worksheets with your Essbase data.

The basics for this tool are simple. First, make sure you are logged into the appropriate Essbase Application | Database. Second, always remember to select the cell on the Microsoft Excel worksheet where you want the member data to begin populating with your member selections. Third, always remember that you can only select members from one dimension at a time with the Essbase member selection tool.

Select the cell on the worksheet where you want to begin populating report criteria data. To load the **Essbase Member Selection** screen click **Essbase | Member Selection...** from the Microsoft Excel main menu toolbar.

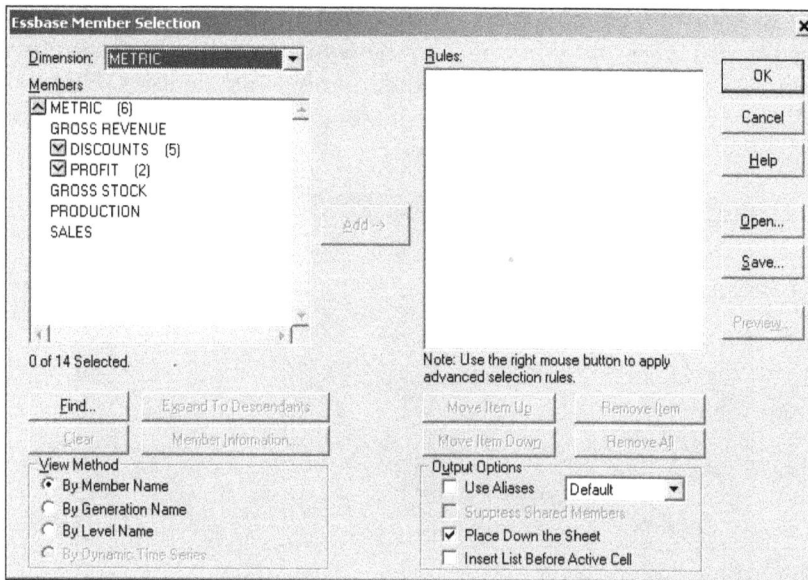

Looking at the preceding screenshot, you will see in the upper left area of the screen a **Dimension** list box. You may select the dimension from which you wish to select members from this list box. The dimension name will then be placed in the **Members** area of the screen where you can click on it to drill down to the levels you need to be at.

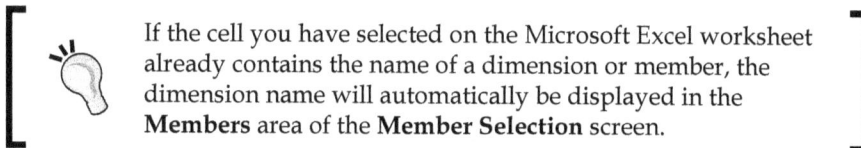

> If the cell you have selected on the Microsoft Excel worksheet already contains the name of a dimension or member, the dimension name will automatically be displayed in the **Members** area of the **Member Selection** screen.

When you click to select a member you can move it to the **Rules** section of the screen by clicking the **Add** button. Or you can simply double-click the member itself.

Below **Members** section of the screen are four buttons. The **Find** button allows you to search the database outline if you are unsure of where a member is in the outline. This function also allows pattern searches so you only need to know part of the name. This is very useful for large dynamically built outlines.

The **Expand to Descendents** button will do just that. It will drill-down on the member you have selected and expand your view all the way to the zero level members. The **Clear** button will clear your selections and the **Member Information** button, when clicked, will open a small display window containing information such as UDAs, and so on, as shown in the following screenshot:

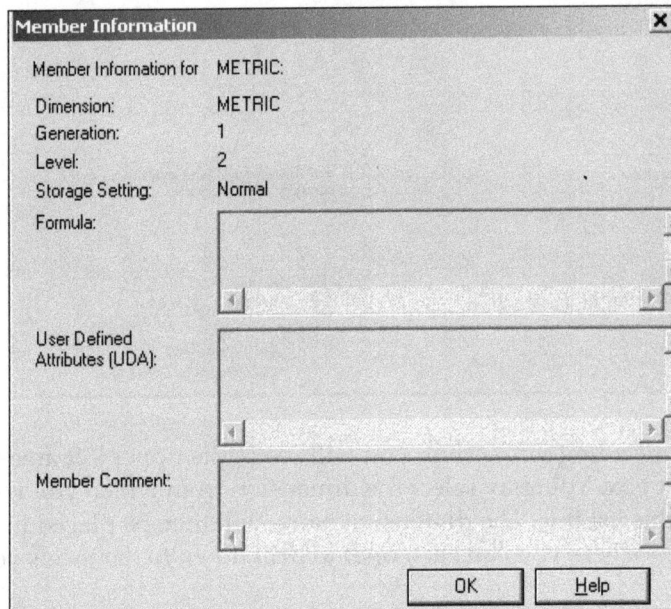

Finally, on the bottom of the left side of the **Member Selection** screen are the options for setting the **View Method**. By now, you should be able to recognize the different choices. For simplicity's sake we will stick with the **By Member Name** setting.

On the right side of the **Member Selection** screen is the **Rules** section. This is where the members you select are moved to so you can verify your selections or apply advanced selection rules to the members.

Once again, Essbase is full of little tricks that make your life easier. If you remember, from the prior screenshot, the **METRIC** dimension is shown in the **Members** area of the screen. The four children of **METRIC** are also shown because the view has been expanded to show this. Let's say you want all four children selected and moved to the **Rules** section of the screen. You could accomplish this in several ways:

- Double-click each individual member to move it to the **Rules** section
- Hold down the *Ctrl* key and click on each individual member to highlight it, then click the **Add** button
- Double-click the **METRIC** member to move it to the **Rules** section, then apply advanced selection rules

Let's go for the third option from the above choices. Double-click the **METRIC** member to move it to the **Rules** section of the **Member Selection** screen. Then right-click to open a small advanced selection rules menu as shown:

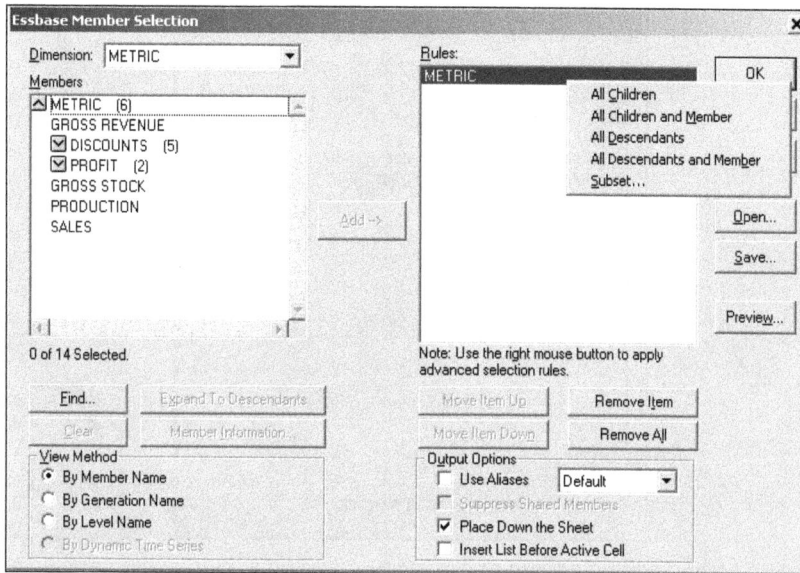

Notice the choices you are offered. You can pick from **All Children**, **All Children and Member**, and more. The one we want to see now is the **Subset** option. Please click on **Subset...** to open the **Subset Dialog** box.

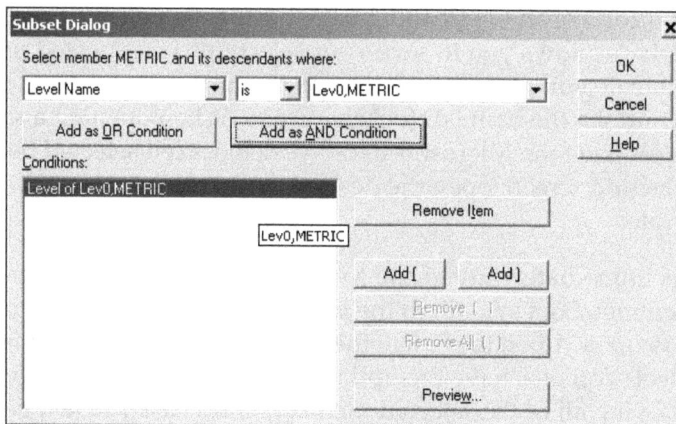

It is in this **Subset Dialog** box that you can really narrow down the member selection criteria. You can use AND/OR operators and parenthesis, as well as pointing to level names, generation names, or any combination.

When you are finished defining your selection rules, you may click the **Preview** button on the **Subset Dialog** box, or click **OK** to return to the **Essbase Member Selection** screen where there is also a **Preview** button.

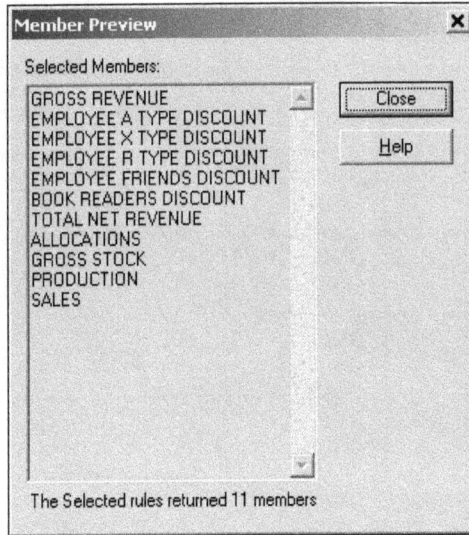

Looking at the above screenshot of the **Member Preview** screen, you can see that the selection rule defined in the **Subset Dialog** box returns the four zero level members of the **METRIC** dimension.

Continuing with the **Member Selection** screen, on the far right side, in addition to the **Preview** button are an **Open** and a **Save** button. Believe it or not, for your convenience, Essbase allows you to save your selections for repeated use. When saving a selection rule you must follow the usual naming conventions for Essbase file objects and limit the file name upto 8 characters. When opening a saved selection rule make sure you have the Microsoft Excel worksheet cell selected before you open the **Member Selection** screen, open the desired saved selection rule file and click **OK**. It's that simple!

The four buttons immediately under the **Rules** pane are for selection manipulation while the selected members are still in the **Rules** pane. You have the options of moving members up or down to change the order in which they are displayed on your worksheet. You also have the options of removing erroneously selected members or removing all of the selected members if it's easier to just begin again.

Finally, there are the **Output Options** checkboxes. These options affect the way Essbase drops the selected members onto the Microsoft Excel worksheet.

If you decide to display your member names using Essbase member aliases, you will also have the option of choosing which alias table to use. Simply check the **Use Aliases** box.

If you choose to **Suppress Shared Members**, Essbase will not return any members that would normally be returned by your selection if they are tagged as **Shared Members** in the database outline. This option is only available if you are viewing the outline in **Level** or **Generation** mode.

If the **Place Down the Sheet** checkbox is checked, Essbase will place the selected members downward vertically, beginning with the active cell on the worksheet. If the box is unchecked Essbase will place the selected members horizontally across the worksheet from left to right, beginning with the active cell.

If you check the **Insert List Before Active Cell** box, Essbase will place the selected members opposite of how they would be placed with the preceding option.

Using the Keep Only function

The **Essbase | Keep Only** function is really great. When you click this function, Essbase will automatically keep all members on the sheet, that are in the same dimension as the members in the selected cells on the worksheet.

This function is perfect if you have selected all cars and pickup trucks for your initial report. You have the zero level members of the **Total Vehicles** dimension as your row header values, as shown in the previous screenshot. If you decide to only show cars (Sedans) on the report, then select the cells with the car member names in them, and click **Essbase | Keep Only**. You can also select multiple rows at the same time and click on **Keep Only**. The report now only contains data for cars as shown in the following screenshot:

Using the Remove Only function

After just reading about the **Essbase | Keep Only** function it should be pretty obvious what the **Essbase | Remove Only** function does.

The **Remove Only** function removes only the members you have selected on your Microsoft Excel worksheet. If we look at the example in the **Keep Only** function, we see that Essbase removed all unselected members of a row or column in the worksheet. **Remove Only** will only remove the members that are selected. Therefore, to keep all of the 4 door car data as in the example above, you would select the **2 Door Sedan** and click on **Essbase | Remove Only**. This will remove the **2 Door Sedan**, leaving you behind the data for the **4 Door Sedan** as shown in the following screenshot:

Zooming in on your data

Here is a nice function to get familiar with. Before we explain how this function works, please remember the setting of the **Essbase Options** screens where there are options to set the **Zoom** function's behavior.

To use the **Essbase | Zoom In** function simply select any parent level members of a dimension listed on your Microsoft Excel worksheet and click **Essbase | Zoom In**. It's that easy.

Let's say your **Essbase Options** for the **Zoom** functions are set to **Bottom Level** and **Keep Selection**. You select the **Total Vehicles** member on your worksheet and click on **Essbase | Zoom In**. Your sheet now has all of the **Zero** level members from the **Total Vehicles** dimension, as well as the **Total Vehicles** member itself as shown in the following screenshot:

Essbase | Zoom In is a nice, convenient way to add new members to your report without a lot of effort.

Zooming out on your data

Perhaps you have noticed a pattern here. We have a pair of functions that basically perform similar, but opposite tasks. The **Essbase | Zoom Out** function performs exactly the opposite task as the **Essbase | Zoom In** function.

Once again, how you have your **Essbase Options** set for the zoom function, will determine how **Zoom Out** behaves.

If you have your **Zoom** options set to **Next Level** and you select a **Zero Level** member on your worksheet, then click **Essbase | Zoom Out**, and Essbase will replace the selected member with the member next up in the outline. Typically this would be a **Parent** member of the selected member. As seen in the following screenshot, if you select Pickup truck and click on **Essbase | Zoom Out,** you update the Microsoft Excel sheet with the parent level member of the Pickup, which in this case is the **Total Vehicles** member as shown:

Pivot Essbase members on your spreadsheet

The **Essbase | Pivot** function is another nice tool in your toolbox. This function pivots members that you have placed on your worksheet as row headers upto columns headers and vice versa. To use this function all you need to do is to select, for instance, a group of row members and then click **Essbase | Pivot** and Essbase will pivot them upto be column members.

Another handy task that **Pivot** will perform for you is to transpose column or row members with another column or row grouping. You will need to have the secondary mouse button functionality enabled in your **Essbase | Options** for this to work.

With the secondary mouse button enabled just click and hold on the member you want to swap and drag it on top of the member you want to swap with. While you are not actually clicking the **Essbase | Pivot** for this functionality Essbase considers it to be a part of the pivot functionality.

Flashback: The Essbase Add-in Undo

Flashback is your Essbase undo function. To use this functionality you need to have the **Enable Flashback** option checked in the **Essbase | Options**.

Immediately after using most of the available Essbase functions in the Essbase add-in, and especially after an **Essbase | Retrieve**, if you are not happy with the results of the task you just executed, all you need to do is click on **Essbase | Flashback** to reset your worksheet back to the way it was prior to the most recent task you performed.

Sadly, you only get one flashback, but it can be a life saver.

> We have found that one of the best times to have the flashback functionality is right after this unfortunate event.
>
> You have just spent a bit of time setting up your worksheet, just the way you want it. You have the row members and the column members set up. You click **Essbase | Retrieve** and the sheet re-arranges itself and wrecks your entire layout. What happened? Well, more than likely, you have the Essbase **Mode** options set to **Free Form** instead of **Advanced Interpretation**.
>
> Not to worry though, just click **Essbase | Flashback** and all of your hard work is restored back to the way it was before your little mishap.
>
> Didn't we say, it's a good idea to always double-check your **Essbase | Options** prior to getting heavily involved in your work?

Locking the data and retrieving

This function is exactly like the **Essbase | Retrieve** function with one huge difference. On top of retrieving the data into your Microsoft Excel worksheet, when clicked, this function will also lock all of the data blocks relative to the member information on the worksheet.

You need to be careful with **Essbase | Retrieve & Lock,** because the locked blocks will remain locked by your ID, until you unlock them with the **Essbase | Unlock** function.

If there are other users of the system that may need to access data locked by you and your worksheet, they will be unable to access it until it is unlocked by you. Also, any background processes, like database calculations or report scripts, will fail when they cannot access the locked data.

Locking the data

We wonder if you can't guess what this function does.

Well, when you click **Essbase | Lock**, Essbase locks all of the data blocks in the database that are needed to represent the data on your Microsoft Excel worksheet.

Again, be careful as the data will remain locked by your ID until you unlock it by clicking on **Essbase | Unlock**.

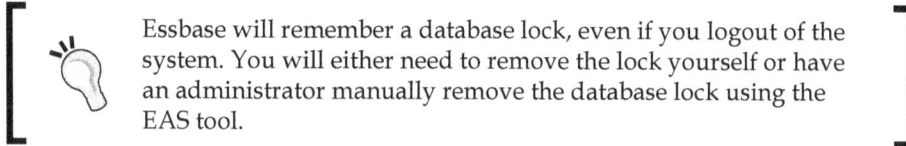

> Essbase will remember a database lock, even if you logout of the system. You will either need to remove the lock yourself or have an administrator manually remove the database lock using the EAS tool.

Unlocking the locked data

The **Essbase | Unlock** function is used to unlock data blocks in the database that have been locked by you.

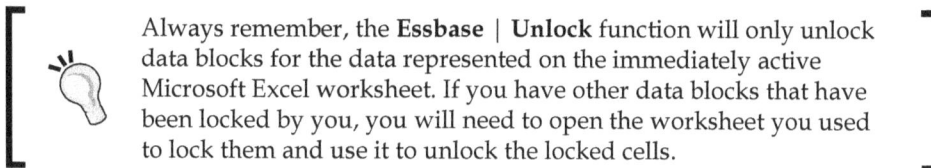

> Always remember, the **Essbase | Unlock** function will only unlock data blocks for the data represented on the immediately active Microsoft Excel worksheet. If you have other data blocks that have been locked by you, you will need to open the worksheet you used to lock them and use it to unlock the locked cells.

Sending your data to the database

This function sends data back to the database. In a relational database this would be known as an **Insert** or an **Update**.

To insert or update data in an Essbase database it is as easy as pulling data into your formatted Microsoft Excel worksheet by performing an **Essbase | Retrieve,** then adding new values or updating existing values. When finished, perform an **Essbase | Send** to save the new values to the database.

It is very important to note that the actual steps to use the **Essbase | Send** function are follows:

1. Perform an **Essbase | Lock**. Essbase will not write to data blocks that are not previously locked.

2. Perform an **Essbase | Send**. The only time that Essbase will automatically unlock the data cells you have locked is after an **Essbase | Send**.

Running a database calculation

To be able to make use of the **Essbase | Calculation** function, your Essbase ID must at least have calculation privileges on the database you are connected to. If you do have the proper database permissions, when you click **Essbase | Calculation,** you will see the small screen shown here:

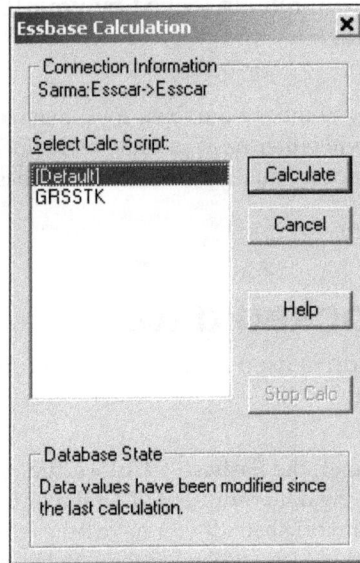

This little screen is actually pretty useful. On top of showing you your current database connection and a little state of the database message, you are allowed to select the specific calculation script you wish to execute and you can click **Calculate** to run it.

There is a **Cancel** button which will close the small screen without executing any calc scripts. There is also a **Stop Calc** button that allows you to attempt to halt an executing database calculation script. The reason we say the **Stop Calc** button attempts to halt the calculation script is because Essbase determines when it is a good and safe time to halt an executing database calculation script.

There is also what is known as the point of no return, where Essbase will decide if it is safer to complete the execution of the calculation script rather than interrupt it.

Retrieving your sheet without data

This is a nice little function, especially if you're just setting up a worksheet and do not really need to look at the resultant data. It is also good if you are worried about large queries and system performance. When you retrieve a worksheet with the **Essbase | Navigate Without Data** function turned on your query will perform exactly as it is supposed to, except that it will not return any data to the spreadsheet. For instance, if you perform an **Essbase | Zoom In**, the sheet will update as far as the member names being displayed, but no data values will be returned.

To use **Essbase | Navigate Without Data** simply click it. The function toggles back and forth when clicked and is either on or off as indicated by a check mark next to the function name on the Essbase menu, as shown in the following screenshot:

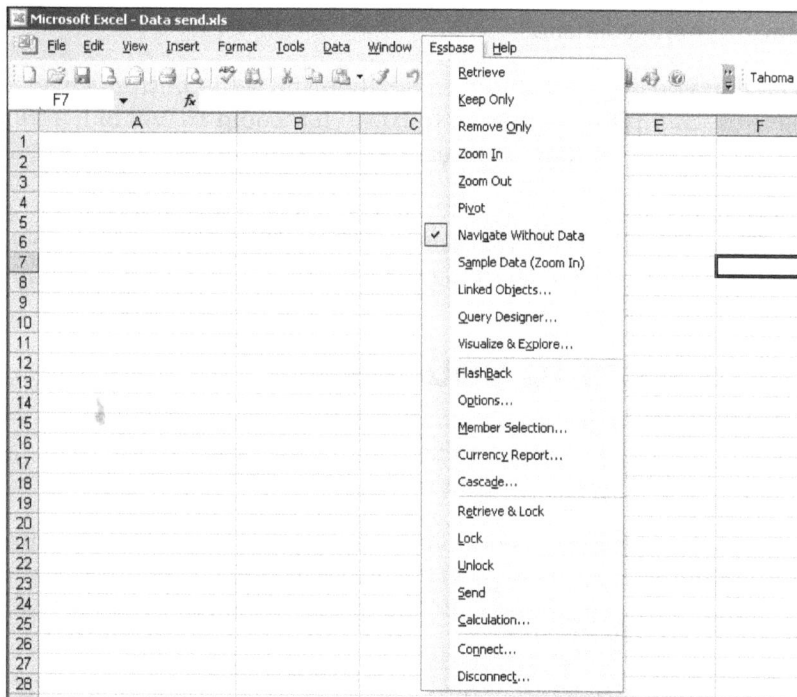

Most of the other functions are one time uses so they do not need an indicator letting you know whether they are active or not. In the case of the **Essbase | Navigate Without Data** function, if it is active you will see a little orange box with a check mark in it next to the function name in the left margin of the Essbase add-in menu. Click the function name again to turn it off.

Zooming in on sample data

This function allows you to return only sample subsets of the actual data that a retrieve may return. The **Essbase | Sample Data (Zoom In)** function depends on how you have two **Essbase | Options** set. First, is the sampling percentage setting on the **Zoom** tab of the **Essbase | Options** screen. Whatever percentage this is set to is the amount of data which will be returned when you **Zoom In** using this function. How much you **Zoom In** is determined by the **Zoom** setting, also on the **Zoom** tab of the **Essbase | Options** screen.

For example, if you click on a member name on your spreadsheet and then click the **Sample Data (Zoom In)** function, your data will be returned as follows: Let's say there are 200 children members under the member you selected for the **Sample Data (Zoom In)** function and your **Zoom In** function is set to **Bottom Level,** and your **Sampling** setting is set to 100%. This **Zoom In** will return all 200 children members into your spreadsheet.

Let's now say that you have the **Zoom In** function still set to **Bottom Level** but this time you have the **Sampling** setting set to 10%. This **Zoom In** will only return the first 20 children members into your spreadsheet. These 20 members are 10% of the 200 that are available.

The **Sample Data (Zoom In)** function works very well for Zoom Ins on particularly large dimensions if you are just checking the data and do not need to see all of it.

Linking objects to your data

In Essbase it is possible to link an object, such as a file object, to a specific data cell in the database. This object can contain information or explanations on or about the data or it can be whatever you want it to be.

The **Essbase | Linked Objects...** command displays the **Linked Objects Browser** dialog box. The **Linked Objects Browser** allows you to create or access linked objects and displays the objects currently linked to the data cell you have selected.

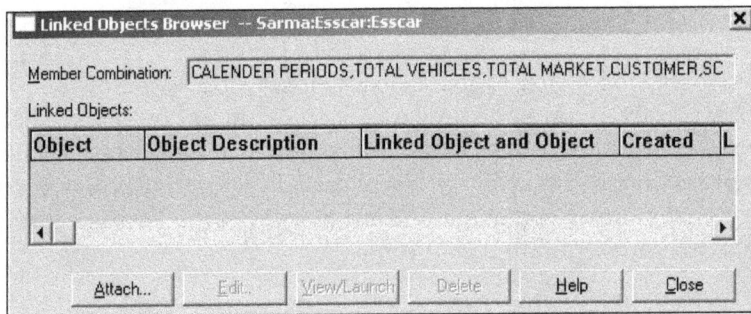

You cannot create linked objects for member combinations containing attributes. Also, you cannot use the **Linked Objects Browser** dialog box in **Free Form** mode.

Creating graphical data representations

When you click on **Essbase | Visualize & Explore...** it will launch the **Hyperion Visual Explorer** (HVE). This option does require a separate license but is about as close to an off-the-shelf data dashboard as you can get.

The HVE helps you explore and analyze data in an Essbase database. But more specifically, it provides an easy to use interface for creating graphical summaries and reports of your data in a highly interactive user interface. These graphical summaries answer questions about market totals, scenario versus scenario comparisons, regional rankings, and buying trends. You can answer with visual representation, any questions there may be regarding the data stored in your company's Essbase databases. The results are high impact and impressive. The biggest difference between the Microsoft Excel add-in and HVE is the Microsoft Excel add-in uses the traditional native connection, where as the HVE uses the specialized multidimensional database query language known as MDX. We will explain MDX in greater detail in a future chapter.

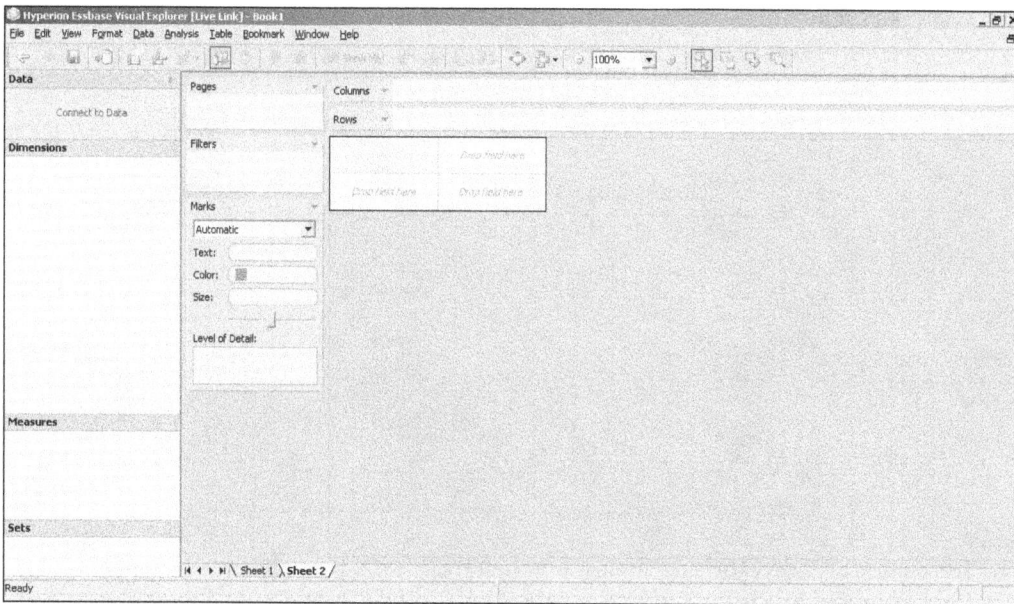

Best of all you will look like a hero using this tool and no one but you will know how easy it was to use.

Using the currency conversion tool

To use the **Essbase | Currency Report...** function you must purchase a separate license for the Essbase currency conversion tool. Unless you have extensive currency conversion needs there are ways to create financial data without it.

The **Essbase | Currency Report...** function enables you to perform ad hoc currency conversions during data retrieval. When you select **Essbase | Currency Report...** the **Essbase Currency Report** dialog box is displayed. If you have implemented a currency conversion application you can use the **Currency Report** command to dynamically perform currency retrievals and currency conversions.

Custom Microsoft Excel workbook reporting

The **Essbase | Cascade...** command allows you to replicate Microsoft Excel worksheets using member combinations. You can have retrieved data flow across multiple Microsoft Excel worksheets in the same Microsoft Excel workbook, or you can create multiple cascaded Microsoft Excel workbooks stored in different locations.

When you select **Essbase | Cascade...** the **Essbase Cascade Options** dialog box is displayed.

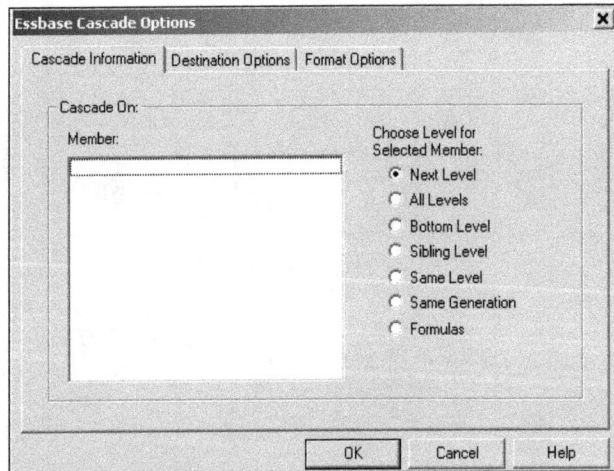

The **Essbase Cascade Options** dialog box has three tabs that allow you to set the formatting and storage options for the cascaded reports you will create:

- **Cascade Information**: On this tab, you select what outline members you want to cascade on and the zoom level you wish to zoom to.

- **Destination Options**: On this tab, you can choose where to store the newly created Microsoft Excel workbooks.

There are options for either opening existing files or overwriting them with new ones. You can make your choices as to creating worksheets in a workbook or creating new workbooks themselves.

Finally, there are naming options for you to take advantage of, including prefix and suffix designations, to be used while naming your workbooks.

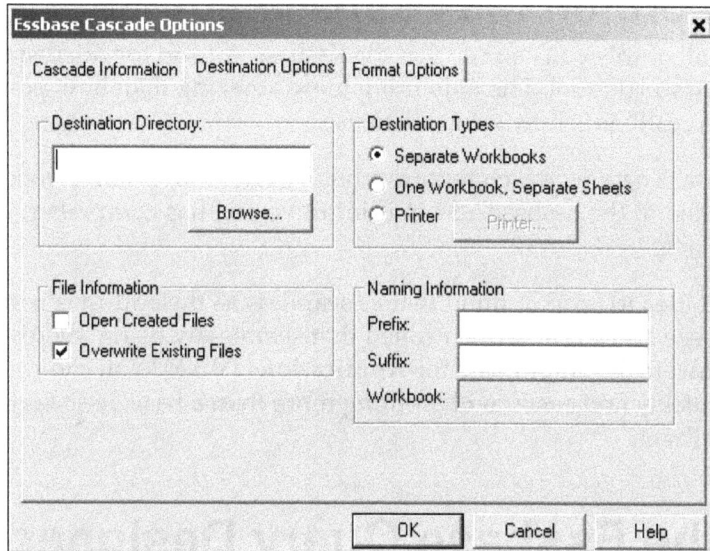

- **Format Options**: This tab allows you to choose your workbook formatting options.

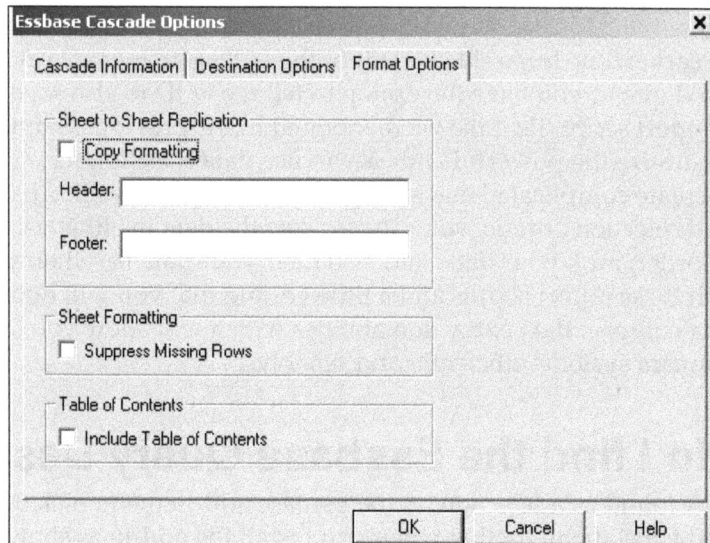

The formatting options include choosing whether to copy the existing workbook formatting, adding custom page headers and footers, suppressing rows that don't contain data from your reports, and including a table of contents with each workbook.

A final word on the Essbase add-in

After reading all of this you can see that the Essbase Add-in for Microsoft Excel is an incredibly powerful tool. The only thing more amazing than how powerful the Essbase add-in really is is how easy it is to use.

Except for a few functions which require a bit of practice to become good at, every function included in the Essbase add-in is intuitive and has comprehensive help that is readily available.

It's also a good idea to keep in mind that as seamless as the add-in is with Microsoft Excel, the Essbase add-in can be controlled that seamlessly using Microsoft Excel's built-in and powerful **Visual Basic for Applications (VBA)**. You can create powerful applications quickly and easily with nothing more than a basic Essbase installation and Microsoft Excel.

Using the Essbase Query Designer

The EQD is a wonderful tool within a tool that allows you to set up reports and spreadsheets with the aid of an easy to use visual interface tool. Once you have a query designed just the way you want it you can save it off and use it over and over again to retrieve your data.

As mentioned earlier, one huge side benefit of the EQD is that when saving your custom designed query, you have the option to tell the EQD to also save the query as an Essbase report script file. Like we mentioned in the previous chapter, this option lets you utilize the powerful and easy to use data selection functionality of the EQD to create complicated and specific report scripts as well. Apart from the complicated selection criteria, you can also sort the data in either ascending or descending order, rank your data, and also filter your data based on your own needs. It is with these report scripts and a little editing that you will find yourself in possession of complex data extraction abilities which will allow you to feed data to downstream systems efficiently and reliably.

Where do I find the Essbase Query Designer

The EQD can be found as a selection on the Essbase add-in menu pick that is added to the Microsoft Excel menu toolbar when you install the add-in as shown:

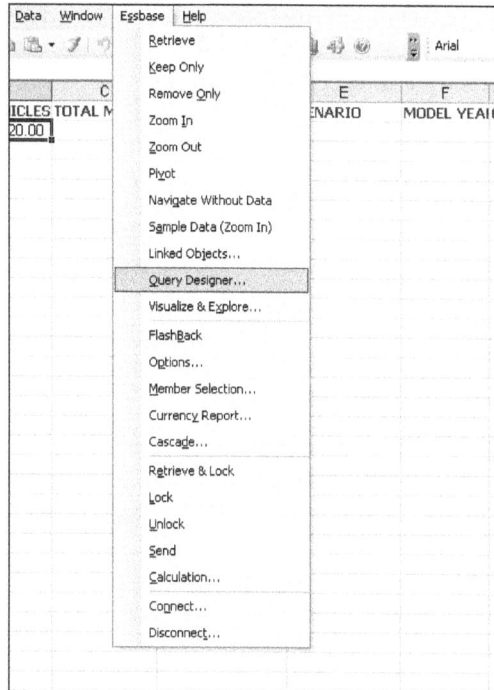

As you can see, finding and accessing the EQD was easy enough. By clicking on the **Query Designer...** selection you are presented with the primary EQD screen shown as follows:

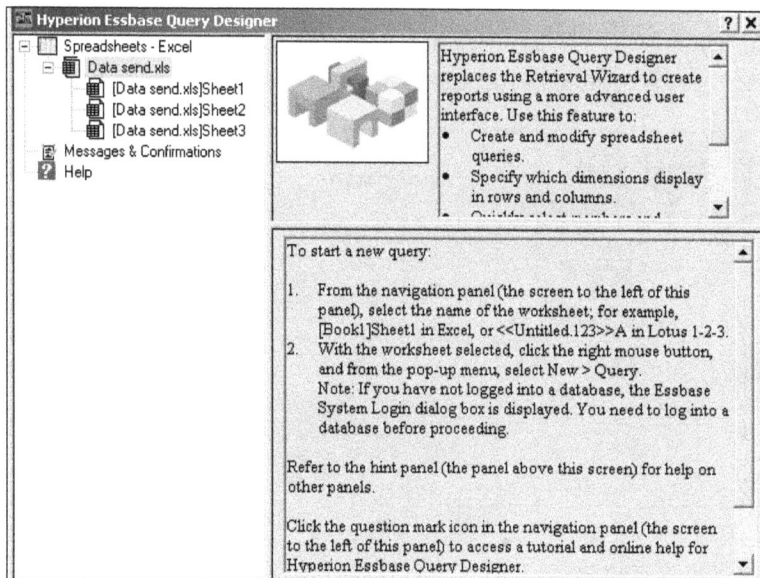

One look at the preceding screenshot and you will see that while the EQD is a very powerful tool, it is also a very user-friendly tool. Oracle has made great strides in creating tools that are intuitive and packed with instructions and help.

Now, looking at the previous screenshot, you see the screen is divided into three panes. Each pane has its own purpose.

- The upper-right pane will always contain information, tips, or even step-by-step instructions, pertinent to the area of the EQD you are currently in.
- The lower-right pane, on the main screen, contains brief instructions on how to open a new query. The lower-right pane on other screens accepts input from you as you build your query. In other words, it is in this area that you make your selections.
- The left pane is your organizational pane and it shows you information about the entire scope of your current Microsoft Excel session. For instance the left pane shows you, in tree format similar to the Essbase Administration Services, what workbooks you have open, what worksheets are available to you in each workbook, and important database outline dimension and member information relative to the queries you are building and the Microsoft Excel workbooks you are building them in.

The active Microsoft Excel workbook that was open is selected in the left pane when you start the EQD. Anytime you select a workbook in the left pane it will display the initial, or main EQD screen.

The three other EQD screens are displayed based on what selection you have made in the left pane.

- By clicking on any worksheet available to EQD, a tree view is displayed in the query information screen as shown in the following screenshot:

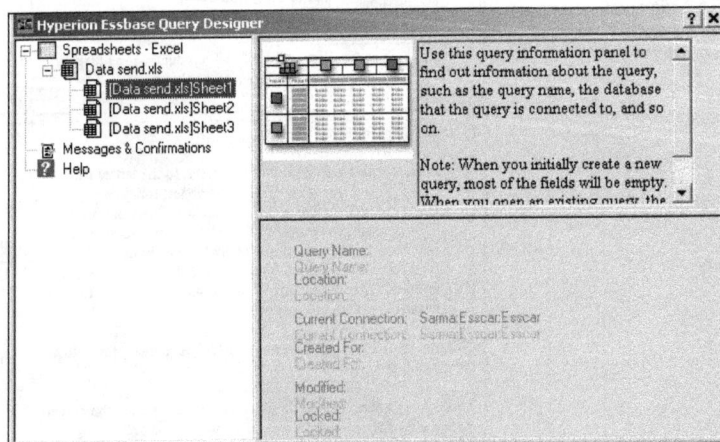

The query information screen contains information about the query itself like its name, location, the database connection, and so on.

- The next screen in the EQD is the **Messages and Confirmations** screen. This screen allows input from you in the form of checkbox selections.

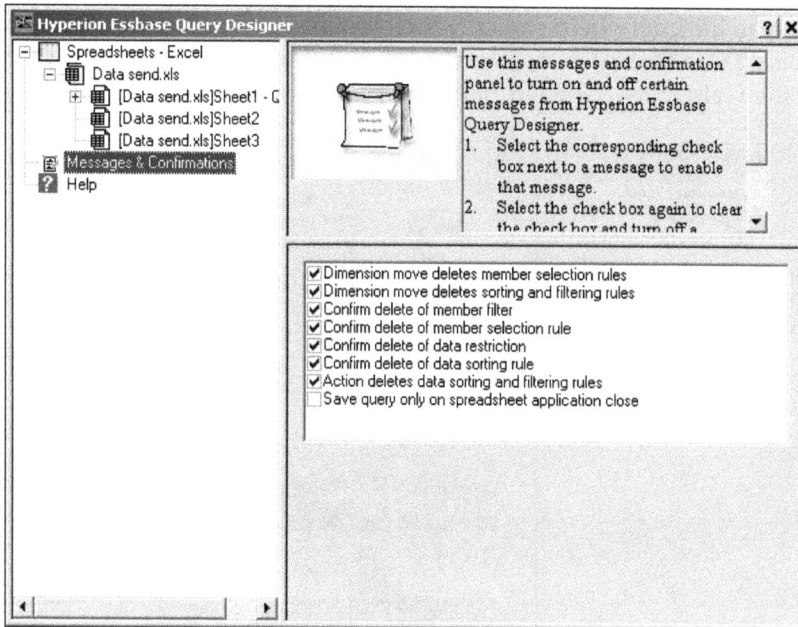

The selections on the **Messages and Confirmations** screen can be very helpful depending on how you select them. As you can see in the preceding screenshot, the selections on the **Messages and Confirmations** screen are fairly intuitive.

For example, the very first checkbox, **Dimension move deletes member selection rules**, will remove member selection rules on a dimension if you move it from a row member to a column member or vice versa, when checked.

Likewise, the second selection, **Dimension move deletes sorting and filtering rules**, will remove any sorting and/or filtering rules on a dimension if you move it from a column member to a row member or vice versa, when checked.

When you read through the rest of the choices you will see they offer similar choices that you can select, depending on how comfortable you are using the EQD. For the most part the **Messages and Confirmations** selections give you the option of message boxes popping up asking for confirmation when you are attempting to perform a function in the query designer.

- There is the query help screen which is shown below. Again, this screen is divided into three panes, as are the rest of the EQD screens. When you click on the **Help** icon in the left pane, the screen will change to the **Help** screen.

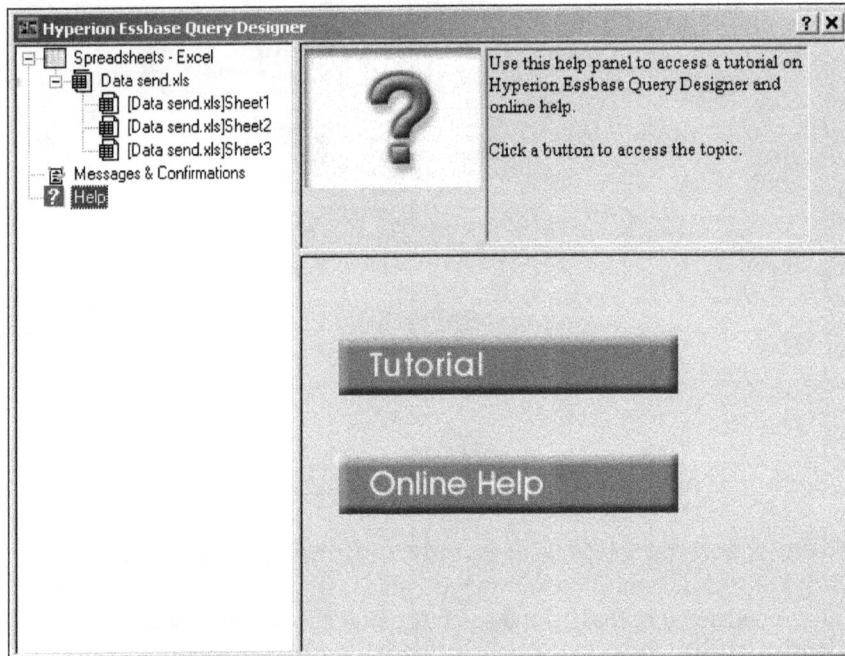

Referring to the usual upper-right pane on the screen, you will see tips on how to use the EQD help. In the lower-right pane are two buttons. These buttons offer you the choice between stepping through an EQD tutorial or activating the EQD online help. This screen is pretty much an intuitive screen that you can best learn how to use by exploring on your own.

Creating a query with Essbase Query Designer

Essbase queries are associated with individual worksheets in a Microsoft Excel workbook. This is not to say that a query cannot be used in several worksheets, it's just that the development of a query must be associated with an individual worksheet.

From any of the EQD screens all you need to do to begin a query is to right-click with your mouse on any worksheet listed in any workbook that is displayed in the left or organizational pane of any of the EQD screens. When you right-click on an available worksheet it will display a menu as seen in the following screenshot:

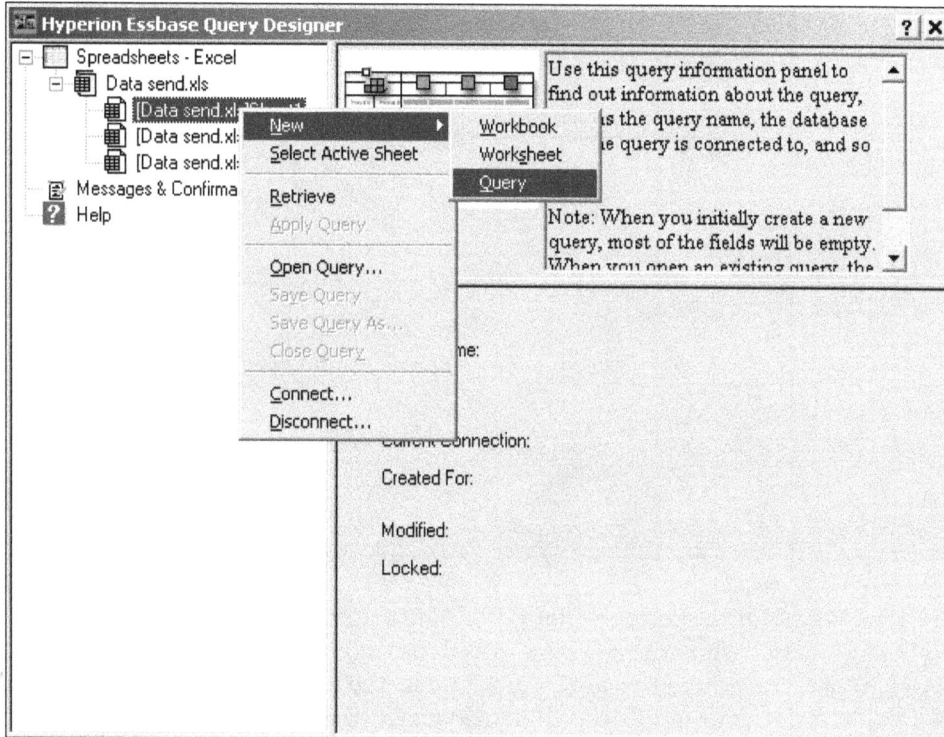

From this menu you will be offered several selections. If you click on **New,** you will be offered three options:

- Create a new Microsoft Excel workbook
- Insert a new worksheet into the active Microsoft Excel workbook
- Create a new Query

There are also options to **Select Active Sheet**, which selects the active worksheet in the workbook. You can choose to **Open Query, Retrieve** data into the active worksheet, or most importantly, **Connect** or **Disconnect** to and from the desired Essbase database. If you are already logged in to Essbase through the active workbook, there is no need to login again through EQD.

Make sure you are logged in one way or another then select **New | Query** to begin creating your Essbase query. The following screenshot shows how the designer will look when you are actually creating or editing an Essbase query:

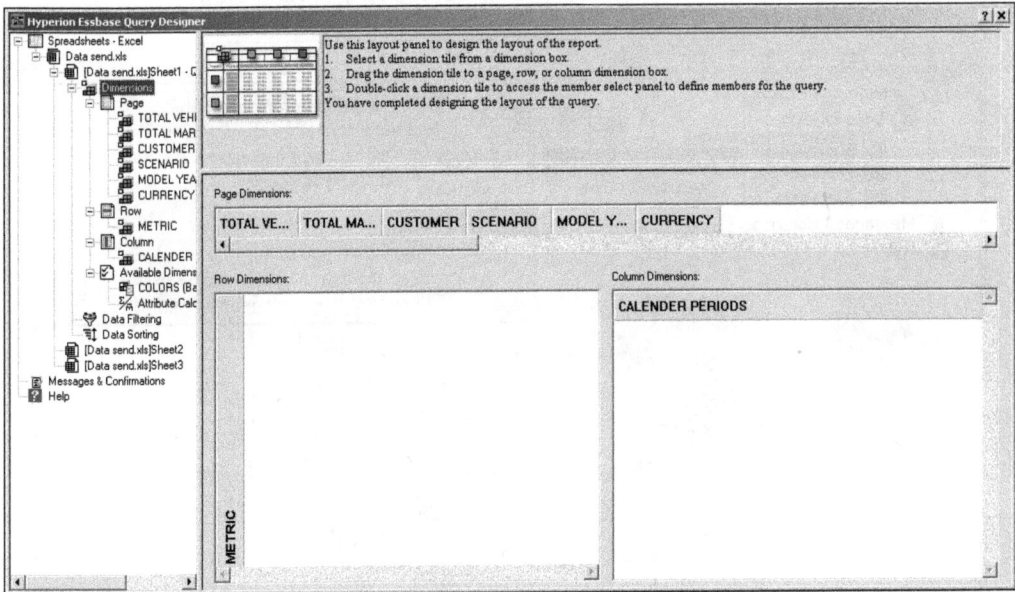

Notice how your EQD screen has changed. There are still three panes common to all EQD screens, but while the left pane is still the organizational screen and the upper-right pane is still the tips and tutorial pane, the lower-right pane now displays a relational view of your database's dimensions. Essbase will drop in place the database dimensions as it thinks they should be. Obviously you will set up your query the way you want to.

There are three sections involved with setting up a query which are identical to how the dimensions are selected when setting up an **Essbase Report Script**.

> Remember, when saving an Essbase query created with EQD, you can also have Essbase save a matching Essbase report script at the same time. This can be a huge help in the creation of a quickly needed Report Script which will need little, if any, additional editing to be used as described at length in the previous chapter.

Page dimensions

Page dimensions are members that only need to be mentioned once on the page header and the resultant report will only contain data for that member. For example, if you were to place the member **Canada** from the **Total Market** dimension as a page dimension, all of the data in the report will be for the **Canada** market.

Row dimensions

Row dimensions are members that populate the report's row headings. For example, if you wanted to create a report that has all of the vehicles listed on the left as row headings, you would drag-and-drop the **Total Vehicles** dimension tile from the **Page Dimension** section to the **Row Dimension** section and tell it to extract the children of the **Total Vehicles** dimension.

Depending on your other choices, the resultant report will contain data displayed with the individual vehicles listed as row headings.

Column dimensions

Just like the row dimensions, column dimensions are the members you use for the column headings on your report. For example, a common way to set up a report that shows a year's worth of data is to have the individual months placed horizontally across the top of the columns. What you would do is drag-and-drop the **Calendar Periods** dimension tile into the **Column Dimensions** section and setup the rule that selects the desired range of months you need.

Sample query

By looking at the previous screenshot you will see that if you were to retrieve data based on the default dimension placement, you would not get a very informative report.

For starters, the page dimensions listed are **Total Vehicles**, **Total Market**, and **Model Year**. Without any changes this will give you a report where all of the data returned would be at the **Total Vehicle**, **Total Market**, and total **Model Year** level. Not a very granular report to say the least. The fact that the **Measures** dimension is placed in the **Row Dimensions** section and the **Calendar Periods** dimension is placed in the **Column Dimensions** section, is the only thing saving this query.

What if we wanted a report that showed us two years of data for all of the vehicles Esscar builds, for all of the markets Esscar sells in, and the most current model years. Here is what we would do:

1. Rearrange the dimension tiles into the sections (as shown in the following screenshot). Also, notice how the left pane now shows the database dimensions listed under the active worksheet that you are creating the query in.

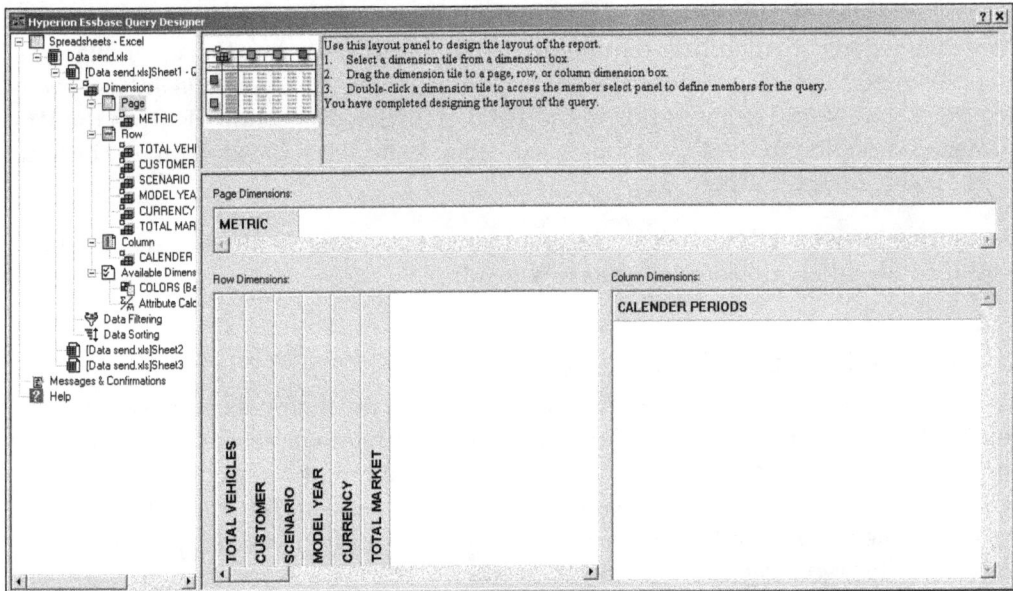

2. We now define selection rules to the dimensions so they return the data we want. Let's begin with the **Page Dimensions**. Double-click on the **METRIC** tile in the **Page Dimensions** section to move to the member selection and selection rules screen. This screen is the same as the screen shown in the previous screenshot. However, now the lower-right pane is divided into two sections, the **Members** section and the **Selection Rules** section. Notice how the **Members** section displays the name of the dimension you double-clicked and all of the children members. Double-click the **Gross Stock** member to place it in the **Selection Rules** section.

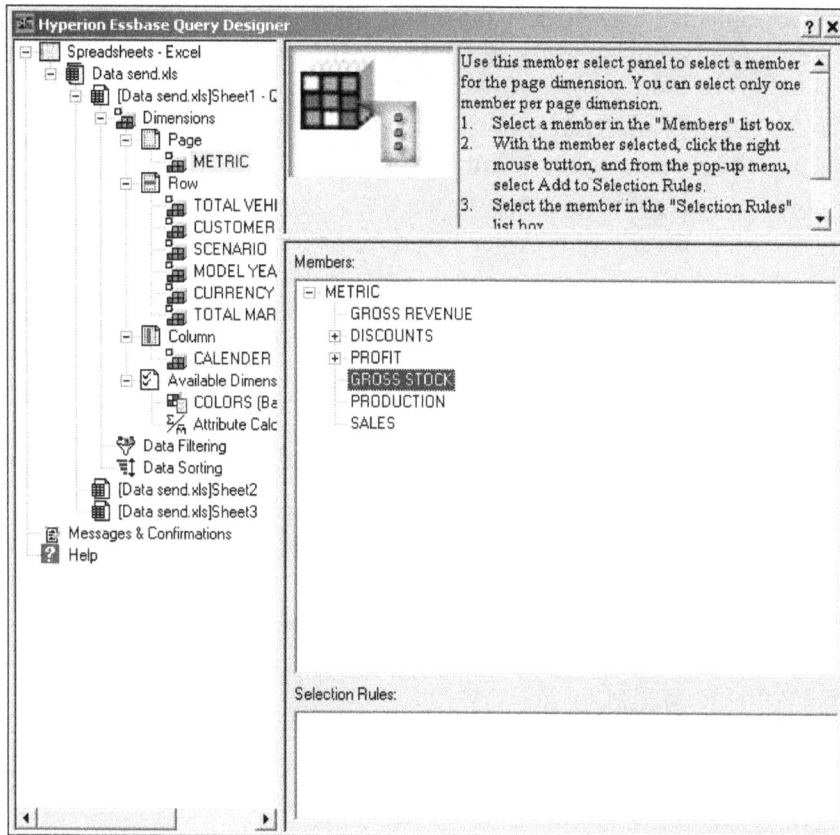

3. Next, click on the **Calendar Periods** dimension listed under the **Column** heading in the left pane. This will populate the **Members** section with the **Calendar Periods** dimension and its immediate children, which are the YEAR's members.

4. Double-click on each year member to have it placed into the **Selection Rules** section of the screen.

5. Right-click on each of the year members. Here you are offered a small menu with available member selection rule criteria. The various member selection rules criteria are as follows:

   i)   **New Member Filter**: Brings you to a new area in the EQD screens where you are allowed to refine your data selection criteria by **Level** or **Generation** and also add **And** and **Or** clauses.

   ii) **Preview…**: When clicked, **Preview…** brings up a small window which will display all database outline members which will be selected by the current rule set.

iii) **Select >**: This option allows you to select a definite rule, such as all children of the given member or all descendents of a given member.

iv) **Delete Selection Rule**: By clicking this option you will delete the currently selected member selection rule.

v) **Delete All Rules**: By clicking this option you will delete all rules for the active query and need to start over adding rules.

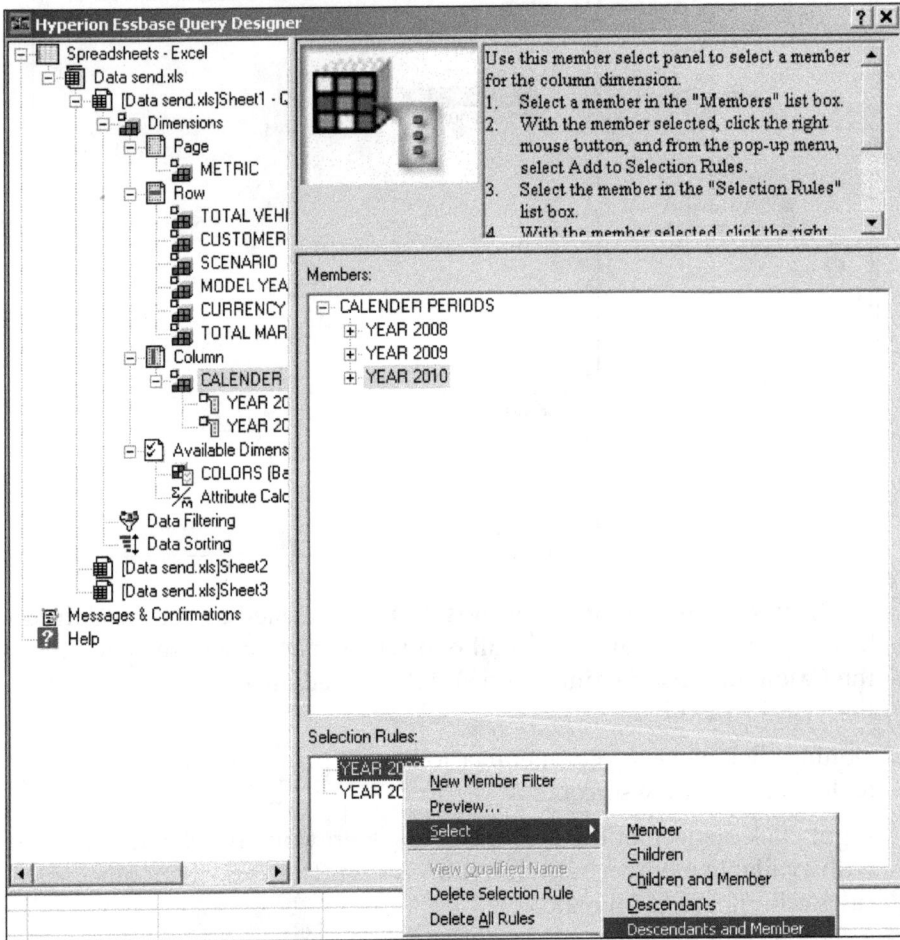

6. Select **New Member Filter** as this option can give you the most control when filtering outline members. Notice how the lower right pane of the EQD screen changes again. This time you are allowed to create a member selection rule based on where the members are in the outline. You can choose between **Level** selection and **Generation** selection and also can use **And** or **Or** clauses as well.

7. In this case we will select **Level 0** members for our criteria, which will return to us all of the month members for the years we have selected.

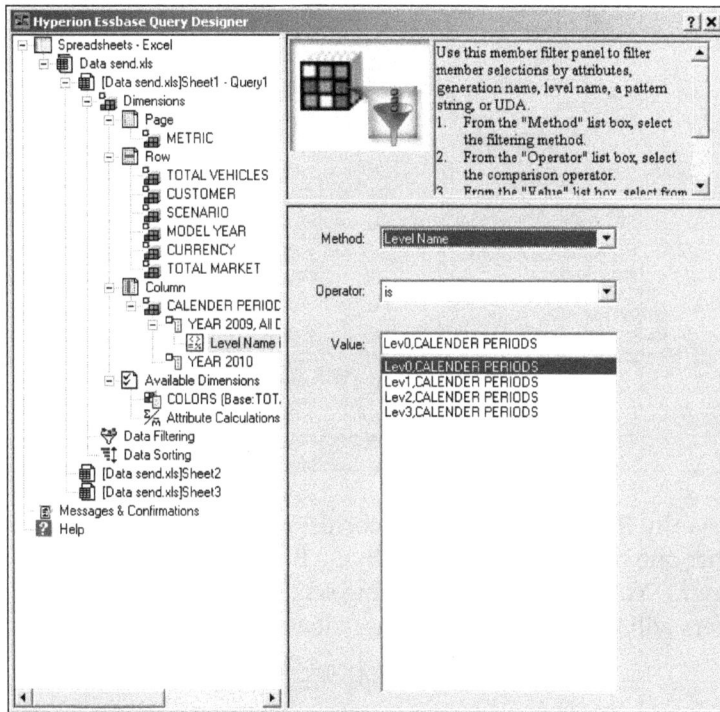

Once you have made your selection(s) click on one of the YEAR members in the left pane to return your screen to the previous configuration. In the next screenshot, you will notice that the lower-right pane has the **Members** section and the **Selection Rules** section.

Notice in the **Selection Rules** section how the selected YEAR members now have the member selection rule you applied to them.

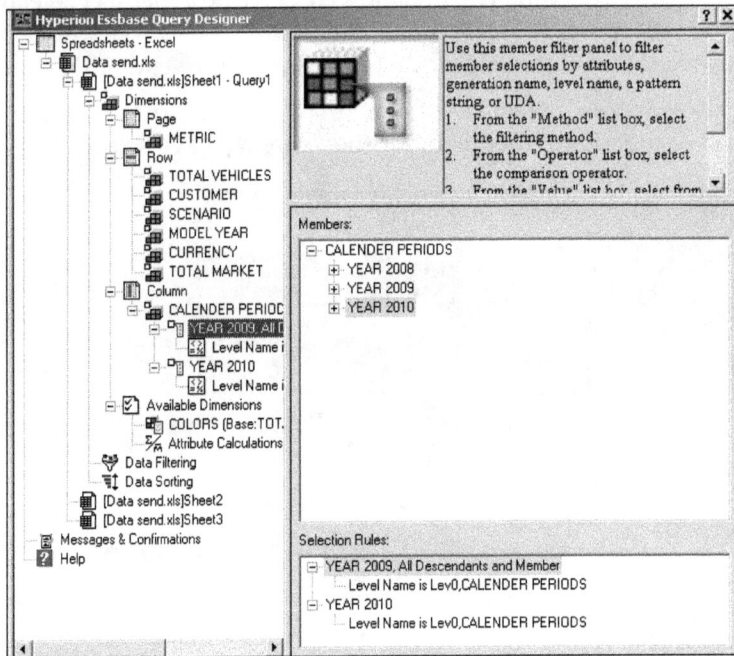

8. Just to verify that the EQD has the correct members selected simply right-click on either one of the year members in the **Selection Rules** section and click on **Preview...**. You will see the following screenshot, showing you exactly which members will be selected in this query using the rules you have defined.

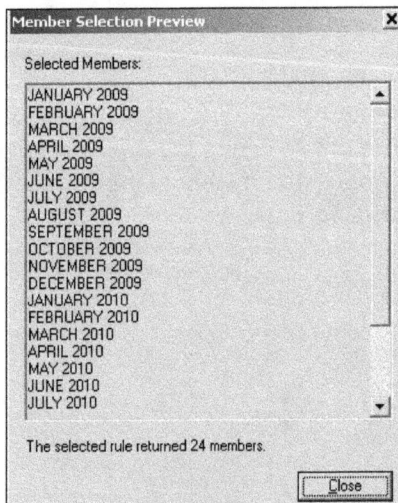

9. Well, we have our **Page Dimensions** and **Column Dimensions** set up. All we need to do now is set up the **Row Dimensions**. Looking at the organizational pane, pay attention to how we have the dimensions that are selected as the **Row Dimensions** arranged. We want to create a report that contains row information for the individual **Markets**, then the individual **Model Years,** and finally the individual **Vehicles**. We do not want to display any data at the total levels for the **Row Dimensions**. Using what you have already learned about Essbase, you know that you want the data to appear top-down in the organizational pane, much like the database outlines. Thus, we want the **Total Market** dimension first, then underneath it we want the **Model Year** dimension, and lastly we want the **Total Vehicles** dimension.

10. Begin row selection by clicking on the **Total Market** dimension in the left pane of the screen. This will place the **Total Market** dimension into the **Members** section of the lower-right pane.

11. Double-click on the **Total Market** dimension to place it into the **Selection Rules** section of the member selection pane.

12. Right-click on the **Total Market** dimension in the **Selection Rules** section and choose **Select** then **Children**. This will give you all of the children of the **Total Market** dimension without giving you the **Total Market** member itself.

13. Now do the same as in the previous three steps for the **Model Year** and **Total Vehicles** dimensions.

14. Once completed your query should look like the following screenshot:

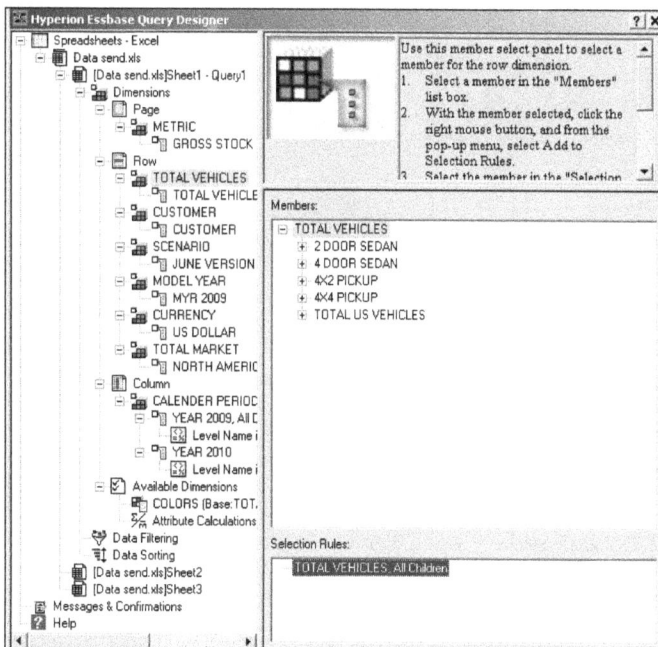

15. Now to test your query you simply right-click on the Microsoft Excel worksheet that you are designing the query under and click on **Apply Query**. The data with the layout you defined will be pulled into the Microsoft Excel worksheet. Remember to also save your query with the same rules as any Essbase file object. You now have a reusable query that you can use anytime by simply opening through EQD and running it.

16. Oh yes when you save the query, Essbase saves it with an .eqd extension and at the same time saves the query as the equivalent Essbase report script with a .rep file extension. The actual query can only be opened by the EQD but the report script can be opened by any ASCII text editor and modified for use with any report script execution method described earlier.

Report script by-product

Previously, we explained the Essbase report script and its usefulness as a reporting tool or as a method of creating extract data from your Essbase database. A desirable and welcome by-product of an Essbase query created with the EQD is a matching Essbase report script.

One of the easiest ways to create an Essbase report script is to use the EQD to design what you would like your report or extract file to look like, then use the simultaneously generated report script file to use and modify as needed. This is your basic Essbase report script:

```
// This Report Script was generated by the Essbase Query Designer
<SETUP { TabDelimit } { decimal 13 } { IndentGen -5 } <ACCON <SYM
<QUOTE <END
<PAGE("METRIC")
<COLUMN("Calendar Periods")
<ROW("Total Market","Model Year","Total Vehicles")
// Page Members
// Selection rules and output options for dimension: METRIC
{OUTMBRNAMES}
"Gross Stock"
// Column Members
// Selection rules and output options for dimension: Calendar
//Periods
{OUTMBRNAMES}
<Link ((<LEV("Calendar Periods", "Lev0,Calendar Periods")) AND (
<IDESC("2009")))
<Link ((<LEV("Calendar Periods", "Lev0,Calendar Periods")) AND (
<IDESC("2010")))
// Row Members
```

```
// Selection rules and output options for dimension: Total Market
{OUTMBRNAMES}
<Link (<CHILD("Total Market"))
// Selection rules and output options for dimension: Model Year
{OUTMBRNAMES}
<Link (<CHILD("Model Year"))
// Selection rules and output options for dimension: Total Vehicles
{OUTMBRNAMES}
<Link (<CHILD("Total Vehicles"))
!
// End of Report
```

In this case, we see by looking at the script, that the page dimension is the METRIC dimension, the column dimension is the Calendar Periods dimension, and the row dimensions are Total Market, Model Year, and Total Vehicles. This will give us a report where the column headings are members from the Calendar Periods dimension, the row headings will be members from the Total Market, Model Year, and Total Vehicles dimensions.

Reading further we also see that since the page dimension is the METRIC dimension, the exact member used is the Gross Stock member.

Continuing down we see that the column headers will be the zero level members of the Calendar Periods dimension and the children of 2009 and 2010.

Lastly, the row headings will consist specifically of the children of Total Market, the children of Model Year, and the children of Total Vehicles.

You can execute this script in Microsoft Excel by simply pasting the code directly into a Microsoft Excel worksheet or you can execute it from an Essbase command script or a MaxL script or even an Essbase API call.

Now any modifications can easily be made to a script that you know works perfectly.

As with all of the other Essbase features that we have gone over in this book, the EQD is intuitive and easy to use. We highly recommend you take the time to play with it and create many queries.

Always pay attention to the informational pane on the EQD screens as it will always adjust to the area you are working in and provide pertinent tips and help.

Summary

Well, there you have it! In this chapter we have learned how you can generate reports using the Essbase Add-in for Microsoft Excel or Visual Explorer or Essbase Query Designer, as well as the capabilities of each type of reporting. What we recommend now is to just start playing with the add-in. Try creating custom data sheets by first performing simple retrieves. Then, as you become more comfortable and confident, you can begin setting up advanced row and column headings by using the double-click and pivoting functions or by using the fully functional Essbase Member Selection tool to populate your spreadsheet's row and column headings. Once you've become adept at setting up good looking spreadsheets and reports, you can start playing around with retrieving data into your sheets, then **Locking** and **Sending** the data back to the database.

Next up, is how to automate your Essbase database system. We will show you an assortment of functionality options included in your Essbase package that allow you to automate routine tasks, from the very basic and menial, to the large and complex. You can turn everyday chores into automatically running batch jobs that do everything from dynamically adding dimension members to the database outline, to loading and calculation data, to actually building presentation and analysis cubes.

8
Automating your Essbase Cube

If you've made it this far and you're still coherent, congratulations! Upto now there has been a tremendous amount of information for you to absorb, all of it necessary. With all that we have presented to you to this point you should be able to take your Essbase journey from a complete installation to a fully functioning Essbase database.

Complimenting your fully functioning Essbase database is your knowledge of the many ways to load and calculate the data in your Essbase database. You also have a good understanding of how to utilize the powerful Essbase Add-in for Microsoft Excel, allowing you to interact with your database and the data contained in it.

In this chapter you will learn that many of the routine tasks required to keep your Essbase system functioning at its best can be automated. Further, many of the routine administrative tasks can be automated and the functionality then provided to your business customers so they can perform for themselves many of the administrative duties that pertain to their business operations. Some of these types of tasks include adding new users, granting permissions, executing data loads, and running database calculations.

This chapter is divided into three main sections and each section speaks to a different method that can be used to automate Essbase functions and commands.

In the first section, we discuss the Essbase command scripts, or Ess-Commands, or simply EssCmds. The Essbase command scripting functionality is a holdover from the very earliest versions of Essbase and was rumored to be phased out completely in Essbase versions higher than version 9.x. We have since found out that Essbase version 11.x will now contain EssCmd functionality to give you more time to convert your scripts to the newer MaxL scripting language. The new MaxL scripting language has replaced EssCmd and provides superior functionality and ease of use. Although we are covering Essbase command scripts here we recommend you use the new MaxL scripting language and the Essbase API instead, especially if you are developing a new system.

The second section is where we discuss the Essbase MaxL scripting language which has been developed to not only replace the aging Essbase command scripting language, but also offer enhanced functionality while providing less cryptic and easier to use command words.

In the third section, we discuss the Essbase Application Programming Interface or API. The Essbase API has evolved over the successive versions into a very powerful set of tools for the developer. What top of the line application package does not include a complete array of API tools? You just have to figure that Essbase would have one of the best available.

The Essbase API can be accessed from Microsoft Visual Basic for Applications, known as VBA, and included with all Microsoft Office components. The API can also be accessed from Visual Basic and COM+ applications, and the API can also be accessed from Java programs. All in all it is a very versatile and extremely useful tool to have in your Essbase toolbox!

Essbase command scripts (EssCmd)

EssCmd is a command-line Essbase interface that can perform operations interactively through a command-line window or through a batch or script file. EssCmd operates independently of any other Essbase analytic services interface, including the EAS tool, the Essbase add-in, or any custom-built application programs.

The Essbase command scripting language, affectionately known as Ess-Command or just EssCmd, is a highly functional set of tools that are used to automate many tasks in the world of Essbase. Although EssCmd has been phased out in the latest versions of Essbase it's still a good idea that you become familiar with EssCmd and what you can do with it. If you ever inherit an existing system that is still using an older version of Essbase chances are that it will have lots of EssCmds in use.

For starters an Essbase command script file object is actually an ASCII text file with a file extension of .scr. As with all Essbase objects you must follow the naming conventions we have previously discussed.

> All Essbase file objects can be named using upto 8 characters, can have no spaces in the name, and must be located in a folder or directory path that does not contain spaces.

Creating an Essbase command script

There is only one way to create a usable EssCmd. Because an EssCmd file object is actually an ASCII text file you can open any text editor and begin entering commands. The text editor is also how you would modify an existing Essbase command script.

Although there is no formal EssCmd script editor supplied with Essbase there is comprehensive help included in the online help that is supplied with the EAS tool.

To access this excellent EssCmd resource simply click **Help | Information Map** to open your web browser and bring up the following screenshot:

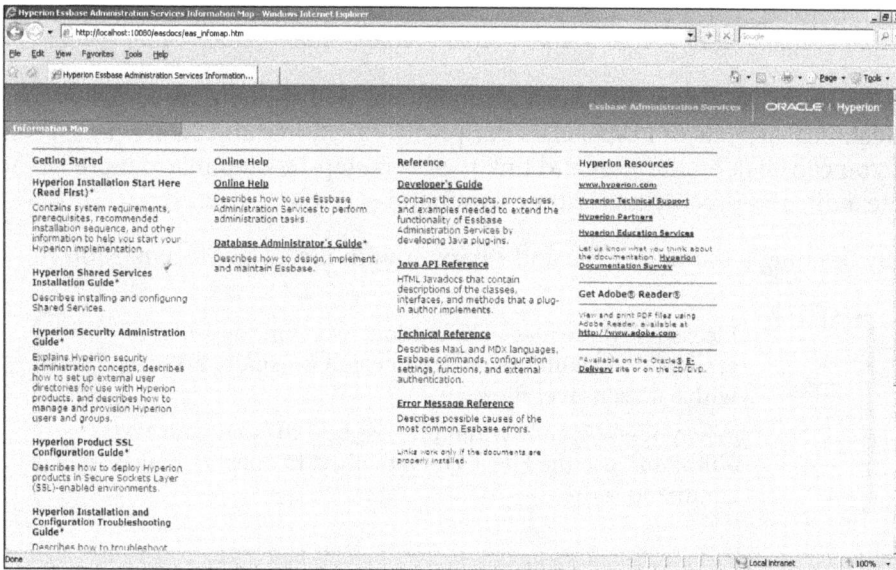

From the **Essbase Administration Services Information Map** screen, click
the **Technical Reference** link under the **Reference** column, to bring up the
following screenshot:

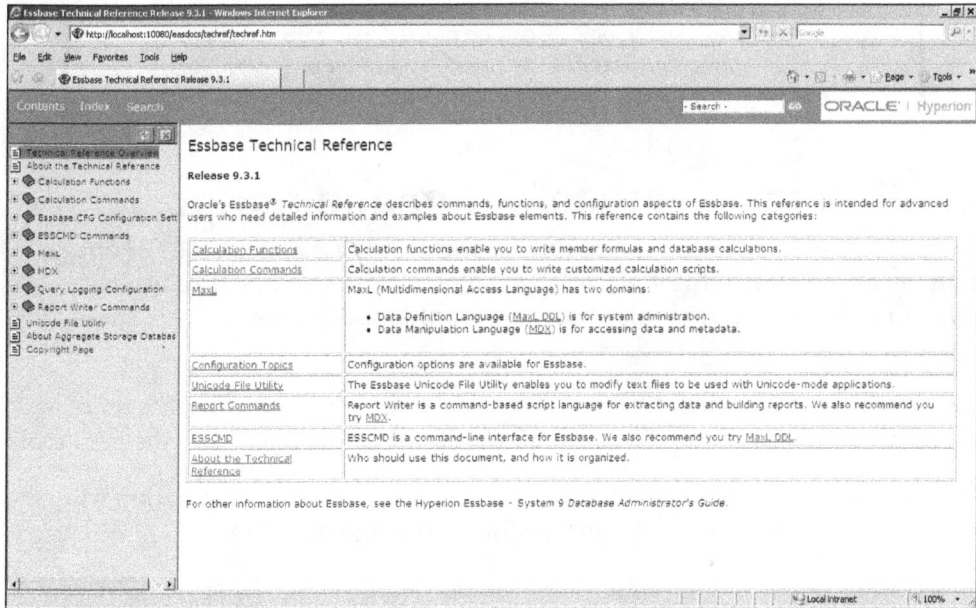

On the **Technical Reference Overview** screen you will see help topics listed for most
of the technical aspects of Essbase, its peripheral functions, and its services. From this
screen you can click on the **EssCmd** link to access step-by-step instructions on how
to create, edit, and execute an Essbase command script.

Begin by opening a blank text file and saving it with the .scr file extension.

> Please use these files with caution. In a Windows-based
> system, a file with the .scr extension is usually associated
> with a screensaver file type.
>
> When opening an EssCmd file, it is best to open your text
> editor and use the **File | Open** method to open an Essbase
> command script.

EssCmd commands and categories

There are over 120 distinct EssCmd commands that do everything from running report scripts and calculation scripts to database outline maintenance and security. The following screenshot shows a complete listing of available EssCmd commands:

```
ADDUSER             EXPORT                    LISTDB                RENAMEOBJECT
APPLYOTLCHANGEFILE  GETALLREPLCELLS           LISTFILES             RENAMEUSER
APPLYOTLCHANGEFILEEX GETAPPACTIVE             LISTFILTERS           REPORT
BEGINARCHIVE        GETAPPINFO                LISTGROUPS            REPORTLINE
BEGININCBUILDDIM    GETAPPSTATE               LISTGROUPUSERS        RESETDB
BUILDDIM            GETATTRIBUTESPECS         LISTLINKEDOBJECTS     RESETOTLCHANGETIME
CALC               GETATTRINFO               LISTLOCATIONS         RESETPERFSTATS
CALCDEFAULT        GETCRDB                    LISTLOCKS             RESETSTATUS
CALCLINE           GETCRDBINFO               LISTLOGINS            RUNCALC
COPYAPP            GETCRRATE                  LISTOBJECTS           RUNREPT
COPYDB             GETCRTYPE                  LISTUSERS             SELECT
COPYFILTER         GETDBACTIVE               LISTVARIABLES         SETALIAS
COPYOBJECT         GETDBINFO                  LOADALIAS             SETAPPSTATE
CREATEAPP          GETDBSTATE                 LOADAPP               SETDBSTATE
CREATEDB           GETDBSTATS                 LOADDATA              SETDBSTATEITEM
CREATEGROUP        GETDEFAULTCALC            LOADDB                SETDEFAULTCALC
CREATELOCATION     GETMBRCALC                LOGIN                 SETDEFAULTCALCFILE
CREATEUSER         GETMBRINFO                LOGOUT                SETLOGIN
CREATEVARIABLE     GETMEMBERS                LOGOUTALLUSERS        SETMSGLEVEL
DELETEAPP          GETPARTITIONOTLCHANGES    LOGOUTUSER            SETPASSWORD
DELETEDB           GETPARTITIONOTLCHANGESEX  OUTPUT                SHUTDOWNSERVER
DELETEGROUP        GETPERFSTATS              PAREXPORT             SLEEP
DELETELOCATION     GETUPDATEDREPLCELLS       PRINTPARTITIONDEFFILE UNLOADALIAS
DELETELOG          GETUSERINFO               PURGELINKEDOBJECTS    UNLOADAPP
DELETEUSER         GETVERSION                PURGEOTLCHANGEFILE    UNLOADDB
DELETEVARIABLE     GOTO                      PUTALLREPLCELLS       UNLOCKOBJECT
DISABLELOGIN       IFERROR                   PUTUPDATEDREPLCELLS   UPDATE
DISPLAYALIAS       IMPORT                    REMOVELOCKS           UPDATEBAKFILE
ENABLELOGIN        INCBUILDDIM               REMOVEUSER           UPDATEFILE
ENDARCHIVE         LISTALIASES               RENAMEAPP            UPDATEVARIABLE
ENDINCBUILDDIM     LISTAPP                   RENAMEDB             VALIDATE
ESTIMATEFULLDBSIZE                           RENAMEFILTER         VALIDATEPARTITIONDEFFILE
EXIT
```

The command list can be rather intimidating to look at but we assure you that all of the EssCmd commands are easily understandable and simple to use. To help you become familiar with the commands and their function, Essbase also groups them by category.

The basic categories of the EssCmd commands are as follows:

- **Using EssCmd**: These commands are used to log in and out of EssCmd, view command lists, pause EssCmd execution, and direct command script output.

- **Application and database administration**: These commands are used to perform database creations and routine administration, and to get information about existing applications and databases.

- **User/Group security**: Use these commands to perform user ID and access group maintenance and administration.

- **Security filters and locks**: These commands can list, copy, and rename database security access filters, and also remove database locks.

- **Database objects**: These commands are used to list database objects and their lock statuses, if any. Also, you can copy and rename database objects, and view or remove URLs, cell notes, or database partitions linked to the database.

- **Outline/Attribute information**: Use these commands to view outline member information, member attribute information, current attribute naming specifications, and to view the outline paging information.

- **Dimension building**: This group of commands can be used to build one or more dimensions from data files or SQL sources. You can build multiple dimensions incrementally and decide how you want the database restructured after the dimension build is complete.

- **Data loading, clearing, and exporting**: Use these commands to load your data from files or from individual records or to clear all data from a database or to export and import data to and from text files.

- **Calculating**: These commands can be used to run calc scripts, execute one or more calc strings, run or change the default database calculation, and view information about calcs associated with outline members.

- **Reporting**: Use these commands to execute report scripts or to run one or more report strings individually.

- **Partitioning**: This group of commands can be used to load or unload data from a database partition or even produce a text file version of a partition mapping.

- **Outline synchronization**: These commands are actually used in conjunction with partitioned databases to keep the target database outline synchronized with changes made to the source database outline.

- **Error and log handling**: Use these commands to set conditional or unconditional error branching from EssCmd scripts, redirection of process information output, specifying what level of detail messages are displayed in, and clearing the application log file when necessary.

- **Currency conversion information**: These commands are used to get information about currency databases linked to the currently selected database.

- **Location aliases**: These commands manage location aliases used in a distributed analytic services environment. Location aliases are names that are used in place of server addresses, applications, databases, user IDs, and passwords.

- **Substitution variables**: Use these commands to manage any substitution variables. Substitution variables are placeholders for information that changes regularly. Use them in calc scripts, report scripts, and the spreadsheet add-in to avoid hard coding.

- **Aliases**: These commands manage and, display the values of alias tables for database outlines. Alias tables contain a listing of member names and their alternate names, or aliases.

- **Integrity and performance**: These commands are used to check database statistics and validate databases against possible corruption.

- **Backing up**: Use these commands to place one or more Application | Databases into *Read Only* mode in preparation for archiving or backup.

Well, there you have it! In a nutshell you have all of the Essbase command script categories. For complete details on how to code each function and what task it performs please refer to the **Essbase Administration Services Information Map** that you access from the EAS **Help** menu pick. There you will find a complete command list with specific details on how to code each function.

Coding a basic EssCmd

Even though you should no longer be writing new Essbase command scripts we would remiss if we did not at least go over the basics. The following instructions will guide you through writing a basic Essbase command script so you will have at least a working knowledge level in case you need it.

Always remember EssCmd logging

First and foremost, in any EssCmd script is the inclusion of script logging. A good output log is invaluable for helping to debug any problems.

The first line in any EssCmd script should be the OUTPUT command. This command toggles on or off the script logging and also allows you to specify where to put the log as shown here:

```
OUTPUT 1 "c:\EssCmd.log"; /* The 1 specifies turning job log output
on and then you code the log's location */
```

Connecting to an Essbase server

Obviously, you will need to be connected to an Essbase server to perform any tasks or functions. In EssCmd there are two ways to login to the server. If your script will only be accessing one specific Essbase database you can code your login command as follows:

```
LOGIN ServerName userID Password appName dbName;
```

This command will log you into a specific Essbase Application|Database, and you will need to log out before you can connect to another Application|Database. The appName and dbName parameters are optional however, and if you plan on performing tasks against several Application|Databases you would login like this:

```
LOGIN hostNode userName password;
SELECT appName dbName;
```

The term hostNode refers to the specific server name or IP address of the Essbase server you wish to connect to.

Using the LOGIN then SELECT method to login allows you to change the Application|Database at any time in your script by using another occurrence of the SELECT command.

Your EssCmd script should now look like this:

```
OUTPUT 1 "c:\EssCmd.log"; /* The 1 specifies turning job log output
                             on and then you code the logs location */
LOGIN hostNode userName password; /* Connect to Essbase server */
SELECT appName dbName; /* Connect to specific application/database */
```

What about error checking

Before we go too much further, we should stress the importance of error checking. Lucky for us the EssCmd library includes an IFERROR command that acts as a GOTO for errors. This can be very important if the next command in a script is dependent on the successful completion of the previous command. Having your script halt execution on an error can prevent all kinds of grief.

It is a good idea to follow all commands in the script with the IFERROR command and you can add your error checking as shown:

```
IFERROR "ERROR"; /* On an error the script will branch to the
                    "ERROR" line */
:ERROR /* Script skips to here and resumes execution */
EXIT; /* In this case we exit the script */
```

Once you have added your error checking, your fledgling script should look like the script below:

```
OUTPUT 1 "c:\EssCmd.log"; /* The 1 specifies turning job log output
                             on and then you code the log's
                             location */
IFERROR "ERROR"; /* On an error the script will branch to the
                    "ERROR" line */
LOGIN hostNode userName password; /* Connect to Essbase server */
IFERROR "ERROR"; /* On an error the script will branch to the
                    "ERROR" line */
SELECT appName dbName; /* Connect to specific application|database */
IFERROR "ERROR"; /* On an error the script will branch to the
                    "ERROR" line */
```

*** Add functional commands here ***

```
OUTPUT 3; /* Turns off script logging */
LOGOUT; /* Logs out the script and exits */

:ERROR /* On an error the script branches to here and
          resumes execution */
EXIT; /* In this case we exit the script */
```

Adding some functional commands

So now you have an EssCmd script that when executed, will turn on logging, log in to a specified Essbase server, select a specified Essbase Application | Database, turn off logging, and log out, all the while checking for errors in the command execution.

You now need to add some commands to the script which will actually do some work! How about if we load a specific Essbase application and database into memory? We will then run the default calculation script against that database. Next, we will unload the database and the application from server memory to conserve system resources. And finally, we will log out and the script will terminate.

To the example script above, we want to add the following commands:

```
LOADAPP appName; /* Loads the specified application into memory */
IFERROR "ERROR"; /* On an error the script will branch to the
                    "ERROR" line */
LOADDB appName dbName; /* Loads the specified database into memory */
IFERROR "ERROR"; /* On an error the script will branch to the
                    "ERROR" line */
```

```
CALCDEFAULT; /* Executes the default calculation on the selected
                 database */
IFERROR "ERROR"; /* On an error the script will branch to the
                    "ERROR" line */
UNLOADDB appName dbName; /* Unloads the specified database
                            from memory */
IFERROR "ERROR"; /* On an error the script will branch to the
                    "ERROR" line */
UNLOADAPP appName; /* Unloads the specified application from memory */
IFERROR "ERROR"; /* On an error the script will branch to the
                    "ERROR" line */
```

Now, let's add these lines to the rest of the script and see what a complete EssCmd
script looks like.

The finished script

Here is what your EssCmd script should look like with all of the commands added.
It is ready to execute and in the next section, we will discuss the ways to execute an
Essbase Command script.

```
OUTPUT 1 "c:\EssCmd.log"; /* The 1 specifies turning job log output
                             on and then you code the log's
                             location */
IFERROR "ERROR"; /* On an error the script will branch to the
                    "ERROR" line */
LOGIN hostNode userName password; /* Connect to Essbase server */
IFERROR "ERROR"; /* On an error the script will branch to the
                    "ERROR" line */
SELECT appName dbName; /* Connect to specific application/database */
IFERROR "ERROR"; /* On an error the script will branch to the
                    "ERROR" line */
LOADAPP appName; /* Loads the specified application into memory */
IFERROR "ERROR"; /* On an error the script will branch to the
                    "ERROR" line */
LOADDB appName dbName; /* Loads the specified database into memory */
IFERROR "ERROR"; /* On an error the script will branch to the
                    "ERROR" line */
```

```
CALCDEFAULT; /* Executes the default calculation on the selected
                database */
IFERROR "ERROR"; /* On an error the script will branch to the
                    "ERROR" line */
UNLOADDB appName dbName; /* Unloads the specified database
                            from memory */
IFERROR "ERROR"; /* On an error the script will branch to the
                    "ERROR" line */
UNLOADAPP appName; /* Unloads the specified application from memory */
IFERROR "ERROR"; /* On an error the script will branch to the
                    "ERROR" line */
OUTPUT 3; /* Turns off script logging */
LOGOUT; /* Logs out the script and exits */

:ERROR /* Script branches to here and resumes execution on error */
OUTPUT 3; /* Turns off script logging */
EXIT; /* In this case we exit the script */
```

Remember, all command lines must end with a semi-colon. If you wish to add comments to the script, you would follow the example below using a /* to begin a comment and a */ to end a comment:

```
/* This is an EssCmd comment line */
```

Executing an EssCmd

There are two easy ways to execute Essbase Commands. First, there is the interactive command line processing where you are logging in and executing commands from the DOS command prompt. Second, is the batch processing method, where you actually launch a batch job from either your desktop PC or on an application server. Let's continue and learn a little bit more about each method.

EssCmd processing from command prompt

Interactive Essbase command prompt mode lets you interactively enter commands at the EssCmd command line and receive short responses. Interactive command line mode is convenient and preferable for short operations that require few commands, no checking for information on the fly, and little error checking.

In interactive mode you manually enter commands on the command line and respond to returned prompts. This is useful when you are performing simple tasks that require few commands. If you are performing more complex tasks that require many commands as well as error handling, consider creating an EssCmd script file to run in a batch job. To launch the EssCmd command line application simply open a DOS command line window and enter the fully qualified path and file name for the `esscmd.exe` as shown in the following screenshot:

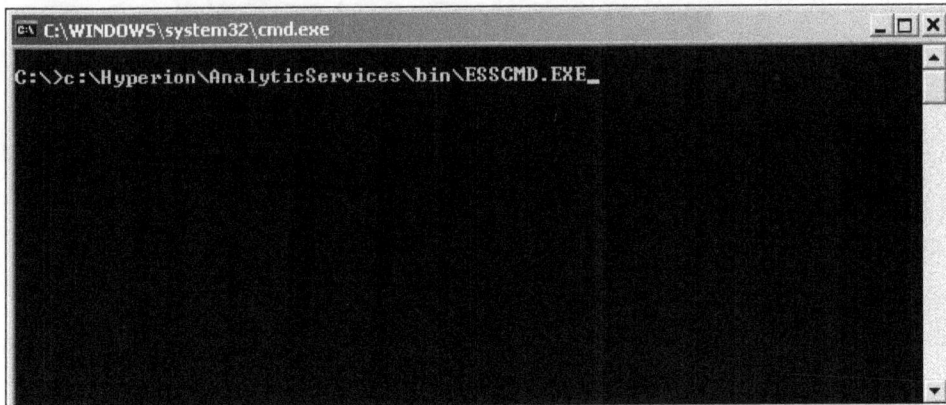

If you have Essbase installed on a Windows client you can register the `esscmd.exe` file as you would a DLL. The registration process alerts you that is has failed yet it still registers the executable.

The benefit here is that you can now call the `esscmd.exe` by its name only. No extension or path needs to be included. This makes starting a command line session easier and if you register it on your application server as well, then it makes coding batch jobs and shell commands easier too.

Once you have entered the `esscmd.exe` command in the command line screen you will see the following:

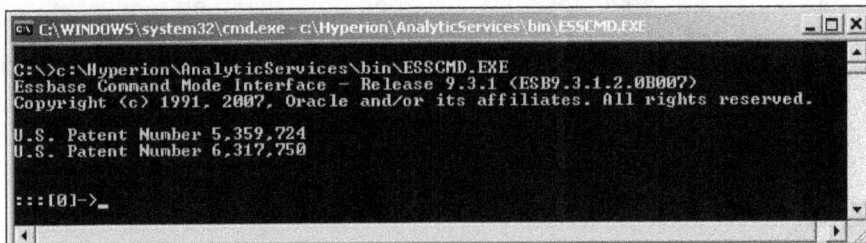

You now have opened the **Essbase Command Mode Interface**. At the command prompt, you can begin entering commands. We suppose the first thing you should do is log in to an Essbase analytic server or else you will just sit there.

You enter your commands exactly as you would type them into an EssCmd script file as illustrated previously in this chapter. Also, remember to always terminate a command line with a semi-colon, just as is required in an EssCmd script file.

EssCmd processing in batch mode

Essbase command batch processing mode lets you automate your routine analytic services maintenance and diagnostic tasks for the server, applications, and databases. You can write a script or batch file and run it from the command line. Or you can call a script from a batch job and run it fully automated.

Batch processing mode is convenient if you frequently use a particular series of repeated commands or if your tasks require many commands and the ability to test for processing errors.

A batch file is an operating system file that can call EssCmd scripts and can also include operating system commands. You can use one batch file to run multiple sessions of EssCmd. This can be a licensing consideration since multiple EssCmd connections connected through the same EssCmd session count as only one license port, thereby saving on potentially expensive system licensing.

You can run a batch file on the analytic server from the operating system command prompt and the file is processed by the operating system. On Windows and Windows NT systems, batch files have `.bat` file extensions. These files can also be scheduled to run automatically from the Task Scheduler, thus fully automating your processes.

To run an Essbase EssCmd script from the DOS command line prompt, simply enter the fully qualified path to the EssCmd script file as shown:

```
ESSCMD C:\Batch.SCR
```

The line above will execute the EssCmd script file named `Batch.SCR`.

To have a batch file execute an Essbase EssCmd script, you would place a line like the following line in a `.bat` file and execute the batch file:

```
ESSCMD C:\Batch.SCR
```

Well there you have it! You may be wondering why such a relatively easy to use set of powerful tools would be getting phased out but just wait until you read the next section on Essbase MaxL scripts. The MaxL scripts are replacing the Essbase command scripts and are a more powerful, easier to use, intuitive, and interactive scripting tool for Essbase.

Essbase MaxL scripts

MaxL is a Multidimensional Access Language developed for Essbase analytics. MaxL, as it is known, is a powerful scripting tool developed for the system administrator of Essbase to perform administrative tasks from the creation of a new user, to adding new security filters, to updating the database outline, to importing data, to executing calculation scripts, and finally to the deletion of a database or an application.

These tasks are very important to do, but remember, if you make a mistake in one of these scripts your entire database cube and all of the data can be lost. Please use extreme caution while executing MaxL statements.

MaxL statements are case sensitive and must always end with a semi-colon.

MaxL supports most of the tasks and functions that you can perform in the EssCmd scripting language and it also supports all of the new functionalities that have been added to the newer versions of Essbase. EssCmd is used extensively in the older versions of Essbase and MaxL is highly recommended for the newer versions of Essbase. EssCmd does not support some of the newer features like ASO and Essbase database security filters.

The MaxL scripting language uses a statement construct syntax which has its own grammar. Every MaxL statement consists of verbs and objects.

Some of the verbs used in a typical MaxL statement are:

- Alter
- Create
- Display
- Drop
- Execute
- Import
- Export
- Grant
- Query
- Refresh

Some of the objects used in a MaxL statement are:

- Application
- Database
- Dimensions

- Calculation
- Data
- Filter
- Location Alias
- Aggregate Build
- Aggregate Process
- Calculation
- Outline
- Partitions
- Tablespace
- Session

The following screenshot shows you the list of all of the available MaxL statements:

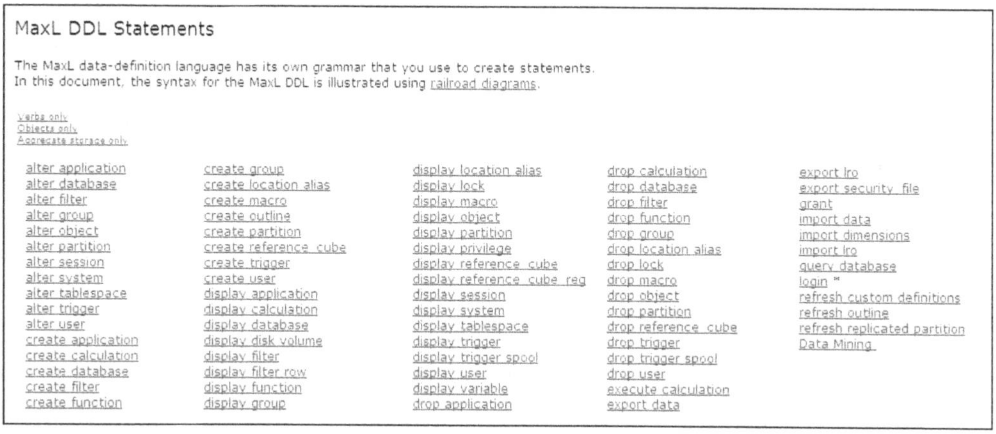

MaxL DDL Statements

The MaxL data-definition language has its own grammar that you use to create statements.
In this document, the syntax for the MaxL DDL is illustrated using railroad diagrams.

Verbs only
Objects only
Aggregate storage only

alter application
alter database
alter filter
alter group
alter object
alter partition
alter session
alter system
alter tablespace
alter trigger
alter user
create application
create calculation
create database
create filter
create function
create group
create location alias
create macro
create outline
create partition
create reference cube
create trigger
create user
display application
display calculation
display database
display disk volume
display filter
display filter row
display function
display group
display location alias
display lock
display macro
display object
display partition
display privilege
display reference cube
display reference cube req
display session
display system
display tablespace
display trigger
display trigger spool
display user
display variable
drop application
drop calculation
drop database
drop filter
drop function
drop group
drop location alias
drop lock
drop macro
drop object
drop partition
drop reference cube
drop trigger
drop trigger spool
drop user
execute calculation
export data
export lro
export security file
grant
import data
import dimensions
import lro
query database
login
refresh custom definitions
refresh outline
refresh replicated partition
Data Mining

Let's walk through some of the MaxL statements which will be used in the day-to-day life of an Essbase administrator.

Logging on to the Essbase server

Obviously, the first step that is required to use MaxL is to log on to the Essbase server. Here is a step-by-step demonstration of how to log on to an Essbase analytic server using MaxL statements.

Syntax:

Login

```
<USERNAME> /* enter your user name or batch id */
```

Identified by

```
<PASSWORD> /* enter your password or batch password */
```

On

```
<HOSTNAME> /*enter the server name */
```

Code Sample:

```
login <USERNAME> identified by <PASSWORD> on <HOSTNAME>;
```

Guess what? You have just written your first MaxL statement. Did we say something new here? Well, we have learned a little bit about a few MaxL statements in earlier chapters of this book, but here we are discussing MaxL for the sole purpose of learning how to use the MaxL scripting language and all of the benefits these commands can bring to the Essbase administrator.

Working with an Essbase application in MaxL

As a part of your weekly or monthly maintenance, you may have routine tasks to perform on the application level. Guess what? You can easily execute repetitive tasks using the MaxL scripting language. A word of caution, the user who performs these MaxL actions should have **System Designer** access or higher.

At the application level you can do some very important actions with MaxL. You can create a new application on the analytic server or you can create a copy of an existing application. You can also alter an application, display an application, and finally even drop an application. Let us see how we can use each of these actions in a MaxL script.

Creating an application

Using the MaxL scripting language you can either *create* a new application or *copy* an existing application. You may wonder why we would need to create an application by using a MaxL script. Well we may need to create a yearly MaxL job which requires you to copy an existing application to a new application as a backup, but also you will need to create a new application to replace the old application for the new year's cycle. Both of these tasks, creating a new application and copying an existing application can be done using the MaxL `Create` statement as shown in the syntax and code sample as follows:

Syntax:

```
create application 'Application_Name' type 'Mode' as  'Application_
Name ' comment 'Comment-String';
```

`'Application_Name'`: Name of the new application should be upto 8 characters long as with all Essbase database objects.

`type`: Indicates whether this application is to be Unicode or not with the default being is non-Unicode mode. Unicode is a system of assigning a unique number to each character regardless of the language or platform. When a database is created using the Unicode convention, users from all parts of the globe, using all different character sets can use your Essbase system without worry of data corruption.

`As 'Application_name' [optional]`: Name of the existing application which will be copied to the new application.

`comment 'Comment-String' [optional`: This is a comment which is given to the application and can be viewed in the application properties screen.

Example 1: In the following example, we are creating a new application. Since we did not mention the Unicode mode, by default, it will be created as a non-Unicode application.

```
Create application ESSCARNW comment 'New Esscar Application';
```

Example 2: In the next example, we are creating a new application which is same as the existing application and will be for the purpose of an application backup.

```
Create application ESSCARBK as ESSCAR comment 'Back up of Esscar
Application';
```

Now that you have seen how we can create an application using a MaxL statement, let us see how we can use the alter application statement in MaxL.

Altering the application

With the **alter** statement, you can set the properties for an application, add, modify, or drop a substitution variable, load or unload an application, enable or disable application start up commands, add an application comment, or clear an application log file.

Keep the following screenshot in mind when you are looking at the MaxL alter application command examples that follow. For reference, whatever that is performed in the script can also be performed through the **Application Properties** screen accessed through the EAS tool.

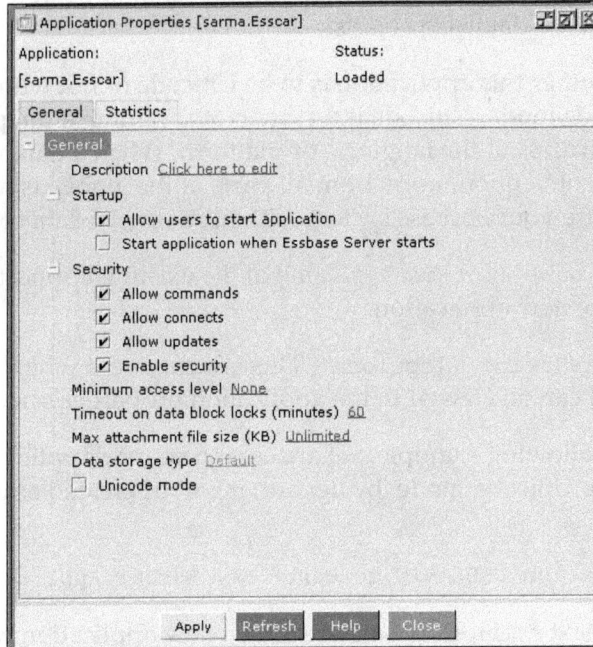

Let's look at a few more commonly used `alter` statements.

Using the SET properties statement

You can set an application's properties using the `alter` and `set` statements. Some of the `set` commands are:

- `set minimum permission`: Grants all authorized users a minimum application permissions level which is valid for all of the databases under this application. This command directly corresponds to the Minimum access level setting in the **Application Properties** screen on the **General** tab.

  Syntax:

  ```
  alter application <App-Name> set minimum permission <READ |
  WRITE | CALCULATE | DATABASE DESIGNER>;
  ```

  Code Sample:

  ```
  alter application 'ESSCAR' set minimum permission read;
  ```

- `set lock_timeout after`: This is the maximum time a user can maintain a database lock if idle. The default lock time out is 60 minutes.

  Syntax:

  ```
  alter application <App-Name> set lock_timeout after integer
  <MINUTES | SECONDS>;
  ```

  Code Sample:

  ```
  alter application 'ESSCAR' set lock_timeout after 75 minutes;
  ```

- `set max_lro_file_size`: You can set a maximum file size of an LRO. This can be either unlimited, or you can specify a file size.

  Syntax:

  ```
  alter application <App-Name> set max_lro_file_size
     <UNLIMITED | LRO SIZE>;
  ```

  Code Sample:

  ```
  alter application 'ESSCAR' set max_lro_file_size 32768b;
  ```

  This code sets the maximum LRO file size to 32KB.

- `set type unicode_mode`: You can convert a non-Unicode into a Unicode mode.

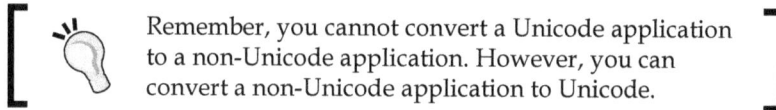

  > Remember, you cannot convert a Unicode application to a non-Unicode application. However, you can convert a non-Unicode application to Unicode.

  Syntax:

  ```
  alter application <App-Name> set type unicode_mode;
  ```

  Code Sample:

  ```
  alter application 'ESSCAR' set type unicode_mode;
  ```

Using load/unload database

These commands will load and unload the databases into or out of system memory.

Syntax:

```
    alter application <App-Name> load database <Db-Name>;
    alter application <App-Name> unload database <Db-Name>;
```

Code Sample:

```
    alter application 'ESSCAR' load database 'ESSCAR';
    alter application 'ESSCAR' unload database 'ESSCAR';
```

Clear application log

A good practice for an Essbase administrator would be to clear the application log as often as possible. If the application log file is allowed to get too large users, a marked decrease in system performance is seen. The good news for the Essbase administrator is that there is no need to log on to the Essbase server through EAS to clear the log file. The system administrator can write a MaxL script and use it to clear the log file on a weekly basis. Be sure to back up the log file for audit trails according to your company's standards.

Syntax:

```
alter application <App-Name> clear logfile;
```

Enable/Disable start up/auto startup

In an application's properties you can set the application to start whenever the Essbase server is started or you can start an application at the first user request to log on. These properties can be set by the administrator with a MaxL command.

```
startup /* Allow user to start Application */
```

If startup is enabled, the users can start the application upon log on. If startup is set to disabled, the users will not be able to log on, if the application is not already started.

Syntax:

```
alter application <App-Name> enable startup;
alter application <App-Name> disbale startup;

autostartup /* Start Application when Essbase Analytical Server
                starts */
```

If autostartup is enabled, the application will start as soon as the Essbase analytic server is started. If autostartup is disabled, the application will not start when the Essbase analytic server is started.

Syntax:

```
alter application <App-Name> enable autostartup;
alter application <App-Name> disable autostartup;
```

The MaxL `alter` statements are some of the more commonly used MaxL statements. Do not let this give you any indication as to the usefulness of every single available MaxL command. You may go for years and never use a command that someone else uses every day. As an Essbase administrator it is upto you to decide what works best in your individual situation.

Display application

This statement displays all of the information about all of the applications on the server or you can specify a specific application.

Syntax:

```
display application all;
display application <app-name>;
```

Drop application

The `drop application` command will drop an empty application. To remove an application that has databases in it, use the `cascade` option and if some of the objects are locked, then you can use the `force` option.

Syntax:

```
drop application <App-Name> cascade;
drop application  <App-Name>cascade force;
```

Working with an Essbase database from MaxL

In the `Database` MaxL object, you can use the same verbs like Alter, Create, Display, and Drop as you have used in the alter application statements, but these are at the database level.

Just like the MaxL statements that are used for altering an Essbase application, there are many MaxL commands that are used to alter an Essbase database as well. And, just like the application level MaxL commands, the database level commands directly correspond to the settings available to you through the EAS tool.

As you are reading through the examples we have used in the following section, keep in mind the details from the following screenshot that shows the **Database Properties** screen.

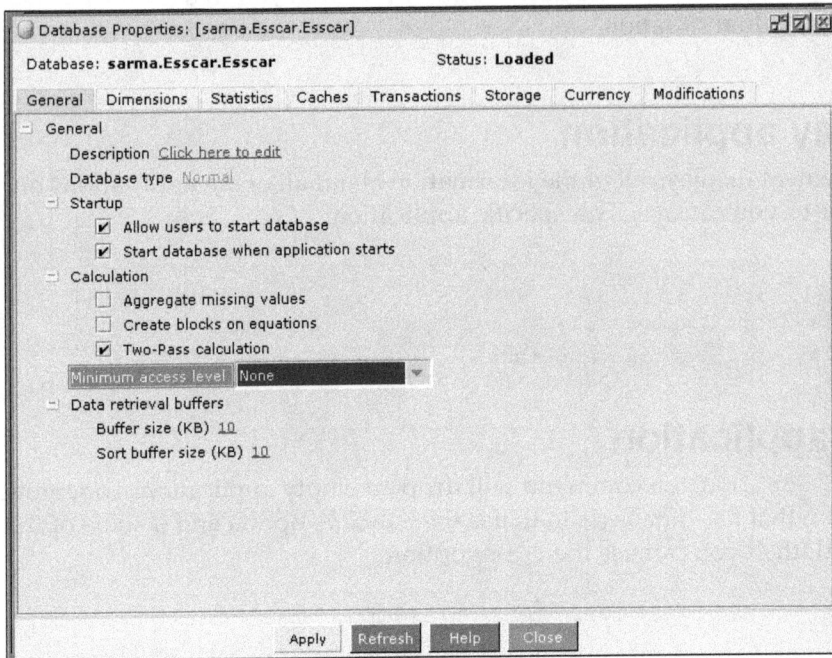

Let's see how each of these MaxL verbs will be used in the Essbase database object.

Creating or replacing a database

Using a MaxL statement you can create a new standard database or a new currency database. With the `create` statement you can also make a copy of an existing database.

Syntax:

This statement is for a standard Essbase database:

```
create database <app-name.db-name>;
```

This statement is for a currency Essbase database:

```
create currency database <app-name.db-name>;
```

Code Sample:

```
create database 'ESSCAR'.'ESSNEW';
replace database 'ESSCAR'.'ESSBKP' as 'ESSCAR'.'ESSCAR';
```

or

```
create database 'ESSCAR'.'ESSBKP' as 'ESSCAR'.'ESSCAR';
```

Altering a database

Just like the application `alter` command there is an `alter` command for the databases.

How about we walk through some of the more commonly used ALTER commands?

Enable/Disable commands

These MaxL commands are used to enable or disable some of the more commonly updated Essbase database properties.

This syntax shows how to enable/disable Essbase database properties:

```
alter database <Dbs-name> enable | disable two_pass_calc |
  aggregate_missing | startup | autostartup | compression >;
```

Code Sample:

```
alter database 'ESSCAR'.'ESSCAR' enable autostartup;
alter database 'ESSCAR'.'ESSCAR' enable two_pass_calc;
alter database 'ESSCAR'.'ESSCAR' disable startup;
alter database 'ESSCAR'.'ESSCAR' disable aggregate_missing;
alter database 'ESSCAR'.'ESSCAR' enable autostartup;
```

Archive commands

An Essbase database can be archived to a file. These MaxL commands are used for archiving a database. Use the `begin archive to file` to begin the archive export and `end archive` to end the archive export of the database. We will talk more about archiving in the next chapter.

Syntax:

```
alter database <db-name> begin archive to file <File-name>;
alter database end archive;
```

Set commands

In MaxL, you can also use the `set` commands. Some of the most widely used `set` commands are `retrieve_buffer_size`, `data_cache_size`, `index_cache_size`, `currency_conversion minimum permission`, `compression`, `lock_timeout`, `implicit_commit_after n blocks`, and many more.

Some syntax and code samples are listed below for the `set` commands.

Syntax:

```
alter database <Db-name> set <SET-COMMAND>;
```

Code Sample:

```
alter database 'ESSCAR'.'ESSCAR' set data_cache_size 4096;
alter database 'ESSCAR'.'ESSCAR' set retrieve_buffer_size 15360;
alter database 'ESSCAR'.'ESSCAR' set currency_database
'ESSCAR'.'ESSCURR'; /* This links a Standard database to its
                        currency database */
alter database 'ESSCAR'.'ESSCAR' set compression zlib;
alter database 'ESSCAR'.'ESSCAR' set note 'DATA IS UPATED on
02/08/2009';
```

Reset database

In MaxL, you can clear the data, LRO objects, and the entire outline in one single statement. Use extreme caution while using this command as there is no undo function to save you.

Syntax:

```
alter database <Db-Name> reset <all | data>;
```

Code Sample:

```
alter database 'ESSCAR'.'ESSCAR' reset all;
alter database 'ESSCAR'.'ESSCAR' reset data;
```

Rename database

Using the alter statement, you can also rename the database to a new name.

Syntax:

```
alter database <Db-name> rename to <new Db-name>;
```

Code Sample:

```
alter database 'ESSCAR'.'ESSCAR' rename to 'ESSCARN';
```

These are some of the commands that you can perform using the ALTER database.

Display database

With MaxL you can display all of the pertinent information about a database in one easy command.

Syntax:

```
display database <all | Db-Name | on application App-name>;
```

Code Sample:

```
display database;
display database all;
display database 'ESSCAR'.'ESSCAR';
```

Drop database

This command is used to delete Essbase databases and if a database has some of its objects locked, then also use the FORCE parameter to unlock those objects.

Syntax:

```
drop database <Db-Name>;
```

Code Sample:

```
drop database 'ESSCAR'.'ESSNEW';
drop database 'ESSCAR'.'ESSNEW' force;
```

Working with data in MaxL

With MaxL statements you can also import data into an Essbase database or export data from the Essbase database to a text file. These two statements are powerful statements and are very widely used.

The import statement not only imports data into the Essbase cube, it is also used t o update dimensions in the outline.

Syntax:

```
import database <app-name>.<db-name>
```

data | dimension: data is used when we are loading data into the cube. Use dimension for updating dimension in the outline.

connect as <Database Username>: Since we are loading the data from a relational database, please specify the user name here.

IDENTIFIED BY <Database password): Specify your relational database password.

USING (Information about the Rules File)

LOCAL | SERVER: Location of the rules file

RULE_FILE

RULE FILE NAME: Name of the rule file

ON ERROR APPEND TO (error File information)

WRITE | APPEND

ERROR FILE NAME: Path for error file C:/book/dataload.err

Code Sample:

```
import database 'ESSCAR'.'ESSCAR' data
connect as 'hypuser' identified by 'password'
using server rules_file 'dSales'
on error write to 'C:/book/dataload.err';
```

The export MaxL statement is used to export the level 0 data, all of the data, or just the input data from the Essbase cube into a text file. This function is mainly used for data retention as per company policy or backing up critical data.

Syntax:

```
export database <app-name>.<db-name>;
```

all | level 0 | input: all indicates all levels of data, level 0 indicates only leaf node data which excludes the aggregated data, and input indicates only input data.

```
data in columns to data_file <File-name>;
```

Code Sample:

```
export database 'ESSCAR'.'ESSCAR' all data to data_file 'C:/book/
export_data.txt';
```

Working with database calculations in MaxL

Using MaxL you can also create database calculation files, display the list of calc files, drop calc files, and execute calc files.

Create calculation

MaxL statements let you create a new calc file or copy an existing calc file from another application on the server.

Syntax:

```
create calculation <Calc-name> <Calc-string | as calc-name>
```

Code Sample:

```
create calculation 'ESSCAR'.'ESSCAR'.'ESSCALC' 'CALC DIM(PRODUCTS,
MARKETS)'
```

Upon execution of the above code a new calc script named ESSCALC will be created within the ESSCAR application.

Display calculation

The display MaxL statement will display the calculation scripts on the analytic server.

Syntax:

```
display calculation <all | <Calc-name> | on application <App-name>
| on database <Db-Name>>;
```

Code Sample:

```
display calculation all;
display calculation on application 'ESSCAR';
```

Execute calculation

The execute calculation MaxL statement will run the specified calc script.

Syntax:

```
execute calculation < Calc-name > | Calc-name on database Db-String
| Calc - String on Db-Name | default.;
```

Code Sample:

```
execute calculation 'ESSBCAR'.'ESSCAR'.'ESSCALC';
execute calculation 'CALC DIM(PRODCTS,MARKET)' on 'ESSACAR'.'ESSCAR';
```

Drop calculation

The `drop calculation` MaxL statement will delete the existing named calc script.

Syntax

```
drop calculation < Calc-name >;
```

Code Sample:

```
drop calculation 'ESSCAR'.'ESSCAR'.'ESSCALC';
```

Working with user privileges in MaxL

Using MaxL statements, the database administrator can create, edit, display, drop, and grant privileges to user IDs.

The basic accesses you can grant to a user ID are the same as defined in either the application properties or the database properties.

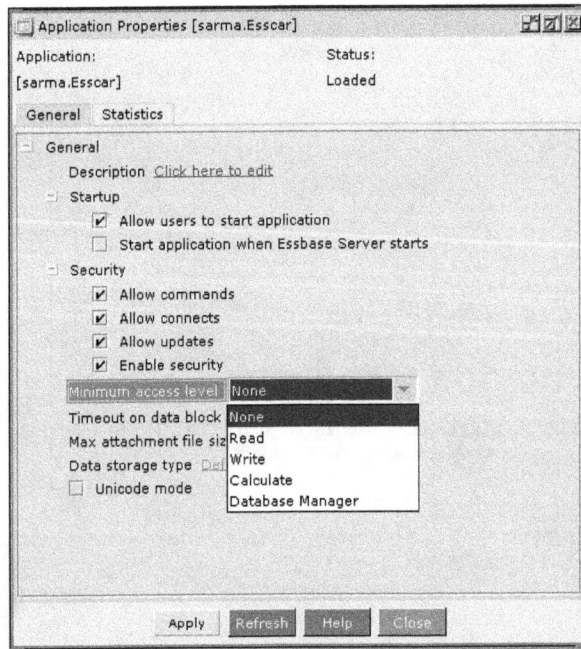

Looking at the previous screenshot you can see the choices provided to you for default access to the Essbase applications or databases. The only difference is if you set the access at the application level, the user will have the selected level of access for all databases within the application. If you grant this same level of access at the database level the ID will have this level of access only at the database level for which it was given.

Create user

Using the MaxL statement, you can create a new user, assign a default password, and associate the user with a database access group.

Syntax:

```
create user <user-name> identified by <password> as <EXISTING
USERNAME> | member of group <group-name>;
```

Code Sample:

```
create user essuser identified by essinit member of group esssales;
```

Alter user

The `alter` MaxL statement lets the administrator edit a user such as: change the group, remove the user from a group, enable the password, disable the password, and reset the user.

Syntax:

```
alter user <user-name> add to group <Group-name>; /* Adds an
    existing  user to an access group */
alter user <user-name> remove from group <Group-name>; /* Removes
    an existing user from an access group */
alter user <user-name> rename to <new user-name>; /* Renames an
    existing user to a new user name */
alter user <user-name> enable; /* Reactivate the user's ID */
alter user <user-name> disable; /* Disable the user ID */
alter user <user-name> set_password <new-password>; /* Set a new
    password for a specified user ID */
alter user <user-name> set_password_reset_days <integer> days | none
| immediate | exact; /* Set the password time to live in days */
alter user <user-name> reset; /* This statement resets the user
    ID. If the user ID is locked then it will be unlocked.
    Unsuccessful password attempts will set to 0 */
```

Code Sample:

```
alter user 'HYPUSER' add to group ESSPROFIT;
alter user 'HYPUSER" RESET;
```

Display user

The `display user` MaxL statement will display the user information like username, last logon date, enables, and password reset days remaining.

Syntax:

```
display user all | <User-name> | in group (all | <Group-name>);
```

Code Sample:

```
display user all;
display user in group all;
display user in group ESSPROFIT;
```

Drop user

The `drop user` MaxL statement will delete the existing user.

Syntax:

```
drop user <user-name>;
```

Code Sample:

```
drop user ESSUSER;
```

Grant user

The `grant user` MaxL statement will grant permissions to the user.

Syntax:

```
grant user SYS-SYSTEM-PRIVILEGE | SYS-SYSTEM-ROLE | APP-SYSTEM-ROLE ON
APPLICATION <APP-Name> | GRANTED-DBS-SYSTEM-ROLE ON DATABASE <Db-name>
| FILTER <Filter-name> | EXECUTE <Calc-name> TO <User-name> | <Group-
name>;
```

Code Sample:

```
grant user administrator to Sarma;
grant user no_access to Joe;
```

Working at the System level with MaxL

The database administrator is sometimes required to clear the Essbase log, unload all the application from the memory, or kill a process which is running. All of these statements can also be performed by the `system` MaxL statement. The `system` MaxL statement has only two actions to `alter` or `display` information.

Alter system properties

Using the `alter system` MaxL statement, you will be able to load and unload an application on the server, clear the Essbase log file, set invalid login limit, set password reset days, enable/disable Unicode, log out all or a specific user session. These changes are all updated at the analytic server level.

Let's see some of the `alter system` statements in use.

Syntax:

```
alter system load application all | <App-Name>;
alter system unload application all | <App-Name>;
alter system clear logfile;
alter system logout session all | <Session-id> | by user <User-name>
   | on application <App-Name> | on database <Db-Name>;
alter system enable unicode;
alter system disable unicode;
```

Code Sample:

```
alter system load application 'ESSCAR';
alter system logout session by user 'SARMA';
```

Display system properties

The `display system` MaxL statement displays the information about the Essbase server.

Syntax:

```
display system version | ports_in_use | expost_directory
   | license_info;
```

Code Sample:

```
display system all;
display system ports_in_use;
```

Substitution variables

Substitution variables can also be updated by using MaxL statements and commands. The following commands adding, updating, and dropping the substitution variables can be at the application, database, or the server level.

- `add variable`: This is used to create a new **Substitution Variable**.

  Syntax:

  Adding variables at Application level — these can be accessed by only the application specified.

  ```
  alter application <App-Name> add variable <variable-Name>
  <variable-value>;
  ```

  Adding variables at Database level — these can be accessed by only the database specified.

  ```
  alter database <App-Name>.<db-name> add variable
  <variable-Name> <variable-value>;
  ```

  Adding variables at the System level – these can be accessed by all of the applications that reside on the Essbase server

  ```
  alter system add variable <variable-Name> <variable-value>;
  ```

  Code Samples:

  ```
  alter application 'ESSCAR' add variable 'sCurrMonth' '200902';
  alter database 'ESSCAR'. 'ESSCAR' add variable 'sCurrMonth'
  '200902';
  alter system add variable 'sCurrMonth' '200902';
  ```

- `set variable`: This is used to update the value of an existing **Substitution Variable**. If the variable is not defined, then use `add variable` first to create a new **Substitution Variable**.

  Syntax:

  Setting variables at the application level

  ```
  alter application <App-Name> set variable <variable-Name>
  <variable-value>;
  ```

  Setting variables at the database level

  ```
  alter database <App-Name>.<db-name> set variable <variable-Name>
  <variable-value>;
  ```

Setting variables at the System level

```
alter system set variable <variable-Name> <variable-value>;
```

Code Samples:

```
alter application 'ESSCAR' set variable 'sCurrMonth' '200902';
alter database 'ESSCAR'. 'ESSCAR' set variable 'sCurrMonth'
'200902';
alter system set variable 'sCurrMonth' '200902';
```

- `drop variable`: This command is used to delete an existing **Substitution Variable**.

  Syntax:

  Drop a substitution variable at the Application level

  ```
  alter application <App-Name> drop variable <variable-Name>;
  ```

  Drop a substitution variable at the Database level

  ```
  alter database <App-Name>.<db-name> drop variable
  <variable-Name>;
  ```

  Drop a substitution variable at the System level

  ```
  alter system drop variable <variable-Name>;
  ```

  Code Samples:

  ```
  alter application 'ESSCAR' drop variable 'sCurrMonth';
  alter database 'ESSCAR'. 'ESSCAR' drop variable 'sCurrMonth';
  alter system drop variable 'sCurrMonth';
  ```

Executing a MaxL statement

Now that you have learned how powerful the MaxL statements are, let's see how we can execute the statements. The MaxL statements can be written in any text editor like Windows Notepad and you then save the file with the `.mxl` extension.

How do we run a MaxL statement? There are a couple of ways this can be accomplished. They are as follows:

- Run MaxL from the command prompt using the MaxL shell
- Executing a MaxL statement from the MaxL editor in EAS

Executing MaxL from Command Prompt

When you install the Essbase client, by default, the MaxL shell executable is provided and is named `essmsh.exe`. This executable will be located in the `bin` folder of the Oracle client home install folder, typically as shown:

`<Hyperion_home>\AnalyticServices\bin`

The extension for a MaxL file is `.mxl`, and the files are ASCII text files, which you can write statements and edit in any common text editor like Windows Notepad.

To execute your script you go to the `bin` folder path and fire off the MaxL script as shown below.

Open a blank Notepad text file and type in these MaxL statements:

```
spool on to 'C:\book\MaxlOutput.txt';     /* This sends all the Maxl
                                              outputs to the File
                                              mentioned */
login hypuser password on localhost;    /* Log in to the Essbase
                                           Server */
create application 'EsscarN';    /* This Step creates the
                                    Application called EsscarN */
create database 'EsscarN'.'EsscarN' as 'Esscar'.'Esscar';
/* This creates the copy of the Database Esscar and new Database name
is EsscarN */
alter database 'EsscarN'.'EsscarN' reset data;
/* This statement will clear all the Pre-existing data */
alter database 'EsscarN'.'EsscarN' set variable 'sCurrMonth' '200902';
/* Sets a variable called sCurrMonth */
import database 'EsscarN'.'EsscarN' data connect as 'hypuser'
identified by 'password' using server rules_file 'dSales' on error
write to 'C:/book/dataload.err';    /* This statement loads the
                                       data into the Cube */
logout;    /* logs out users session */
exit;      /* Exits from Maxl */
```

Save the file with the `.mxl` extension then open the Command Prompt and run your `MaxL script` from the prompt as shown in the following screenshot.

> If you type `ESSMSH` in the command prompt and the MaxL prompt does not show up, then go to the **Environment Variables** and add the path below:
>
> `<Hyperion-home>\AnalyticServices\bin\essmsh.exe.`
>
> After you add this into the path, you will be able to run MaxL from anywhere in the DOS prompt.

```
C:\WINDOWS\system32\cmd.exe                                    _ □ ×

   MaxL Shell completed

C:\Data>essmsh test.mxl

   Essbase MaxL Shell - Release 9.3.1 (ESB9.3.1.2.0B007)
   Copyright (c) 2000, 2007, Oracle and/or its affiliates.
   All rights reserved.

MAXL> login reader password1 on sarma;

     ERROR -      103 - Unexpected Essbase error 1051293.
     ERROR - 1051293 - Login fails due to invalid login credentials.

MAXL> logout;

        essmsh error: Not logged in to Essbase

   MaxL Shell completed

C:\Data>
```

Oops! There is an error and it looks like we have a wrong password in there.
But if there is an error message this is how you will see the error message.

Now let us change the password and rerun the script.

```
C:\WINDOWS\system32\cmd.exe                                    _ □ ×

C:\Data>essmsh test.mxl

   Essbase MaxL Shell - Release 9.3.1 (ESB9.3.1.2.0B007)
   Copyright (c) 2000, 2007, Oracle and/or its affiliates.
   All rights reserved.

MAXL> login reader password on sarma;

   OK/INFO - 1051034 - Logging in user [reader].
   OK/INFO - 1051035 - Last login on Saturday, May 23, 2009 10:08:30 AM.
   OK/INFO - 1241001 - Logged in to Essbase.

MAXL> logout;

        User reader is logged out

   MaxL Shell completed

C:\Data>
```

In the previous screenshot, you can now see that the script ran successfully without
any error messages. In the next section let us see how we can do the same while
using the EAS tool.

Executing MaxL from EAS

The EAS comes with plenty of tools and utilities. Believe it or not EAS also has a
MaxL editor where you can type all of the MaxL statements and execute the MaxL
scripts. In the EAS MaxL editor you do not need to specify the login commands as
you are already logged onto the Essbase analytic server through EAS.

Here are the steps to execute MaxL from the EAS MaxL editor:

1. Within EAS, click on **File | Editor | MaxL Script Editor.** The MaxL script editor will be opened.

2. The `import database` MaxL statement should be used to load the data, as shown in the following screenshot:

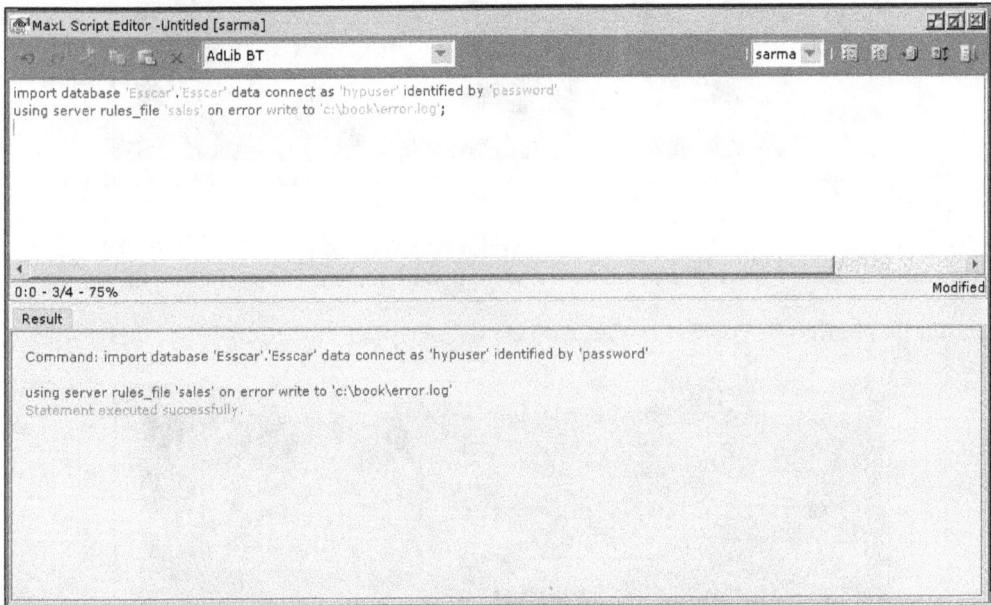

This is how you can execute your MaxL scripts from within EAS. In the next section we will discuss how you can make use of the powerful Essbase API to write highly functional backend programs for your Essbase applications.

Essbase Application Programming Interface (API)

The Essbase Application Programming Interface or API, is a programmatic interface between your client or your application server and the Essbase analytic server. The Essbase analytic server manages the transfer of data between client and analytic server or the application server and analytic server over your network.

Using programs coded by you to make calls to functions within the Essbase API, data or results are returned from the Essbase servers you are connected to. The Essbase API contains much of the same functionality that the Essbase software included with your system contains.

Typically you don't need to be concerned with where the physical Essbase server machine is located on the network when writing a program that uses API calls. Locating the server and transferring the data, is all handled by the API through TCP/IP connections.

Installing the Essbase API

The API functionality is automatically installed and available to clients and application servers from the Essbase analytic server when you install the Essbase analytic software on your server.

To install the API software on a client machine, you simply need to make sure the API selection is checked during your routine installation of the Essbase add-in. If the desktop machine in question has the Essbase add-in already installed, but not the Essbase API libraries, you can perform a complete reinstallation of the Essbase add-in without harming your current add-in installation. When you get to the installation step where it asks if you want to perform a routine or custom installation, select **Custom.** Then, on the next screen, select only the Essbase API.

For application server installation, the process for older versions would be just like the steps for a client PC for the API only. Simply perform a custom installation and select only the Essbase API for installation. Newer versions of Essbase (6.x and higher) are shipped with an Essbase Runtime Client which will install all of the required API libraries onto the target machine and support Essbase API functionality.

You now have the Essbase API on all of the machines in your network and can begin programming Essbase functions from the Essbase API.

What you should know to use the Essbase API

As you are already aware, this entire book is intended for use by IT professionals that have at least some level of experience and understanding of database usage and programming. Basic programming knowledge and experience with object-oriented programming is required to really understand how to code effective programs that take full advantage of the Essbase API functionality.

There are three distinct sets of API programming libraries for your programming convenience. There is a full Visual Basic library of API functionality, a full C library of API functionality, and a full Java function library as well.

For the sake of consistency throughout this book and the usability in Microsoft Excel VBA, we will discuss the Visual Basic or VB API library of functions. Complete documentation can be found in the online technical reference included with and accessible from the EAS tool.

Oracle Essbase also supports a complete Java API framework with a vast array of predefined packages and functions that allow the Essbase installation to exist on a distributed server environment that supports a full web-based application. Custom functions and controls are also supported. In order to run the Java API you need to install the Hyperion provider services. Much more information about the Java API can be found in the N-tier Application Programming Interface guide included with your Oracle Essbase installation package.

> Remember that COM+ objects are written in VB code, and any API functionality can be written into one as easily as into a formal Visual Basic program.
>
> The benefit of COM+ objects is that their functionality can be available on a server to support client calls, as well as web-based calls.

What functions are available in the Essbase API

There is a vast array of functionality available in the Essbase API. In the easily available Essbase API documentation the API functions are divided into two functional group categories.

The first category is the Visual Basic Main API group of functions. These functions perform tasks that you would perform during day-to-day operations.

Visual Basic Main API Function Categories

Visual Basic Main API Functions (listed categorically).

- Alias Table Functions
- Application Functions
- Attributes Functions
- Database Functions
- Database Member Functions
- File Functions
- Group Administration Functions
- Initialization and Login Functions

- Linked Reporting Object Functions
- Location Aliases Functions
- Miscellaneous Functions
- Object Functions
- Partition Functions
- Security Filter Functions
- Substitution Variable Functions
- User Administration Functions

As you can see from the previous list, the main API functions offer quite an assortment of functions that can make your life easier. There are functions for setting all kinds of application and database properties and attributes. There are functions for database maintenance and user maintenance. There are even file functions, security functions, and database object functions. There are also many database related functions.

The second category of Essbase API functions is the Visual Basic Outline API group of functions. As the name suggests, this category of API functions is more specifically targeted to the Essbase database outline.

Visual Basic Outline API Function Categories

Visual Basic Outline API Functions (listed categorically).

- Alias Table
- Attributes
- Dynamic Time Series
- Generation Name
- Level Name
- Member Administration
- Member Alias
- Member Formula
- Member Traversal
- Outline Administration
- Outline Query
- Set-up/Clean
- User Attribute

From the previous list you can see that the Outline API functions allows you specific Essbase database outline functionality.

With the combined functionality of both API categories written into a comprehensive enough of a program that you can practically build, populate, and use an Essbase application/database without ever touching the actual EAS tool.

Essbase API programming tips

A good coding style to adopt when writing code in any programming language is the indented or nested coding style. This style is recommended the world over for writing easy to follow written code instructions. The indented or nested coding style allows for easier debugging and enhancing of your code, now and in the future. The nested coding style also helps ensure that you will remember to follow the opening of a function with the closing of a function.

Essbase nested coding style examples

Here is a representative example of the nested coding style and the obvious benefits
of employing such a method or style.

```
Begin action 1
      Begin action 2
          Begin action 3
              Perform action 3
          End action 3
          Begin action 4
              Perform action 4
          End action 4
      End action 2
End action 1
```

This example should illustrate nicely why the nested style is the preferable code
writing style. The next example will now put the previous example into Essbase
functionality context so it makes sense for you. Most Essbase API functions usually
must be started or opened and after completion of the task they must be ended
or closed.

```
Initialize the API
      Login to a server
          Connect to a database
              Open a database outline
                  Browse the outline
              Close the outline
              Open a report
                  Modify & save the report
              Close the report
          Disconnect from a database
      Logout from the server
Terminate the API
```

Typically, the group of Essbase API calls or functions illustrated in the previous
example would be embedded in a VB subroutine so that it would actually look
more like this:

```
Sub BrowseOutlineAlterReport()
Initialize the API
      Login to a server
          Connect to a database
              Open a database outline
                  Browse the outline
              Close the outline
              Open a report
                  Modify & save the report
```

```
          Close the report
        Disconnect from a database
      Logout from the server
  Terminate the API
  End Sub
```

As you can see each Essbase API call has an ending or terminating call that must be executed when the desired function has completed.

> Many code editors support the nested coding style by automatically indenting the next line of written code to the same indentation as the previous line making nested code writing even easier. The Visual Basic editor supports nested code writing and Oracle Essbase recommends you use the nested coding style when coding Essbase API functions.

Essbase API function declarations

For your convenience your Essbase package comes with a VB code module that has all of the Essbase API functions and declarations already coded for you. All you need to do is add the module to your VB/VBA/COM+ project then start coding the API calls and functions. The file's name is esb32.bas and is a wonderful time saver.

As you can see in the previous screenshot, the Essbase supplied API declaration module includes all of the necessary global variables and other API related structures, as well as all of the API function calls. What a nice thing to have!

How to code an API function

In the following example, we will code an Essbase API function that returns database information into an Essbase private type structure named DBINFO:

```
Sub GetDataBaseInfo(Appname as String, DBName as String)
            'Pass Application name and Database name to VB subroutine

Dim sts as ESB_STS_T 'Dimension return code variable
Dim hCtx as ESB_HCTX_T 'Dimension API handle context
Dim DbInfo as ESB_DBINFO_T 'Dimension DB information variable

sts = EsbGetDatabaseInfo (hCtx, Appname, DBName, DbInfo) 'Execute
                                                    'API function

If sts = ESB_STS_NOERR ' Test API function return code
       Call DisplayDatabaseInformation 'Branch to new subroutine on
                                    'satisfactory return code
End If

End Sub
```

After a successful call to the Essbase API EsbGetDatabaseInfo function, the **DbInfo** structure will be populated with a variety of database information for the database that was passed to the function. The following is an example of the variable structure showing what database information is returned.

```
Type ESB_DBINFO_T
```

ElapsedDbTime	As Long	'Elapsed database time
DataFileCacheSetting	As Long	'Data File Cache size database
DataFileCacheSize	As Long	
DataCacheSetting	As Long	
DataCacheSize	As Long	'run-time size of the Data cache
IndexCacheSetting	As Long	
IndexCacheSize	As Long	'size of the Index cache
IndexPageSetting	As Long	
IndexPageSize	As Long	'run-time size of an Index Page
nDims	As Long	'number of dimensions

AppName	As String * ESB_APPNAMELEN	'application name
Name	As String * ESB_DBNAMELEN	'database name
Country	As String * ESB_MBRNAMELEN	'country dimension
Time	As String * ESB_MBRNAMELEN	'time dimension
Category	As String * ESB_MBRNAMELEN	'category dimension
Type	As String * ESB_MBRNAMELEN	'type dimension
CrPartition	As String * ESB_MBRNAMELEN	'curr partition member
DbType	As Integer	' Database Type
Status	As Integer	'database load status
nConnects	As Integer	'number of users connected
nLocks	As Integer	'number of blocks locked
Data	As Integer	'data loaded flag
End Type		

There sure is a lot of information passed back from this call. Now do you remember back a little bit that the variable name used in this API call is DbInfo? Yes, the variable DbInfo, dimensioned using the variable structure above, now contains all of the data that is listed in the ESB_DBINFO_T structure.

To read any of the information returned in this structure, the steps are very easy. For instance, if you want to read how many users are connected to the database you returned the information from just code: variable = DbInfo.nConnects and your variable will now contain the number of users connected to the database. You can also use DbInfo.nConnects elsewhere in your program depending on how you dimensioned it.

Essbase API code sample blocks

It seems that for most good programmers, the only difference between programming languages is the syntax of the code itself. Let's face it, logic is logic, and If means If and End If means End If in all programming languages. The syntax may vary though, as we've all seen End If or End-If or ENDIF.

You have probably sensed that Oracle has created quite a product with Essbase and you are correct. You have probably also gotten the idea that Oracle is very thorough and has prepared well written and easy to understand system documentation. Well, we'd have to say you are correct once again. The following is a picture of a typical API function reference found in the Oracle Essbase API Reference that can be found online or accessed through the EAS tool.

The following example is an exact representation of how the Essbase API Function Reference looks, when accessed through EAS. It also looks very similar when accessed through the Internet.

EsbInit

| Description | Syntax | Parameters | Return Value | Notes | Access | Example | See Also |

Description

EsbInit() initializes the Essbase VB API and message database. The ESB_INIT_T structure passed to this function includes a number of initializatio parameters, including the name of the message database, the flag indicating whether to use a customized error handler, the maximum message sta to be used by this error handler, the name and location of your help file, and version number.

Syntax

```
EsbInit (pInit, phInst)

pInit   As ESB_INIT_T
phInst As Long
```

Parameters

pInit	Pointer to Essbase VB API initialization structure.

Return Value

The ESB_INIT_T structure passed to this function includes a number of initialization parameters, including the name of the message database, error handler, the name and location of your help file, and version number.

EsbInit() returns an instance handle in *phInst*. The returned instance handle allows multiple applications to independently access the VB API (for DLLs onl The instance handle should be preserved and passed to the **EsbLogin()** and **EsbTerm()** functions.

Notes

- You *must* call this function before any other Essbase VB API functions.
- If any field in the initialization structure is an empty string or zero (as appropriate), the API uses a default value for those parameters.
- ESB_TRUE and ESB_FALSE are global variables. Assign them integer values as demonstrated in the example.

Access

This function requires no special access.

Example

```
Declare Function EsbInit Lib "ESBAPIW.DLL" (Init As ESB_INIT_T, hInst As Long) As Long

Sub ESB_Init ()
   Dim hInst As Long
   Dim Init As ESB_INIT_T
   Dim sts As Long

   ESB_FALSE = 0
   ESB_TRUE  = 1

   '***********************
   ' Define init structure
   '***********************
   Init.Version = ESB_API_VERSION
   Init.MaxHandles = 10
   Init.LocalPath = "C:\ESSBASE"
   ' Use default message file
   Init.MessageFile =""
   ' Use EsbGetMessage to retrieve
   ' messages
   Init.ClientError = ESB_TRUE
   Init.ErrorStack = 100

   '********************
   ' Initialize the API
   '********************
   sts = EsbInit (Init, hInst)
End Sub
```

```
EsbLogin()
EsbAutoLogin()
EsbTerm()
EsbGetMessage()
```

As you can see from the actual Essbase API Reference images, the guidance and instructions are very helpful. You get a complete explanation of the function and tasks it can perform. You get an example showing exactly how to code the function. Many times we will just copy and paste the example into an actual subroutine and modify as needed. You also get information on any special requirements the function may have. For instance the `Init` function must be performed before any other Essbase API function. Best of all you get a list of any related functions that are either required to accompany the subject function or are similar and may be a better fit for what you are trying to accomplish.

The sample API subroutine explained

What we will do now is take the VB subroutine from the previous example and show you how it would look in a real program.

```
Sub BrowseOutlineAlterReport()
ESB_Init 'Initialize the API
     ESB_Login(Server, UserID, Password, hInst) 'Login to server
         ESB_SetActive(hCtx, ApName, DbName) 'Connect to a database
             ESB_OtlOpenOutline 'Open a database outline
                 ESB_OtlRestructure 'Restructure the outline
             ESB_OtlCloseOutline 'Close the outline
         ESB_ClearActive 'Disconnect from a database
     ESB_Logout 'Logout from the server
ESB_Term 'Terminate the API
End Sub
```

You have just completed our instruction for the Essbase API section of this chapter. We know that you now feel confident that you can take advantage of the Essbase API functionality and make your life a lot easier.

> Because the Essbase API functions execute on the analytic server, the same tasks or functions that could be performed through EAS or the Microsoft Excel add-in will almost always execute substantially faster than on the client.

Systems built with extensive use of automated Essbase API functionality are usually more reliable since there is no need for a human to be in there messing things up. This same reason also seems to make the automated systems more stable as well.

All in all, it is better to plan for the long haul and do some of the hard work up front in terms of writing code. This method of system development does nothing but keep paying you back with long term dividends.

Summary

Well that should just about put you over the top. You have a system built with the best multidimensional OLAP software available and now it's nearing a lights out operation with you automating the majority of your routine database maintenance and administration tasks. How can you contain yourself?

As with the other chapters in this book we can honestly tell you that even if this book were one thousand pages long, we would be barely scratching the surface of the knowledge and experience you can gain from plain old tinkering around with Essbase. Do yourself a real favor and play!

Next up in Chapter 9, is a comprehensive array of Essbase system tips and tricks. These items will help you when it comes to performance tuning your application, database and server configuration, memory management for server and client and much more.

.

Advanced Techniques

9

Well here we are at a place in this book where the information being presented to you is not so much mandatory as it is optional, and it can be used as needed. In actuality, the default settings with your Essbase installation are perfectly adequate for most applications. It is only when your needs start to expand beyond the ordinary that you will find yourself looking for ways to tweak your Essbase system performance.

In this chapter you will find a variety of database and system settings and adjustments that will help you keep your Essbase database running at top performance.

While we highly recommend that you actually read this entire chapter the first time through, it can also be used as a handy reference if and when you feel you may need to enhance your current system's performance or make improvements that will allow for trouble free growth in your system.

Performance tuning your database

Unlike many of the more typical relational database applications, Essbase has many more database administrator options that can drastically affect the performance and reliability of your Essbase database system.

Perhaps it's time to repeat what we've said before, "Essbase is an art, not a science." There, we'll let that sink in a little bit.

What we mean by the previous and often repeated statement is that most of the time your experience and good judgment can be far more valuable when giving consideration to tuning your Essbase database than any stale old list of hard-coded formulas.

When you actually get to tuning your system always keep in mind that what you read here, learn from others, or even glean from Oracle system documentation, is in most cases to be taken as guidelines for your own individual situation.

The actual actions you'll be performing, when you are tuning your database, are items like adjusting several optional cache sizes through both the EAS and in the Essbase system configuration file or `Essbase.cfg`. You may also be taking steps to alter the order of the dimensions in the database outline.

> We know this isn't really performance related but it is very important! If there were anything that could be considered as a weakness anywhere in Essbase, it would be the Essbase security file or `Essbase.sec`.
>
> Because this file is more or less open all the time for system I/O operations, there is a high potential for the file to become corrupted in the event of a power outage or other serious event.
>
> If you do encounter a situation where the server needs to be rebooted unexpectedly, we highly recommend that before you restart the server or the Essbase service, you make a backup copy of the `Essbase.sec` file. The file itself can be found in the `Essbase\bin` folder.

The shape of your database outline

What are they talking about when we refer to the shape of an Essbase outline? How can an Essbase database outline have a shape? Well conceptually every Essbase database outline has a shape. What you want to be concerned with is what shape your outline has.

Believe it or not, the shape of your outline is one of the most important considerations for overall database performance, but it is still a guideline. There will be times when this guideline simply will not work for you.

Everyone knows what an hourglass looks like, right? An hourglass is wide at the ends and narrow in the middle. Well in most cases, you want your Essbase database outline to have the shape of an hourglass, really.

The hourglass outline

Here is what we mean by all of this shape nonsense. The shape is determined by the size and storage type of the dimensions in the Essbase database outline. It is generally recognized in the Essbase community that the optimal arrangement for your database outline is as follows:

- Largest **Dense** dimensions ← **Most members**

- Smallest **Dense** dimensions ← **Least members**

- Smallest aggregating **Sparse** dimensions ← **Least members and usual consolidations**

- Largest aggregating **Sparse** dimensions ← **Most members and usual consolidations**

- Non-aggregating **Sparse** dimensions ← **Can have many or few members but little to no consolidations**

By looking at the following screenshot, you will see the recommended dimension structure, as seen in the EAS **Database Properties** screen:

Database Properties: [sarma.Esscar.Esscar]

Database: **sarma.Esscar.Esscar**   Status: **Loaded**

General | Dimensions | Statistics | Caches | Transactions | Storage | Currency | Modifications

Number of dimensions 9

Dimension	Type	Members in Dimension	Members Stored
CALENDER PERIODS	Dense	52	52
METRIC	Dense	14	12
CUSTOMER	Sparse	3	3
SCENARIO	Sparse	3	3
MODEL YEAR	Sparse	3	3
CURRENCY	Sparse	4	4
TOTAL VEHICLES	Sparse	19	16
TOTAL MARKET	Sparse	33	32
COLORS	Sparse	3	0

Apply   Refresh   Help   Close

Notice how even with relatively few members, the database outline has the dimensions structured as recommended, wide at the ends and narrow in the middle. Just like an hourglass.

The reason for this is the same as was given in Chapter 5 on calculation scripts. The structure of the database is extremely important to the functioning of the database. What the hourglass shape will tend to do is help keep the database block size down to manageable levels for optimal performance during calculations and data loads.

While this database outline shape methodology will work for most situations, there are times when it will not. For example, in a large parts database, you may need to place your parts dimension last, regardless of the fact that it may have many parent/child consolidations.

Database block size

As previously mentioned, database block size is an important and integral part of overall database performance. From calculating the database, to retrieving data into a Microsoft Excel spreadsheet, bigger data blocks in an Essbase database usually mean slower performance. Of course, the number and type of dimensions directly affect the database data block size.

The suggested ideal database data block size is between 50KB and 200KB. The really ideal block size is less than 100KB or in the 50KB to 80KB range. The number of dense dimensions in the database greatly affects the data block size, so the ideal recommended number of data dimensions in an Essbase database should be from 5 to 7. Of course, there are times when these recommendations are just not possible, but most applications will fit within these parameters.

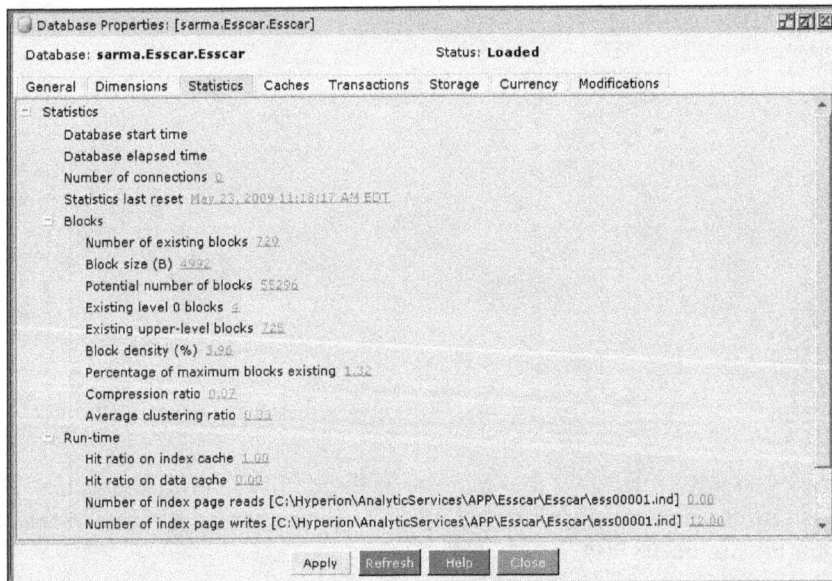

Looking at the previous screenshot you can see the **Statistics** page of the **Database Properties** screen from the EAS tool. This screen tells you all there is to know about your database data block set up. It will be on this screen you will verify if the changes you have made to your Essbase outline have actually helped with block size, block usage, or block density.

Database configuration settings

There are many database caches and settings available to help you with optimizing your database.

As you know, optimally storing your data is the job of a properly configured database outline. A properly configured outline can also have an effect on calculation performance, data load performance, and data retrieval performance.

Data retrieval buffers

When it comes to loading, retrieving, calculating, and extracting your data, performance optimizing is the job of caches and buffers. During reporting, data retrieval cache and buffer settings are used to obtain optimal retrievals of the data.

One pair of settings that you cannot go wrong with is the **Data retrieval buffers** settings, found on the **General** tab of the **Database Properties** screen (seen below).

The memory used by these buffers is only allocated when an Essbase retrieve is executed from a Microsoft Excel spreadsheet or when an Essbase report script is executed. Because of this you can increase the retrieval buffer and the retrieval sort buffer sizes until you get the results you need, all the way upto the maximum size of 100,000 KB, which is 100MB. Best of all you will not rob the system of memory when they are not in use. These data cache settings are particularly useful when you are reporting on or retrieving larger amounts of dynamically calculated data.

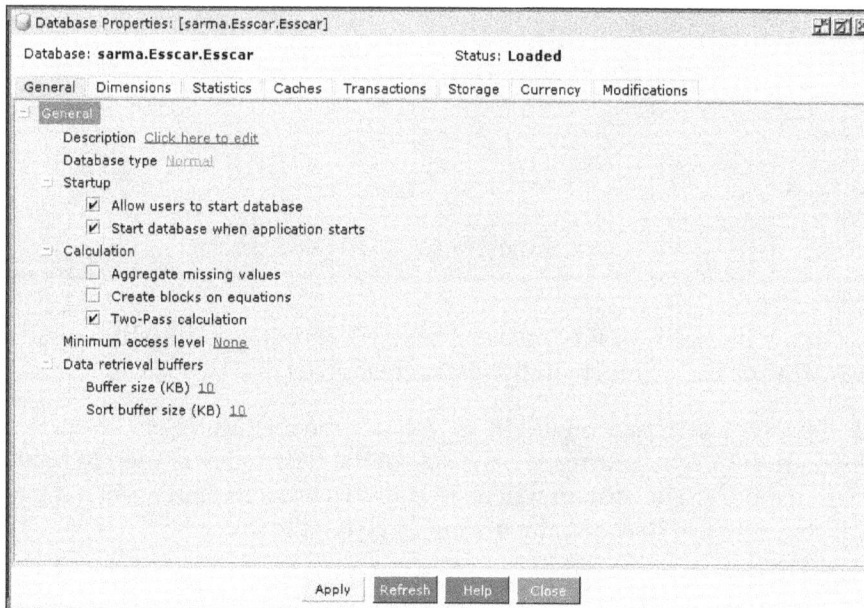

Data cache settings

On the **Caches** tab of the **Database Properties** screen (seen below), you will find an assortment of database cache settings that are configurable by the administrator through EAS.

The first option, **Cache memory locking,** will actually retain the memory needed for the database caches at all times. In order to set the **Cache memory locking** to true, you should use the **Direct I/O** memory setting on the **Storage** tab. The **Direct I/O** setting uses the memory set by the **File Cache** and does not consume Essbase server memory when not in use. By default, this is set to false. While this may give slight improvement during data loads, we have never noticed any real difference in day-to-day operations by checking this option. You may as well let the system enjoy the use of the memory until it is needed by one of these caches.

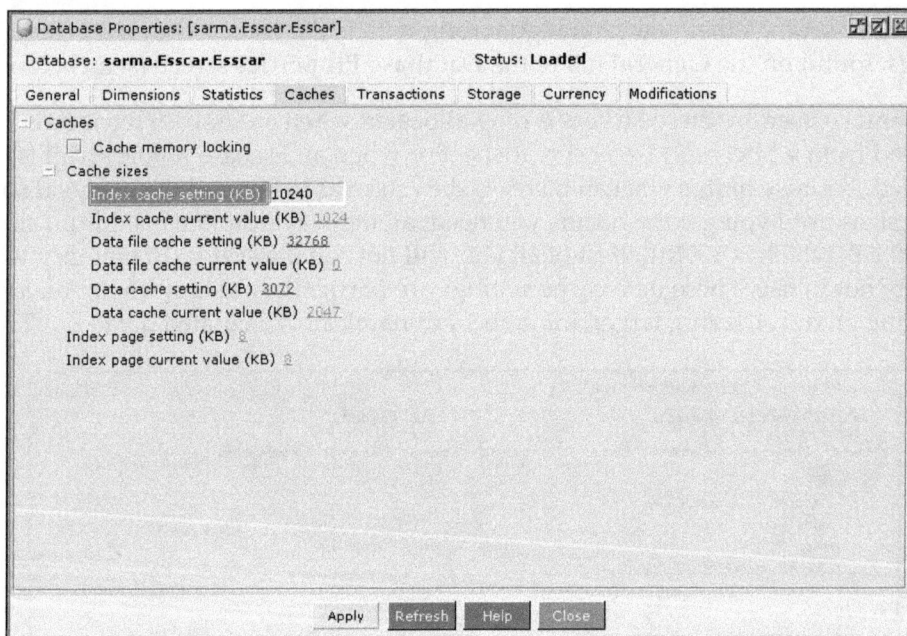

One thing you will notice about Essbase is that it is certainly not bashful. Essbase will almost always use as much of the system resources that you allow.

For the **Index cache setting,** you might as well use the maximum of 10240KB, which is 10MB. The **Index cache setting** sets the size of the buffer that is used to hold index page files in memory. The system will only grab this extra memory when it needs it and it will certainly use it, especially during large data loads.

The **Data file cache setting** is the size of the buffer used to load the database page files into memory. This setting is only relevant if you have your database set to **Direct I/O**. **Buffered I/O** is the default and on all but the largest of data loads has tweaking this setting made any noticeable difference. The **Data file cache setting** can be set as large as the combined total size of all of the database page files. On a 30GB database setting, the page file cache size may not be practical, or even possible, especially if you only have 16 GB of system RAM!

For the **Data cache setting**, it is usually fine left where it is at the default setting of 3072KB. The recommended maximum size is 0.125 times the size of the **Data file cache setting**. Only change this setting if you are experiencing performance issues and have many concurrent users accessing the database.

The **Index page setting** is a static number and cannot be set by you. Oracle has determined that 8KB is sufficient for a database index page size.

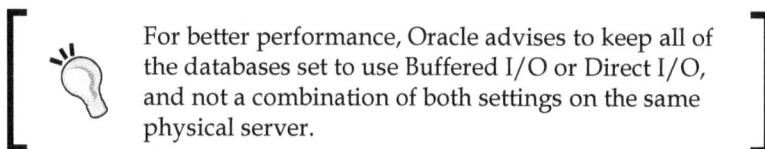

> For better performance, Oracle advises to keep all of the databases set to use Buffered I/O or Direct I/O, and not a combination of both settings on the same physical server.

Data load and storage settings

We will now briefly cover the available options for optimizing your system's data loading and data storage capabilities. As is always recommended, the default settings are in most cases, more than adequate, so you should make any changes carefully and test each one fully to determine if the change is warranted or not.

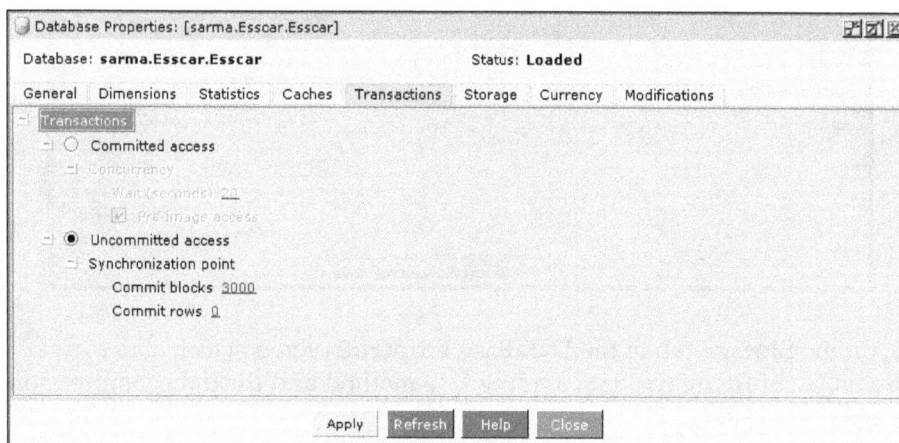

On the **Transactions** tab of **Database Properties** screen (seen in the previous screenshot), you will see options for **Committed access** and **Uncommitted access**. If you select **Committed access** Essbase will hold all of the data blocks involved in a transaction until the changes or updates are committed to the system. This can be a problem for you because Essbase will keep duplicates of the data blocks until the time they are committed and you will temporarily need double the actual space that you really need for data storage. Essbase does this in case of the need for a rollback.

The default setting for transactional access is **Uncommitted access**. As is true with most Essbase settings, the default setting in this case is more than adequate for most systems, and the default setting of 3000 for **Commit Blocks** works well too. Even in larger systems, we haven't been able to notice measurable differences when playing with this setting.

The 3000 Commit Blocks setting means that Essbase will commit or make permanent updates to data blocks for three thousand data blocks at a time. This means that if a calculation is interrupted, for example, that all of the work upto the point of interruption will not be lost. All work that has completed, in 3000 data block increments, will actually be saved to the database.

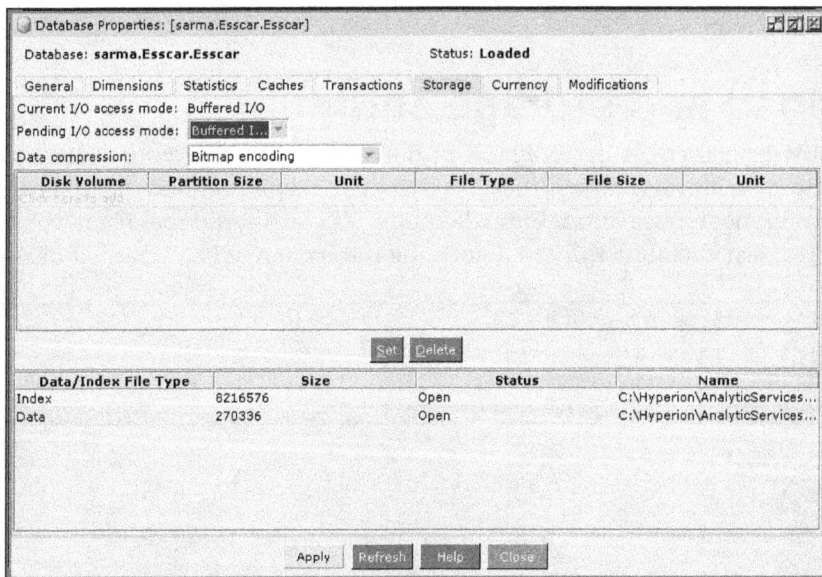

Finally, on the **Storage** tab of the **Database Properties** screen (seen above), we are allowed to configure the data loading I/O method and the data compression for storage.

As usual, the default Essbase setting for data load I/O, **Buffered I/O**, is more than adequate for most data load operations. **Buffered I/O** takes advantage of the file cache settings discussed earlier and only in cases where there is an extremely large amount of data to load will it be noticeable that the system needs to swap in and out of virtual memory.

The **Direct I/O** setting is best for extremely large data loads. **Direct I/O** bypasses the cache and accesses system memory directly. If your system has lots of extra memory available, this option can provide a real boost to the data loading performance.

Data compression can also be a factor in system performance and once again Essbase has several options for you. Obviously, the **No Compression** setting can be the quickest for I/O because there is no extra process time required to compress or uncompress the data as it is read. This is not recommended at all because the size of even an average database would grow to unmanageable proportions very quickly.

Can you guess what the best all-around compression setting is? Yes, it is the Essbase default setting for **Bitmap encoding**, what else? Overall, this setting uses space the most efficiently when compared to other available compression types and has a lower than average I/O cost as well.

Essbase does offer **Run-Length encoding** as well, and this setting may be preferable for databases that have very low block density. Of course, you will need to do some experimenting to see if this type of data compression is right for your situation.

Lastly, Essbase offers you the choice of **ZLIB** compression. **ZLIB** compression can be useful if the density of your data blocks is extremely high. Again, you will need to experiment with this setting.

Partitioning databases

If you are at all familiar with database terminology, you know that partitioning a database, either relational or multidimensional, is almost always done as a performance consideration. In the relational database world, you are usually taking one very large database and partitioning it into smaller, more manageable databases.

In the Essbase multidimensional world, there are several reasons for partitioning:

- To split a large, cumbersome database into smaller, more manageable pieces or slices

- To create, in one database, selected pieces or slices of data from several similar but unrelated databases

- To provide a consolidated look at an overall enterprise process

- To control data level security more effectively
- To increase system performance when retrieving high use data

Caution:

Partitioning databases is a very real method of improving performance. You must be very careful not to get carried away and have too many source databases included in your partitioned target database. Essbase will load into memory all source databases in a transparent partition and this can actually have a negative effect on system performance!

Essbase offers three types of database partitioning options. They are:

- **Replicated**: A replicated database partition copies a portion of the source database to be stored in a target database. Users can access the target database as if it were the source. The database administrator must occasionally refresh the target database from the source database.
- **Transparent**: A transparent partition allows users to manipulate their data that is stored in a target database as if it were part of the actual source database. The remote data is retrieved from the source database each time the users of the target database request it. Write backs to the target database also flow through back to the source database.
- **Linked**: A linked partition enables users to navigate from one data value in one database to a subset of the data in another database. The two databases may contain very different outlines.

As you can see there are three very different partitioning methods available to you with your Essbase system. This may sound tired by now, but truly, even partitioning your databases is something that is really only needed on the largest of systems. Partitioning is a valid performance tuning consideration for sure but its use should be governed more by your Essbase knowledge and experience than by any sort of formula that says if your database is this size it should do this or that.

Let us consider the first scenario, where the database is large and cumbersome and you need to split the data. In this scenario we have 5 years worth of data in the database. For the earliest 3 years of the data, the users do not need to use it on a day-to-day basis for analysis but only need it once in a while. This scenario seems to be best suited for the transparent partition where we partition the data by the time dimension. We are going to have the *Current* and *Prior* years in one cube and the remaining 3 years in a different cube. Let us call the *Current* and *Prior* year cube our **ESSCAR** cube and the *Prior* cube the **ESSCARP** cube. Current and Prior year data will be loaded into the **ESSCAR** and the prior 3 year's data will be loaded into the **ESSCARP** cube. In this example, the **ESSCARP** database or cube is the source data and **ESSCAR** database is the target database. Now, let's see step-by-step how we set up the transparent partition.

1. Using EAS, open the **ESSCAR** application and expand the **ESSCAR** database. Select the **Partitions** menu pick and then click on the **Action | Create new partition on "ESSCAR"**. You will then see the **Create Partition for Block Storage Application** screen as shown below.

   On the **Type** tab, select the **Partition** type. In this case select, **Transparent** partition and then click on the **Connection t**ab.

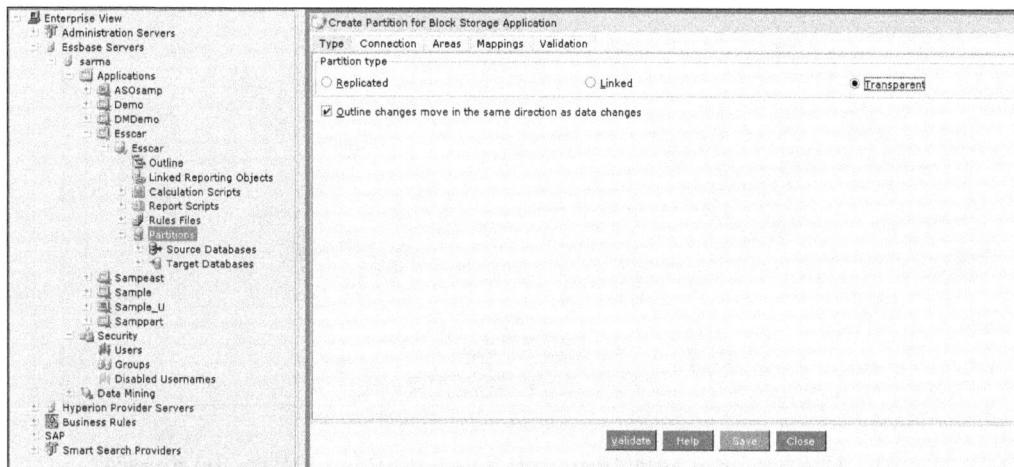

2. On the **Connection** tab, you will need to enter the information about the server, source database, target database, username, and password. We suggest that for current separation of duties policies, you create a separate batch id for this process. In the source database, we have selected **EsscarP** as target database and **Esscar** as the source database.

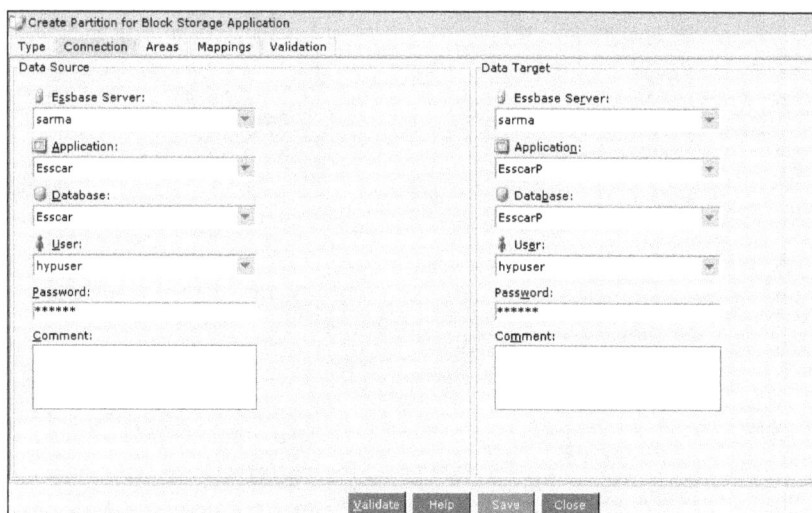

3. Click on the **Areas** tab to link members between the target and the source. On this screen, you can add data selection information in three different methods that we describe here:

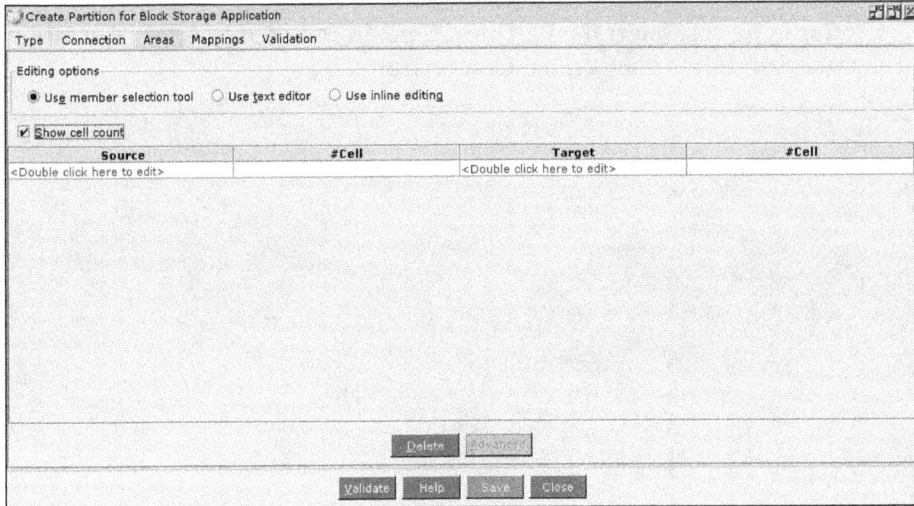

i) **Use member selection tool**: If you double-click on the **Source** heading, or the **Target** heading you will see the **Area Mapping Member Selection** screen where you can select the source outline members and the target database outline members for which you want to map together.

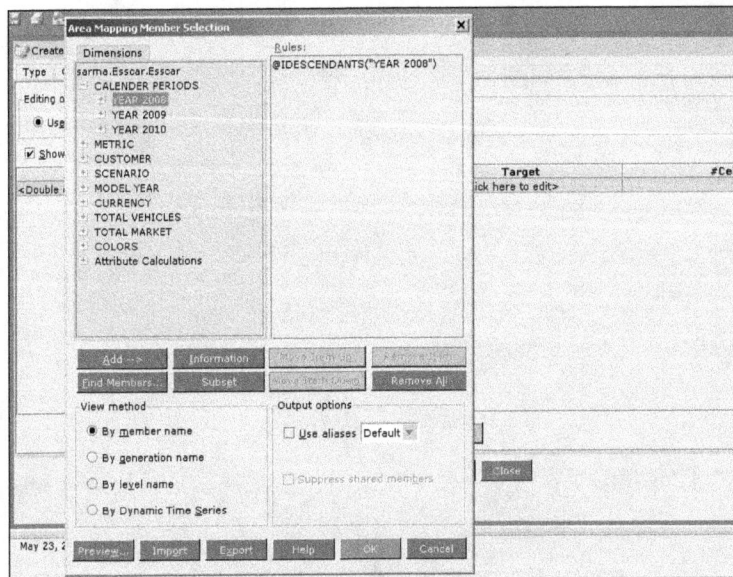

ii) **Use text editor**: In the text editor screen, you can type in the source or target member names. You can also select the **Show Cell Count** checkbox which will help you validate your database outline selections by allowing you to verify matching cell counts between the source and target database outlines. Verifying that the cell counts match is how Essbase determines you have correctly defined the slice of data that is to be used by the source and target databases. If the cell counts do not match there is reason to believe you have a data mismatch and will need to re-examine your data mappings.

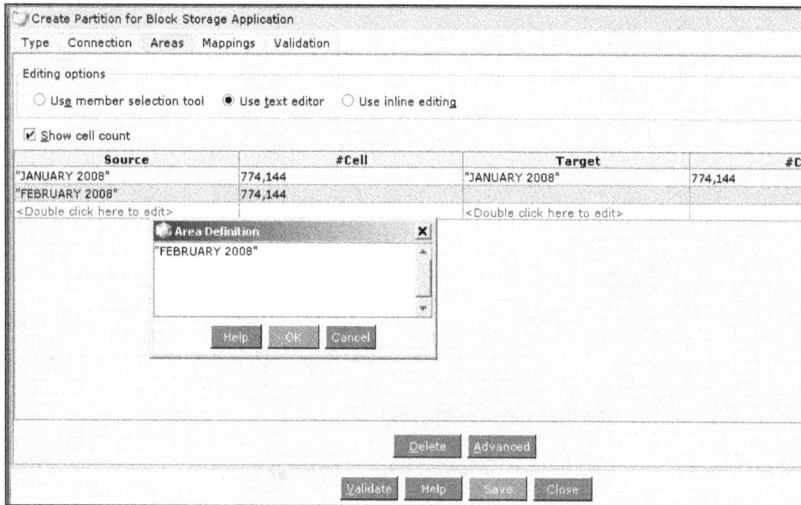

iii) **Use inline editing**: Inline editing allows you to enter more than one member name to map between the source and target members as shown in the following screenshot:

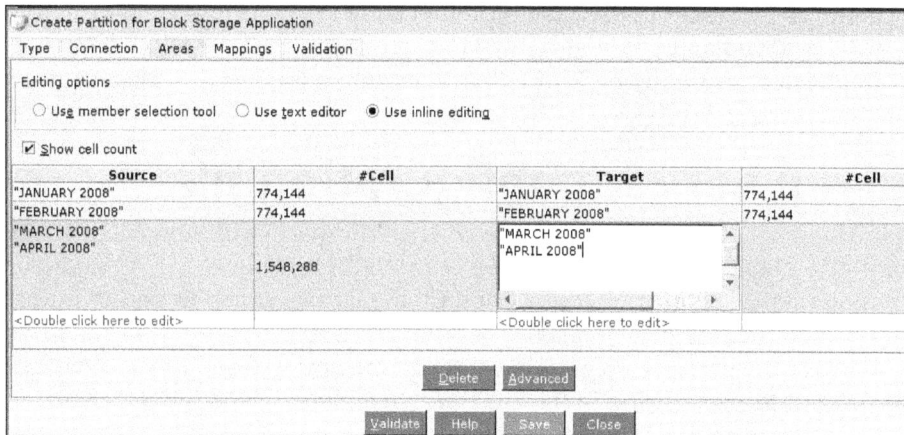

4. On the **Mappings** tab you can mention the member name if the outline contains different member names or the same member name with different names. The source and the target members can be defined in this screen.

5. After you have completed the four steps to set up a partition definition, you can click on the **Validate** button. If you have successfully set up your partition you will see a message box saying your partition is valid and you can then save the partition. If there is an error it will prompt you with an error message as shown in the following screenshot:

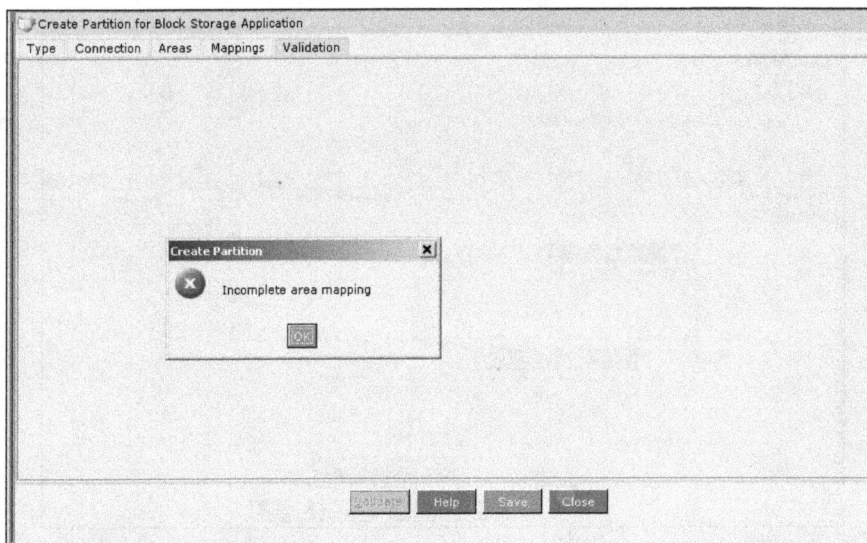

The error message in the previous screenshot says that the area mappings are incomplete. You must go back and click on the **Areas** tab and correct the error by ensuring you have matching source and target partition definitions and then you can click on the **Save** button. If there are no errors the partition will then be saved and you will be able to make use of the partitions. To create a **Replicated** partition or a **Linked** partition you would follow these same steps.

Analytic server configuration file

This is the big one! The essbase.cfg file is where most of your advanced techniques will come into play. The essbase.cfg file is an ASCII text file and can be edited using any standard text editing tool. Found on the Essbase analytic server in the essbase\bin folder, the heart and soul of your performance tuning will be in there. In fact, many of the performance tuning settings the you will set through the EAS will have a counterpart setting in the essbase.cfg file.

> **A word to the wise:**
>
> Always make a backup copy of the essbase.cfg file before you make any changes to it. The essbase.cfg file is a critical system file used by the Essabse analytic server, and there are entries in there that affect whether the service will start or not. Just in case.

First of all, there are literally dozens of optional statements that can be used in the essbase.cfg file as shown in the screenshot below. However, do not be alarmed, if you do not have each of the available statements represented in the essbase.cfg file. As usual, Essbase has a default setting for almost all of them.

AGENTDELAY	DLTHREADSPREPARE	NETDELAY
AGENTDESC	DLTHREADSWRITE	NETRETRYCOUNT
AGENTDISPLAYMESSAGELEVEL	DYNCALCCACHEBLKRELEASE	NETTCPCONNECTRETRYCOUNT
AGENTLOGMESSAGELEVEL	DYNCALCCACHEBLKTIMEOUT	NODENAME
AGENTPORT	DYNCALCCACHECOMPRBLKBUFSIZE	NOMSGLOGGINGONDATAERRORLIMIT
AGENTTHREADS	DYNCALCCACHEMAXSIZE	NUMERICPRECISION
AGGRESSIVEBLKOPTIMIZATION	DYNCALCCACHEONLY	OUTLINECHANGELOG
AGTSVRCONNECTIONS	DYNCALCCACHEWAITFORBLK	OUTLINECHANGELOGFILESIZE
AUTHENTICATIONMODULE	EXCEPTIONLOGOVERWRITE	PARCALCMULTIPLEBITMAPMEMOPT
CALCCACHE	EXCLUSIVECALC	PIPEBUFFERSIZE
CALCCACHEHIGH	EXPORTTHREADS	PORTINC
CALCCACHEDEFAULT	FORCEALLDENSECALCON2PASSACCOUNTS	PORTUSAGELOGINTERVAL
CALCCACHELOW	GRIDEXPANSION	PRELOADALIASNAMESPACE
CALCLIMITFORMULARECURSION	GRIDEXPANSIONMESSAGES	PRELOADMEMBERNAMESPACE
CALCLOCKBLOCK	HAENABLE	QRYGOVEXECBLK
CALCMODE	HAMAXNUMCONNECTION	QRYGOVEXECTIME
CALCNOTICE	HAMAXNUMSQLQUERY	REFERENCECUBESIZELIMIT
CALCOPTFRMLBOTTOMUP	HAMAXQUERYROWS	SECURITYFILECOMPACTIONPERCENT
CALCREUSEDYNCALCBLOCKS	HAMAXQUERYTIME	SERVERPORTBEGIN
CALCPARALLEL	HAMEMORYCACHESIZE	SERVERPORTEND
CALCTASKDIMS	HARAGGEDHIERARCHY	SERVERTHREADS
CCTRACK	HARETRIEVENUMROW	SET COPYMISSINGBLOCK
CLEARLOGFILE	HASOURCEDSNOS390	SHAREDSERVICESLOCATION
CRASHDUMP	ISHFIXTHRESHOLD	SHAREDSERVICESREFRESHINTERVAL
CSSREFRESHLEVEL	IDMIGRATION	SILENTOTLQUERY
CSSSYNCLEVEL	IMPLIEDSHAREONMINUS	SQLFETCHERRORPOPUP
DATACACHESIZE	INCRESTRUC	SSAUDIT
DATAERRORLIMIT	INDEXCACHESIZE	SSAUDITR
DATAFILECACHESIZE	JVMMODULELOCATION	SSINVALIDTEXTDETECTION
DELAYEDRECOVERY	LOCKTIMEOUT	SSLOGUNKNOWN
DELIMITEDMSG	LOGINFAILUREMESSAGEDETAILED	SSPROCROWLIMIT
DELIMITER	LOGMESSAGELEVEL	SUPNA
DEXPSQLROWSIZE	LROONSHAREDMBR	TARGETASOOPT
DIRECTIO	MAXFORMULACACHESIZE	TARGETTIMESERIESOPT
DISABLEREPLMISSINGDATA	MAXLOGINS	TIMINGMESSAGES
DISKVOLUMES	MEMSCALINGFACTOR	TRIGMAXMEMSIZE
DISPLAYMESSAGELEVEL	MULTIPLEBITMAPMEMCHECK	UNICODEAGENTLOG
DLSINGLETHREADPERSTAGE	NETBINDRETRYDELAY	UPDATECALC
		VLBREPORT

That is quite an impressive list of configuration settings. You may even recognize some of them based upon our earlier discussions. Keep in mind that the essbase.cfg file can contains settings that have no real effect on system performance management, but they do set configurations for other aspects of system control. The proper syntax and use of each statement can be found in the **Essbase Technical Reference**, but we will show you a few of the more important ones.

Following we have an example of an actual `essbase.cfg` file. As you can see, you can place comments anywhere in the file by beginning the line with a semi-colon. Multiple comment lines require each line to begin with a semi-colon. Statement lines are simply the statement itself, followed by a space, then the parameter. The statement line itself does not need to be terminated by a period or semi-colon as other scripts in Essbase need to.

Although it does not say this is mandatory anywhere in the Essbase documentation, we have always kept the statement entries in the `essbase.cfg` file all uppercase so there is no confusion as to what character is what.

```
; ++++++++++++++++++++++++++++++++++++++++++++++++
; Begin Essbase configuration file for the ESSCAR server
;
; Dynamic calc support for the ESSCAR application
; due to large numbers of members being dynamically calculated
DYNCALCCACHEONLY ESSCAR FALSE
DYNCALCCACHEWAITFORBLK ESSCAR FALSE
;
; Sets the max number of error rows to be written from
; any single data load or process
DATAERRORLIMIT 5000
;
; Allows the use of DIRECT I/O when possible
DIRECTIO TRUE
;
; Sets the number of blocks locked by a database calculation
; and corresponds to the setting in the calc script itself
CALCLOCKBLOCKHIGH 50000
CALCLOCKBLOCKDEFAULT 30000
CALCLOCKBLOCKLOW 10000
;
; Sets the delay time and number of retries allowed for a connection
; to the analytic server
NETDELAY 2000
NETRETRYCOUNT 4000
;
; Allows the use of a database calculator cache
CALCCACHE TRUE
;
; Sets the size of the calculator cache for high, default and low
; cache sizes. Use of cache size determined in calc script
CALCCACHEHIGH 200000000
CALCCACHEDEFAULT 100000000
```

```
CALCCACHELOW 50000000
:
; Sets up the analytic server to use multiple threading during
; data loads
DLSINGLETHREADPERSTAGE FALSE
DLTHREADSPREPARE 2
DLTHREADSWRITE 2
;
; +++++++++++++++++++++++++++++++++++++++++++++++++++
```

Configuration categories

As you can see, making entries into the essbase.cfg file is a relatively easy task. However, making good entries is where your Essbase knowledge and experience pays off.

The following is a listing of the configuration categories and their general usefulness:

- **Ports and connections**: Most of these settings are obviously to help your Analytic Server manage itself on the network and with other components.

- **Logging and error handling**: These settings help Essbase determine things like the level of detail in an output log or the maximum number of lines written during a process.

- **Calculation**: The calculation settings category has many settings that help with system performance, mainly during calculation execution.

- **Hybrid analysis**: These settings do more for the configuration of Essbase's interaction between itself and a backend relational database. This type of data querying is known as hybrid analysis.

- **Query management**: These settings help with the special needs of installations that make use of partitioned databases and heavy hybrid analysis methods. There is not a lot here for overall system performance.

- **Memory management**: Now, here is a good category! We like this one so much that we have given it its own separate section in this chapter. A definite positive impact on system performance can be gleaned from these settings.

- **Data import/export**: Like the category name indicates, you can help improve the overall performance of your data loading and data exporting processes.

- **Miscellaneous**: While some of these settings will end up being necessary for your own installation, there really isn't any performance enhancing settings in the miscellaneous category.

Configuration settings to consider

Here are a few essbase.cfg file settings you should consider using when first having concerns about system performance.

> Always remember, you can add a new statement to the essbase.cfg file at any time by simply opening it in any text editor. After you have added or removed the necessary statement, you save and close the file.
>
> The new settings will take effect the next time the Essbase service is started or restarted on the server.

Ports and connections

In this section, we will talk about the server agent threads, net delays, and agent delays. These settings, added to the Essbase server configuration file, can help improve the performance of your system as well as to help improve the network connectivity:

- AGENTTHREADS: Specifies how many threads the server may spawn for connections. If you have a low number of paid licenses, you would set this setting a little higher than average. The default is five for maximum performance.

- AGENTDELAY: The higher you set this setting the longer the Essbase service will wait to process requests from connections. Obviously, the higher the AGENTTHREADS setting, the higher you should set this setting.

- AGTSVRCONNECTIONS: Specifies the maximum number of concurrent connections to the analytic server. A lower number usually means faster system response time.

- NETDELAY: Specifies the delay in milliseconds, of how long the analytic server will wait between retries on failed network requests.

- NETRETRYCOUNT: Specifies the number of times the analytic server will retry a failed network request.

Logging and error handling

In this section, we will talk about how you can set the limits for data load errors as well as the level of detail captured in the output error messages.

- DATAERRORLIMIT: Specifies the maximum number of rows written to the log for individual processes. The default is 1,000 and the maximum is 65,000. Your experience will help you decide how much information you need in the log.

- AGENTLOGMESSAGELEVEL: Specifies to Essbase what level of detail is to be written to system logs. The more knowledgeable you become, the less information you will require to monitor your system, thereby keeping the logs smaller and improving system performance.

Calculation

Here we will talk about the settings that will best help improve the run-time and overall performance of your Essbase calculation scripts.

- CALCCACHE: Tells the analytic server whether to use a calculator cache. When set to true, you can also set the CALCCACHELOW, CALCCACHEDEFAULT, and CALCCACHEHIGH settings that can be used in any database calculation scripts.

- CALCLOCKBLOCK: Specifies how many data blocks Essbase will lock at one time during a calculation. There are mixed feelings on the setting because a higher number of locked blocks seems like it would finish faster, but does more and smaller chunks actually finish quicker? This is where testing and experience come into play.

- DYNCALCCACHEONLY: Specifies to the analytic server if Essbase can use memory outside of the dynamic calc memory to complete its tasks. This may not be a good idea because Essbase may tend to wait if allowed for more memory causing the process to actually slow down.

- CALCPARALLEL: This specifies how many parallel threads are allowed at one time while calculating the data. Essbase recommends that the maximum number of parallel threads be one less than the total number of processors on your server. For example, if your server has 8 processors you would code 7 as your maximum number of threads to use.

    ° For 32 bit: Block storage option, you can select between 1 to 4

    ° For 64 bit: Block storage option, you can select between 1 to 8

    ° For Aggregate Storage option, you can select in between 1 to 8 with 2 being the default.

    Syntax:

    CALCPARALLEL [APPNAME] [DBNAME] N

- EXCLUSIVECALC: This specifies if concurrent calculations are allowed on the same database.

    Syntax:

    EXCLUSIVECALC TRUE | FALSE

- **UPDATECALC**: This specifies if intelligent calc is turned on or off by default.

  Syntax:

  ```
  UPDATECALC TRUE | FALSE
  ```

Data import/export

In this section we will walk through the settings you can use to improve the system's performance while loading data into your cube or while extracting data from your cube.

- **DLSINGLETHREADPERSTAGE**: This setting tells Essbase to use Single Thread or use the number of threads specified in the DLTHREADSPREPARE and DLTHREADSWRITE. This can be set for an individual application or for the entire analytic server.

  Syntax:

  ```
  DLSINGLETHREADPERSTAGE [APPNAME] [DBNAME] TRUE | FALSE
  ```

- **DLTHREADSPREPARE**: This setting tells Essbase how many threads to prepare to use for a data load. This is a definite performance enhancer and it is recommended you specify a number that is one less than the total number of processors on your server.

  Syntax:

  ```
  DLTHREADSPREPARE n
  ```

- **DLTHREADSWRITE**: This setting is used with the DLTHREADSPREPARE setting and specifies the number of threads to actually use during a data load. Again, the number should be one less than the number of processors on your server.

  Syntax:

  ```
  DLTHREADSWRITE n
  ```

  Code Sample:

  ```
  DLSINGLETHREADPERSTAGE ESSCAR ESSCAR TRUE
  DLTHREADSPREPARE 2
  DLTHREADSWRITE 3
  ```

  In the above example, DLSINGLETHREADPERSTAGE is set to TRUE, so this tells the Essbase server to use a single thread for the Esscar application for data loading and the DLTHREADPREPARE and DLTHREADSWRITE will not used.

  ```
  DLSINGLETHREADPERSTAGE ESSCAR ESSCAR FALSE
  DLTHREADSPREPARE 2
  DLTHREADSWRITE 3
  ```

In the above example, DLSINGLETHREADPERSTAGE is set to FALSE, so this tells the Essbase server not to use single threaded data loading on the Esscar application and the DLTHREADPREPARE and DLTHREADSWRITE settings are used.

These settings will improve the performance of the Essbase data loads.

Well, there you have it. What was going to be a little bit about the essbase.cfg file has turned into quite a long-winded affair. That's okay, because there is a lot to know, and a lot that can have a positive effect on your operations.

Memory management

Oh look, here is more information that could be in the essbase.cfg section. Yes, that is true, but memory management is probably the most important task you can perform to keep your Essbase system running smoothly and efficiently.

It's no secret that everything in life is a give and take. With Essbase, it gives you unparalleled capacity for slicing and dicing large amounts of data, all the while performing real time calculations on the fly. What Essbase takes for this is unbelievably large amounts of memory to deliver this functionality with anywhere near acceptable response times.

Before we talk about some of the essbase.cfg settings you can use to help control your system's memory usage we want to discuss a few other things you can do:

1. Make sure all of your applications and databases are set to only start when there is a request for data and not when the analytic service starts. For every started database, Essbase will reserve the memory necessary for that database and there will be that much less memory available for the rest of the system.

2. Create a small job that will run periodically and stop applications and databases that are not actively in use, because in Essbase, once the application or database is started, the only thing that stops it is a server shutdown, the administrator, or by a command from a script or job.

3. Monitor and adjust all caches and buffer settings, since they all use memory.

4. Make judicious use of the config.mem file located in the ArborPath\Bin folder. This file allows you to set a maximum amount of memory to be used by either specific applications or by all applications on the server. If an application uses its maximum allotment of memory, it will either shutdown or slow way down and attempt to process with what it has. This is a very important setting because you do not want one application sucking all of the memory out of the system and halting the other databases and their processes.

One of the single largest users of system memory is the database outline itself. By its very nature, the larger the outline, the more server memory is consumed just to load the database into memory.

We highly advise using extreme care in determining the data elements and data categories you will use for your database outline.

Fewer dimensions are always preferable to more dimensions. For every new dimension in the outline the potential size of the data and the actual size of the outline grow exponentially. It is always better to have fewer dimensions with lots of members, than it is to have more dimensions with less members. Think about it!

essbase.cfg memory settings

Let's now take a look at those `essbase.cfg` memory specific settings that will directly affect the performance of your Essbase system:

- `MULTIPLEBITMAPMEMCHECK`: Tells analytic services to enforce the size limit for the amount of memory that is used for the calculator cache when analytic services selects the multiple bitmap cache option.

- `VLBREPORT`: Tells Essbase to dynamically determine the retrieval buffer size, between 100KB and 10MB, for retrievals from databases without Dynamic Calc, Attribute, or Dynamic Time Series members. This memory is only used when needed, so it does not take away from continuous system resource availability.

- `TRIGMAXMEMSIZE`: This setting tells Essbase how much memory it can use to perform the trigger function. While the triggering function is a great feature, it can be very memory intensive at the expense of other system operations. This memory is reserved by the application that has the trigger set up and is no longer available to the rest of the server.

- `SSPROCROWLIMIT`: Controls the maximum number of spreadsheet rows analytic services processes on an individual user spreadsheet request from Microsoft Excel. The default is 250,000, which is extraordinarily high for a spreadsheet request. You do not want a spreadsheet retrieval slowing down your entire server, so we recommend starting with 5,000 rows, and increasing as needed from there.

- CALCLIMITFORMULARECURSION: Now here is a little known setting. What it does is prevent the server from executing calculation scripts that perform recursive operations deeper than the system specified number of 31 levels. If you add this setting to the `essbase.cfg` file with a `TRUE` parameter, the system will enforce the 31 level rules. If you add this setting with a `FALSE` parameter, there will be no limit, and a lowly database calculation script could actually be responsible for bringing down your analytic server. Try explaining that to your boss! Besides, rarely do you code a calculation script that even uses half that many levels.

- DATACACHESIZE: This sets the data cache size for all of the new databases that are created on the server. This cache holds the data blocks in memory. This cache setting is not applied to all of the existing databases that are already created on the server. The data cache size can be specified in Bytes (B), Kilobytes (K), Megabytes (M), or Gigabytes (G). This will take place after the analytical service is restarted or after the server reboot.

  Syntax:

  `DATACACHESIZE n`

  n is an integer value in B, K, M, or G

  Code Sample:

  `DATACACHESIZE 4M`

  This sets the data cache size to 4 Megabytes for all new databases that are created after the service is restarted with this setting.

- DATAFILECACHESIZE: This sets the data file cache size for all of the new databases that are created on the server. This cache holds the data files in the memory. The data file cache size can be specified in Bytes (B), Kilobytes (K), Megabytes (M), or Gigabytes (G). This will take place after the analytic service is restarted or after a server reboot.

  Syntax:

  `DATAFILECACHESIZE n`

  n is an integer value in B, K, M, or G

  Code Sample:

  `DATAFILECACHESIZE 400M`

  This sets the data file cache size to 400 Megabytes for all of the new databases that are created after the service is restarted to have a data file cache size of 400 MB.

- `INDEXCACHESIZE`: This sets the index cache size for all of the new databases that are created on the server. This cache holds the index pages in the memory. The index cache size can also be specified in Bytes (B), Kilobytes (K), Megabytes (M), or Gigabytes (G). Again, this setting will take effect after the analytic service is restarted or after a server reboot.

  Syntax:

  `INDEXCACHESIZE n`

  n is an integer value in B, K, M, or G

  Code Sample:

  `INDEXCACHESIZE 400M`

  This sets the index cache size to 400 Megabytes for all new databases that are created after the service is restarted.

Well, that wraps it up for the system memory and its management. We know you've heard this before, but here it goes. Always buy the most memory you can afford at the time you are purchasing it. If you believe you will do fine with 32 GB, then buy 64GB.

Summary

Goodness, you must be an Essbase expert by now! No, there is no such thing as an Essbase expert. In real life, maybe an Essbase Guru would most accurately describe someone who is more proficient with Essbase than others.

By now, we believe that you now realize that Essbase is not all about reading and memorizing recommended settings and sizes, but instead Essbase is more about using what resources you have available to you to get the job done. A Guru is someone who possesses far more than just the so-called technical knowledge. A Guru is also someone who possesses intelligence and wisdom.

Yes, someone could create a test for Essbase to gauge your overall technical knowledge, but what really counts is your good judgment based on your experience. Figuring out how to accomplish the same task several different ways based on the situation is how you advertise your Essbase Guru-ability (is that even a word).

Here is an example of Essbase Guru-ability. Consider that you are a reasonably capable technical person who now has Essbase knowledge added to his repertoire of skills. You are performing a large data load from a relational database (we're talking Gigabytes). It seems like the load is taking much too long to complete. What do you do?

Well, you know that a multi-threaded process will execute faster than a single-threaded process. You also know that there are specific data load settings that you can use in the essbase.cfg file that may help alleviate this performance issue. Then, you remember that you read about the DLSINGLETHREADSPERSTAGE, DLTHREADSPREPARE, and DLTHREADSWRITE settings that can be coded in the essbase.cfg file. These settings allow you to set up your data loads to use multiple-threading while processing. You quickly make the appropriate entries in the essbase.cfg file, restart your server, and start your data load process again. You are now amazed and happy that the data load processes to completion significantly faster.

Just remember these now familiar words on your long and exciting Essbase journey, "Essbase is an art, not a science."

Next up, we jump into a discussion on a relatively new database structure concept. First rolled out with Hyperion Essbase version 7.x, the Aggregate Storage Option (ASO) is an option that is gaining considerable ground as a means to provide your business customer with superior system performance, while still delivering the expected Essbase level of data quantity, quality, and integrity.

10
Essbase Analytics Option

Welcome to the exciting world of Essbase Analytics known as the Aggregate Storage Option (ASO).

In the first nine chapters of this book, we have taken you from being a competent IT professional that is an Essbase novice, to that same competent IT professional who is now a capable Essbase programmer/administrator as well. All along this journey, we've been using the Block Storage Option (BSO) database architecture.

We have presented all of the instructions, teachings, and examples based on the BSO, in Essbase. All of the efficient methods of processing, performance tuning, and database design have been geared towards using the BSO. In fact, prior to Essbase version 7.x, your only option was the use of the BSO architecture for building Essbase applications.

Well, now you're ready to take everything one step further. You see, the BSO architecture used by Essbase is the original database architecture as the behind the scenes method of data storage in an Essbase database. Remember, we have already discussed that the block construction can be conceptually compared to a Rubik's Cube for how the data is stored in the cells of a data block, like the cells of color on a Rubik's Cube. The ASO method is entirely different.

Let's learn all about the ASO which is now also used to store data in an Essbase database. We will learn exactly what ASO is, how it works, and when to use ASO instead of BSO. We will explain the use of the special industry standard multidimensional data query language known as MDX that is employed by Essbase, and is particularly effective with ASO. Finally, we'll go over the pros and cons of ASO and BSO.

What is ASO

ASO is Essbase's alternative to the sometimes cumbersome BSO method of storing data in an Essbase database. In fact, it is BSO that is exactly what makes Essbase a superior OLAP analytical tool but it is also the BSO that can occasionally be a detriment to the level of system performance demanded in today's business world.

In a BSO database, all data is stored, except for dynamically calculated members. All data consolidations and parent-child relationships in the database outline are stored as well. While the block storage method is quite efficient from a data to size ratio perspective, a BSO database can require large amounts of overhead to deliver the retrieval performance demanded by the business customer.

The ASO database efficiently stores not only zero level data, but can also store aggregated hierarchical data with the understandings that stored hierarchies can only have the no-consolidation (~) or the addition (+) operator assigned to them and the no-consolidation (~) operator can only be used underneath **Label Only** members. Outline member consolidations are performed on the fly using dynamic calculations and only at the time of the request for data. This is the main reason why ASO is a valuable option worth consideration when building an Essbase system for your customer.

Because of the simplified levels of data stored in the ASO database, a more simplified method of storing the physical data on the disk can also be used. It is this simplified storage method which can help result in higher performance for the customer.

Your choice of one database type over the other will always depend on balancing the customer's needs with the server's physical capabilities, along with the volume of data. These factors must be given equal consideration

Creating an aggregate storage Application|Database

Believe it or not, creating an ASO Essbase application and database is as easy as creating a BSO application and database. In case you have forgotten how to do it from the information we've given you in earlier chapters, all you need to do is follow these simple steps:

1. Right-click on the server name in your EAS console for the server on which you want to create your ASO application.

2. Select **Create application | Using aggregate storage** as shown in the following screenshot:

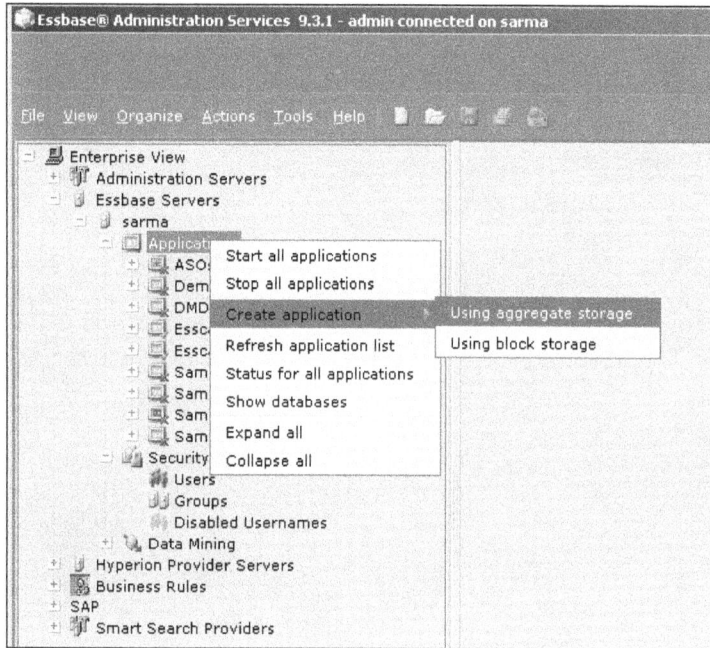

3. Click on **Using aggregate storage** and that's it. The rest of the steps are easy to follow and basically the same as for a BSO application.

To create an ASO application and database, you follow virtually the same steps as you do to create a BSO application and database. However, there are some important differences, and here we list a few:

- A BSO database outline can be converted into an Aggregate Storage database outline, but an Aggregate Storage database outline cannot be converted into a Block Storage database outline.

Steps to convert a BSO application into an ASO application:

° Open the BSO outline that you wish to convert, select the Essbase database and click on the **File | Wizards | Aggregate Storage Outline Conversion** option. You will see the first screen **Select Source Outline**. The source of the outline can be in a **file system** or on the **Essbase Server**. In this case, we have selected the OTL from the **Essbase Server** and then click **Next** as shown in the following screenshot:

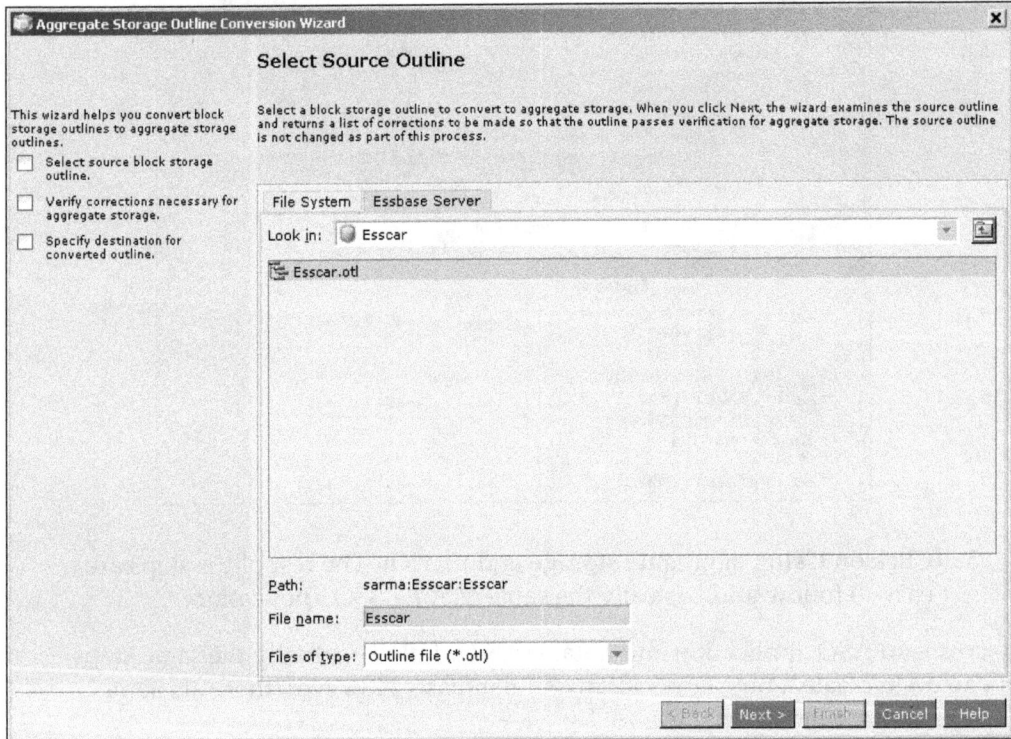

° In the **Next** screen, the conversion wizard will verify the conversion and display a message that the conversion has completed successfully. Click **Next**.

° Here, Essbase prompts you to select the destination of the ASO outline. If you have not yet created an ASO application, you can click on the **Create Aggregate Storage Application** on the bottom-right corner of the screen as shown in the next screenshot:

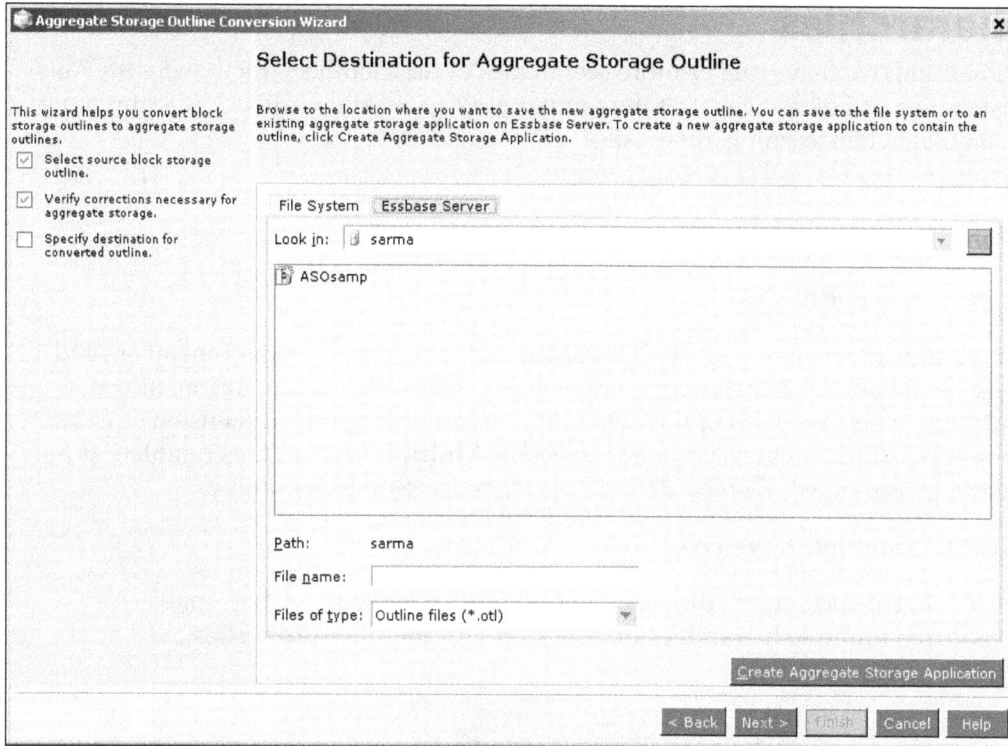

Enter the **Application** and the **Database** name and click on **OK.** Your new ASO application is created, now click on **Finish**. Your BSO application is now converted into an ASO application. You may still need to tweak the ASO application settings and outline members to be the best fit for your needs.

- In an ASO database, all dimensions are **Sparse** so there is no need to try to determine the best **Dense/Sparse** settings as you would do with a BSO database.

- Although Essbase recommends that you only have one Essbase database in an Essbase application, you can create more than one database per application when you are using the BSO. When you create an ASO application, Essbase will only allow one database per application.

There is quite a bit to know about ASO but have no fear, with all that you know about Essbase and how to design and build an Essbase system, it will seem easy for you.

Keep reading for more valuable information on the ASO for things like, when it is a good time to use ASO, or how do you query ASO databases effectively, or even what are the differences between ASO and BSO. If you understand the differences, you can then understand the benefits.

Hierarchies

Dimensions can have one or more hierarchies of the members. Included with your installation of Essbase, you get the sample ASO application called ASOsamp to use as a guide when learning about ASO.

In ASO, there are two types of hierarchies:

- Stored hierarchies
- Dynamic hierarchies

An outline dimension in an ASO database can have any number of members and these members can only be set as either stored members or dynamic members. They can even have both of the hierarchies. In order to set the dimension to have both types of hierarchies, you need to enable **Multiple Hierarchies Enabled**. If no hierarchy is defined, then by default it is tagged as **Stored** hierarchy.

To enable multiple hierarchies, follow these steps:

1. Right-click on the dimension or member name you wish to enable the multiple hierarchies on. Click on **Edit member properties…**.

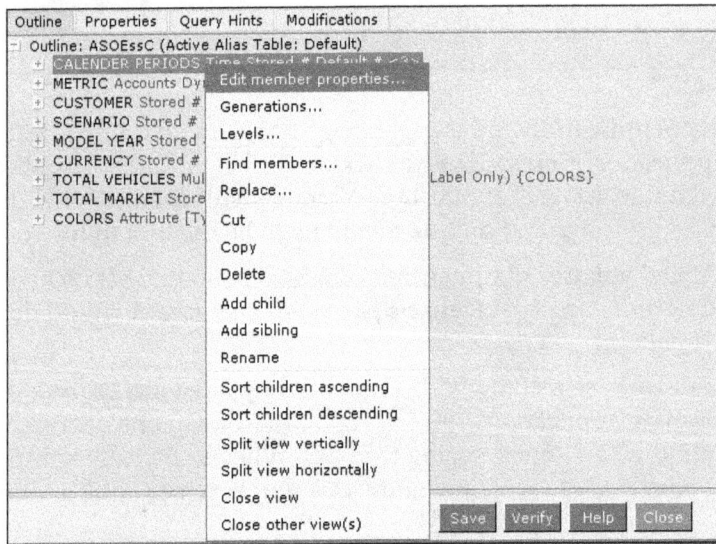

2. On the **Member Properties** screen, under the **Hierarchy** section, select **Hierarchies Enabled** from the **Hierarchy** list box:

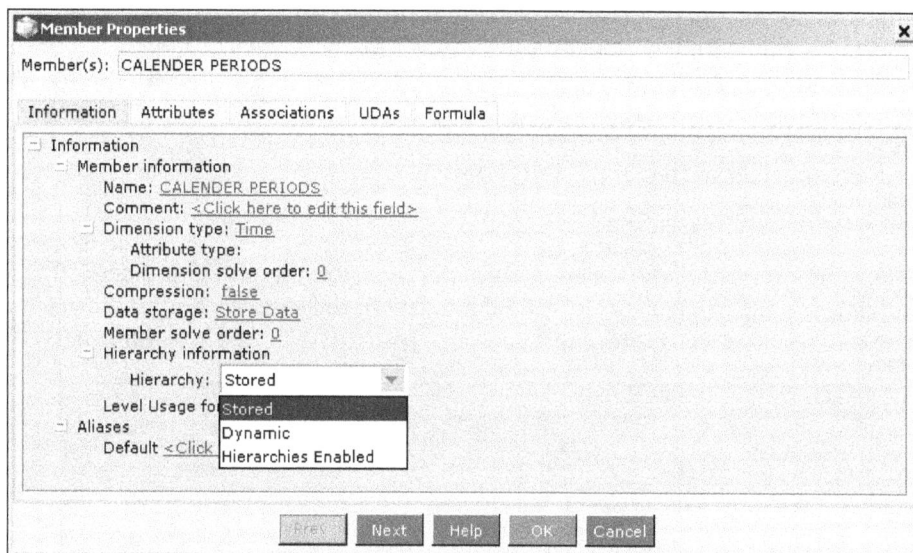

Stored hierarchies

Using **Stored** hierarchies, the data is aggregated based on the outline structure. The data aggregation and data retrieval is faster. There are a few restrictions when using **Stored** hierarchies:

- Stored hierarchies cannot have member formulas.

- Stored hierarchies can have the **no-consolidation (~)** operator for **Label-only** members. A member that is label only is merely in the outline as a place holder or to be informational and does not store data. A good example of this is our **Calendar Periods** dimension. While the root member **Calendar Periods** is useful to have for information, the data would make no sense rolled upto this level.

Dynamic hierarchies

Using **Dynamic** hierarchies, the data is not aggregated but is calculated at the time of the data retrieval. Since the data is calculated at the time of retrieve, the response time for the output is longer. The account dimension is always tagged as **Dynamic** hierarchies and you cannot change the account dimension to stored hierarchy. The advantages of the **Dynamic** hierarchies are:

- Dynamic hierarchies can have formulas.
- Dynamic hierarchies can have any consolidation operator.

The following screenshot shows an example of how the **Dynamic** and **Stored** hierarchies are used in the sample ASO database. In the sample ASO database's case, you can see that the **Time** dimension has **MultipleHierarchies Enabled**:

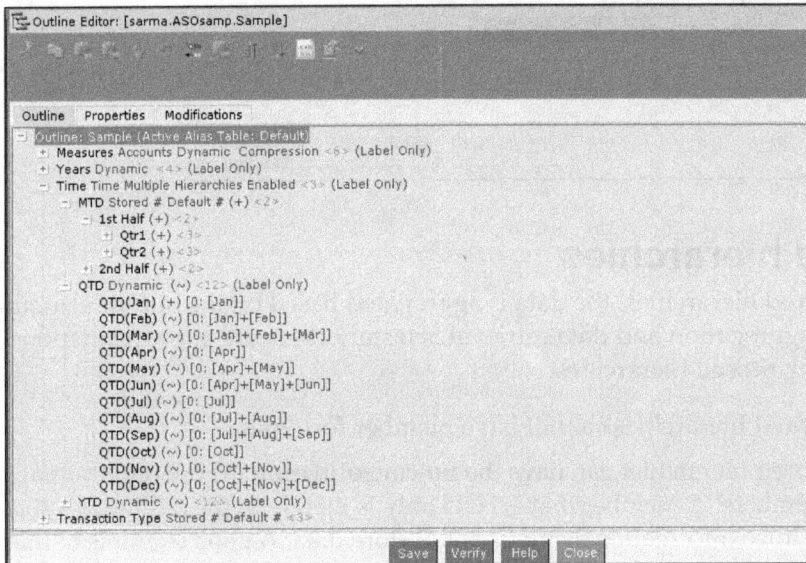

Outline paging

This is one major difference between a Block Storage application and an Aggregate Storage application that provides a noticeable boost in performance. Unlike a BSO application, where the database outline must be loaded into memory as a single element, the database outlines in ASO databases are created and stored in what can be considered a page-able format. This means that instead of Essbase loading the entire database outline into memory, the page-able outline can be loaded into memory either one page or section at a time. This can free up resources and can help make data retrieval and data aggregations faster by reducing the amount of memory consumed by large database outlines.

Aggregation

There is no need for complex calculation scripts in an ASO database. Now, you may be wondering how the data gets aggregated without performing any calculated aggregation? How fast will my data get retrieved? In an ASO database, the data gets loaded only into the *level 0* (leaf node) cells. When the user attempts to retrieve data at a level higher than the zero level, the data is dynamically aggregated. Also, remember a good portion of this aggregated data is not physically stored in the database. As the database size increases, the dynamic aggregation consumes more time. In order to improve the database performance, you may need to pre-aggregate the data.

MDX query language

So is now a good time to spring a new scripting language on you? Of course it is!

Okay, so it's not really a whole new language, it's just a piece of the MaxL scripting language we haven't gone over with you yet.

You may recall how we've gone over the MaxL scripting language previously. Well, the MaxL scripting language actually has two pieces. These MaxL pieces are known as MaxL DDL for Data Definition Language, which is the piece you are already familiar with and MaxL MDX for Multidimensional Expressions.

Why have we not explained something like MDX in-depth already? The reason is that while the DDL piece of MaxL contains many powerful functions that are written in relatively easy to understand syntax and it can easily replace the Essbase Command scripting language (EssCmd) as your primary tool for automating database maintenance and support processes, the MDX piece of MaxL is more of a data querying language. Yes, MDX is very powerful as is DDL, but its usefulness can be debated since there are several other methods of querying data in Essbase that are just as effective and easier or more convenient to use. The Essbase Reports scripting language with the aid of the Essbase Query Designer, is one example that comes to mind as an effective data querying tool. MDX also supports the XML for Analysis (XMLA) API.

MDX however, has its place and its place is where it is best suited. The place for MDX is querying ASO Essbase databases.

MDX functions for ASO

As we said earlier, the MDX data query language is a useful tool in its own right. In most cases, the MDX language has equivalent functions for each member set function found in the Essbase Calculation Script language or the Essbase report script language. The following screenshot shows the complete list of MDX data query functions available:

Abs	Except	LastChild	PrevMember
Aggregate	Exp	LastPeriods	Rank
Ancestor	Extract	LastSibling	RelMemberRange
Ancestors	Factorial	Lead	Remainder
Attribute	Filter	Leaves	Right
Avg	FirstChild	Left	Round
BottomCount	FirstSibling	Len	RTrim
BottomPercent	FormatDate	Level	Siblings
BottomSum	Generate	Levels	Stddev
Case	Generation	Ln	StddevP
Children	Generations	Log	StrToMbr
ClosingPeriod	GetFirstDate	Log10	StrToNum
CoalesceEmpty	GetLastDate	Lower	Subset
Concat	Head	LTrim	SubString
Contains	Hierarchize	Max	Sum
Count	IIF	Median	Tail
Cousin	InStr	MemberRange	ToDate
CrossJoin	Int	Members	ToDateEx
CurrentMember	Intersect	Min	Today
CurrentTuple	Is	Mod	TopCount
DateDiff	IsAccType	NextMember	TopPercent
DatePart	IsAncestor	NonEmptyCount	TopSum
DateRoll	IsChild	NonEmptySubset	Truncate
DateToMember	IsEmpty	NTile	TupleRange
DefaultMember	IsGeneration	OpeningPeriod	Uda
Descendants	IsLeaf	Order	Union
Distinct	IsLevel	Ordinal	Upper
Dimension	IsSibling	ParallelPeriod	Value
DrilldownByLayer	IsUda	Parent	WithAttr
DrilldownMember	IsValid	Percentile	xTD
DrillupByLayer	Item	PeriodsToDate	
DrillupMember	Lag	Power	

Now, look at the functions listed here. They look like a hybrid between Essbase member selection functions and typical SQL functions found in any relational database.

Unfortunately, after all of the hard work we've been through getting you to think and act like an Essbase programmer/administrator, we don't want you to slip back into the relational way of thinking. This is only acceptable when querying an ASO database, because it is indeed set up somewhat similar to a relational database in terms of data structure.

Take a close look at the functions, most of them are intuitive as to their function and you will also notice a complete array of functions that are suspiciously similar to the column functions in relational SQL. Again, this is because an ASO database does not store the complete set of data like a BSO database does. ASO only physically stores the data at the lowest levels and is a lot like a relational database where you depend heavily on functions such as SUM, MAX, and ABS to massage the data as it is delivered to you.

MDX function examples

Here, we will show you the same data query function twice. One will be in the format used by the Essbase Calculation Script language and the other example will be in the MDX data query language. The reason for this is to illustrate how vastly different each language is.

The @ANCEST function is a very commonly used function. In an Essbase database, where the data is stored at all levels, you can easily ask for the ancestor member. In an ASO database however, the data in most cases is dynamically calculated, so you have to ask for it in a different way so Essbase can interpret your request properly.

- **Essbase Calculation Script**

  Syntax:

  ```
  @ANCEST (dimName, genLevNum, [ mbrName])
  ```

  Example:

  ```
  @ANCEST(Product,2,Sales)
  ```

- **MDX Query Language**

  Ancestor

  Example:

  ```
  (
    Sales,
    Ancestor(
      Product.CurrentMember,
      Product.Generations(2)
    )
  )
  ```

The command above assumes you are keying off of the member currently selected. What will be returned is the value of Sales from the ancestor of the member in the product dimension and the Generation level 2.

MDX query syntax

To make querying an ASO database more relational and SQL like, you can actually write your queries like you would in a relational database using SQL.

Looking at the following examples, you can see that the SELECT statement is almost identical to that of a query written in SQL. Because the data is stored similarly, the query language is similar. That way, you won't forget when you're querying an Essbase BSO database or an Essbase ASO database.

Typical MDX query structure:

```
SELECT [<member_name>,[ <member_name>]]
  FROM [<Essbase_database_name>]]
 WHERE [<dimension_name.member_name>
       [, <dimension_name.member_name>]]
```

Syntax:

```
SELECT  Sales,Stocks
FROM    EssCar
WHERE   Calendar Periods.June, Model Year.2010
```

Typical SQL Query Structure

```
SELECT  column_name>[, <column_name>...]
FROM    table_name
WHERE   value = value [and value = value]
```

Syntax:

```
SELECT  Sales, Stocks
FROM    MARKET_INFO_TBL
WHERE   Month = June and ModelYear = 2010
```

Well, this should put you in a good place for querying an ASO database. The Essbase Technical Reference included and installed with the EAS on your client PC contains all of the information you need on the actual query functions and member set functions.

As with everything else in this book, the only way you will get proficient is to play around in the database.

Executing an MDX query

Now, here is a question that is begging to be asked. How do we execute an MDX query?

The answer is easy enough. You execute an MDX query in exactly the same fashion as you execute any MaxL statement. Remember, both DDL and MDX are really MaxL scripts. The only difference between MaxL DDL and MaxL MDX is the editor used through the EAS tool.

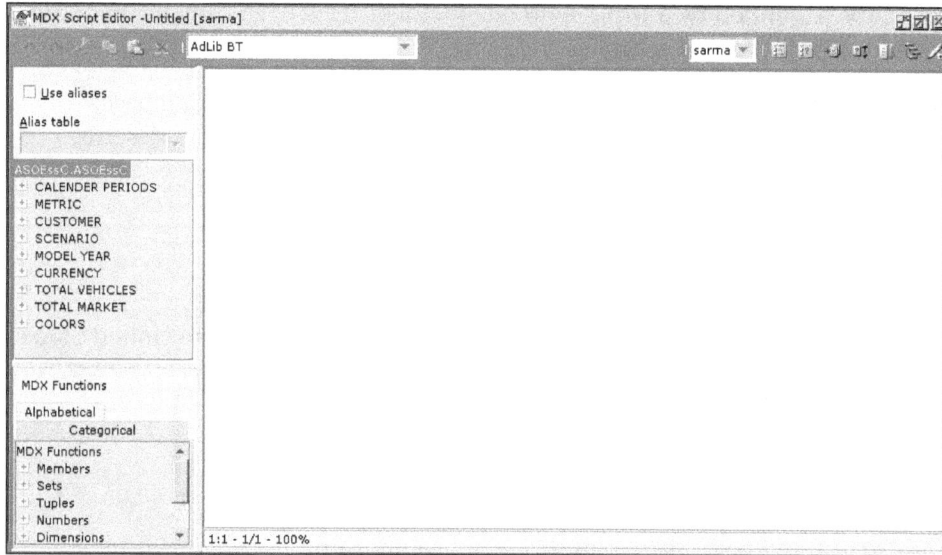

In the previous screenshot, we showed you the MDX editor that you can access from the EAS tool by clicking on the **Editors** menu selection and then selecting MDX.

When you are using the MDX editor, you have the same nice features as the other editors that are included in the EAS tool. It is through the editor that you can also execute your MDX statements.

The other way to execute your MDX statements is through the command line prompt. This is exactly like you were shown earlier in this book for the MaxL DDL statements.

Honestly, if it wasn't for the major outline differences between an ASO database and a BSO database, you could travel through your entire Essbase career and not really need the MDX piece of MaxL. Because the ASO database structure can actually be at least conceptually compared with a relational database more than a multidimensional database, it's a good idea to get friendly with MDX.

Tuples and Sets

A **Tuple** is a collection of members from different dimensions that represent a slice of data from the database. A tuple can contain one member from each dimension. A tuple should be wrapped in parentheses when written. In theory, each cell in the Essbase cube is defined by a tuple with one member from each dimension. A single member is also considered a tuple.

A tuple is an easy way to describe a slice of data from an Essbase database. A correctly written tuple can contain very few actual words, but can describe a large amount of data.

Here is an example of a tuple:

```
(Total Market. United States)
```

The tuple above will return all data at the Total Market level for the United States.

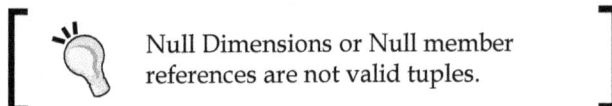

> Null Dimensions or Null member references are not valid tuples.

Sets are an ordered collection of tuples. A set can be empty, have one tuple, or it can have more than one tuple. Duplicates of tuples are allowed. Sets are enclosed in curly brackets.

Here is an example of a set:

{CALENDER PERIOD.2008}—defines one Tuple

{CALENDER PERIOD.2008, CALENDER PERIOD.2007}—defines sets of two Tuples

Pros and cons of ASO and BSO

As you have seen earlier in the chapter, there are some differences between the ASO and the BSO. Even though there are differences, we would like the reporting output to be the same and the analyst who is running the report should not even know to which type of database he is connected. Let us take some time to look at a few of the pros and cons between these two types of databases.

Pros and cons of BSO

The Essbase BSO is the original format of the Essbase database technology. The BSO is also the mainstay for Essbase as it offers robust, full-featured functionality. Here we will describe what we feel are some of the positive features of the BSO as well as some of the not so positive features for you.

Pros

Listed below are just a few high-level features that we feel makes the Essbase BSO a good choice:

- Several databases stored in one application.
- No reserved names for application and database names.
- Account dimension supports all types of calculations and attribute members.
- Calculation scripts are supported.
- Uncomplicated write back ability.
- Formulas are allowed in all dimensions with no restrictions.
- Outline changes do not automatically clear data values, even if a data source is used to both modify members and load values. Therefore, incremental data loads are supported for all outlines.
- Currency conversion is supported.

Cons

Listed below are a few high-level features that we feel you may need to be wary of when using the Essbase BSO:

- For better performance, the outline dimensions must be defined as **Dense** or **Sparse**, based on data density, which can sometimes be difficult to get exactly right.
- Database calculation—calculation script or outline consolidation.
- Calculation order will need to be defined in the calc scripts and is predetermined in a default outline calculation.
- Unrestricted write back ability which can be dangerous if care is not exercised.
- No automatic update to values after data load. Necessary calculation scripts need to be specially executed, including any default calculations.
- Sometimes requires large amounts of resources.

Pros and cons of ASO

The ASO is fast becoming the standard for extra large Essbase databases. Where the need for high speed data retrieval for reporting and analysis can eclipse the need for full-featured functionality, ASO fills in nicely. Here we will describe what we feel are some of the positive features of the ASO as well as some of the not so positive features for you.

Pros

Listed below are just a few high-level features that we feel makes the Essbase ASO a good choice:

- Easy optimization, massive data scalability, reduced disk space, and upto 100 times faster.
- Database creation is accomplished by either migrating a BSO outline or defined as new after application creation.
- Outline dimensions will not need to be designated as dense or sparse.
- Outline is validated every time a database is started.
- Database calculation or aggregation of the database can be predefined by defining aggregate views.
- Calculation order is not relevant for database calculation, but is relevant for dynamic calculation formulas.
- Limited write back ability.
- At the end of a data load, if aggregation exists, the values in aggregation are recalculated and updated automatically.
- Aggregate storage database outlines are page-able. This feature significantly reduces memory usage for very large database outlines.

Cons

Listed below are a few high-level features that we feel you may need to be wary of when using the Essbase ASO:

- Aggregate storage applications have some limitations that do not apply to block storage applications with regard to consolidations, calculations, and overall robust functionality.
- Can store only one database per application.
- Names reserved for table spaces cannot be used as application or database names.

- Accounts dimension does not support time balance members and association of attribute dimensions.

- On non-account dimensions, there are restrictions on label only members and dynamic time series members. Members tagged as dynamic hierarchies have no restrictions on the consolidation settings. Stored hierarchy members can only be tagged as label only or (+) addition.

- Non-account dimensions support only consolidation operator (+) addition

- Calculation scripts are not supported.

- Formulas are allowed only on account dimension members and allowed with certain restrictions.

- Only *Level 0* cells whose values do not depend on formulas in the outline are loaded.

- Data values are cleared each time the outline is structurally changed. Therefore, incremental data loads are only supported for outlines that do not change.

- Currency conversion is not supported without the use of special MDX queries. This method can have a negative effect on performance.

As you can see, there are some substantial differences and some very good reasons to use one type of database over another. To give you our idea of the ideal application of ASO and BSO, read below:

- ASO Database: The ASO database is ideal for dynamically built Essbase cubes that are usually *Read Only* and used for reporting, presentation, and analysis. This type of database would also tend to have a rather large outline where at least one dimension has a significant amount of members. A parts dimension or product dimension comes to mind.

  Behind this ASO database would be a large BSO parent Essbase database, from which the dynamic ASO databases are built on the fly.

- BSO Database: The BSO database is ideal for virtually any size cube, but where performance is not necessarily the number one priority. Accuracy and completeness of data would be the main consideration.

  The BSO database is ideal as the large parent database where users from many different departments can trigger jobs which will dynamically build ASO reporting cubes on an as needed basis. The typical BSO database is ideally suited for financial analysis applications.

Of course, these are just one possibility or scenario. The beauty of Essbase is that you can do most anything with it. Heck, you could easily have a large Oracle relational database as the backend data source for your ASO cubes.

The possibilities are endless!

Summary

We hope you have found the information in this chapter as fun, exciting, and useful as we have. As we've said repeatedly throughout this book, it should be no wonder to you why Oracle Essbase is the number one data analytics tool in the world! It's almost as though Essbase is a product that is never finished, because just when you think it can't get any better, it gets even better!

You should now have a good understanding of the two very different but complimentary Essbase database architectures. The BSO is the old standby foundation in the world of Essbase, and the ASO is the streamlined speedster.

The differences in many cases between ASO and BSO are minor, but their affect can be dramatic. The BSO utilizes the standard data block method of storing data, while the ASO uses the aggregate method. The BSO is built for rugged and robust computing and analysis. The ASO is built for high speed, high volume data analysis and reporting.

We're sure you see by now that whether you use ASO, BSO, or both together, you can be confident you have made the right choice.

Yes, there are several imitators out there. There are some that are even pushing their product for free. We are confident you will agree with us that when all is said and done, Essbase is the clearly superior tool. Read on in fact, for an introduction to some of the new components available in what is now a suite of Essbase applications.

11
Essbase System 9 Components

Here we are at the last chapter of this outstanding book. It has taken ten, occasionally long, chapters to get you to a point where you are proficient and capable in the exciting world of Oracle Essbase.

A lot has changed with Essbase since the early days back in the 1990's. Essbase itself has grown and flourished into the world's leading OLAP analytic software and now includes all of the bells and whistles you'd expect and more.

The purpose of this chapter is to go over some exciting new additions to the Essbase family. No longer is it just Essbase, the multidimensional OLAP database. The future of Essbase, beginning with Essbase version 9.x, is now Essbase System 9.

Essbase System 9 is now a suite of analytical applications or components of which Essbase is the cornerstone. Some of the components enhance the overall abilities of the suite and some are targeted more to specific computing purposes.

Overview of System 9 components

When Oracle purchased Hyperion and several other companies, they set out to organize their product catalog and bring together a standardized naming convention as well as standardized software versioning. The Essbase suite of tools and applications is no exception as Essbase version 9.x has become Essbase System 9, and there never really was a commercially released Essbase version 8.x. Oracle now has plans to further integrate the Essbase suite of tools and components into their product catalog and we'll just need to wait and see how this plays out with version 11 and beyond.

What we are giving you in this chapter is a high level look at each new Essbase tool or component and also a slightly lower level look at the hot new additions to the Essbase family. Not to detract from any of the other Essbase family members, but the new Oracle Smart View, for one, is an awesome tool to have in your toolbox.

Essbase Analytic Services (Essbase agent)

The term Essbase analytic services, while commonly thought to refer to the Essbase suite of applications, actually refers to the common Essbase system structure that is built around the Essbase analytic database engine technology.

We know this sounds confusing, but here is how it works. In your Essbase toolbox, you can have many different tools. Some of them are optional and can be added at an additional expense and some of them must be included from the beginning for proper system installation. No matter what tools you want to add to your Essbase toolbox, the Essbase agent or Essbase analytic services must be included and it is the cornerstone of the Essbase suite of applications.

The Essbase agent is what you install on your server in order to make it an Essbase analytic server. The Essbase agent is what you use to build, deploy, and maintain your Essbase databases.

In a nutshell, Essbase analytic services is the heart and soul of your Essbase system.

Essbase Planning

Also known as Hyperion Planning or even Oracle Planning, Essbase Planning is a centralized Microsoft Excel and web-based planning and forecasting tool that combines data from various internal business activities such as finance, marketing, and so on, into one integrated tool. Planning uses the data to provide a closer look at the company's overall business operations and helps improve the forecast predictability accuracy.

Planning makes use of Essbase in an ingenious way. The data for each business activity is stored in its own custom Essbase database or cube. Several business activities can share the same cube and have their own set of dimensions and members. Therefore, Essbase must be started and running in the background so Planning can access the cubes. The various Planning functions are then supported by Planning's seamless accessing of the data from the Essbase cubes and by using the stored business rule feature to apply the customer defined business rules to the data for planning and analysis purposes.

The storing of complex business rules to facilitate proper analysis of the data is a huge benefit of Oracle Planning and is accomplished within the module by utilizing a small space on a relational database such as an Oracle or SQL server database.

With the aid of pre-packaged process modules, Essbase Planning can also greatly shorten the length of time typically required for budget and forecast cycles, thus lowering the total cost of ownership for this product.

Essbase analytics

It's funny, but the word analytics is being tossed about rather often these days. Pretty much anything you do with OLAP or multidimensional database tools, can be termed analytics.

In Essbase however, Essbase analytics, to some, usually refers to Essbase's other database engine, the ASO database engine. The reason given for this is that the typical Essbase ASO database is primarily used for presentation, analysis, and reporting which are all analytic functions. The Essbase BSO database, while analytic itself, can also be considered transactional as well.

The Essbase analytics nickname dates back to the advent of the ASO database architecture when all you had was the BSO architecture. The new ASO architecture was the analytic tool.

Yes, it's funny how Essbase is an analytical package and inside that package is an analytic piece but that's just how it is.

Try not to get hung up on the terminology here though. When considering your options, you need to look at all of the same things you have always looked at. How large will the system be? What are the business customer's requirements? What type of system am I building here?

When you answer these questions, it will matter less what you call what you are doing than choosing the right tools.

Hyperion Application Link/Oracle Application Link

The name pretty much says it all. Hyperion Application Link is a suite of ETL tools that allows the user or programmer to integrate Oracle products, like Essbase, with other third party software packages, especially transactional database packages.

Hyperion Application Link (HAL) can integrate all of your data loading and ETL functions into one place and offer improved performance.

When gathering data for your Essbase application, you may encounter data from many different sources. HAL allows you to set up a link to your favorite Oracle database using an ODBC connection. HAL will also allow you to load data from conveniently delivered flat files too. In fact, you can usually accomplish just about all of your data loading needs for your Essbase System 9 installation by using HAL.

Oracle Business Rules

This tool can be a tremendous time saver. The Oracle Business Rules tool allows the programmer to create, store, execute, and manage complex business rules as specified by the business customer and as it relates to the business process and the data. All of this is accomplished by using an easy to understand user interface with graphical depictions of the various elements that go into a rule.

Imagine a business process that dictates the values for next month's sales commitments as follows:

- If the actual sales for the prior month are not received by the 15th of the current month, then the committed sales for the current month are to equal the sales number that was forecasted from the prior month.

- If the actual sales for the prior month are received by the 15th, then the number used for the current month's committed sales will be equal to the prior month actual sales * 1.15.

This is just one example of a business rule being automatically executed against the data for the users of the system. There are endless possibilities on how to make good use of this tool.

The advantages of the Oracle Business Rules tool are clear, especially in today's fast-paced business world where static structures in data load and calculation scripts need almost continual modifying. With the Hyperion Business Rules tool, the dynamic nature of the business can more effectively be supported with the creation of minimal maintenance dynamic rules.

Oracle Reports

Oracle Reports is a powerful new tool for creating reports that presents complex financial analytic data in an easy to read, professional looking, graphical format. The reports you create can contain many elements such as colorful charts, graphs, and even text box objects.

Creating reports is quick and easy and objects embedded in one report can be linked to appear in another report.

Essbase Shared Services

Essbase Shared Services or Shared Services is a component of Oracle's Essbase Foundation Services. Shared Services is a standardized infrastructure framework that facilitates the deployment of other Essbase System 9 components and also simplifies the ongoing system maintenance of those components.

Shared Services provides a central framework for creating and maintaining users. It can also be used for managing user security across all Oracle Essbase modules, including external authentication.

One nice feature of Shared Services is that you can build your applications for easy user ID set up and maintenance. If you are able to use external authentication or network authentication, where Essbase allows the network to authenticate the user ID, your password maintenance is all but eliminated and a user who has access to the network can also access any Essbase application that you have given him or her access to. If you plan to use Essbase authentication, the user ID is authenticated by the Essbase analytic server at login time.

Finally, Essbase Shared Services provides the capability of managing the migration of components from your test environments to your production environments. You perform the development and testing in the Dev environment and then use the Shared Services tool to copy the objects to the Prod environment.

Oracle Essbase Provider Services

Oracle Essbase Provider Services is a middle tier data source provider between an Essbase Server and Smart view, XMLA, and/or Java API. The following figure shows the Provider Services architecture:

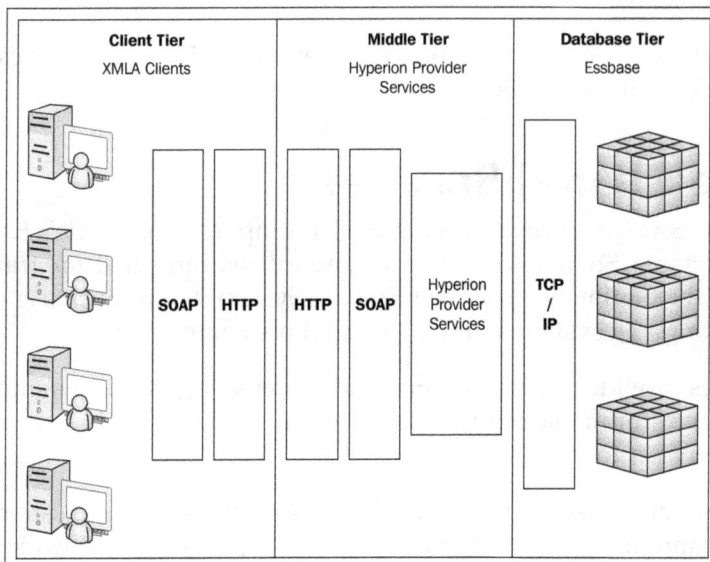

As you can see, Provider Services is a three-tiered architecture. One of the other special features is that you can configure Oracle Provider Services from the EAS tool. When you are working with Smart View for Microsoft Office, you will have the option of selecting Oracle Provider Services to connect to the Essbase analytic server.

Essbase Smart Office

Essbase Smart Office or more commonly known as Essbase Smart Space, is a unique new tool in the world of real-time analytic analysis and reporting.

The most amazing feature of Essbase Smart Office is that it offers the first gadget-based user interface. Smart Office consists of a set of configurable gadgets that run on the business customer's PC desktop and provide continuous access to financial, operational, and performance related data. Additionally, Smart Office contains a toolkit that can be used for creating additional gadgets and data services that constantly keep the user upto date.

The following screenshot says it all for this tool. Can you imagine how happy your customers will be with this scene on their desktop? You will probably have many new co-workers which will call you friend.

Here comes the awesome part. Smart Office can also act like a sort of desktop instant messenger tool or collaboration tool, where users can notify one another on the fly of changes in business processes, task completions, or anything else that can affect their performance.

Oracle Essbase Financial Reporting

This tool can be easily compared to a conductor in an orchestra. With it's easy to use, user friendly graphical user interface, Oracle Essbase Financial Reporting gets high grades on its usability factor.

While advanced users will enjoy the intuitive, quick and easy, drag-and-drop method for creating impressive reports, even the most computer illiterate users can produce high level, executive quality reports with just a little practice.

Take a look at the following screenshot to see an example of how easy and intuitive using Oracle Essbase Financial Reporting really is:

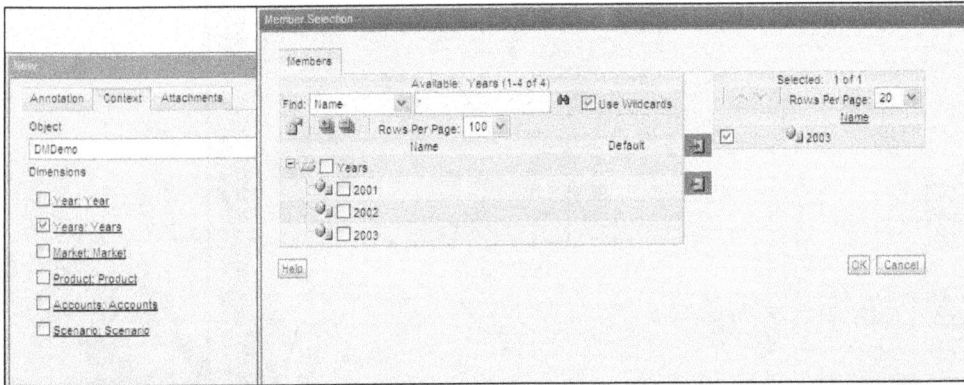

On top of the reporting capabilities, Oracle Financial Reporting also has functionality that allows the user to schedule batch report generation, distribute reports, and divert reports to a holding area. Then, to complete the process, Oracle Financial Reporting can be used to send notifications to specified recipients when their reports are ready.

Smart View for Microsoft Office

As you know, Oracle Essbase comes with an Add-in tool designed to be used in Microsoft Excel. It is this add-in that is one of Essbase's biggest strengths and also makes all of the various data analysts very happy.

Oracle, being the industry leader that they are, did not stop with the Essbase Add-in for Microsoft Excel. Oracle realized that in addition to making the data analysts very happy, it would probably be a good idea to make the flashy sales people and the big shot executives very happy as well.

With Essbase version 9.x and higher, Oracle has introduced a new product called Smart View. Oracle Essbase Smart View, simply put, is like an Essbase Add-In for the entire Microsoft Office suite of applications.

In today's world of on demand this and real time that, just imagine a tool that allows you to go into a meeting with your beautifully prepared Microsoft PowerPoint presentation that itself is now directly connected to the Essbase database. Your presentation will always have up-to-the-second and accurate data. Also, imagine that you need to send a quick email to your team alerting them to some data condition that needs immediate attention. Well, your email can also connect directly to the database and will contain up-to-the-second data.

In the following screenshot, you can see how Smart View will dynamically update values in a Microsoft Excel object embedded in a Microsoft Word document. You can do this with PowerPoint and Outlook email as well.

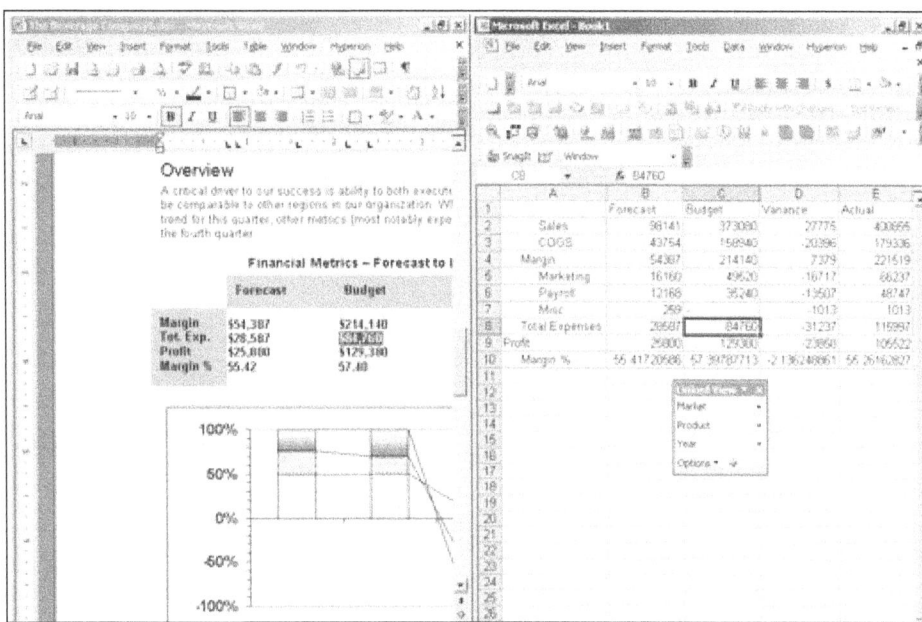

Wait, there's more. No more trying to hastily update Microsoft Word documents in a pinch either. You guessed it, embedded into your document is a dynamic connection to your Essbase database.

Oracle Smart View also works effortlessly with Microsoft Excel.

Summary

As you can see, the Oracle Essbase family is about as complete as one could possibly want or need it to be. It seems that if there is ever a need that is unfulfilled in the Business Intelligence arena, Oracle will fill it and fill it better than anyone else.

One stop shopping has never been true than it is with Oracle. Whatever your Business Intelligence, OLAP, or Analytic computing needs, there is an Oracle Essbase product that will satisfy your requirements better than any other product. When multiple products are used together as part of the Essbase System, they are truly unbeatable.

Just remember, it all started with Essbase and Essbase is still the OLAP, Business Intelligence, and Analytic foundation today.

A New Essbase Companion— Oracle Smart View

As you know, Oracle Essbase comes with an add-in tool designed to be used in Microsoft Excel. It is this add-in that is one of Essbase's biggest strengths. As you also know, it is this add-in that makes all of the various data analysts very happy as well.

Oracle, being the industry leader, they are, did not stop with the Essbase Add-in for Microsoft Excel. They realized that in addition to making the data analysts happy, it would probably be a good idea to make the flash and dash executives happy as well.

Oracle has introduced, with Essbase version 9.x, a new product called Smart View. Oracle Smart View, simply put, is like an Essbase Add-in for the entire Microsoft Office suite of applications.

In today's world of on demand this and real time that, just imagine a tool that allows you to go into a meeting with your beautifully prepared Microsoft PowerPoint presentation that is directly connected to the Essbase database. Your presentation will always have up-to-the-second and accurate data. Also imagine that you need to send a quick email to your team alerting them to some data condition that needs immediate attention. Well, your email can also connect directly to the Essbase database and will contain upto the second data!

Wait, there's more! No more trying to hastily update Microsoft Word documents in a pinch either. You guessed it, embedded into your document is a dynamic connection to the Essbase database!

Oh, and in case you are wondering, Oracle Smart View works effortlessly with Microsoft Excel too! Does it get any better than this?

Smart View is like having your cake and being able to eat it too! Now, let's jump in and see how we can make the best use of Oracle Smart View for reporting your data.

Reporting with Oracle Smart View

The installation of Smart View is very easy. Along with Oracle Smart View, you will also need to install Oracle Shared Services, formerly the Oracle Hub, or Oracle Provider Services. Smart View can be used with all Oracle products, such as Essbase, Oracle Planning, and Financial Reporting.

When installing Oracle Smart View in Microsoft Excel, there is no need to uninstall the Essbase Add-In, you can simply install right on top of it. After Smart View is installed you should see an **Hyperion** menu pick on the main toolbar in Microsoft Excel, this will be in addition to the Essbase menu pick. You should now also see the Hyperion menu pick on the toolbars for Microsoft Word, Microsoft PowerPoint, and on any of the other Microsoft Office components you have installed on your computer.

By clicking on the Hyperion menu pick added to your toolbar, you see a listing of the entire menu available to you as shown in the following screenshot:

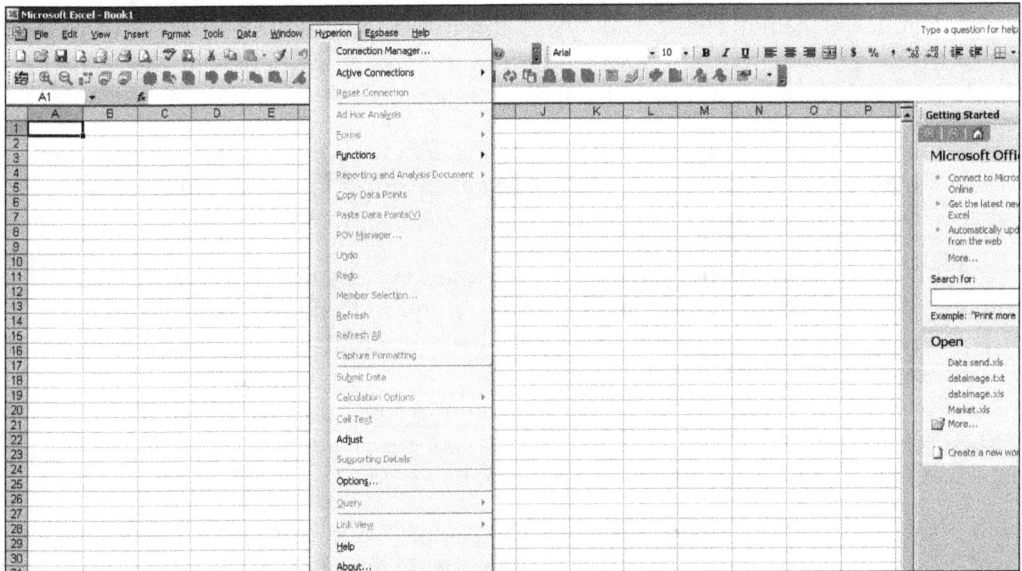

Adding a data source with the connection manager

Before you can even begin to retrieve data from your Essbase database or through your Oracle Planning module, you will need to define a data source to Smart View for each connection. This needs to be done individually for each Microsoft Office application in which you will be using Smart View.

To add a data source, click on **Hyperion | Connection Manager.**

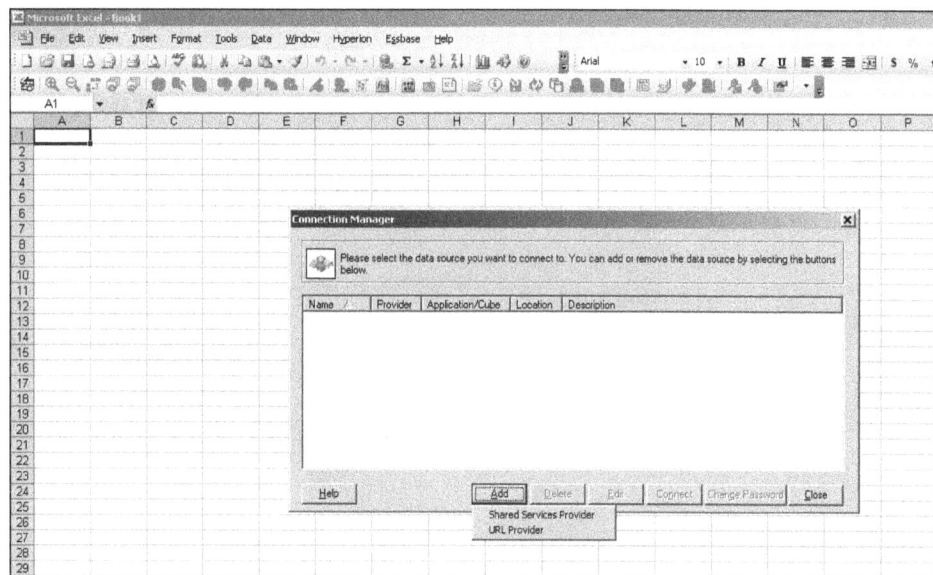

You will then be asked to connect using either **Shared Services Provider** or **URL Provider**. In this example, we have chosen **URL Provider** and in the next screen you see a list box with several URL locations.

In the list box, you will see **Hyperion Provider** and **Hyperion Reporting and Analysis**. To connect to Essbase, Oracle Planning, or Oracle Financial Management use **URL Provider** and for Financial Reporting, Production Reporting, or Web Analysis use **Hyperion Reporting and Analysis**. Since we are connecting to Essbase, we have selected **URL Provider**.

For **URL Location**, you need to provide the location where Hyperion Provider is actually running. If your Hyperion Provider is installed on your client, then it would be running on your localhost and you need to provide the URL address.

For Essbase, the default URL location is:

`http://localhost:13080/aps/SmartView`

For Oracle Planning, the default URL location is:

`http://localhost:8300/HyperionPlanning/SmartView`

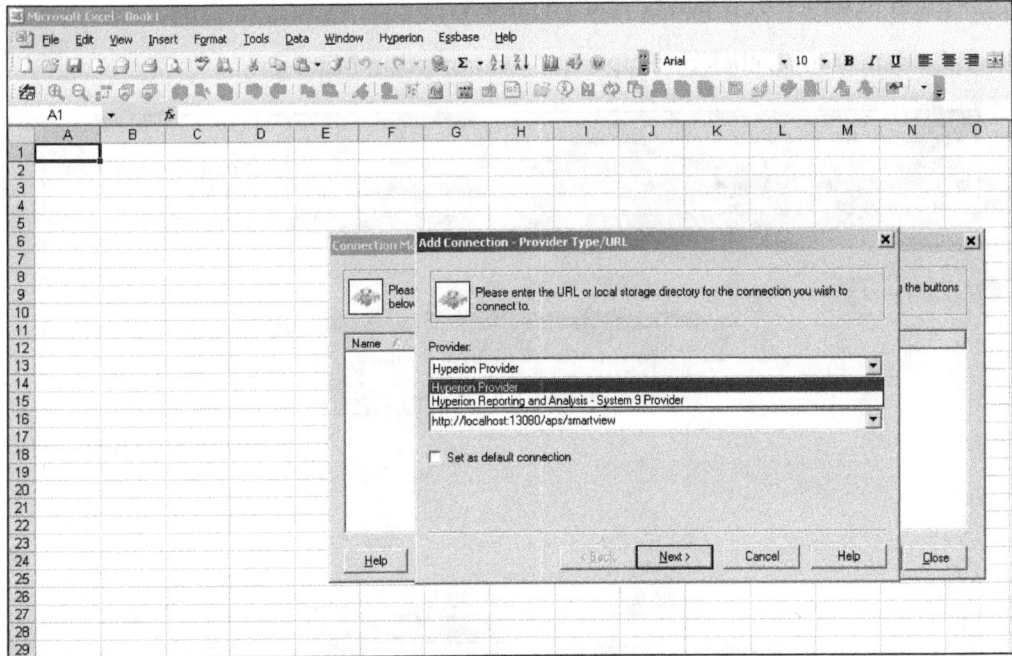

Once the **Provider** and **URL Location** are entered, please click on the **Next** button to proceed.

On the next screen you will see the Essbase server. When you click on the server the system will prompt you to enter your Essbase user name and password to connect to the Essbase server as shown in the following screenshot:

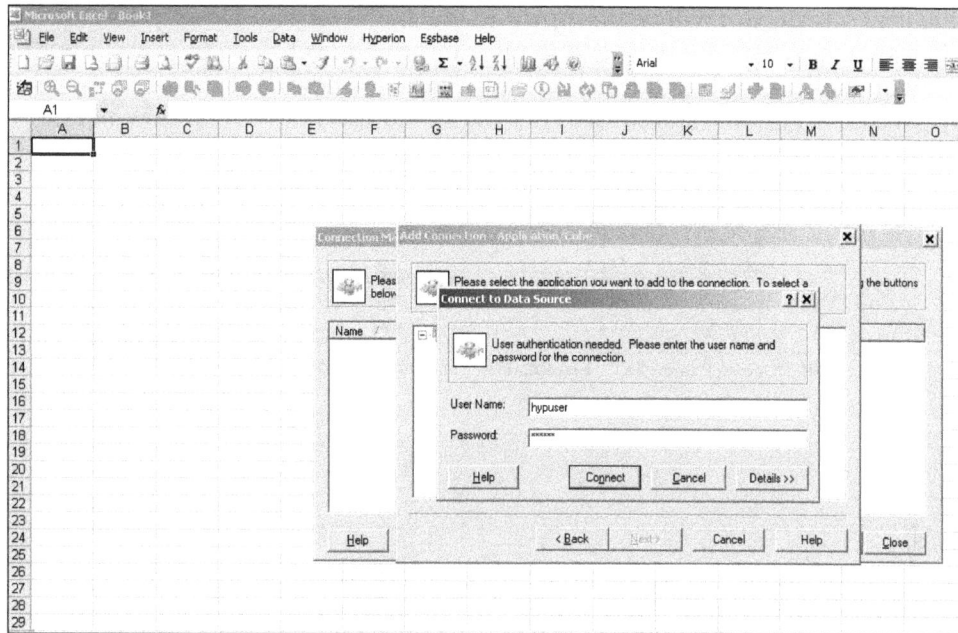

After you have entered your user ID and password click on the **Connect** button and in the next screen you will see a list of the available applications and databases on the Essbase server. Select the application and database to which you want to establish the connection and click on **Next**.

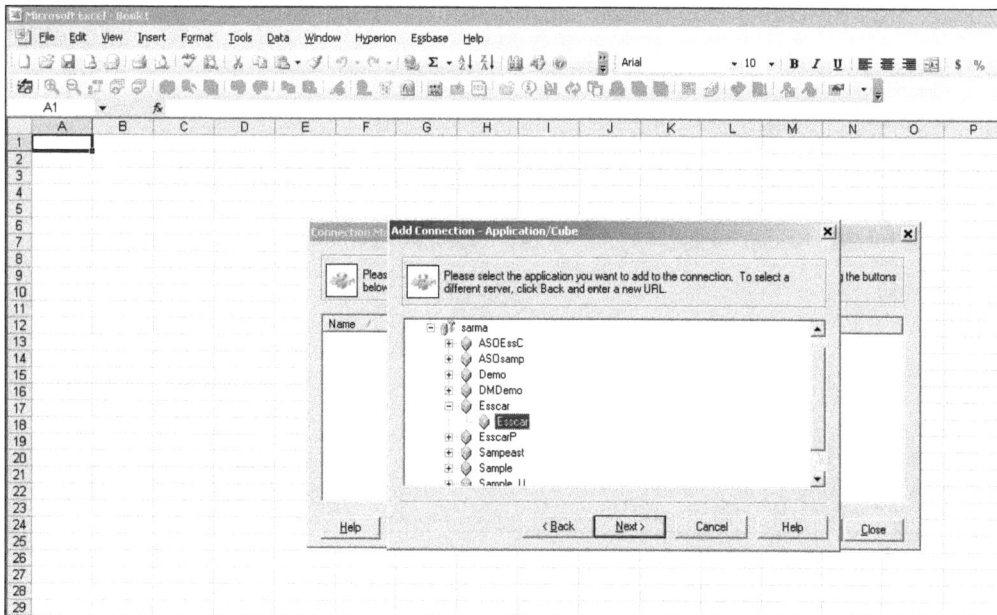

On the next screen, you will be prompted to enter a **Name** and **Description** for the data source. When you have entered this information click on the **Finish** button and you are now done. You have successfully added a new data source for Smart View. To connect to this data source click on the **Connect** button as shown in the following screenshot:

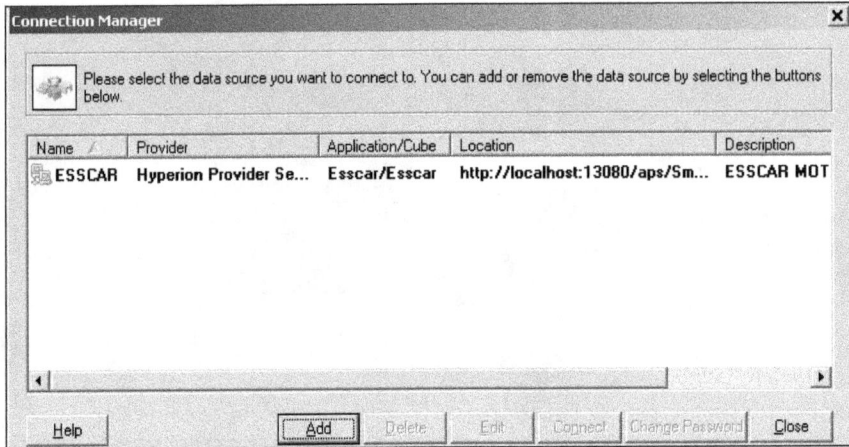

In order to establish a connection to the Essbase server, you will be asked to enter your user name and password. Once you have entered the correct information, you can click on the **Connect** button and you will be successfully connected to the Essbase cube. You are now ready for happy reporting. The following screenshot shows the connection manager after the connection is established:

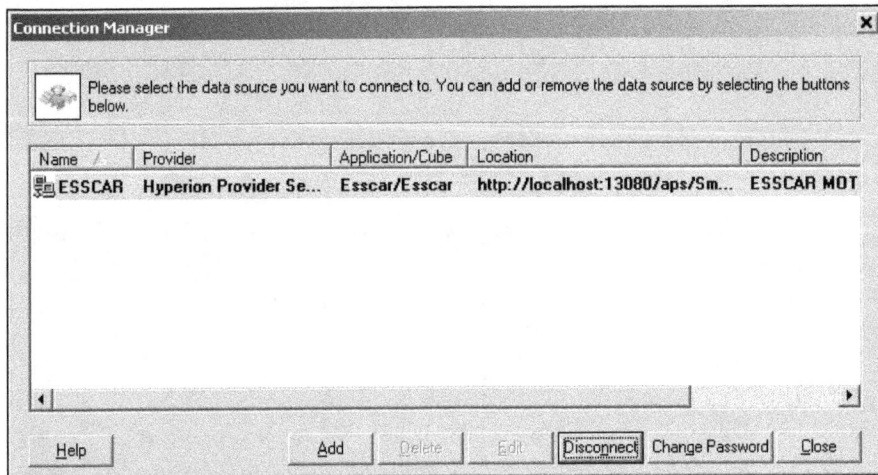

If you have the Essbase Add-in installed on the same PC, we need to remove the **Enable Double-Clicking** option from the **Essbase | Options | Global** tab in Microsoft Excel.

Steps to update the Essbase Add-in option:

1. Open Microsoft Excel and click on **Essbase | Options.**

2. Click on the **Global** tab.

3. Uncheck the **Enable Double-Clicking** checkbox.

4. Click on **OK**.

The next screenshot shows the **Essbase | Options | Global** tab and I assume you are quite familiar with this screen, as we have discussed it in the add-in section of this book:

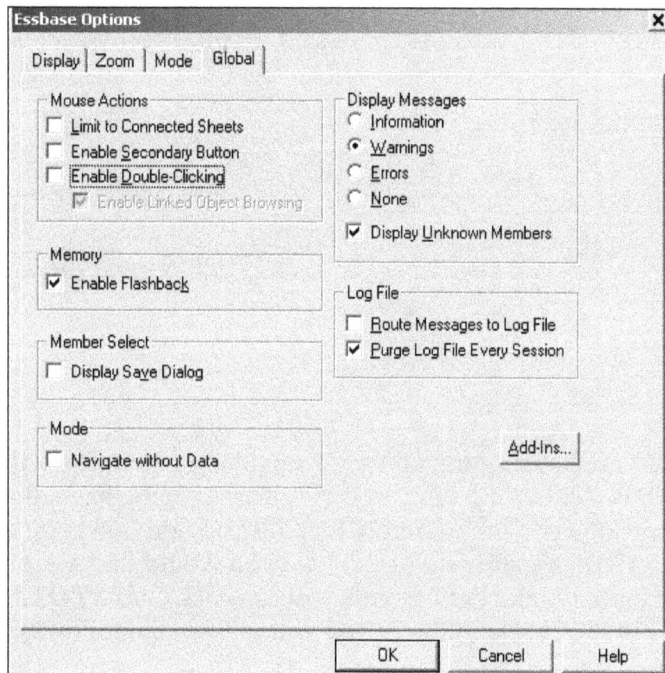

Retrieving data using Smart View in Microsoft Excel

Now that you have established a connection with the Essbase server, you are ready to retrieve data. With Smart View, you can generate reports using the **Free Form** or you can do your own **Ad-Hoc** reporting. Using the **Free Form** reporting option, like we talked about for the Microsoft Excel Add-in, you can define the row and column member names and click on the **Hyperion | Refresh** button and you will see the data as shown in the following screenshot:

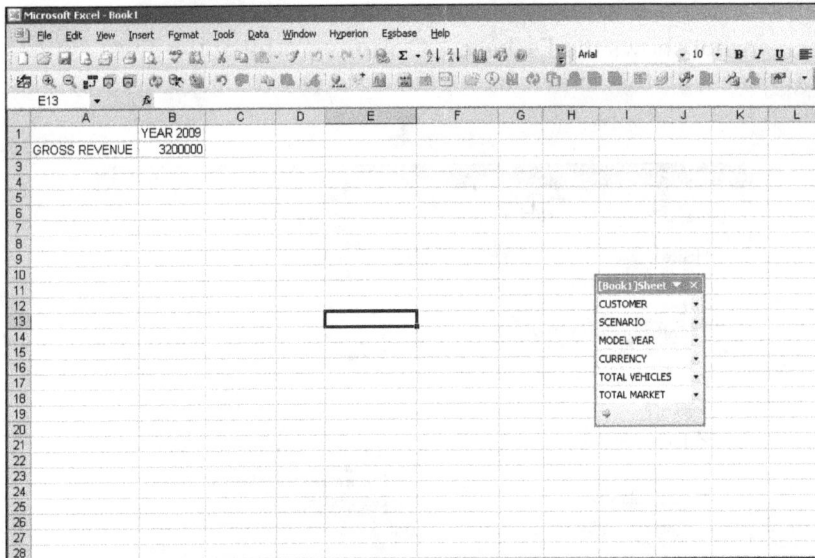

If you notice in the previous figure, you see a small box called **[Book1]Sheet** that is nothing but a **POV (Point of View)**. The POV has all of the page dimension information for the data you are currently looking at. Right now, you are viewing data for **TOTAL MARKET** and you decide that you would like to see the data at a specific market level. On the POV screen, you can click on the **TOTAL MARKET** drop-down box and then click on the **...** and you will see the following **Member Selection** screen:

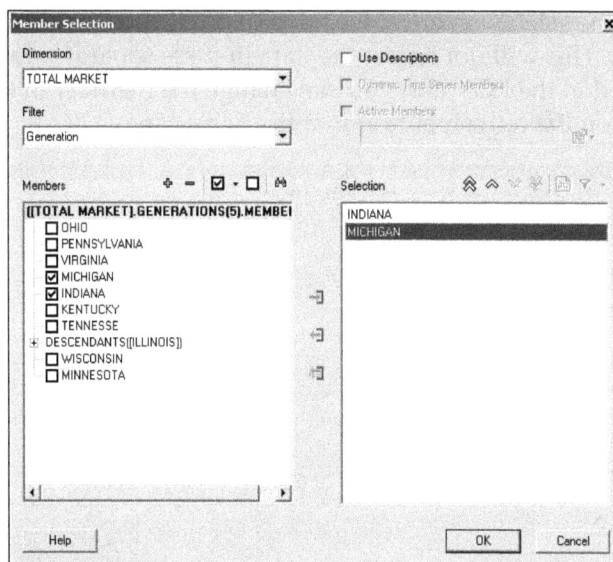

In the **Member Selection** screen, you can see all of the available members for the dimension you have selected listed in the **Members** list box (which is on the left hand part of the **Member Selection** screen) and you can see all of the members you have selected in the **Selection** list box (right-hand side of the **Member Selection** screen). In the **Member Selection** screen, you can also select different dimensions by clicking on the **Dimension** drop-down list. You can also set **Filters** for the members you have selected to narrow your selection further. The filter can be at the Children, Descendants, Level, or Generation of the member you have selected.

In this example, we have filtered the selection by the **Generation** and displayed the report of all of the members in Generation 5. Select all returned members by clicking on the select all button ☑ and then click on the add button ⇥ to add the members into the selection list. Click on **OK** to return back to Microsoft Excel.

On the Microsoft Excel sheet, click the refresh button ⟳ on the POV. The data will then be refreshed.

As you can see in the selection above, we have selected three members from the market dimension. This will not report the data in three separate sheets, but the members are stored in the POV and you can change the member in the POV anytime and click on the refresh button to refresh the data.

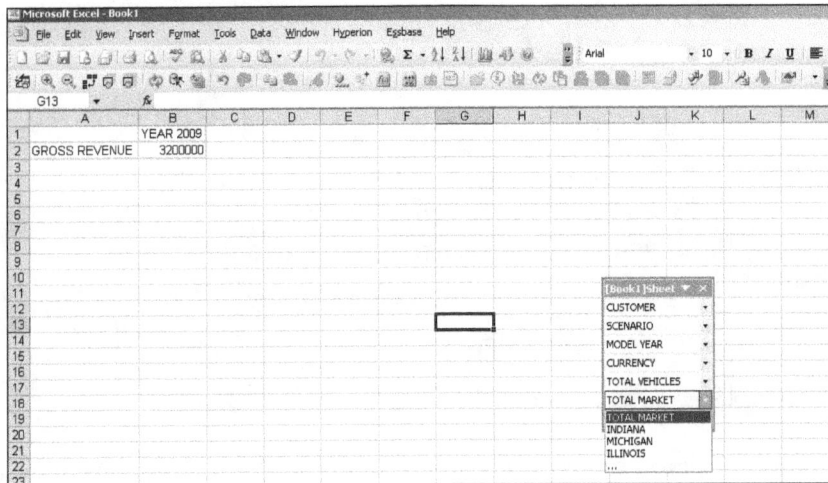

The Free Form reporting is the same as the Free Form reporting that we have talked about previously in the chapter on the Essbase Add-In. However, the difference is that in Smart View, you will have a POV selection through which you can change your other member selections. In the next section, we will learn little more about the POV Manager.

POV Manager

You can also report the data in Microsoft Excel using the POV Manager. Once you have established a connection to the Essbase database, click on **Hyperion | POV Manager**. The **POV Manager** screen will be opened and you will see two folders, one is called **Active** and the other is called **Saved**.

If you click on the **Active** folder you will see the current active connections. If you are connected to two data sources you will see two connection names in the **Active** folder. If you select a connection now in the right side of the POV Manager, you will have two selections, one is the **Connection** and the other is **POV** (seen in the following screenshot). In the **Connection** block you will see information about the data source that this connection is associated with and in the **POV block** you will see all of the dimension information along with the default members selected. On the **POV** block the left side is the dimension information and right-hand side is the selected member information. If you double-click a member in the POV, the **Member Selection** screen will be displayed and you can change the member information.

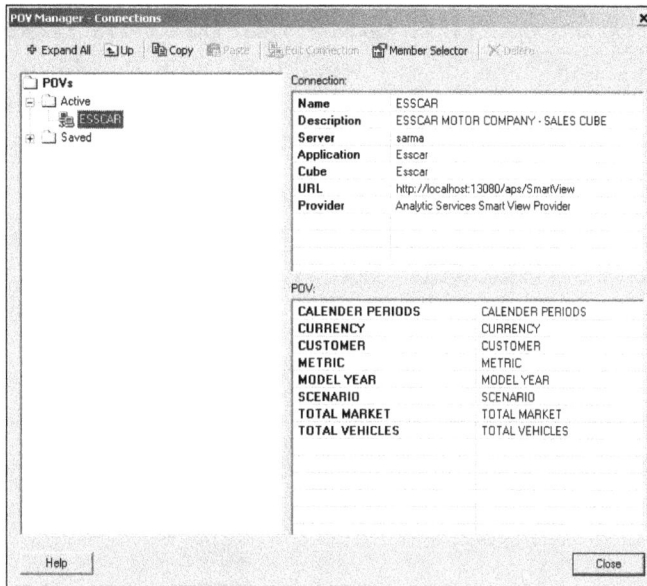

In the **Saved** folder, you have a folder which has the same name as the Microsoft Excel workbook name and inside that folder there are three folders called **Sheet 1**, **Sheet 2**, and **Sheet 3.** These folders correspond with the number of sheets in your workbook. Inside each individual sheet folder you can save the connection information and POV for that sheet. Once you save the Microsoft Excel file the connection information is also saved and this can be used by the business user to save and then share their queries with other users.

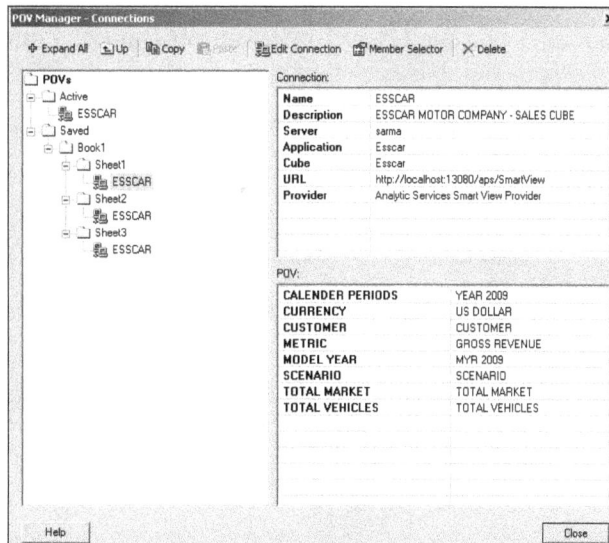

Submitting data and calc scripts in Smart View

Like the "Lock and Send" data update method in the Essbase Add-in, you can also send data to the Essbase database by clicking on the **Hyperion | Submit Data** button. Let's say we have a member called **Dealer Adjustments** in our **Measures** dimension and we allow the business analysts to enter adjustments to this member using Microsoft Excel. All they need to do is click on **Submit Data** to send the data to the Essbase database. The moment the business analyst enters the January 2009 Dealer Adjustments data in Microsoft Excel, the spreadsheet cell shows the information in yellow, indicating that this information has been edited and needs to be sent to the server, as shown in the next screenshot:

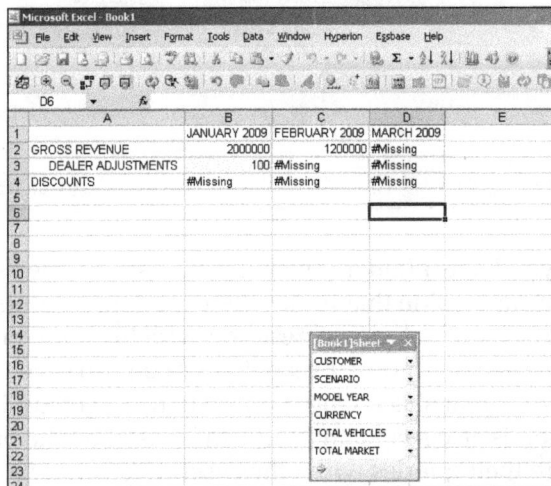

The moment the user clicks on the **Hyperion | Submit Data**, the information is submitted to the Essbase database as shown:

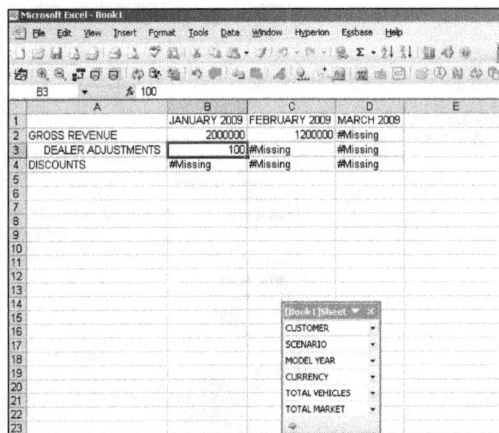

As you can see from the previous screenshot, the data is submitted to the database server but the data has not been rolled upto its parent which is **TOTAL DISCOUNTS**. In order to roll up the data, you need to execute a calc script.

Click on the **Hyperion | Calculation Options | Calculate** and you will see the calculation scripts screen as shown:

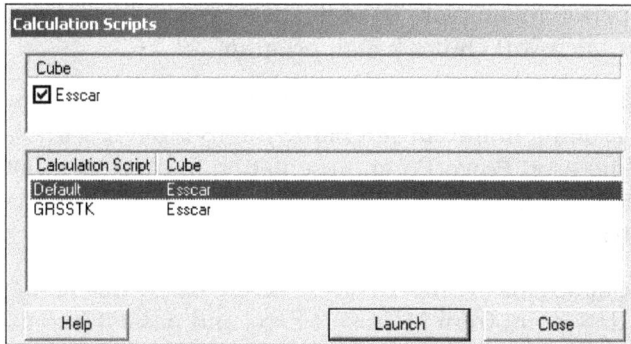

In this screen you can see all of the available **Calculation Scripts** for the Essbase database you are connected to. In this case we select the default calc and click on **Launch**. When the Calc has completed, the data is rolled upto the higher parent levels. If you run the report for the **TOTAL DISCOUNTS** now, you will see the data is rolled up as shown in the following screenshot:

Using Smart View in other Microsoft Office products

This is one of the coolest features in Smart View. When you install Smart View, it will be integrated into all of the Microsoft Office products loaded on your PC. If you open Microsoft Word you will see a Hyperion menu item, open Microsoft PowerPoint and you will see a Hyperion menu pick, what the heck, you will even see the Hyperion menu pick in your Microsoft Outlook mail program.

Let's say you are meeting with the Finance Director monthly, to show how good or bad the company is doing in the current market. This is never a fun task. Chances are you will create a Microsoft PowerPoint presentation. With Smart View, all you need to do is just click to refresh the data every month and you will get the most current data from the Essbase database into your presentation.

Let's see how we can do this in Smart View. There are a couple of ways to do it. You can copy the data point from Microsoft Excel and paste it into the Microsoft PowerPoint presentation or just create a new data point in the Microsoft PowerPoint presentation. It's that easy!

1. First, explore how we can do it by copying the Data Points from Microsoft Excel to Microsoft PowerPoint.

2. Select the cell whose data point you want to copy and click on **Hyperion | Copy Data Points.**

3. Open the Microsoft PowerPoint in the menu item and click on **Hyperion | Paste Data Points.**

You will now see a message on the Microsoft PowerPoint screen saying **NEED REFRESH** as shown in the following screenshot:

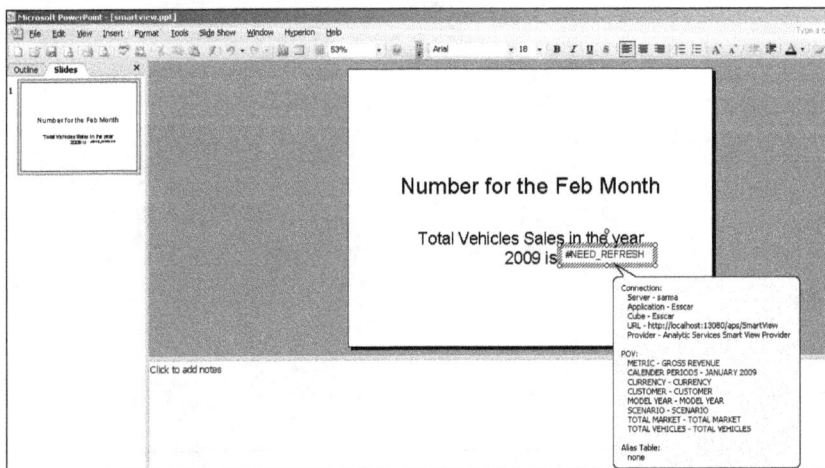

If you look closely at the previous screenshot, you will see the connection detail which tells you all of the information about the members that are chosen for this Data Point. Since your connection is already established in Microsoft Excel, you do not need to reconnect in Microsoft PowerPoint. In order to see the new data, click on **Hyperion | Refresh**, you will see the data in Microsoft PowerPoint (as seen below) and you are now ready for the meeting.

> ### Number for the Feb Month
>
> Total Vehicles Sales in the year
> 2009 is 2000000

Another way of calling the Essbase data from other Microsoft Office products is by using the Smart Tags option. These Smart Tags are turned off by default but you can always turn them on.

On the **Tools** menu, click on the **Auto Correct Options**, and then click on the **Smart Tags** tab and select the **Label Text with Smart Tags** checkbox to enable the Smart Tags.

Now that the Smart Tags are enabled, let's modify our Microsoft PowerPoint presentation to show the data by **Market**. In Microsoft PowerPoint, just enter **SmartView** and you will see a small **i** on the top of the Smart View as shown in the following screenshot:

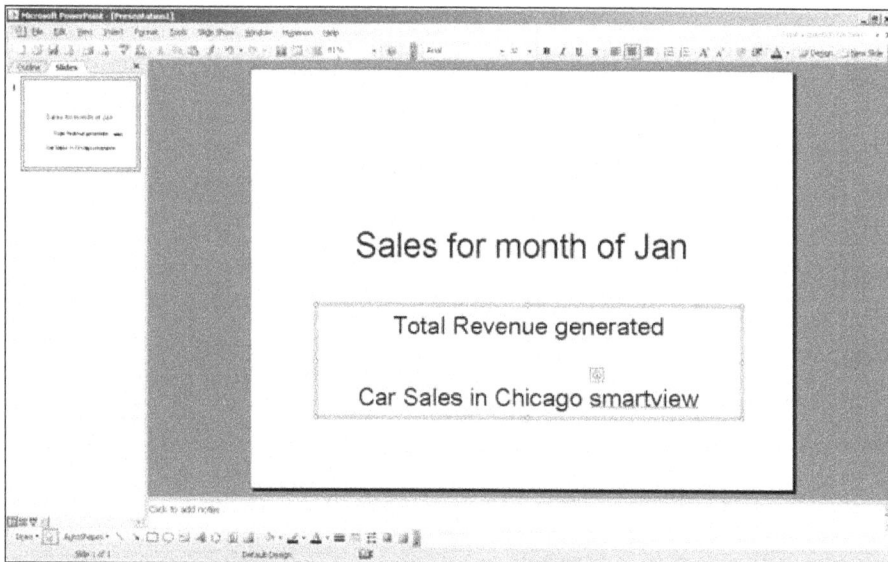

Click on the "**i**" tag and then click on the **Functions | Connection Name (Esscar) | HsGetValue** option. This function is used to return a data point for all of the members you have selected. Upon clicking on this, you will see a **Member Selection** screen where you can make all of the selections as shown in the next screenshot:

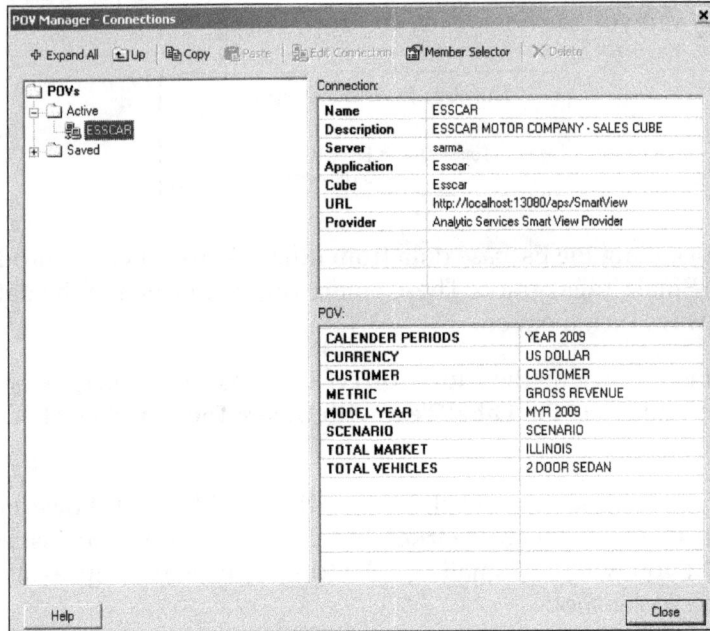

Click on **OK** after you have made all of the selections you need and you will see the data pulled into your Microsoft PowerPoint presentation (as seen below):

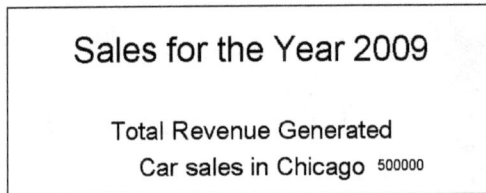

Sales for the Year 2009

Total Revenue Generated
Car sales in Chicago   500000

Well that wraps it up for Hyperion Smart View. With the already outstanding Essbase Add-in for Microsoft Excel and now the addition of Smart View there is virtually no limit to what you can do in the world of Business Intelligence.

Stay tuned as Oracle has even more new and exciting products coming down the pipe.

Index

Symbols

A

about 359, 360
essbase.cfg, memory settings 360-362

Microsoft Excel
calculation script, running 209, 211

Microsoft Excel add-in
add-in spreadsheet options, setting 250, 251
add-in xll file, locating 244, 245
calculation function 268
Cascade... command 272
currency conversion tool, using 272
Currency Report... function 272
data, retrieving from Essbase 249, 250
data, sending to database 267
Essbase add-in 274
Essbase add-in, reloading 244
Essbase cascade options, dialog box 272-274
Essbase, connecting to 246
Essbase, connecting to from Microsoft Excel 247, 248
Essbase, disconnecting from 248
Essbase members, selecting for query 258-263
Essbase Query Designer (EQD), launching 249
flashback, Essbase add-in undo command 266
graphical data representations, creating 271
Keep Only function, using 263
lock function 267
navigate without data function 269
Pivot function 265
Remove Only function, using 264
reporting with 243
retrieve function 266
retrieve & lock function 266
send function 267
unlock function 267
worksheet, disconnecting from database 249
zoom in function 264, 265
zoom out function 265

Microsoft Excel VBA
calcScript parameter 212
calculation script, running 211
parameters 212
SheetName parameter 212

synchronous parameter 212

miscellaneous function
about 186
@CALCMODE() function 186
@CONCATENATE()and@SUBSTRING() function 187

mode tab, Essbase options
formula preservation section, keep only or remove only 256
formula preservation section, retain on keep and remove only 256
formula preservation section, retain on retrieval 256
mode section, update mode 255
retrieval section, advanced interpretation 255
retrieval section, free form 255

modifications tab, Essbase database 58
Multidimensional Access Language. *See* **MaxL**
MULTIPLEBITMAPMEMCHECK, essbase.cfg memory settings 360
multiplication (*) operator 79

N

navigate without data function 269
NETDELAY, essbase.cfg file settings 356
NETRETRYCOUNT, essbase.cfg file settings 356
network setup
developer client 29
end-user pc 29
Essbase server 28
raw data 28
Never Consolidate (^) operator 79
no dimension type, standard dimension 71
Non-Unicode applications 42, 43
normal (non-currency) database, Essbase database 47

O

OLAP 31
OLAP analytical solutions
and traditional data analysis applications, differences 31, 32
Online Analytical Processing. *See* **OLAP**

T

text files
  delimited text files 124
  fixed column width text files 124
Time dimension 66
Time dimension, EssCar database outline
  Dynamic Time Series member, adding 114
time dimension type, standard dimension
  70
Total Customer dimension 34
Total Market dimension 35
Total Vehicles dimension 33, 65, 66
traditional data analysis applications
  and OLAP analytical solutions, differences
    31, 32
transactions tab, Essbase database 56
transparent database partition, setting up
  348-352
transparent partition 48
TRIGMAXMEMSIZE, essbase.cfg memory
  settings 360
tuple 378
Two-pass Calc 189-191

U

UDA
  about 111-113
  rules 113
Unicode applications 42, 43
unlock function 267
UPDATECALC, essbase.cfg file settings
  358
User Defined Attributes. *See* **UDA**
user privileges, MaxL
  user, altering 319, 320
  user, creating 319
  user, displaying 320
  user, dropping 320
  user, granting 320
  working with 318, 319

V

valid consolidation operators
  addition (+) operator 79
  division (/) operator 79

multiplication (*) operator 79
Never Consolidate (^) operator 79
percent (%) operator 79
subtraction (-) operator 79
valid consolidation operators (~)
  Exclude from Consolidation (~) operator 79
Visual Basic Main API group, functions
  328, 329
Visual Basic Outline API functions 329
VLBREPORT, essbase.cfg memory settings
  360

W

worksheet, Microsoft, Excel add-in 249

X

XMLA 373
XML for Analysis. *See* **XMLA**

Z

zoom in function 264, 265
zoom out function 265
zoom tab, Essbase options
  hybrid analysis option, enable hybrid
    analysis 254
  member retention section, include section
    254
  member retention section, remove unse-
    lected groups 254
  member retention section, within selected
    group 254
  sampling section 254
  zoom in section, all levels 254
  zoom in section, bottom level 254
  zoom in section, next level 254

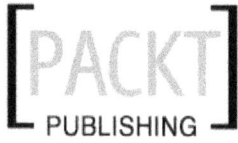

Thank you for buying
Oracle Essbase 9
Implementation Guide

About Packt Publishing

Packt, pronounced 'packed', published its first book "*Mastering phpMyAdmin for Effective MySQL Management*" in April 2004 and subsequently continued to specialize in publishing highly focused books on specific technologies and solutions.

Our books and publications share the experiences of your fellow IT professionals in adapting and customizing today's systems, applications, and frameworks. Our solution based books give you the knowledge and power to customize the software and technologies you're using to get the job done. Packt books are more specific and less general than the IT books you have seen in the past. Our unique business model allows us to bring you more focused information, giving you more of what you need to know, and less of what you don't.

Packt is a modern, yet unique publishing company, which focuses on producing quality, cutting-edge books for communities of developers, administrators, and newbies alike. For more information, please visit our website: www.packtpub.com.

Writing for Packt

We welcome all inquiries from people who are interested in authoring. Book proposals should be sent to author@packtpub.com. If your book idea is still at an early stage and you would like to discuss it first before writing a formal book proposal, contact us; one of our commissioning editors will get in touch with you.

We're not just looking for published authors; if you have strong technical skills but no writing experience, our experienced editors can help you develop a writing career, or simply get some additional reward for your expertise.

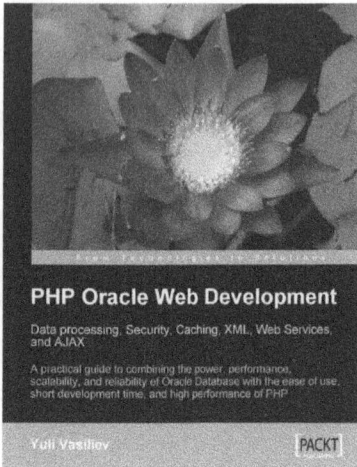

PHP Oracle Web Development: Data processing, Security, Caching, XML, Web Services, and AJAX

ISBN: 978-1-847193-63-6   Paperback: 396 pages

A practical guide to combining the power, performance, scalability, and reliability of the Oracle Database with the ease of use, short development time, and high performance of PHP

1. Program your own PHP/Oracle application

2. Move data processing inside the database

3. Distribute data processing between the web/ PHP and Oracle database servers

4. Create reusable building blocks for PHP/ Oracle solutions

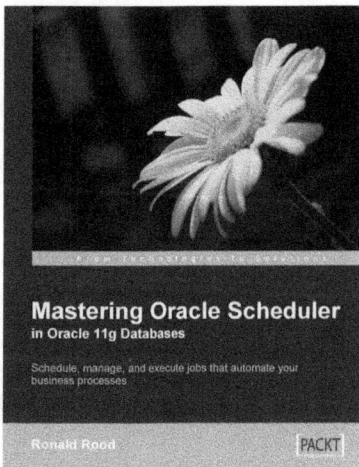

Mastering Oracle Scheduler in Oracle 11g Databases

ISBN: 978-1-847195-98-2   Paperback: 240 pages

Schedule, manage, and execute jobs that automate your business processes

1. Automate jobs from within the Oracle database with the built-in Scheduler

2. Boost database performance by managing, monitoring, and controlling jobs more effectively

3. Contains easy-to-understand explanations, simple examples, debugging tips, and real-life scenarios

Please check **www.PacktPub.com** for information on our titles

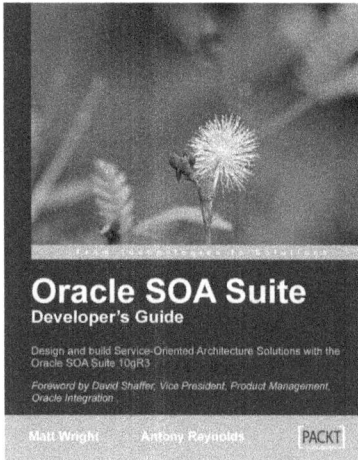

Oracle SOA Suite Developer's Guide

ISBN: 978-1-847193-55-1   Paperback: 652 pages

Design and build Service-Oriented Architecture Solutions with the Oracle SOA Suite 10gR3

1. A hands-on guide to using and applying the Oracle SOA Suite in the delivery of real-world SOA applications.

2. Detailed coverage of the Oracle Service Bus, BPEL Process Manager, Web Service Manager, Rules, Human Workflow, and Business Activity Monitoring.

3. Master the best way to combine / use each of these different components in the implementation of a SOA solution.

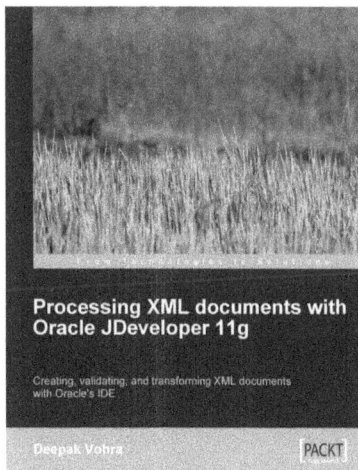

Processing XML documents with Oracle JDeveloper 11g

ISBN: 978-1-847196-66-8   Paperback: 384 pages

Creating, validating, and transforming XML documents with Oracle's IDE

1. Will get the reader developing applications for processing XML in JDeveloper 11g quickly and easily

2. Self-contained chapters provide thorough, comprehensive instructions on how to use JDeveloper to create, validate, parse, transform, and compare XML documents.

3. The only title to cover XML processing in Oracle JDeveloper 11g, this book includes information on the Oracle XDK 11g APIs.

Please check **www.PacktPub.com** for information on our titles